82-190

W9-CET-788

THE BEATLES

Books by Hunter Davies

Here We Go Round the Mulberry Bush
The Other Half
The New London Spy
The Beatles: The Authorized Biography

THE BEATLES

by Hunter Davies

112 8490

The man who traveled with the Beatles for
sixteen months to write their *authorized*
story in 1968 brings old and new
fans up-to-date with this revised
edition of the best-selling biography

McGRAW-HILL BOOK COMPANY

New York • St. Louis • San Francisco

567890 DODO 83210

Library of Congress Cataloging in Publication Data

Davies, Hunter, 1936–
The Beatles.
1. The Beatles.   2.   Rock musicians—England
—Biography.
ML421.B4D38   1978   784′.092′2   [B]   77-25031
ISBN 0-07-015463-5

For Brian Epstein

Grateful thanks are also due to their mums, dads,
relations, friends and all who sailed with them, in
Liverpool, Hamburg, and London, and gave so much
time and help with this book. I am also indebted to
Mrs. Queenie Epstein, Clive Epstein, Peter Brown,
Geoffrey Ellis, Neil Aspinall, Mal Evans, Tony Barrow,
and everyone else associated with them through
Nems Enterprises and Apple; and to George Martin,
Dick James, and Sir Joseph Lockwood; and to Richard
Simon and all at Curtis Brown. And to Margaret. Not
forgetting John, Paul, George, and Ringo, without whom.

Contents

Introduction

It is now ten years since this book first came out, way back in 1968 when the world was very, very young. Time scales have become so concertina-ed these days that the sixties are already yellow round the edges, a hazy time we scarcely remember. Yet such is the desire for nostalgia that we are already reviving the sixties, bringing back the memories, making them a subject now for camp recall. Did it ever really happen, the phenomenon called the Beatles? It did indeed. And this is the book that, in 1968, tried its jumpy, jagged best to describe how it all came to pass.

Re-reading it is almost as eerie as examining the early Beatles photographs that appear later in this book. My children—like John's and Paul's and Ringo's children—can have no idea what Beatlemania was. What did you do during Beatlemania, Daddy? I screamed. Were they like the Osmonds, Daddy? I don't wish to answer that. All one can say, hand over heart, is that there has been nothing like the Beatles, before or since. The latter is the more surprising. One would have thought that the trail they blazed would have been not merely followed by others— which it was—but developed, extended, improved. Nothing on the same scale has taken their place. There have been good performers in the last ten years. There have been some good songs written. There have been some interesting new waves. But no group has been so creative or inventive or had such an impact on their generation as the Beatles. They appeared in 1963 and started to split up in 1969—seven years of amazing creativity that saw the production of around 150 songs, songs the whole world sang, until the next one came out. At least twenty of them have become classics and will go on as long as there is popular music.

Many books have been written and will be written about the Beatles, many of them by people more musically qualified than I, all trying to explain the phenomenon of their music. I didn't try. I was the fly on the wall, living with them for eighteen months during 1966–1967, going back over their trail, trying to piece together as assiduously as possible every element in their success. I was criticized by some at the time for not standing back far enough, for not trying to analyze and evaluate. I'm glad I didn't. I would probably have gotten it horribly wrong. Most of all, I'm glad I didn't make any predictions. They would very soon have been disproved by events.

At the time, I honestly didn't think the Beatles would split up. This probably shows in the book, though I tried to keep my feelings out of it. They seemed to get their creative strength from one another. Of course, I didn't think they would go on forever either and become geriatric pop stars, climbing on stage with the aid of crutches. The Beatles had already given up touring well before the end of the book; and it was obvious the whole idea of Beatlemania, and all that had gone with it, was the very last thing they wanted. I presumed they would eventually go their own way as people and even as performers but I felt that as *composers* they would never want to go it completely alone. I was wrong.

I always felt, and still do, that the Beatles as blokes were ordinary blokes put into an extraordinary situation, but that as composers they were always special. I thought being special would keep them together —at least as composers. What I imagined would finally happen (way back in my sixties reveries) would be that they'd all get killed in a car crash. Their seven years had been so dramatic—and people associated with them, like Brian Epstein, had ended their lives so dramatically— that surely the Beatles would be bound to go out in a cloud of glory. I didn't want it to happen soon, but when it did, I was sure it would be final and fantastic.

However, I found it hard enough at the time keeping track of the facts to worry about predictions. The facts themselves were changing all the time and certain parts of the book were out of date by the time it was published. The book was simply what had happened to them up to that stage. I wasn't to know that the best had been. I based the facts on their own memories and the memories of the chief participants. When one deals with people, there is no such thing as one absolute truth. The truth is divided by the number of people involved.

All the same, I still believe all the events described in this book to be true. There might be a little too much trivia, which I would cut out if I were writing it now, but there are no lies, not as far as I know. And if I were writing the book again now, I would try to improve the style.

It seems so jumpy and staccato, probably because I kept on putting off actually writing the book, concentrating on amassing notes and interviews from every quarter. I was enjoying living the book so much that I didn't want to end the experience by calling a halt to the field work and sorting out the chapters. I almost started on the final writing when *Sergeant Pepper* began, but fortunately I held back. When that was finished, I threw the book together rather too quickly—hence a certain clumsiness. I tracked down John Lennon's father only at the last minute, which is why the first chapter is particularly jumpy.

Although I am confident no serious mistakes crept in, under close examination, I'd have to admit that quite a few important truths were omitted. Now it can be told. . . .

Luckily, to spare too many blushes, John has in recent years been going round the world saying what a bastard he was as a Beatle, revealing the awful things he really did, so the truth, such as he now sees it, is already out. (Personally, I think he's overcompensating, having felt guilty for conning the public during the early Beatle days when Brian Epstein pushed their clean, wholesome, lovable image.) John has also been quoted as saying that this book was a whitewash. Well, he read it before it was published the first time—as did the other three—and I made the few minor corrections they requested. Only George requested any lengthy changes and this was in the last section where he thought I hadn't given enough space to his thoughts on religion. (He also thought I wasn't taking them seriously enough.)

The troubles began when their then sidekicks at Apple tried to clean up the book, cut out the bad language, the stories about John thieving, references to drugs, and the like. Back in the sixties, one didn't write about such things as one does today. Their efforts were in the main resisted—but I never want to go through that sort of infighting again.

Out of courtesy, I also let their parents read through the early childhood sections, which concerned them personally. As you will see, I include in these chapters what the boys themselves remembered of their childhood. This was where the fun started. The worst, from my point of view, came from John's Aunt Mimi, the lady who brought him up. She denied most of John's views of his childhood, maintaining he was always sunny and bright. You will notice that Chapter 1 ends limply and rather abruptly with a remark about John being "as happy as the day was long." This was at Mimi's insistence. I'm not saying that she is mistaken—that was the truth as she chose to see it. John chose to see his childhood as one long fight against the world. Who is to say which view was the truth? Anyway, Mimi kicked up a fuss. She also told John that she had never heard him swear in his childhood so she certainly was not going to have him swearing in this book, swearing about his childhood or about any other time. I have a letter which John sent me, asking me to take out a couple of stories and to cut the swearing, just to keep Mimi happy. That, I suppose, could be counted as a whitewash. All the same, I feel every reader is still able to form a clear picture of John's childhood.

I think any reader over the age of fifteen, even in 1968, must have been well aware of what really happened in the dressing rooms after Beatle concerts. Groupies are a cliché today, as we know from so many films and books. The Beatles were no different. They just had more to pick from than most. It was the job of the road managers to say you, you, not you, get lost, you and then you five minutes later. In 1968, three of the four Beatles were happily married, as far as the outside world was aware. The wives naturally did not want such things mentioned—nor did the Beatles. Goodness knows what Aunt Mimi would have thought. Personally, I don't regret not having been able to get in the sex sagas, though the hints were there, between the lines.

One thing I did regret was not being able to say that Brian Epstein was homosexual. I thought I made it fairly implicit, saying at the end of Chapter 15 that he had only one girlfriend, then continuing to talk about his unhappy love affairs. There was also the memorable phrase which describes him as a "gay bachelor."

If he had lived, Brian would have allowed me to spell it out. He had told me so, having begun to feel he could come to terms with himself publicly, knowing it was a vital part of his personality. It certainly explained many of his actions, his fussing over the Beatles, preening and pruning them, mothering them. The tragic thing was that a lot of his love for them was one-sided. They didn't know, nor want to know, about his masochistic, self-destructive, nightlife, which rarely, alas, gave him any pleasure.

However, as he'd only recently died when the book came out and as so many close members of his family refused to believe the truth about him, I was persuaded to steer clear of the subject. Today, many homosexuals in public life take little care to disguise the truth about themselves. In most cases, it's irrelevant; with Brian Epstein it mattered. One of the strangest of the Beatles sagas is how such a person as Brian Epstein came to be interested in them in the first place. What attracted a public-school, well-brought-up, middle-class Jewish boy, a rising businessman who loved Sibelius and had shown not the slightest personal interest in any sort of pop culture? What made him go along to see four scruffy, working-class yobboes in a smelly underground coffee bar? He fancied them—that was the simple explanation, though I was never able to spell it out. Most of all, he fancied John, jumping around in his leather gear and big cowboy boots. (The gossip, years later, was that he fancied Paul, as Paul was always supposed to be the prettiest Beatle, but that couldn't have been further from the truth. He liked men butch and aggressive, even when they didn't like him—often *because* they didn't like him—sexually.)

Brian Epstein gave the Beatles to the world when others more worldly had already passed them by. They created themselves, their music and their performances, but in the wrong hands—nasty, grasping, short-term hands—their national launching would have been very different. The popular explanation was that Brian was simply a very smart Jewish businessman. He'd seen the money in them. In truth, he wasn't a great businessman, as was shown later when many of his deals had to be rearranged. He wasn't materialistic. Brian Epstein loved the Beatles, in every sense of the word. That's all there was to it.

I have to admit I still love them. My heart has stood still back in the good old days. There's not a Beatle number I don't like. "Why Don't We Do It in the Road?" might not get into my Top 100, but there are certainly at least fifty Beatle songs that for me will never go stale. I can never decide which one album I would take to a desert island—*Hard Day's Night, Help, Rubber Soul,* or *Sergeant Pepper.* I still feel honored to have been present during the composition and recording of *Sergeant Pepper,* the greatest artistic event of the sixties.

Two years ago, my house was burgled and, among other things, all my Beatle records were stolen, many of them personal presents. They left behind some Beethoven and Sibelius, stuff I hadn't played since school. It was a gang of kids, so the police said. Old singles are now changing hands at double the original price—as I discovered when I had to replace them. Hold tight to your old records. Hold tight to your old memories.

There are now Beatle conventions held regularly in America, in Britain, and in other parts of the world, get-togethers of fans who swap memories and memorabilia. Luckily, I've still got my old copies of *Beatles Monthly,* old posters, sheet music, and those funny plastic records they used to give out at Christmas to the paid-up fans. Commercially, the Beatles are still a gold mine. Their own records get reissued and make the Top Ten in the charts and rubbish they recorded years ago as a back-up group in Hamburg have been brought out with great success. "Yesterday" has to date been recorded by other artists 1,200 times.

My thirteen-year-old daughter is a Beatles fan (without any prompting from me) and so are many girls in her class. They know the words to all their favorite songs, and they vie with each other to learn numbers the others still haven't heard of. They never saw them perform, of course, and have no idea of their individual personalities, and they can never imagine the impact they had when they first arrived, but they accept their songs as songs and like them. It used to be said, back in the very early days of Beatlemania, that it was the media that did it, building them all up, forcing them upon a gullible public, which was crazy, even at the time. Today's teenagers, like yesterday's, do their own discovering of the Beatles, even if the degree of public mania is now a little less.

Not long after this book first appeared, I was asked by *The Times* of London to write their obituary. Every year the metal gets dragged out and the yellow galleys brought up to date as new marriages, new events, are added. I have tried in a new last chapter to this book, a brief postscript, to cover some of the events of these last ten years and consider why it was they split up; but in all honesty I have very little interest in these later, post-Beatles activities. I am closest to Paul, see him regularly, and delight in his family and in the success of Wings. I saw Ringo quite often until he was divorced and moved away from my neighborhood in North London. I get obscene and obscure notes and cuttings from John in New York from time to time. George I never see. I moved on to do ten other books on completely different topics and have resisted all temptation to do a second volume on the end of the Beatles. Their end as Beatles turned out to be far from glorious. It was their rise that mattered. This is the story of their rise.

Hunter Davies
London
September 1977

Liverpool

Liverpool is up in the top left-hand corner of England just above the
bump on the map which is called Wales. Liverpool looks out from its
corner over to Ireland, and beyond that to America. There are a lot of
Irish and a lot of Welsh in Liverpool. The Irish are said to be witty and
the Welsh are said to be good singers.

The singing and the wit didn't get started until the nineteenth century.
Until then, nothing much happened in Liverpool: Its first charter dates
back to 1207 but most things today date back only to the Industrial Revolution. In 1830 the world's first passenger railway started in Liverpool
and ten years later the Cunard Steamship Company sent out the world's
first ocean liners. For a hundred years after that, Liverpool was all go.
Since the Second World War, and the decline of the Lancashire cotton
industry, things haven't been so booming. The population today is 712,-
040, not much more than it was in 1901.

But Liverpool is still a proud, bustling city. The city fathers can point
to many proud achievements. The Corporation puts out leaflets which
tell that the clock faces of the Royal Liver Building are bigger in diam-
eter than those of Big Ben, that Liverpool had the first Medical Officer
of Health in Britain in 1847 and that both the RSPCA (Royal Society
for the Prevention of Cruelty to Animals) and the NSPCC (National
Society for the Prevention of Cruelty to Children) had their beginnings
in Liverpool. And for present-day achievements, there's the new Roman
Catholic Cathedral, which has more stained glass than any other cathedral in the world, and Liverpool's nine Members of Parliament, one of
whom is Mr. H. Wilson.

But since the war, if the British man in the street has ever thought
about Liverpool he has thought about none of these great achievements.
In British mythology, Liverpool has three things which it is famous for
—soccer, fighting, and comedians. The list of Liverpool comedians in-

1

cludes Tommy Handley, Robb Wilton, Arthur Askey, Ted Ray, Ken Dodd, Norman Vaughan, and Jimmy Tarbuck, but they are all of purely British interest. Rex Harrison, also a Liverpudlian, is better known than any of these to audiences outside Britain, but his person is far from being Liverpudlian.

Fanny Hill was born, fictionally, in Liverpool. She was quite a comic. Matthew Arnold died there and so did William Huskisson, President of the Board of Trade, in the world's first-ever train accident, back in 1830.

Liverpool still has a nineteenth-century look. The central public buildings and monuments all have that yearning classical grandeur the Victorians loved. The Adelphi Hotel in name and in soul is a period piece, though it's trying desperately to be grand. Many of our heroes in this book used to meet at the Adelphi. Outside, of course. Our heroes and their friends and relations are not very grand.

Lime Street Station is another Liverpool meeting place that will figure prominently in our tale. Ladies of the street, such as the famous Maggie May, used to get their best pickings in Lime Street, before they were driven under cover, back to the docks or over the water. "Over the water" in Liverpool means people who live over the Mersey in Cheshire. Cheshire is very posh. None of our heroes lived in Cheshire.

The landmark for all Liverpool water jaunts is the Pier Head. The boats go everywhere, simply across the water, or to Wales, to Ireland, or to America. It is dominated by the huge Royal Liver Building, which is very black and dirty. It has the famous green Liver bird perched on top, with wires to hold it down as it would obviously have flown off years ago to somewhere warmer and cleaner. There also is a big black statue of Edward VII on horseback. Apart from that, the Pier Head is very disappointing. It's just a big empty, very windy square, bounded on one side by the pier. But it also contains the main bus terminal for the city. Most ordinary Liverpudlians spend a lot of their lives around the Pier Head, especially our heroes.

All those great ships and railways, all those funny comedians, even all that fighting and soccer, have paled beside our heroes. In the minds of millions who had never heard of Liverpool before—and even to those who had—Liverpool is now known as the place our four heroes came from.

PART 1: LIVERPOOL

Chapter 1: John

Fred Lennon, John's father, was brought up in an orphanage. "It was the best orphanage in the whole country, the Bluecoat in Liverpool. We wore top hats and tails. I got a very good education."

He had been orphaned in 1917 at the age of five when his father, Jack Lennon, had died. Jack Lennon had been born in Dublin but had spent most of his life in America as a professional singer. He had been an original member of the Kentucky Minstrels. After he retired, he returned to Liverpool, where Fred was born. Fred Lennon left the orphanage at fifteen, with his good education and two new suits to get him through life. He became an office boy.

"I did well as an office boy. You might think I'm big-headed, but I'm not. I'd only been there a week when the boss sent to the orphanage for three more boys. He said if they had only half the vitality I had, they'd be all right. They thought I was terrific." Terrific or not, by the age of sixteen Fred had left office work for the sea. He became a bellboy and eventually a waiter.

"I soon became headwaiter, of course. I was their best, but I had no ambition. There was one ship, the *Moreton Bay,* which would never leave Liverpool unless Freddy Lennon was on board. They had to take me or there would have been a mutiny!"

He met Julia Stanley before he went to sea. It happened just a week after he'd left the orphanage.

"It was a beautiful meeting. I was wearing one of my two new suits. I was sitting in Sefton Park with a mate who was showing me how to pick up girls. I'd bought myself a cigarette holder and a bowler hat. I felt that really would impress them. There was this little waif we had our eye on. As I walked past her, she said, 'You look silly.' I said, 'You look lovely,' and I sat down beside her. It was all innocent. I didn't know anything. She said if I was going to sit beside her, I had to take that silly

5

hat off. So I did. I threw it in the lake. I haven't worn a hat from that day to this."

Fred and Julia went out together, during Fred's spells ashore, for about ten years. He says her mother "loved the bones of his body" but that her father didn't care for him very much. But he had taught Julia to play the banjo.

"Me and Julia used to play and sing together. We'd have been the tops today. One day she said to me, 'Let's go and live together.' I said we wouldn't just live together. Me, I'd been brought up in orphanage. I said we had to put the banns up and get married properly. She said, 'I bet you won't.' So I did, just for a joke. It was all a big laugh, getting married."

The Stanley family didn't think it much of a laugh. They considered themselves a definite cut above Fred Lennon. They looked upon themselves as respectable lower-middle-class.

"We knew that Julia was going out with Fred Lennon," says Mimi, one of Julia's four sisters. "He was handsome, I'll admit. Some people even said he had a perfect profile. But we knew he would be no use to anyone, certainly not our Julia." According to Mimi, neither of her parents cared for Fred or the bones of his body. They wouldn't let him into the house. Mimi was working away in North Wales as a secretary when she heard the awful news about Fred and Julia. She came home at once —to calm down her mother, so she says.

The marriage had taken place on December 3, 1938. No parents were present. Fred turned up first, outside the Adelphi Hotel at ten in the morning. There was no sign of Julia, so he went off and tried to borrow a pound from his brother.

"Julia still hadn't turned up when I got back. I rang her at the Trocadero where she was working as an usherette and spoke to one of her mates. They all loved me at the Troc. They used to say to me if you ever fall out of love with Julia, I'll be waiting."

Julia did turn up and they spent their honeymoon at the cinema. Afterward Julia went back to her home and Fred went back to his. The next day Fred got on a ship and went off to the West Indies for three months.

When Fred came back, they managed to get rented accommodation on their own. Then Fred was off again, leaving Julia, who found that she was pregnant. It was the summer of 1940. Liverpool was under heavy bombing. No one knew where Fred Lennon was. Julia went into the Maternity Hospital in Oxford Street to have her baby. He was born during a heavy air raid on October 9, 1940, at seven in the morning and he was called John Winston Lennon. Winston was the result of a momentary fit of patriotism.

"The minute I saw John," says Mimi, "that was it. I was lost forever. A boy! I couldn't get over it. I went on and on about him, almost forgetting Julia. She said, 'All I've done is have him.' "

When John was eighteen months old, Julia, who had moved back with her parents, went down to the shipping office one day to pick up her money from Fred, which somehow had been coming through. She was told the money had stopped. "Fred had deserted ship," says Mimi. "No one knew what had happened to him."

Mimi says that was really the end of the marriage, though they didn't separate until a year or so later. She had always expected that Fred would desert Julia.

"Julia eventually met another man whom she wanted to marry," says Mimi. "It would have been difficult to take John along as well, so I took John. I wanted him, of course, but it did seem the best thing to do. Both Julia and Fred wanted me to adopt him. I've got letters from them saying so. But I could never get them both down to the office together to sign the forms."

Fred Lennon's version of his "desertion" and what happened to his marriage is naturally a bit different. He says he was in New York when the war broke out. He heard he was to be transferred to a Liberty ship as an assistant steward instead of a headwaiter. "It meant I would lose my rating. I didn't mind getting involved in the war, but I couldn't put up with losing my rating, could I? The captain of the passenger ship I'd been working on advised me what to do. He said, 'Freddy, go and get drunk and miss your boat.' "

This is what Fred did; and he ended locked up on Ellis Island. He was told again to join a Liberty ship. Fred said he wanted to be headwaiter on the *Queen Mary*. He was at last marched onto a Liberty ship heading for North Africa. When they arrived there, Fred was put in jail.

"One of the cooks on board had said to me one day to go and get a bottle from his room. I was drinking it when the police arrived. I was supposed to have broached the cargo. I hadn't. It had all happened before I got on board, but the whole crew got off, except me. Stealing by finding, that was what it was. I defended myself, but it didn't do no good."

Fred spent three months in jail. Naturally, he says, his money to Julia stopped. He hadn't any to send her, but he did send her some letters.

"She loved my letters. I said to her, there's war on; go out and enjoy yourself, pet. That was the biggest mistake of my life. She started drinking and going out and enjoying herself. And I'd told her to."

John has vague memories of his days living with the Stanleys, being looked after by his mother while Fred was at sea, although he could not have been more than four years old at the time. "One day my grandad took me for a walk to the Pier Head. I had a new pair of shoes on and they hurt me all the way. My grandad slit the heels with a pen knife so they would be comfortable."

He did get the impression from his mother that she and Fred had had some happy times. "She told me about them always larking around and laughing. I think Fred must have been popular. He used to send us ship's concert lists with his name on singing 'Begin the Beguine'."

Julia, according to her sisters, was always singing as well. "She was gay, witty and full of fun," says Mimi. "She never took life or anything seriously. Everything was funny, but she couldn't see into people until it was too late. She was more sinned against than sinning." Fred went back to sea again, after Julia had gone to live permanently with the new man and John went with Mimi. During one leave Fred decided to go and visit John at Mimi's house. "I rang up from Southampton and spoke to John on the phone. He must have been getting on for five by then. I asked him what he was going to be when he grew up, that sort of thing. He spoke lovely English. When I heard his scouse accent years later, I was sure it must be a gimmick."

Fred arrived in Liverpool, worried sick, so he says, about John, and went to visit Mimi. "I asked John how he'd like to go to Blackpool and go on the fair and play in the sea and the sand. He said he'd love it. I asked Mimi if I could. She said she couldn't refuse. So I set off with John for Blackpool—intending never to come back."

Fred and the five-year-old John spent some weeks in Blackpool, staying with a friend of Fred's. "I had bags of money at the time. You couldn't go wrong in those days, just after the war. I was on lots of rackets, mainly bringing back black market stockings. They're probably still selling the stuff in Blackpool I brought over."

The friend he was staying with in Blackpool was planning to emigrate to New Zealand. Fred decided to go with him. All the preparations were made, when one day Julia arrived at the door.

"She said she wanted John back. She'd now got a nice little home and decided she wanted him. I said I was now so used to John I was going to take him to New Zealand with me. I could tell she still really loved me. I said why didn't she come with me? We could start again. She said no. All she wanted was John. So we argued and I said, well, let John decide.

"I shouted to John. He runs out and jumps on my knee. He clings to me, asking if she's coming back. That's obviously what he really wanted. I said no, he had to decide whether to stay with me or go with her. He said me. Julia asked again, but John still said me. Julia went out of the door and was about to go up the street when John ran after her. That was the last I saw of him or heard of him till I was told he'd become a Beatle."

John went back to Liverpool with Julia, but not to stay with her. It was his Aunt Mimi who wanted him back. He moved in, for good this time, with Mimi and George at their house, Mendips, number 251 Menlove Avenue, Woolton, Liverpool.

"I never told John about his father and mother," says Mimi. "I just wanted to protect him from all that. Perhaps I was overanxious. I don't know. I just wanted him to be happy."

John is very grateful to Mimi for what she did. "She was obviously very good to me. She must have been worried about the conditions I was brought up in and must have been always on at them to think about me, telling them to make sure the kid's safe. As they trusted her, they let her have me in the end, I suppose."

John soon settled down with Mimi. She brought him up as her son. She was a disciplinarian and stood no nonsense, but she never hit him or shouted at him. Her worst punishment was to ignore him. "He always hated that. 'Don't 'nore me, Mimi,' he used to say."

But Mimi allowed his personality to develop. "We were always an individual family. Mother never believed in being conventional, and neither do I. Just because most people have lunch at one, it didn't mean to say we had. We just had meals when we felt like them." But Uncle George, who ran the family dairy business, was the weak link, if John wanted to be spoiled. "I used to find notes John had left under George's pillow: *Dear George, will you wash me tonight and not Mimi,* or *Dear George, will you take me to Woolton Pictures.*"

Mimi allowed John only two outings of that sort a year—one to the Christmas pantomime at the Liverpool Empire and the other to a Walt Disney film in the summer. But there were smaller treats, such as Strawberry Fields, a local Salvation Army girls' hostel which each summer had a big garden party. "As soon as we could hear the Salvation Army band starting, John would jump up and down shouting, 'Mimi, come on. We're going to be late.' "

John's first school was Dovedale Primary. "The headmaster told me this boy's as sharp as a needle. He can do anything, as long as he chooses to do it. He won't do anything stereotyped." John was reading and writing after only five months at school, though his spelling was funny even then. Chicken pox was always chicken pots. "He went on holiday to my sister's in Edinburgh once and wrote me a card saying *Funs are getting low*. I've still got it."

Mimi wanted to take John to and from Dovedale school herself, but he wouldn't allow it. After his third day, he said she was making a show of him and she hadn't to come any more. So she had to content herself by walking secretly behind him out of school, keeping about twenty yards behind, shadowing him to see that he was all right.

"His favorite songs were 'Let Him Go, Let Him Tarry' and 'Wee Willy Winkie.' He had a good voice. He used to sing in the choir at St. Peter's Woolton. He always went to Sunday school and was later confirmed when he was fifteen."

Until the age of fourteen, Mimi gave him only five shillings a week pocket money. "I tried to teach him the value of money, but it never worked. 'Uncle George has to work for his money,' I said to him. 'No he doesn't,' said John. 'All his men do the work.'" To get any extra money, John had to work for it by helping in the garden. "He always refused to until he was really desperate. We'd hear the shed door being furiously opened, then he'd get the lawn mower out, in a terrible temper, and race across a few feet of the lawn at about sixty miles an hour, then storm in for his money. But money didn't really mean anything to him. He didn't care about it. He was always generous beyond belief when he had any."

John started writing his own little books when he was about seven. Mimi still has bundles of them. His first series was called "Sport, Speed and Illustrated. Edited and Illustrated by J. W. Lennon." It contained jokes, cartoons, drawings, pasted-in photographs of film stars and footballers. It had a serial story which ended each week with "If you liked this, come again next week, it'll be even better."

"I was passionate about *Alice in Wonderland* and drew all the characters. I did poems in the style of the Jabberwocky. I used to *live* Alice and Just William. I wrote my own William stories, with me doing all the things. When I did any serious poems, like emotional stuff later on, I did it in secret handwriting, all scribbles, so that Mimi couldn't read it. Yes, there must have been a soft soul under the hard exterior. *Wind in the Willows,* I loved that. After I'd read a book, I'd relive it all again. That was one reason why I wanted to be the gang leader at school. I'd want them all to play the games that I wanted them to play, the ones I'd just been reading."

As a little boy, he had golden hair and looked very like his mother's side of the family. People always mistook him for Mimi's real son, which she liked. If they were strangers, she never contradicted them. Mimi was very protective, looking after him all the time, trying not to let him mix with what she called common boys.

"I was coming down Penny Lane one day and I saw this crowd of boys in a ring, watching two boys fighting. 'Just like those common Rose Lane scruffs,' I said. This was another school, not John's. Then they parted and out came this awful boy with his coat hanging off. To my horror, it was Lennon.

"John always liked me telling him that story. 'Just like you, Mimi. Everybody else is always common,' he used to say."

In his playing with kids around the street, Mimi says he always had to be the boss. But at school it was much more serious. He had his own gang, which led to brawls and physical fights with everyone, just to prove he was the best. Ivan Vaughan and Pete Shotton, his two closest friends at school, say he seemed to be perpetually fighting. Mimi quite approved of these two friends, as they both lived locally, in the same sort of semis, but not of some of the others.

"I made friends with a boy whose mother was a semi-prostitute," says John. "The rest of her kids had been taken off her. This boy eventually went to prison. Mimi wasn't very pleased. She tried to save me from such a bad family. I did fight all the way through Dovedale, winning by psychological means if ever anyone looked bigger than me. I threatened them in a strong enough way to beat them, so they thought I could.

"I used to go thieving with this kid, pinching apples. We also used to ride on the bumpers of tram cars in Penny Lane and ride miles on the back of the tram, without paying. I'd be shitting myself all the time, I was so scared. I was the kingpin of my age group. I learned lots of dirty jokes very young; there was this girl who lived near who told me them.

"The sort of gang I led went in for things like shoplifting and pulling girls' knickers down. When the bomb fell and everyone got caught, I was always the one they missed. I was scared at the time, but Mimi was the only parent who never found out. Other boys' parents hated me. They were always warning their kids not to play with me. I'd always have smart-alec answers if I met them. Most of the masters hated me like shit. As I got older, we'd go on from just stuffing rubbish like sweets in our pockets from shops and progressed to getting enough to sell to others, like ciggies."

On the surface, his environment at home with the loving, kind but firm Mimi seemed good enough. But although she never told him about himself, there were the vague memories of the past in his mind and also, as he grew older, more and more unanswered questions which worried him.

"On Julia's visits, he did once or twice ask me things," says Mimi. "But I didn't want to tell him any details. How could I? He was so happy. It would have been wrong to say your father's no good and your mother's found someone else. John was so happy, singing all the time."

John remembers beginning to ask Mimi and being always given the same sort of answers. "Mimi told me my parents had fallen out of love. She said my dad was so heartbroken he couldn't face coming back. She never said anything directly against him, except that he didn't send her any money.

"I soon forgot my father. It was like he was dead. But I did see my mother now and again and my feeling never died off for her. I often thought about her, though I never realized that all the time she was living no more than five or ten miles away. Mimi never told me. She said she was a long, long way away.

"My mother came one day to see us in a black coat with her face all bleeding. She'd had some sort of accident. I couldn't face it. I thought, that's my mother in there, bleeding. I went out into the garden. I loved her but I didn't want to get involved. I suppose I was a moral coward. I wanted to hide all feelings."

John might have thought that he was stifling all his worries and his feelings, but Mimi and his other three aunts—Anne, Elizabeth, and Harriet—say that to them John was completely open and sunny-natured. They say that John was as happy as the day was long.

Chapter 2: John and the Quarrymen

Quarry Bank High School, when John started there in 1952, was a small suburban grammar school in Allerton, Liverpool, not far from Mimi's house. It had been founded in 1922. It is not as big or as well-known as the Liverpool Institute in the middle of the City, but it still has a good reputation. Two of its old boys went on to become Labour Government ministers—Peter Shore and William Rodgers.

Mimi was pleased that he was at a local grammar school rather than one in the City. She thought she would be able to keep an eye on him. Pete Shotton went with him to Quarry, but Ivan Vaughan, his other close friend, went instead to the Institute, much to his relief. He was the only academic one of John's gang. He knew that going with John would make all schoolwork impossible. But he was still accepted as a member of John's gang after school hours. He began to bring boys back from his school to join John's gang. "The first one I brought was Len Garry. But I didn't bring many. I was always very selective about people I brought to meet John."

John has a clear image of his first day at Quarry. "I looked at all the hundreds of new kids and thought, Christ, I'll have to fight all my way through this lot, having just made it at Dovedale.

"There was some real heavies there. The first fight I got in I lost. I lost me nerve when I got really hurt. Not that there was much real fighting. I did a lot of swearing and shouting, then got a quick punch. If there was a bit of blood, then you packed in. After that, if I thought someone could punch harder than me, I said okay, we'll have wrestling instead.

"I was aggressive because I wanted to be popular. I wanted to be the leader. It seemed more attractive than just being one of the toffees. I wanted everybody to do what I told them to do, to laugh at my jokes and let me be the boss."

13

He was caught with an obscene drawing his first year. "That really set me up with the masters." Mimi also found an obscene poem he'd written. "She said she never looked through my things, but I knew she did. She found this one in my drawer. I said I'd just been made to write it out for another lad who couldn't write very well. I'd written it myself, of course. I'd seen these poems around, the sort you read to give you a hard on. I'd wondered who wrote them, and thought I'd try one myself.

"I suppose I did try to do a bit of schoolwork at first, as I often did at Dovedale. I'd been honest at Dovedale, if nothing else, always owning up. But I began to realize that was foolish. They just got you. So I started lying about everything."

From then on, after the first year, it was Lennon and Shotton versus the rest of the school, refusing all disciplines or imposed ideas. Pete thinks that without John as his permanent ally he might have gone under and been forced to follow the school line, though John probably wouldn't have. "But with two of you," says Pete, "it's a lot easier to stick to what you believe in. When you've had a bad time, there's someone to laugh with. It was laughs all the time. We never stopped, all the way through school. It was great."

Pete says most of their escapades don't sound as funny in retrospect, but they still make him laugh when he thinks about them.

"We must have been very young this first time when we had to go to the Deputy Head for having done something bad. He was sitting at his desk writing when we came in and made me and John stand either side of him. As he was sitting down there, telling us off, John started tickling the hairs on his head. He was almost bald, but with a few wisps across the top. He couldn't understand what was tickling him and kept on putting his hand up to rub his bald head as he was telling us off. It was terrible. I was doubled up. John was literally pissing himself. Really. It started to run down his trousers. He had short trousers on, that's why I know we must have been pretty young at the time. The piss was dripping on to the floor and the Deputy Head was looking round and saying 'What's that, what's that?' "

John had a gift for art, which he always managed to do well, despite everything else. Pete in turn was good at math. John was jealous of Pete's interest in math, which he could never do, and always tried to spoil it for Pete. "He always tried to ruin my concentration by putting drawings in front of me. Some were obscene, but they were mostly just funny and I'd burst out. 'Look at Shotton, Sir,' the rest of the class would shout as I was in hysterics.

"If I had to stand at the front of the class for some reason, when the master had his back to everyone, John would stand up and hold up a drawing behind the master's back for me to see. I'd no chance. I couldn't stop laughing at him."

Even when they were up before the Head for their very first caning, John was completely unoverawed by authority. "John had to go in first while I waited outside the Head's door. I was in agony, all up tight, worrying what was going to happen to me. I seemed to wait hours, but it was probably only a few minutes. Then the door opened and John came out—crawling on the floor on his hands and knees, giving great exaggerated groans. I burst out at once. I hadn't realized at first that the Head had two sets of doors. John was crawling out of the lobby place where no one could see him from inside. I had to go into the Head next, still with a smile on my face, which of course they never like."

John got steadily worse from year to year. By the third year, having started near the top of the first form, he had been demoted to the B stream. His reports contained remarks like: "Hopeless. Rather a clown in class. A shocking report. He is just wasting other pupils' time." There was a gap for parents to put in their comments. On this one Mimi wrote: "Six of the best."

Mimi kept on at him all the time at home, but she didn't know how badly he was doing or how uncooperative he was at school. "I only got one beating from Mimi. This was for taking money from her handbag. I was always taking a little, for soft things like Dinkies, but this day I must have taken too much."

He was becoming closer to his Uncle George all the time. "He had taken some time to accept me, I think. I don't think he was as keen as Mimi to take me in the first place, but we got on fine. He was nice and kind and simple. He loved Mimi like nothing else, but she could be tough with him. I once felt very sorry for him when he'd been out to get some fish for the cat and had fallen off his bike. Mimi was only interested in the cat fish when he came, not his bruises."

In June 1953, when John was almost thirteen, Uncle George had a hemorrhage and died. "It happened quite suddenly one Sunday," says Mimi. "He hadn't had a day's illness in his working life. On the Monday he was dead, cirrhosis of the liver. John had been very close to him. In any little rows we'd had, George had always been John's friend. They went out a lot together. I was often jealous when they had good times. I think John was very shocked by George's death, but he never showed it."

"I remember coming home the day Uncle George died," says John. "Mimi was crying over the carrots. She used to take in students at the time. They were sitting around, trying to look sad, but knowing they weren't going to get a proper meal and Mimi would be suffering for months.

"I didn't know how to be sad publicly, what you did or said, so I went upstairs. Then my cousin Lelia arrived and she came upstairs as well. We both had hysterics. We just laughed and laughed. I felt very guilty afterwards."

Around the time of Uncle George's death someone else had appeared on the scene who was becoming more and more important in John's life —his mother Julia. She had always kept in touch with Mimi, though Mimi never told John anything about her. Not long after he had started at Quarry she started coming to Menlove Avenue, making sure first that John was around. She was obviously fascinated to see him growing up, developing, becoming a personality. She had by then two daughters herself, by the man she had gone to live with and was still living with. She never got divorced from Fred Lennon.

"Julia gave me my first colored shirt," says John. "I started going to visit her at her house. I met her new bloke and didn't think much of him. I called him Twitchy. But he was all right, really. Julia became a sort of young aunt to me, or a big sister. As I got bigger I had more rows with Mimi. I used to run away and go and live with Julia for a weekend, or eventually a few weeks."

Both Pete Shotton and Ivan Vaughan, John's two constant friends, have very vivid memories of Julia arriving in John's life and the effect she had on them all. Pete remembers starting to hear about Julia when they were in about the second or third year at Quarry Bank. They were both by then constantly being warned about the terrible things that would be ahead of them. Pete's parents and John's Aunt Mimi were always warning them. But they laughed at these warnings, on their own. Then Julia came along and laughed with them openly at masters, mothers, and everyone.

"She was great," says Pete. "A groove. She'd just say forget it when we'd tell her what was going to happen to us. We loved her. She was the only one who was like us. She told us the things we wanted to hear. Like us, she did everything for laughs."

She turned out to live in Allerton and they often went to visit her after school. Sometimes she came to see them. "We met her once with a pair of knickers over her head like a headscarf. The knicker legs hung down over the back of her shoulder. She pretended she didn't realize when people stared at her. We just fell over.

"Another time we were walking up the street with her and she was wearing a pair of spectacles with no glass in. She would meet people and they wouldn't realize. As she was talking to them, she'd put her fingers through the glasses to rub her eye. People would stare in amazement."

Ivan thinks it was the arrival of Julia which really helped to mess John up. She made him a rebel, encouraged what was there, laughed at everything he did. Mimi had been strict with him, but no more than lots of mothers, making sure he didn't smoke or drink and that sort of thing. Julia said completely the opposite. Said all the things were smashing, egging him on all the time. Mimi had to give way a bit to keep John, but he naturally preferred Julia, which was why he was always running away to stay with her. She had been the black sheep, at least the wild one, in a very conformist family. She wanted John, who was like her anyway, to be the same.

John was by now in 4C; his first time in a C stream, the bottom stream. "I was really ashamed this time, being with the thick lads. The B stream wasn't bad, because the A stream had all the drips. I started cheating in exams as well. But it was no good competing with all the mongols and I did as badly as ever."

Pete Shotton had also come down each form with him. "I wrecked his life as well," John says. By the final term of the fourth year John dropped right down to twentieth in the class, the bottom of the bottom class. "Certainly on the road to failure," wrote one master on his report.

In John's fifth year, a new headmaster arrived, Mr. Pobjoy. He soon found that Lennon and Shotton were the ones to look out for, the school's leading troublemakers. But he genuinely seems to have had some contact with John, which the previous headmaster and most teachers by this time did not. They knew only too well what he was like.

"But he was a thorough nuisance, full of practical jokes. I didn't really understand him. I did cane him once myself, I'm sorry to say. Sorry because I am against corporal punishment. I inherited the system, but soon did away with it. I can't remember what I caned him for."

Mr. Pobjoy was rather surprised when John failed all his O levels. "I thought he was capable of passing. He only failed them all by one grade, which was probably one of the reasons I helped to get him into the Art College. I knew he was good at art and felt he deserved the chance."

Mimi went to see the headmaster when John's future was at stake. "He asked me what I was going to do with him. I said, 'What are *you* going to do with him? You've had him five years.' "

Mimi liked the idea of the Art College, though she probably didn't realize how lucky he was to get in. "I wanted him to be qualified to earn a living in a proper manner. I wanted him to *be* something. At the back of my mind I was thinking of his father and how he had turned out, but of course I could never say that to John."

Looking back now at his school years, John has absolutely no regrets. "I've been proved right. They were wrong and I was right. They're all still there, aren't they, so *they* must be the failures. They were all stupid teachers, except one or two. I never paid attention to them. I just wanted a cheap laugh. There was only one master who liked my cartoons. He used to take them home to his digs with him.

"They should give you time to develop, encourage what you're interested in. I was always interested in art and came top for many years, yet no one took any interest. I didn't even know there was a part of the Art College for fourteen-year-olds. I was disappointed at not getting Art at General Certificate of Education, but I'd given up. All they were interested in was neatness. I was never neat, I used to mix all the colors together. We had one question which said do a picture of 'Travel.' I drew a picture of a hunchback, with warts all over him. They obviously didn't dig that.

"But I'd say I had a happy childhood. I came out aggressive, but I was never miserable. I was always having a laugh. It was all imagining I was Just William, really."

Toward the end of his days at school, John had become interested in pop music, although pop music was something Mimi had always discouraged. She never liked him singing pop songs which as a little boy he picked up from the radio. She preferred him to sing nursery rhymes or hymns. John had no musical education or training of any sort. But he did teach himself to play the mouth organ, after a fashion. One of Mimi's students had given him an old one which he tried to play to them, just to show off.

"I would have sent him to music lessons," says Mimi, "the piano or violin, when he was very young. But he didn't want that. He couldn't be bothered with anything which involved lessons. He wanted to do everything immediately, not take time learning. The only musical encouragement he ever got was from a bus conductor on the way from Liverpool to Edinburgh. We packed him off with his cousins in Edinburgh each year to stay with my sister. He'd got a battered old mouth organ from somewhere and played it all the way there, driving everybody mad, no doubt.

"But the conductor was greatly taken by him. When they got to Edinburgh, he said come down to the bus station tomorrow morning and I'll give you a really good mouth organ. John couldn't sleep that night, and he was down there first thing. It was a real good one as well. John must have been about ten at the time. It was the first encouragement he ever had. That conductor didn't know what he started."

The sort of pop songs John did listen to, when he listened to any, were by Johnny Ray and Frankie Laine. "But I didn't take much notice of them." Nobody really took much notice, at least not boys in Britain of John Lennon's age. Pop music, up to the mid-1950s, was all somehow remote and had no connection with real life. It all came from America and was produced by very show-businessy professionals in lovely suits with lovely smiles who sang lovely ballads, mainly for shopgirls and young mums.

Then three things happened. On April 12, 1954, Bill Haley and his Comets produced "Rock around the Clock." It took a year for it to have any effect on Britain. But when it did, as the theme song of the film *Blackboard Jungle,* rock and roll hit Britain and cinema seats started to be ripped up.

The second event occurred in January 1956 when Lonnie Donegan produced "Rock Island Line." This had little connection with the wild rock music, despite the title. What was new and interesting was the fact that it was played on the sort of instruments anyone could play. Lonnie Donegan popularized skiffle. For the first time, anyone could have a go, with no musical knowledge or even musical talent. Even the guitar, the hardest instrument in a skiffle group, could be played by anyone who mastered a few simple chords. The other instruments, like a washboard, or tea-chest bass, could be played by any idiot.

The third and in a way the most exciting event in pop music in the fifties, and the most influential single person in pop at any time until the Beatles themselves, was Elvis Presley. He also appeared in the early part of 1956. By May his "Heartbreak Hotel" was top of the charts in fourteen different countries.

In a way it was obvious that someone like Elvis should happen. You just had to look at Bill Haley in the flesh, podgy, middle-aged-looking and definitely unsexy, to realize that this new exciting music, rock 'n' roll, had eventually to have an exciting singer to go with it. Rock was the music which excited all kids. Elvis was the exciting singer singing the exciting songs. "Nothing really affected me until Elvis," says John.

Elvis was the first to hit the new teenage market, long before anyone had started to call it a teenage market, or even realize it was there. He wasn't singing phoney, slushy ballads, with a nice smile or a quiet cry, for the ladies, but outright provocative, sexually exciting songs. Kids everywhere felt it was aimed at them.

All the Beatles, like millions of lads of the same age, were affected. They all have the same sort of memories, of groups springing up in every class at school and in every street at home. There were overnight about a hundred dances in Liverpool with skiffle groups queuing up to perform. It was the first time for generations that music wasn't the property of musicians. Anyone could get up and have a go. It was like giving painting sets to monkeys. Some of them were bound to produce something good sometime.

John Lennon didn't have a guitar or any instrument when the craze first began. He took a guitar off a boy at school one day but found he couldn't play it so he gave it back to him. But he knew that his mother, Julia, could play the banjo, so he went to see her. She bought him a secondhand guitar for £10. It had on it "Guaranteed not to split." He did go for a couple of lessons, but never learned. Instead Julia taught him some banjo chords. The first tune he learned was "That'll Be the Day."

He had to practice behind Mimi's back at home. She wouldn't have him in the house with his guitar. He had to stand in the glass porch at the front, playing and singing to himself. "A guitar's all right, John," Mimi used to tell him, ten times a day. "But you'll never earn your living by it."

"We eventually formed ourselves into a group from school. I think the bloke whose idea it was didn't get in the group. We met in his house first time as well. There was Eric Griffiths, guitar; Pete Shotton on washboard; Len Garry, Colin Hanson on drums; and Rod on banjo. Our first appearance was in Rose Street—it was their Empire Day celebrations, out in the street, they all had this party. We played from the back of a lorry. We didn't get paid or anything. We played at blokes' parties after that, or weddings, perhaps got a few bob. But mostly we just played for fun."

Len Garry was the boy from the Liverpool Institute, not from Quarry like the rest of them. Ivan was still in the gang, though he had no musical ability at all, not that the rest had much. "I hung around and played the tea chest now and again, but I wasn't really part of the group."

They called themselves the Quarrymen, naturally enough. They all wore Teddy-boy clothes, had their hair piled high and sleeked back like Elvis. John was the biggest Ted of all. Most mothers warned their sons about him, once they saw him or even when they didn't see him but just heard the stories.

In these early months of the Quarrymen in early 1956, when John was supposedly sticking in hard at school, it was all very half-hearted and irregular. They wouldn't play for weeks. People were always coming and going, depending on who turned up at the party, or who wanted to have a go. "It was all just a joke," says Pete Shotton, "setting up a group. Skiffle was in, so everybody was trying to do something. I was on washboard because I had no idea about music. I was John's friend, so I *had* to be in."

With John being the leader, there were constant rows, which also led to people leaving. "I used to row with people because I wanted them out. Once you had a fight, that was the end and you had to leave the group." Over at the Liverpool Institute, the same sort of thing was happening, groups growing up like mushrooms, though Ivan Vaughan had brought Len Garry over from the Institute into John's group. It seemed to go down well.

On June 15, 1956, he took along another friend from his school to meet John. "I knew this was a great fellow," says Ivan. "I only ever brought along great fellows to meet John."

The occasion for the meeting was the church fete at Woolton Parish Church, not far from John's house. He knew the people there and had got them to let his group perform. Ivan had talked a lot at his school about John and his group. He knew that his friend was interested in that sort of thing, though Ivan himself wasn't.

"Mimi had said to me that day," says John, "that I'd done it at last. I was now a real Teddy boy. I seemed to disgust everybody that day, not just Mimi. I was looking the other day at the photograph of myself taken at Woolton that day. I look such a youthful young lad." What happened that day is a bit cloudy to John. He got roaring drunk, though he was still several years under age. Others remember it very well, especially the friend Ivan brought along—Paul McCartney.

"That was the day," says John, "the day that I met Paul, that it started moving."

Chapter 3: Paul

Paul was born James Paul McCartney on June 18,1942, in a private ward of Walton Hospital, Liverpool, the only Beatle to be born in such luxury. His family were ordinary working-class and it was the height of the war when even relatively poor people had less than usual. But Paul arrived in state because his mother had been the Sister in charge of the maternity ward in which he was born. She was given the star treatment when she went back to have Paul, her first baby.

His mother, Mary Patricia, had given up hospital work just over a year previously, when she'd married his father, and had become a health visitor. Her maiden name was Mohin and, like her husband, she was of Irish extraction, but some way back.

Jim McCartney, Paul's father, began his working life at fourteen as a sample boy at A. Hannay and Co., cotton brokers and merchants in Chapel Street, Liverpool. Unlike his wife, Jim McCartney was not a Catholic. He has always classed himself as an agnostic. He was born in 1902, one of three boys and four girls.

It was considered very lucky when he left school and got a job in cotton. The cotton industry was at its height and Liverpool was the center of its importation to the Lancashire mills. Getting into cotton you were reckoned settled for life.

As a sample boy Jim McCartney got 6 shillings a week. He had to run round to prospective buyers letting them see bits of cotton they were interested in buying. Hannay's imported the cotton, graded and classified it, then sold it to the mills.

Jim did well at the job and at the age of twenty-eight was promoted to cotton salesman. This was considered a big success for an ordinary lad. Cotton salesmen usually had more of a middle-class background. Jim was always neat and dapper with a gentle open face. When he got his

22

big promotion, they put him up to £250 a year. Not a great salary, but reasonable.

Jim was too young for the First World War and too old for the Second, although with the use of only one ear—he broke an eardrum falling off a wall when he was ten—he would not have been liable anyway. But he was liable for some sort of war work. When the Cotton Exchange closed for the war, they sent him to Napiers, the engineering works.

In 1941, at the age of thirty-nine, he got married. They moved into furnished rooms in Anfield. Paul, their first child, was born the next June. Jim's wife Mary was then thirty-two. Jim was working at Napiers during the day and fire-fighting at night when Paul was born. He was able to go in and out of the hospital as he liked, instead of the normal visiting hours, since his wife had worked there.

Jim was allowed in straight away, even before the baby had been washed. "He looked awful, I couldn't get over it. Horrible. He had one eye open and he just squawked all the time. They held him up and he looked like a horrible piece of red meat. When I got home I cried, the first time for years and years." Despite his wife's medical work, he'd never been able to suffer illness of any sort. The smell of hospitals made him nervous, a fear he has passed on to Paul.

"But the next day he looked more human. And every day after that he got better and better. He turned out a lovely baby in the end."

One day when Paul had been out in the garden at home, his mother discovered some specks of dust on his face and said they must move. The work at Napiers on the Sabre engines was counted as working for the Air Force, so through that he was able to get a house on the Knowlsely Estate, Wallasey. These were council houses, but some were reserved for Air Ministry workers. "We used to call them half houses, they were such small, diddy houses, with bare bricks inside. But it was better than furnished rooms with a young baby."

Jim's work at Napiers came to an end before the war finished and he was moved to a job in Liverpool Corporation Cleansing Department as a temporary inspector, going round making sure the dustbin men did their job properly. Jim got little money with the Corporation and his wife went back to health visiting for a while, till the birth of her second child, Michael, in 1944.

But she never really liked health visiting as much as nursing. It was too much nine-to-five, like an office job. So eventually she went back to mid-wifery. She took two domiciliary midwife jobs, which meant living on large estates and looking after all the mothers-to-be in that one area. There was a council house thrown in with the job. The first post was in

Western Avenue, Speke, and the second in Ardwick Road. She was called out every night. Jim says she worked far too hard, more than she should have done, but she was always overconscientious.

Paul's earliest memory, probably from around the age of three or four, is of his mother. He remembers someone coming to the door and giving her a plaster dog. "It was out of gratitude for some delivery she had done. People were always giving her presents like that.

"I have another memory of hiding from someone, then hitting them over the head with an iron bar. But I think the plaster dog was the earliest." One of his other early memories of his mother is when she was trying to correct his accent. "I talked real broad, like all the other kids round our way. When she told me off, I imitated her accent and she was hurt, which made me feel very up tight."

Paul started primary school—Stockton Wood Road Primary—when they were living in Speke. His mother decided against a Roman Catholic school because she had seen too many as a health visitor and didn't like them. Michael soon followed at the same one. "I remember the headmistress saying how good the boys were with younger children," says Jim, "always sticking up for them. She said Michael was going to be a leader of men. I think this was because he was always arguing. Paul did things much quieter. He had much more nonce. Mike stuck his neck out. Paul always avoided trouble."

When the school became overcrowded, the brothers were moved out to another primary school in the country, Joseph Williams Primary School at Gateacre.

Paul perfected his quiet diplomacy even more as he got older, still always doing things quietly—like his mother—instead of noisily like Michael. "I was once hitting Michael for doing something," says Jim. "Paul stood by shouting at Mike, 'Tell him you didn't do it and he'll stop.' But Mike didn't and admitted he had done it, whatever it was. But Paul was always able to get out of most things."

"I was pretty sneaky," says Paul. "If I ever got bashed for being bad, I used to go into their bedroom when they were out and rip the lace curtains at the bottom, just a little bit, then I'd think 'That's got them.' "

Paul easily passed the Eleven Plus and went to the Liverpool Institute, the best-known of Liverpool's grammar schools. It was founded in 1825 as a Mechanics' Institute, which is how it got its name. Liverpool Art College, which shares the same building, was part of the Institute until the 1890s. The University of Liverpool also shares the same origins. It became an ordinary boys' school, giving up all adult classes, around the turn of the century. Michael passed for the Institute as well, but he eventually ended up in the lowest stream. Paul did very well and was always in the top forms.

"He was able to do his homework while watching TV," says Jim. "I used to tell him not to, that he couldn't possibly do both. But I once asked him exactly what had been on, and he knew, and he'd also done an essay. He was smart enough easily for a University. That was always my intention for him. Get a B.A. or a B.Sc. behind his name, then he'd be okay. But when he knew what was in my head, Paul tried to stop himself doing well. He was always good at Latin but when I said he'd need the Latin for a University, he started slacking up."

At the Institute, Paul became about the most sexually precocious boy of his year, knowing what it was all about, or almost, even from his early years. "I once did a dirty drawing for the class. I was the lad who did them. It was folded so you just saw the head and the feet of a woman, but when you opened it out, she was all naked. The full schoolboy bit, with pubic hair thrown in, not that I had any idea what that looked like. By mistake I left it in the top pocket of my shirt. This was the pocket I used to keep my dinner tickets in and my mother always searched it before washing as I often left some.

"I came home one day and she held it out to me. 'Did you do this?' I said no, no, honest, no. I said it was Kenny Alpin, a boy in our class. He must have put it there. I'd tell you if I'd done it. I kept it up for two days. Then I admitted it. The shame was terrible."

After the first year, when he got 90 per cent for Latin, he got fed up with schoolwork. "It was nice and easy that first year. I kept myself clean and eager because it seemed the thing to do. Then it all became woolly. Never once in my schooldays did anyone ever make it clear to me what I was being educated for, what the point of it was. I know my dad went on about needing certificates and all that, but I never listened to that. You heard it so often. We had masters who just hit you with rulers, or told us a lot of shit about their holiday in Wales or what they did in the Army.

"Homework was a right drag. I just couldn't stand staying in on a summer night when all the other kids were out playing. There was a field opposite our house in Ardwick and I could look out the window and see them all having a good time. There weren't many other kids from the Institute living round our way. I was called a college pudding, fucking college puddin' was what they said.

"All I wanted was women, money, and clothes. I used to do a bit of stealing, things like ciggies. We'd go into empty shops, when the man was in the house part at the back, and take some before he came in. For years, what I wanted out of life was £100. I thought with that I could have a house, a guitar, and a car. So, if money had been the scene, I'd have gone wild."

However, Paul wasn't all that useless at school. In 1953, he got a school prize for an essay—a special Coronation prize, a book called *Seven Queens of England* published by Heinemann, which he still has. He always got good marks for all his essays. "I remember a school inspector once asking me how I could write such a technical essay about potholing. I'd heard it all on the earphones in bed. They were marvelous, just lying in bed listening to the radio. Did incredible things to your imagination."

Jim had rigged up a set of receivers for each of the boys in bed, as an attempt to get them to bed early, keep them there, and stop them from fighting. They did fight a lot, but not more than most brothers. Michael used to call Paul "fatty" to annoy him. He had been beautiful as a baby. "He had big eyes and long eyelashes," says Jim. "People used to say 'Oh, he'll break all the girls' hearts one of these days.'" But as an early teenager he went through a chubby stage.

The McCartneys moved from Ardwick when Paul was about thirteen. His mother gave up being a domiciled midwife, though she later went back to being a health visitor. They got a council house at 20, Forthlin Road, Allerton, where Paul spent all his boyhood from then on. It is in the middle of a low terrace row, a bit poky and insignificant, but neat and clean. Menlove Avenue was now just two miles away.

They hadn't been at Forthlin Road very long—Paul was just fourteen —when his mother suddenly started to suffer pains in her breast. They went on for about three or four weeks, coming and going, but she put it down to the menopause; she was then forty-five. "It must be the change," she used to say to Jim. She told various doctors but they agreed that was what it was and told her to forget it. But she kept having pain, and more and more seriously.

One day Michael came into the house suddenly and found her crying. He thought it was because he and Paul must have been doing something they shouldn't have been doing—"We could be right bastards." But he never asked her what it was. She never told them. But she decided this time to see a specialist. He diagnosed cancer. They operated and she died. It had all happened within a month of the first serious pains.

"It just knocked me down," says Jim. "I couldn't understand it. It was awful for the boys. Michael especially was still only twelve and very close to her. They didn't break down or anything. It just hit them very slowly."

"I can't remember the details of the day we were told," says Michael.

"All I can remember is one of us, I don't remember who, making a silly joke. For months we both regretted it."

Paul remembers what it was. "It was me. The first thing I said was 'What are we going to do without her money?' " But they both cried on their own in bed that night. For days afterward Paul prayed for her to come back. "Daft prayers, you know; if you bring her back, I'll be very, very good for always. I thought, it just shows how stupid religion is. See, the prayers didn't work, when I really needed them to, as well."

The two boys moved out for a few days, during the funeral, to stay with their Aunt Jinny. "I think Dad didn't want us to see him breaking up," says Paul. "It was a bit of a drag at Aunt Jinny's. We both had to sleep in the same bed."

Jim was left with the biggest problem. He'd never done much in the house, as his wife was so well organized. He was now left at fifty-three to bring up two boys of fourteen and twelve through perhaps their most difficult years. He had money problems. As a midwife his wife had made more than he, as Paul had so cruelly mentioned. By 1956, Jim's salary was only around £8 a week. Every other working man was at least feeling the beginnings of affluence, but the cotton trade, in which you were supposed to be secure for life, was having a very tough time.

Two of Jim's sisters helped a great deal—Aunt Milly and Aunt Jinny. One of them would come one day a week to Forthlin Road to clean out the house properly. And when the boys were young, they often popped round in the evening to let them in from school.

"The winters were bad," says Jim. "The boys had to light the fires themselves when they came home from school. I did all the cooking. The biggest headache was what sort of parent was I going to try to be. When my wife had been alive, I'd been the one who chastised them. I delivered the hard stuff when it was needed. My wife had done the soft stuff. If we sent them to bed without their supper, it would be her who took something up to them in bed later, though it would probably be my idea. Now I had to decide whether to be a father or a mother or both, or rely on them and just be friends and all help each other.

"I had to rely on them a lot. I would say, 'Don't come in when you come home from school unless one of your aunts is here.' Otherwise, they would have their friends in and wreck the place. I'd come home and find five eggs gone. They wouldn't let on at first, saying they didn't know what had happened to them. Then they'd say, oh yes, we did give the lads a fried egg each. By and large, they were quite good. But I missed my wife. It knocked me for six when she died."

Michael particularly doesn't know how his father managed it. "We were terrible and cruel. He was bloody marvelous. And all that time without a woman. I can't imagine. Paul owes a lot to his dad. We both do."

Both of them used to mock his two pet bits of homespun philosophy. "Here he comes, with his two *ations*," they used to say. Jim used to tell them that the two most important things in life were toleration and moderation. "Toleration *is* very important," says Jim. "They would laugh at people with infirmities, as kids do. I'd explain to them how *they* wouldn't like it. And moderation, it causes a lot of trouble. You're always hearing people say, 'I'd string the bugger up,' without thinking carefully about what would be the best for someone."

Jim always did think about what was the best for people. He has a natural charm and courtesy with everyone, but it's not just the salesman's cozy touch; it's much deeper and more genuine than that. In the hands of a less thoughtful or considerate father, his sons could easily have broken out when their mother died.

From his mother Paul seems to have inherited his capacity for hard work and dedication. He is the sort of person who can always get things done, when he wants to. In some ways Paul despised school and the whole system of passing on processed rules as much as John did. But there was a part of him which didn't want to let himself down. He could always turn on the hard work, even in little bursts, enough to get him through. John became completely bolshie and uncooperative. Paul could never be that.

His brother Michael thinks there was one direct result in Paul of their mother's death. "It was just after Mother's death that it started. It became an obsession. It took over his whole life. You lose a mother—and you find a guitar? I don't know. Perhaps it just came along at that time and became an escape. But an escape from what?"

Chapter 4: Paul
and the Quarrymen

As a child Paul showed no particular interest in music. Both he and his brother Michael were sent once for a couple of piano lessons, but nothing happened. "We made the mistake of starting them in the summer," says Jim. "The teacher used to come to the house and all the kids would be knocking at our door all the time, wanting them to come out and play. So I made them go to the teacher's house, but that didn't last long." Jim also wanted Paul to join Liverpool Cathedral choir. "I made him go, but he deliberately cracked his voice in the audition. Later on he did join St. Chad's Choir, near Penny Lane, for a while."

Later still Paul was given an old trumpet by an uncle, on which he managed to pick out tunes, teaching himself. This talent for picking up music came from his father. As a boy Jim had taught himself to play the piano. Of all the Beatles' fathers, Paul's was the only one with any experience of being a musician.

"I never had any lessons. I just used to pick out chords on an old secondhand piano someone gave us when I was about fourteen and living in Everton. It came from North End Music Stores—Nems—I can remember the name on it. I had good rhythm and could knock out most tunes. I never disgraced myself."

Not long after he started work, Jim McCartney began a little ragtime band to play at works dances. This was around 1919, when he was seventeen. Their first public performance was a dance in St. Catherine's Hall, Vine Street, Liverpool. "We thought we would have some sort of gimmick, so we put black masks on our faces and called ourselves 'The Masked Melody Makers.' But before half time, we were sweating so much that the dye was running down our faces. That was the beginning and end of the Masked Melody Makers."

Instead they called themselves "Jim Mac's Band." They all wore dinner jackets with paper shirtfronts and cuffs. "They were very good. You could buy paper cuffs twelve for a penny. No one could tell the difference. I ran that band for about four or five years, just part time. I was the alleged boss, but there was no distinctions. We played once at the first local showing of the film *The Queen of Sheba*. We didn't know what to play. When the chariot race started we played a popular song of the time called 'Thanks for the Buggy Ride.' And when the Queen of Sheba was dying we played 'Horsy Keep Your Tail Up.' "

When the Second World War came, and a family, Jim packed in his playing career, although he often played a bit on the piano at home. "Paul was never interested when I played the piano. But he loved listening to music on his earphones in bed. Then suddenly he wanted a guitar, when he was fourteen. I didn't know what made him want it."

His guitar cost £15 and Paul couldn't get anything out of it at first. There seemed to be something wrong with it. Then he realized it was because he was left-handed. He took it back and got it altered. "I'd never been really keen on the trumpet. But I liked the guitar because I could play it after just learning a few chords. I could also sing to it at the same time."

He'd followed pop music since he was about twelve, like most of his friends. The first concert he went to was Eric Delaney's Band's at the Liverpool Empire when he was twelve. At fourteen he queued up in his lunch hour from school to see Lonnie Donegan. "I remember he was late arriving. He wrote out little notes for the factory girls explaining it was his fault they were late back as he'd kept them waiting. We used to hang around the stage door waiting for anybody and get their autographs. I once queued up for Wee Willie Harriss's autograph."

He also went to the Pavilion. "That was where they had the nude shows. They would strip off absolutely starkers. Some of them were all right as well. It was funny, letting us in at that age. But it was just good clean dirty fun."

Like John and the others, Paul was influenced by the skiffle phase and Bill Haley's early rock numbers, but, like John again, not until Elvis Presley was he really bowled over. "That was the biggest kick. Every time I felt low I just put on an Elvis and I'd feel great, beautiful. I'd no idea how records were made and it was just magic. 'All Shook Up'! Oh, it was beautiful!" When he got his guitar, he tried to play Elvis numbers or whatever else was popular. His best impersonation was of Little Richard.

"I used to think it was awful," says his father. "Absolutely terrible. I couldn't believe anybody was really like that. It wasn't till years later, when I saw Little Richard on the same bill as the Beatles, that I realized how good Paul's impersonation was."

"The minute he got the guitar, that was the end," says Michael. "He was lost. He didn't have time to eat or think about anything else. He played it on the lavatory, in the bath, everywhere."

There was another friend from his class, Ian James, from the Dingle, who also got a guitar about the same time. He and Paul used to go around together, with their guitars. They played to each other, teaching each other bits they'd learned. "We used to go round the fairs," says Paul. "Listening to the latest tunes on the Waltzer and trying to pick them up. We also tried to pick up birds. That never worked. I haven't got the flair for picking them up like that." Both Paul and Ian James wore the same sort of white sports jackets, after the pop song "A White Sports Coat." "It had speckles in it and flaps over the pockets. We use to have black drainies as well. We used to go around everywhere together dressed the same and think we were really flash. We both had Tony Curtis haircuts. It took us hours to get it right."

Jim McCartney tried to stop Paul dressing the way he did, but didn't get very far. "Paul was very clever," says Michael. "When he bought a new pair of trousers, he'd bring them home for Dad to see how wide they were and he would say okay. Then he would take them back and get them altered. If Dad noticed afterwards, he'd swear blind they were what he'd agreed."

"I was very worried he'd turn out a Teddy boy," says Jim. "I had a dread of that. I said over and over again that he wasn't going to have tight trousers. But he just wore me down. His hair was always long as well, even then. He'd come back from the barber's and it would just look the same and I'd say, 'Were it closed, then?' "

Paul was just as interested in girls as the guitar. "I got it for the first time at fifteen. I suppose that was a bit early to get it. I was about the first in my class. She was older and bigger than me. It was at her house. She was supposed to be baby-sitting while her mum was out. I told everybody at school next day, of course. I was a real squealer."

Paul remembers vividly that day in the summer of 1956 when Ivan mentioned that he was going to Woolton Parish Church to see this group he sometimes played with, though he wasn't actually playing with them that day. Paul said yes, he'd come along and see them. Might be a few girls to pick up.

"They weren't bad," says Paul. "John played the lead guitar. But he played it like a banjo, with banjo chords, as that was all he knew. None of the others had even as much idea as John how to play. They were mostly just strumming along. They played things like 'Maggie May,' but with the words a bit different. John had done them up himself as he didn't know them all.

"They were playing outdoors in a big field. John was staring round as he was playing, watching everybody. He told me afterwards that it was the first time he tried sussing an audience—you know, sizing them, seeing whether it was best to twist a shoulder at them or best not to move at all. I was in my white sports coat and black drainies, as usual. I'd just got them narrowed again during the dinner hour from school. They were so narrow they knocked everybody out.

"I went round to see them afterwards in the church hall place. I talked to them, just chatting and showing off. I showed them how to play 'Twenty Flight Rock' and told them all the words. They didn't know it. Then I did 'Bee Bop a Loo,' which they didn't know properly either. Then I did my Little Richard bit, went through me whole repertoire in fact. I remember this beery old man getting nearer and breathing down me neck as I was playing. 'What's this old drunk doing?' I thought. Then he said 'Twenty Flight Rock' was one of his favorites. So I knew he was a connoisseur.

"It was John. He'd just had a few beers. He was sixteen and I was only fourteen, so he was a big man. I showed him a few more chords he didn't know. Ian James had taught me them really. Then I left. I felt I'd made an impression, shown them how good I was." Pete Shotton, however, doesn't recall Paul making any big impression. Pete, being completely unmusical, was a bit harder to impress by "Twenty Flight Rock," however brilliantly executed.

"I didn't really take in Paul that first meeting," says Pete. "He seemed very quiet, but you do when you meet a group of new blokes for the first time. I wasn't really jealous of him, not at first. He was so much younger than us. I didn't think he was going to be a rival. Me and John were still the closest pals. I was always John's friend. 'Cos I loved him, that's why."

"About a week later Paul went over to Menlove Avenue on his bike to see Ivan. He cycled up through the golf course from Allerton. On the way back he met Pete Shotton. Pete said they'd been talking about me. Did I want to join their group? I said okay, right."

John remembers mulling over the meeting with Paul in his mind afterward, before he decided on anything. It was unusual for him to think things out instead of barging on with whatever he wanted. "I was pissed that day," says John. "So I probably wasn't all that clued up. I was very impressed by Paul playing 'Twenty Flight Rock.' He could obviously play the guitar. I half thought to myself 'He's as good as me.' I'd been kingpin up to then. Now, I thought, if I take him on, what will happen? It went through my head that I'd have to keep him in line if I let him join. But he was good, so he was worth having. He also looked like Elvis. I dug him."

Paul's first public performance as a member of the Quarrymen was at a dance at the Conservative Club in Broadway. Paul was going to do his own little solo bit that evening, probably "Twenty Flight Rock," but something happened and he didn't.

But later on, after the dance, he played for John a couple of tunes he had written himself. Since he'd started playing the guitar, he had tried to make up a few of his own little tunes. The first tune he played to John that evening was called "I Lost My Little Girl." Not to be outdone, John immediately started making up his own tunes. He had been elaborating and adapting other people's words and tunes to his own devices for some time, but he hadn't written down proper tunes till Paul appeared with his. Not that Paul's tunes meant much—nor John's. They were very simple and derivative. It was only them coming together, each egging the other on, that suddenly inspired them to write songs for themselves to play. From that day they never stopped.

"I went off in a completely new direction from then on," says Paul. "Once I got to know John it all changed. He was good to know. Even though he was two years older than me and I was just a baby, we thought the same sort of things."

What happened in the subsequent months was that John and Paul got to know each other. They spent all their time together. They both stayed away from school and went to Paul's house, while his dad was out at work, and ate fried eggs and practiced guitar chords. Paul showed John all the ones he knew. John's banjo chords, taught him by Julia, were obviously useless. As Paul is left-handed, after he had shown John what to do, John had to go home and do it in the mirror on his own, then get it the right way round.

Pete Shotton began to feel a bit out of it. "My days with the group soon came to an end," says Pete. "We were playing at someone's party in Smithdown Lane. It was a right pissup really. John and I got hilarious, laughing like mad at each other's jokes. Then he broke my washboard over my head. I lay there, in tears, with it framed round my neck. That was the end of me with the Quarrymen. It wasn't the life for me any more, playing in a group. Apart from feeling no good, I didn't like standing up there. I was too embarrassed."

Ivan Vaughan had long since left the group, though he was still a friend of John's at home and of Paul's at school. Paul began to think more and more of the possibility of another great friend of his from his school joining the group. He had taken up skiffle and rock and Elvis about the same time, but was coming on even better than most people at the guitar. He thought he would bring him along to see John. He was even younger than Paul, but he didn't think that would matter, he was so good.

Ivan Vaughan was annoyed when he did. Ivan had taken along first of all Len Garry and then Paul McCartney from the Institute to meet John. He looked upon the procuring as his prerogative. He didn't like the idea of Paul taking someone else along. This new friend was not just much younger, but he didn't even make any pretense at being an intellectual, the way Paul did. George Harrison, as the friend was called, was a real out-and-out Teddy boy. Ivan couldn't understand why the Quarrymen should be interested in him.

Chapter 5: George

George Harrison is the only Beatle to come from a large family and the only one whose family background was normal and undramatic. He is the youngest of the four Beatles and the youngest of the four children of Harold and Louise Harrison. He was born on February 25, 1943, at 12 Arnold Grove, Wavertree, Liverpool.

Mrs. Harrison is stocky, jolly, very friendly and outgoing. Mr. Harrison is thin and thoughtful, precise and slowly deliberate. He left school at fourteen and worked for a firm which made mangles, the sort once used by housewives on washday. He got 7/6 a week for taking them round on a hand cart, then dragging them into people's houses. He wanted to join the Navy, but his mother wouldn't let him. His father had been killed at Mons during the First World War and he thinks this put her off all services. But she allowed him to join the merchant navy. He was at sea from 1926 to 1936 as a steward with the White Star Line.

He met his wife Louise in 1929. "No, let me tell this story," she said. "It's the funniest thing you ever heard. As my girl friend and I were going down this alleyway one night, there was three boys we didn't know who whistled at us. We just ran on. We were looking for some boys we did know but they weren't there. On the way back, these other three were still standing around. One said to me, 'Give us your address, then. I'm going to Africa tomorrow and I'll send you a bottle of scent.' I thought, well, it'll be a bottle of scent. So I gave him the address, but one of the other boys, who hadn't spoken to me, leaned over and snatched it out of his hand.

"The next evening, one of my brothers said to me, 'Hey Lou, there's a fellow hanging around our front.' I was dead scared, because my dad went furious if boys hung around. He said unless I came out in five minutes, he was going to knock at the door. So I went out and told him to go to blazes. I told him it was the other fellow I'd given my address to any-

35

way, not him. He went away, but came again the next night. He just started to haunt me. Eventually I had to go out with him."

They did go out for a while, but Harold went back to sea not long afterward. "What a pandemonium his first letter caused. It had the White Star flag on, so I knew it must be him. There was a deaf-and-dumb man in the kitchen the day it came, getting a can of water. My mother was always very kind to everyone.

"Letters were very rare in those days; at least we never got any. This deaf-and-dumb man bent down and picked up my letter, even though he couldn't read. I could see it said *Miss Louise French* and I tried to grab it from him. But somebody else snatched it. It went round everybody before I got it, with everyone howling at all the kisses."

Harold and Louise were married on May 20, 1930. Not in a church, but in Brownlow Hill register office. She was a Catholic but he was not. Her father had originally come from Wexford in Ireland and had originally spelled his name the Irish way, with a *ff*. He was six two and he was at one time a commissionaire at New Brighton Tower. He then became a lamplighter, which he was until he died.

"When he was away during the First World War, my mother became a lamplighter herself. She was up a lamp post one day and somebody accidentally took the ladder away. She was left hanging by her hands from the bar and had to fall in the end. She was eight months pregnant as well. But the baby was lovely. Nine pounds."

Harold and Louise moved into 12 Arnold Grove, Wavertree, when they got married and lived there for eighteen years. It was a simple terrace house, two up and two down, and cost ten shillings a week. It is just a few miles away from the areas in which John Lennon and Paul McCartney were living.

Harold was still at sea and Louise was working as an assistant in a greengrocer's, a job she kept up until shortly before the birth of their first child, Louise, in 1931. Their second child, Harold, was born in 1934. Not long after, Harold Sr. decided to leave the merchant navy. He was fed up anyway, but most of all he wanted to see more of his children. "I was by then a first-class steward on £7.7.0 a month. Twenty-five shillings of that a week was sent home for my wife. I never had enough money, even when we got some 'good bloods' on board. I did a lot of cruises and this is what we called people with money who gave us big tips. So in my spare time I used to cut people's hair. I was trying to save up in order to come ashore and look for a job."

"He used to write home and tell me how hard the life was," says Mrs.

Harrison. "He would take his trousers off at night, hang them on the line, but before they'd stop swinging, he was in them again."

Harold came ashore in 1936. There was a slump on. He was on the dole for fifteen months. "With two kids, I was allowed twenty-three bob a week. Out of that there was the ten-bob rent to play, plus coal and food for all of us."

In 1937 he managed to get a job as a bus conductor and in 1938 became a bus driver. In 1940 Peter was born and in 1944 along came George, the fourth child and third son. "I went upstairs to see him that first day," says Mr. Harrison. "I couldn't get over it. There he was, a miniature version of me. Oh no, I thought. We just couldn't be so alike."

"George was always very independent," says Mrs. Harrison. "He never wanted any assistance of any kind. When we used to send him to Mrs. Quirk's the butcher's we'd give him a note but he'd throw it away the minute he got outside our house. Mrs. Quirk used to see his little face coming over the counter and know who it was. 'Haven't you got a note?' she would say. 'I don't need one,' George'd say. 'Three quarters of best pork sausages please.' He'd not be much more than two and a half when he did that. All the neighbors knew him."

They had a great deal of trouble getting George into primary school. The worst of the bulge years were starting. All the schools were full. "I tried a Roman Catholic school. He'd been baptized a Catholic. But they said I'd have to keep him at home till he was six, then they might be able to take him. He was so intelligent and advanced, so I just sent him to ordinary state primary school."

This was Dovedale Primary, the same school which John Lennon was already at. He was two and a half years older and three classes ahead of George. They never met. But Peter Harrison, one of George's brothers, was in the same year as John Lennon and in the same year as Jimmy Tarbuck, the Liverpool comedian.

"I took him to school that first day, across Penny Lane," says Mrs. Harrison. "He wanted to stay dinners right from the beginning. The next day, as I was getting my coat off the hanger, he said, 'Oh no, I don't want you to take me.' I said, 'Why not?' He said, 'I don't want you to be one of the nosy mothers, standing round the gate talking.' He's always been against nosy mothers. He used to hate all the neighbors who stood around gossiping."

George's first home memory is of buying live chickens for sixpence, along with his brothers Harold and Peter, and bringing them home. "Mine and Harold's both died, but Peter's was kept in the back yard and grew and grew. It was massive and wild. People were so scared of it they came round to the front door instead of the back. We ate it for Christmas. A fellow came and strangled it for us. I remember it hanging on the line after he'd done it."

George was six when they moved from Wavertree to a council house in Speke. "It was very nice and modern. It seemed fantastic to me, after a two-up-and-two-down terrace house. You could go from the hall to the sitting room, then into the kitchen, then into the hall again and back into the sitting room. I just ran round and round it all that first day." The house was number 25 Upton Green, Speke. They'd put their name down for a council house eighteen years previously, in 1930, when Lou was a baby.

"It was a brand-new house," says Mrs. Harrison, "but I hated it from the minute we moved in. We tried to keep the garden nice, but kids just wrecked it. They stole your plants in the middle of the night. It was a sort of slum-clearance area, but they'd mixed up the good and bad families together, hoping the good would lift the rest up."

"After we passed the scholarship," says George, "the teacher asked us who thought they had passed. Only one person put his hand up. He was a little fat lad who smelled. It was very sad, really. He turned out to be about the only one who didn't pass.

"Smelly kids like that were the sort teachers made you sit next to as a punishment. So the poor smelly kids really did get screwed up. All teachers are like that. And the more screwed up *they* are, the more they pass it on to the kids. They're all ignorant. I always thought that. Yet because they were old and withered you were supposed to believe they weren't ignorant." George started at the Liverpool Institute in 1954. Paul McCartney was already there, a year ahead. John Lennon was in his fourth year at Quarry Bank High School.

"I was sad leaving Dovedale. The headmaster, Pop Evans, told us that we may feel smart big boys now, but at the next school we'd be the little boys once again. It seemed such a waste. After all that hustling to be one of the big lads. The first day at the Institute Tony Workman leapt on my back from behind a door and said, 'Do you want a fight, lad?' "

After a short spell of feeling lost and out of it, during which he tried to do a bit of homework and fit in, George gave up being interested in schoolwork. "I hated being dictated to. Some schizophrenic jerk, just out of training college, would just read out notes to you which you were expected to take down, and I couldn't read them afterwards anyway. They never fooled me. Useless, the lot of them.

"That's when things go wrong, when you're quietly growing up and they start trying to force being part of society down your throat. They're all trying to transfigure you from the pure way of thought as a child, forcing their illusions on you. All those things annoyed me. I was just trying to be myself. They were trying to turn everybody into rows of little toffees."

At the Institute, George was known from the beginning as a way-out dresser. Michael McCartney, Paul's brother, was a year below him. He remembers George always having long hair—years before anybody else did.

John Lennon's rebellion took the form of fighting and causing trouble. George did it by his dress, which annoyed masters just as much. But one of the reasons George had long hair was that he always hated getting his hair cut. To save money, his father had always cut the family's hair, as he had done in the merchant navy. By this time the shears were old and blunt. "He used to hurt them," says Mrs. Harrison, "and they hated it." "Yes, perhaps they were a bit rough," says Mr. Harrison. "Rough? You're joking, boy," says his wife.

"George used to go to school with his school cap sitting high on top of his hair," says Mrs. Harrison. "And very tight trousers. Unknown to me, he'd run them up on my machine to make them even tighter. I bought him a brand-new pair once and the first thing he did was tighten them. When his dad found out, he told him to unpick them at once. 'I can't, Dad,' he said. 'I've cut the pieces off.' George always had an answer. He once went to school with a canary-yellow waistcoat under his school blazer. It belonged to his brother Harry, but George thought he looked terrific in it.

"Going in for flash clothes, or at least trying to be a bit different, as I hadn't any money, was part of the rebelling. I never cared for authority. They can't teach you experience; you've got to go through it, by trial and error. You've got to find out for yourself you shouldn't do certain things. I always managed to keep a bit of individuality. I don't know what made me do it, but it worked. They didn't get me. Looking back, I feel pleased they didn't."

So for the first three years he was in continual trouble. " 'Harrison, Kelly, and Workman, get up and get out,' that's all I used to hear. If it wasn't that I was being sent to go and stand in the chewer's corner."

When winkle-pickers came in, George had a monster pair in blue suede. "One of the masters, Cissy Smith, went on at me about them. We called him Cissy because he was always smoothly dressed, in things like purple silk shirts. He said, 'They're not school shoes, Harrison.' I wanted to ask him what *were* school shoes, but didn't."

Cissy Smith's real name was Alfred Smith and he was the brother of John Lennon's Uncle George. "I didn't discover that for years later either. I had hysterics when John told me." In his fourth year or so at the Institute, George began to stay out of trouble more. "I learned it was best to keep cool and shut up. I had this mutual thing with a few masters. They'd let me sleep at the back and I wouldn't cause any trouble. If it was nice and sunny, it was hard to keep awake anyway, with some old fellow chundering on. I often used to wake up quarter to five and find they'd all gone home long ago."

Harry, George's eldest brother, was by this time finished school and had become an apprentice fitter. Lou, his sister, was at training college, and Peter was about to start a job as a panel beater—that is, beating out panels in a car factory.

Harold, George's father, was still a bus driver, but he had also become a successful union official. He started to spend a lot of time at Finch Lane, the Liverpool Corporation social center for conductors and drivers. By the 1950s he was the MC for most of their Saturday-night socials, introducing the guests.

"One of the earliest comedians we launched was Ken Dodd. We'd seen him at the club, having a drink, and we knew he was very funny, but he was always too nervous to go on stage. But he eventually went on. He did this act, 'The Road to Mandalay' with shorts on and one of those pith helmets. It was a riot. I don't think he's half as funny now."

Harold Harrison was naturally pleased that George was at last appearing to stick in at school. He was the only one of his three sons to have got into a grammar school, so he wanted him to do well. As a hard-working, meticulous union official, he wished he had had the chances George was getting. He saw education the way John's Aunt Mimi and Paul's dad Jim did, as the only way, not just to self-advancement but to success and respectability in the world as well. That was the only way you got a good secure job.

A good secure job is what most parents want for their children, but particularly people of Harold Harrison's generation. He had been through the worst of the depression days of the thirties, when he had been out of work for years and forced to bring up a family on meager dole money.

George's individualism and anti-authority don't seem to have come from his father. At least his father's tough early life probably drove into him the need for steadiness. But his mother was always an ally. She wanted all her children to be happy. It didn't matter really what their interests were, as long as they enjoyed doing them. Even when George became interested in something patently pointless, a hobby that nobody could ever make anything of, which clearly didn't lead to security or respectability, his mother still encouraged him.

Mrs. Harrison isn't just jolly and outgoing. In her own way, unlike all the other Beatle parents, she is one of nature's ravers.

Chapter 6: George
and the Quarrymen

Mrs. Harrison was always interested in music and dancing. With her husband she ran a learners' dancing class—mainly ballroom dancing—at the Finch Lane bus conductors' and drivers' club for almost ten years. George showed no interest in music as a child, as far as his parents can remember. "But he would always give you an entertainment if you asked him," says Mrs. Harrison. "He would get down behind a chair and do you a puppet show."

It wasn't until George was about fourteen that he suddenly came home and started covering bits of paper with drawings of guitars. "One day he said to me, 'This boy at school's got a guitar he paid £5 for, but he'll let me have it for £3; will you buy it for me?' I said, 'All right, Son, if you really want.' I had a little job by then. I'd gone back to working at a greengrocer's, the job I'd done before I was married."

The first person to make any impression on George musically was Lonnie Donegan, who was a big influence. "I'd been aware of pop singers before him, like Frankie Laine and Johnny Ray, but never really taken much interest in them. I don't think I thought I was old enough for them. But Lonnie Donegan and skiffle just seemed made for me."

His first guitar was the one his mother bought for him from the school friend who'd got bored. After the first excitement of buying it, it lay in a cupboard for about three months, forgotten.

"There was a screw holding the neck to the box part," says George. "In trying to play it, I took it off and couldn't get it back on again. So I put it away in the cupboard. Then one day I remembered about it again and got Pete to fix it for me."

"George tried to teach himself," says Mrs. Harrison. "But he wasn't making much headway. 'I'll never learn this,' he used to say. I said, 'You will, Son, you will. Just keep at it.' He kept at it till his fingers were bleeding. 'You'll do it, Son, you'll do it,' I said to him. I sat up till two or three

42

in the morning. Every time he said, 'I'll never make it,' I said, 'You will, you will.' I don't know why, really, I encouraged him so much. He wanted to do it, so that was enough for me. I suppose at the back of my mind I remembered all the things I wanted to do as a girl, but nobody encouraged me.

"So when it came to George, I helped all I could. Eventually he was way beyond anything I could understand. 'You don't understand about guitars, do you, Mum?' he said to me once. I said no, but you stick in, I'm sure you'll make it. Keep at it. He said no, he didn't mean that. He needed a new guitar, a better guitar. He said it was like playing a mouth organ. There are certain notes you just can't get because it's not a good enough mouth organ. Well, he'd come to that stage with this three-pound guitar.

"So I said sure, I'll help you to buy a new one. He got one, £30 it cost. Electric as well, or something. Peter had also taken up the guitar. He had one first, in fact, now I think about it. A broken one which he got for five bob. He glued it and put it together and put strings on and it was great."

"My mum did encourage me," says George. "Perhaps most of all by never discouraging me from anything I wanted to do. That was the good thing about her and my dad. If you tell kids not to, they're going to do it in the end anyway, so they might as well get it over with. They let me stay out all night when I wanted to and have a drink when I wanted to. I'd finished with all that staying-out-all-night-drinking bit when everybody else came to it. Probably why I don't like alcohol today. I had it all by the age of ten."

"One day George came home and said he'd got an audition, at the British Legion Club in Speke," says Mrs. Harrison. "I told him he must be daft. He hadn't even got a group. He said don't worry, he'd get one."

George did get a group for his big night at the Speke British Legion. He got his brother Peter on guitar, his friend Arthur Kelly on guitar and two others, one on a tea chest and another on a mouth organ. He himself was on guitar. They all left the house one by one, ducking down behind the hedge. George didn't want all the nosy neighbors to know what they were doing.

They got to the hall and found that the real artists hadn't turned up. Not only did they get their audition, they had to go straight on and play all night as there was no one else there.

"They were so excited when they came home, all shouting together," says Mrs. Harrison. "I couldn't make out at first what happened. Then they showed me the ten bob they'd got each, their first professional engagement. The poor boy on the tea chest looked awful. His fingers were bleeding from playing. The blood was all over the tea chest. They called themselves The Rebels for that night. They had it painted on in red. But I can't remember them playing together again."

George didn't play in a proper group, although he did odd nights sitting in with other groups until, through Paul, he joined the Quarrymen. He first got talking to Paul shortly after he had started at the Institute. They used to meet on the same bus journey. George remembers the day his mother paid his and Paul's fare. But when the skiffle phase arrived and they both had guitars, they became closer friends.

"Paul came round to my house one evening to look at the guitar manual I had, which I could never work out. It was still in the cupboard. We learned a couple of chords from it and managed to play 'Don't You Rock Me Daddy O' with two chords. We just used to play on our own, not in any group, just listening to each other and pinching anything from any other lad who could do better."

They began to spend most of their spare time together, even during the holidays. This started long before Paul had met John and the Quarrymen. Paul appears to have been with the Quarrymen for at least a year before George joined them, probably not until 1958. No one remembers the exact date, but the joining probably didn't happen immediately. George, after all, was very young, even though he was getting better all the time as a guitarist and was getting numerous stand-in dates. He'd taken a Saturday-morning job at a butcher's and one of the full-time shop assistants there was in a group. George did several jobs with this group. Through them he met a drummer called Pete Best.

"I first saw the Quarrymen when they were playing at the Wilson Hall at Garston. Paul was playing with them and said I should come and see them. I'd probably have gone anyway, just for the night out and to see if I could get in any groups. With knowing Paul, I got introduced to John.

"There was this other guitarist in another group that night, Eddie Clayton. He was great. John said if I could play like that, I could join them. I played 'Ranchee' for them and John said I could join. I was always playing 'Ranchee' for them. We'd be going somewhere on the top of a bus with our guitars and John would shout out, 'Give us "Ranchee," George.' "

"But George never thought he was any good," says Mrs. Harrison. "He was always saying that, telling me about all the people who were so much better than he was. I told him he could be, if he stuck in."

John remembers that it was George's youth which made him take some time before asking him to join. "It was too much, too much. George was just too young. I didn't want to know him at first. He was doing a delivery round and just seemed a kid. He came round once and asked me to go to the pictures with him but I pretended I was busy. I didn't dig him on first sight, till I got to know him. Mimi always said he had a low-Liverpool voice, a real whacker. She said, 'You always seem to like lower-class types, don't you, John?'

"George wanted to join us because he knew more chords, a lot more than we knew. So we got a lot from him. Every time we learned a new chord, we'd write a song round it. We used to sag off school and go to George's house for the afternoon. George looked even younger than Paul, and Paul looked about ten, with his baby face."

George says he probably did deliberately hang around John a lot. John was by this time about to start the Art College, but as deliberately aggressive and working-class as ever, despite all Mimi's upbringing.

"I was very impressed by John," says George. "Probably more than Paul, or I showed it more. I loved John's blue jeans and lilac shirt and sidies. But I suppose I was impressed by all the Art College crowd. John was very sarcastic, always trying to bring you down, but I either took no notice or gave him the same back, and it worked."

"Meeting Paul was just like two people meeting," says John. "Not falling in love or anything. Just us. It went on. It worked. Now there were three of us who thought the same."

There were still other members of the Quarrymen, who came and went, either because they couldn't put up with John's tongue or got bored. They needed other people, when they got their occasional dates, as three guitars don't make a group, even in those days. They desperately needed a drummer but no one they picked up, however useless, ever seemed to stay.

They were moving out of the skiffle era as a group. The skiffle phase anyway was waning. Tea chests and washboards were just a bit amateurish. All of them anyway preferred rock 'n' roll and Elvis in particular and this was the style they were trying to copy, listening to new records on the radio and trying to reproduce the same chords or sounds at home. John, as the leader, tried to get bookings from all the little one-man managements who were cashing in on the group craze. But he was finding it very difficult to get regular bookings. There were so many groups, and most of them far better than the Quarrymen.

But they now had two homes to go to—George's almost any time they liked, and Paul's, especially when his dad was out—where they could practice, write music, or just draw and mess around. Mimi was certainly not going to have any Teddy boys from a rock group coming to

Menlove Avenue. Paul, unlike George and John, had his natural charm and classless *persona,* but it didn't fool Mimi.

"He used to come to my front door," says Mimi. "He'd be on his bike which he'd lean against the fence. He would look over at me with his sheep eyes and say 'Hello, Mimi. Can I come in?' 'No, you certainly cannot,' I'd say." Mimi was even more against George, when she heard about him.

"John used to go on and on about George, what a nice boy he was and how I'd like him. He went to great lengths to impress me with George. 'Give you anything, George,' he'd say.

"I eventually said he could come in one day. He arrived with a crew cut and a pink shirt. I threw him out. Well, it wasn't done. I might have been a bit old-fashioned, but schoolboys dressing like that! Up till John was sixteen I always made sure he wore his regulation school blazer and shirt."

John and Paul practiced at George's house in Upton Green. The Harrisons came in one day to find George in the tightest pair of jeans they'd ever seen.

"Harold went spare," says Mrs. Harrison. "When he saw them, he went over the moon. George said John had just given them to him. Then he jumped up and pranced round the room. 'How can I do my ballet without tight jeans?' he said, dancing all over the place. We had to laugh at him in the end. George never gave any cheek, but he always got round us."

The first time Mrs. Harrison actually met John Lennon she was in the kitchen when George brought him home. " 'Here's John,' George shouted. 'Hello, Mrs. Harrison,' John said, coming forward to shake my hand. Well, I don't know what happened next. He somehow fell and as he did, fell on top of me and we both landed on the settee. Dad came in at that moment. You should have seen his face when he saw John on top of me! 'What the devil's going on here?' George said, 'It's okay, Dad. It's only John.'

"John was always a bit of a fool. He was never miserable, just like me."

Chapter 7: John at Art College

John had started at Art College in the autumn of 1957.

"I went for the interview before I'd heard about my O levels. (O, or Ordinary, levels are examinations taken at sixteen by grammar-school students.) I took work I'd been doing on my own. The other lads trying to get in were all neat fuckers, neat letterers. I could never do neat lettering. The lettering bloke said no, he didn't want me, but the painting teacher liked me, he got me in. The new head at Quarry, Mr. Pobjoy, had put a good word in for me as well.

"They all thought I was a Ted at Art College when I arrived. Then I became a bit artier, as they all do, but I still dressed like a Ted, in black with tight drainies. Arthur Ballard, one of the lecturers, said I should change a bit, not wear them as tight. He was good, Arthur Ballard, he helped me, kept me on when others wanted to chuck me out.

"I wasn't really a Ted, just a Rocker. I was imitating Teds, pretending to be one. I was never a real one, with chains and real gangs. If I'd met a proper Ted I'd have been shit-scared. Yet all the parents always thought I was a real Ted, a bad influence on their kids. I got more confidence and just used to ignore Mimi. I ran away for longer spells. Wore what clothes I wanted. I was always on at Paul to ignore his dad and just wear what he wanted.

"I never liked the work. I should have been an illustrator or in the painting school because it seemed groovy. But I found myself in lettering. I didn't turn up for something, so they just put me in that. They might as well have put me in sky diving for the use I was at lettering. I failed all the exams. I stayed on because it was better than working. I was there instead of going to work.

"I always felt I'd make it, though. There were some moments of doubt, but I knew something would eventually happen. When Mimi used to throw things away I'd written or drawn, I used to say, 'You'll regret that when I'm famous,' and mean it. I didn't really know what I wanted to be, apart from ending up an eccentric millionaire. I fancied marrying a millionairess, and doing it that way.

"I had to be a millionaire. If I couldn't do it without being crooked, then I'd have to be crooked. I was quite prepared to do that—nobody obviously was going to give me money for my paintings. But I was too much of a coward to be a crook. I'd never have made it. I did plan to knock off a shop with another bloke, do it properly for a change, not just shoplifting. We used to look at shops at night, but we never got round to doing it."

Julia, John's mother, whom he was spending more and more time with, still approved of the life he was leading. She had now almost taken over from Mimi in his life. He relied on her, because she spoke the same language, liked the same things, hated the same sort of people.

"I was staying with Julia and Twitchy this weekend," says John. "We were sitting waiting for her to come home, Twitchy and me, wondering why she was so late. The copper came to the door, to tell us about the accident. It was just like it's supposed to be, the way it is in the films. Asking if I was her son, and all that. Then he told us, and we both went white. It was the worst ever thing that happened to me. We'd caught up so much, me and Julia, in just a few years. We could communicate. We got on. She was great. I thought, fuck it, fuck it, fuck it. That's really fucked everything. I've no responsibilities to anyone now.

"Twitchy took it worse than me. Then he said, 'Who's going to look after the kids?' And I hated him. Bloody selfishness.

"We got a taxi over to Sefton General where she was lying dead. I didn't want to see her. I talked hysterically to the taxi driver all the way, just ranted on and on, the way you do, just babbled on. The taxi driver just grunted now and again. I refused to go in and see her. But Twitchy did. He broke down." The accident had happened outside Mimi's house in Menlove Avenue.

"I always went out with her to the bus stop," says Mimi. "But this night she left early, at twenty to ten. She went out on her own. A minute later there was a terrible screeching. I flew out and she was dead, knocked down by a car outside my house. I never told the rest of the family the exact spot. They all went past it so often, it would have hurt them too much.

"But Julia isn't dead to me. She's alive as ever. I've never been near her grave, nor Mother's. They're both alive to me. I love them so dearly."

When Julia died, Pete Shotton says, it must obviously have been a terrible tragedy for John. "But he never showed it. It was like when masters beat him up. He never gave anything away. His exterior never showed his feelings." All John's friends knew about the road accident as soon as it happened. Another friend, Nigel Whalley, had been the last to speak to Julia as she came out of Mimi's house to cross Menlove Avenue for the bus. There were tram lines in the middle of Menlove in those days.

"John never talked about Julia or how he felt," says Pete. "But he took it out of his girls. He gave them hell. I remember one of them shouting at him, 'Don't take it out of me 'cos your mother's dead!' "

Mrs. Harrison, George's mother, remembers the effect it had on John. They were still practicing a lot at George's house, the only house where they got endless hospitality and encouragement.

"I remember when I'd given them all beans and toast one evening. It was several months before John's mother died and he was just getting really close to her. I overheard him say to Paul, 'I don't know how you can sit there and act normal with your mother dead. If anything like that happened to me, I'd go off me head.'

"When John's mother did die, he didn't seem to go off his head, but he wouldn't come out. I forced George to go round and see him, to make sure he still went off playing in their group and just didn't sit and brood. They all went through a lot together, even in those early days, and they always helped each other. George was terrified that I was going to die next. He'd watch me carefully all the time. I told him not to be so silly. I wasn't going to die."

Other students at the Art College at the same time as John say Julia's death did make him worse, less interested in other people's feelings, more cruel in his humor.

Thelma Pickles was one of his girl friends at the time, nothing serious, just one of the many people who were in his crowd. Most of them were in awe of him in a way, amazed by his attitude to life because they'd never come across such a personality before.

"John never had any money. He was a real bum, borrowing from everybody all the time, getting people to buy him chips or drinks, or cadging ciggies. He must still owe people pounds. But he has a sort of magnetic personality and could always get money out of people. He was outrageous, and said things people would be scared to say. He could be very cruel. Walking down the street he would go *Boo* in front of old people. And if he saw anyone who was crippled or deformed, he'd make loud remarks, like 'Some people will do anything to get out of the Army.'

"He used to do a lot of cruel drawings as well. I thought they were marvelous. He did one of some women cooing over some babies, saying weren't they lovely. All the babies were deformed, with hideous faces. It was really very cruel. The day the Pope died he did lots of cartoons of him looking really awful. He did one of the Pope standing outside some big pillars outside Heaven, shaking the gates and trying to get in. Underneath it said, 'But I'm the Pope, I tell you.' John had a complete disrespect for everything. But he always had an audience round him. There was one girl who was crazy about him. She used to cry over him.

"He was very self-conscious about his glasses and would never wear them even at the pictures. We went to see *King Creole,* an Elvis film, but he still wouldn't put them on. There was a big sexy advert on for nylons, and he couldn't see that either and I had to tell him what it was."

Thelma picked up from John, she says, the idea that Mimi was very cruel and strict to him. She naturally thought Mimi sounded terrible. "She wouldn't let him go anywhere and only gave him half a crown a day to spend. She was overstrict. We spent hours drinking, or just standing around in the Crack [a pub next to College]. But John couldn't do much drinking on half a crown, could he?

"I never took his music seriously. He would say he'd written this new tune and I would think that was pretty fantastic, someone writing a tune, but I couldn't see what good it was. I knew it took miracles to get anywhere writing bits of tunes, so what was the point? I knew he *could* be famous, at something, but I didn't know what. He was so different and original. But I just couldn't see what he could be famous at. Perhaps a comedian, I thought."

John agrees with most of Thelma's memories of him at Art College. He remembers it all flatly, with little nostalgia or amusement. That was just how it was. "I had to borrow or pinch, as I had no money at college," he says. "So I used to cadge all the time, usually from spaniels like Thelma.

"I suppose I did have a cruel humor. It was at school that it first started. We were once coming home from a school speech day and we'd had a few bevvies. Liverpool is full of deformed people, the way you have them in Glasgow, three-foot-high men selling newspapers. I'd never really noticed them before, but all the way home that day they seemed to be everywhere. It got funnier and funnier and we couldn't stop laughing. I suppose it was a way of hiding your emotions, or covering it up. I would never hurt a cripple. It was just part of our jokes, our way of life."

Two new people came into John's life at Art College. The first was Stuart Sutcliffe. He was in the same year but unlike John showed genuine promise, and keenness, as an artist. "Stu's work was great. He helped me to draw."

Stu was slight and slender, artistic and highly strung, but very fierce and individualistic in his views. He and John became immediate friends. Stu admired John's presence, the fact that he created an atmosphere around him with his dominant personality. John in turn admired Stu's talent for art, which was better than his, and also Stu's greater knowledge of and feeling for art. He knew much more than John about what was happening in the art and design world. Stu couldn't play any instrument and knew little about pop music, but he was completely bowled over when he heard John and his group play in the Art College at lunchtimes.

"Stu used to watch us everywhere we went. He was always saying how good we were when nobody else was very impressed."

George and Paul especially appear to have been slightly jealous of Stu and his influence over John, not that outsiders could see how much John admired Stu. John picked on Stu all the time, hurt him when he could, even though they were inseparable. Paul, following John's lead, also used to pick on Stu, even though Paul was influenced by Stu as well. Paul was always interested in art and he, like John, got from Stu a lot of new ideas and fashions. The other important friend John made at Art College was Cynthia, now his wife.

Thelma Pickles, who was already a girl in John's circle and like him a bit of a tearaway, couldn't understand what John saw in Cynthia.

"Cynthia was so quiet," says Thelma. "A completely different type from us. She came from over the water, the posh part, from a middle-class area. She wore a twin set. She was very nice, but I just couldn't see her suiting John. He used to go on about her, telling us how marvelous she was. I just couldn't see it. I left college for a year, and when I was away I heard they were going strong. I thought that would settle him down, calm him a bit, but it didn't turn out that way at all."

Cynthia Powell was in the same year as John from the beginning, and in the same special class. They both chose lettering as their craft. But for well over the first year they took no notice of each other and moved in completely different circles, she the rather shy and refined very respectable girl from over the water, he the loudmouthed Liverpool Teddy boy.

"I just thought he was horrible. My first memory of ever looking at him properly was in a lecture theater when I saw Helen Anderson sitting behind him stroking his hair. It awoke something in me. I thought it was dislike at first. Then I realized it was jealousy. But I never had any contact with him, apart from him stealing things from me, like rulers and brushes. He looked awful in those days as well. He had this long tweed overcoat which had belonged to his Uncle George and his hair all greased back. I didn't fancy him at all. He was scruffy. But I didn't get a chance to know him, anyway. I wasn't one of his crowd. I was so respectable, or I thought I was."

"She was a right Hoylake runt," says John. "Dead snobby. We used to poke fun at her and mock her, me and my mate Jeff Mohamed. 'Quiet please,' we'd shout. 'No dirty jokes. It's Cynthia and Phyllis.' She was another one of the Hoylake crowd. I wasn't in with them. I used to hang around with the other loudmouths."

They had their first bit of proper conversation in a lettering class one day. "It came out that we were both shortsighted. We talked a bit about it. John doesn't remember that at all, do you?" John said "No." "Very disheartening. But I do. It was after that I found myself getting into the class early, so that I could sit next to him. I used to hang around outside afterwards, hoping to bump into him.

"I didn't make any advances at all. It was just something I felt. John didn't know at all. I wasn't seeming to push at all. I couldn't do that. I don't think he even realizes now how often I used to hang around on the off chance of seeing him." They met, properly, at Christmastime in their second year, 1958.

"We had a class dance," says John. "I was pissed and asked her to dance. Jeff Mohamed had been having me on, saying 'Cynthia likes you, you know.' As we danced I asked her to come out to a party the next day. She said she couldn't. She was engaged."

"I was," says Cynthia. "Well, almost. I'd been going out with the same boy for three years and was about to get engaged. John got annoyed when I said no. So he said come and have a drink afterwards at the Crack. I said no at first, then I went. I wanted to really, all the time."

"I was triumphant," says John. "Having picked her up. We had a drink then went back to Stu's flat, buying fish and chips on the way." They went out every night after that, usually in the afternoon as well, going to the pictures instead of lectures.

"I was frightened of him. He was so rough. He wouldn't give in. We fought all the time. I thought if I give in now, that'll be it. He was really just testing me out. I don't mean sexually, just to see if I could be trusted, to prove to him that I could be."

"I was just hysterical," said John. "That was the trouble. I was jealous of anyone she had anything to do with. I demanded absolute trust from her, just because I wasn't trustworthy myself. I was neurotic, taking out all my frustrations on her. She did leave me once. That was terrible."

"I'd had enough," says Cynthia. "It was getting on my nerves. He just went off and kissed another girl."

"But I couldn't stand being without her. I rang her up."

"I was sitting by the phone, waiting for him."

But John was still as inconsiderate as ever, even after that incident. He went off once on a bus to London for the weekend.

"He went just like that," says Cynthia, "without telling me."

"I didn't."

"You did. It was a college trip, but there was still no need to go."

"Yeh, okay, I was like that. I used to take her dinner money off her, which her mother had given her, and go off and get pissed."

"I wasn't in a hurry to introduce John to my mother. I wanted to prepare her for the shock. He was never overpolite and he looked so scruffy and like a Teddy boy. My mother played it cool. She was good, really, though I'm sure she was hoping for it to peter out. But she never tried to stop it. The teachers warned me about going out with him, that my work was beginning to suffer. My work did go to pot and they were always on at me. Molly, the cleaning woman, once caught John hitting me, really clouting me. She said I was a silly girl to get mixed up with someone like that."

"I was in a sort of blind rage for two years," says John. "I was either drunk or fighting. It had been the same with other girl friends I'd had. There was something the matter with me."

"I just kept hoping he'd get over it, but I wondered if I could stick it long enough to find out. I blamed his background, his home, Mimi, and the College. College just wasn't the place for him. Institutions aren't made for John."

Chapter 8: From Quarrymen to Moondogs

The name Quarrymen had gone by the end of 1959. Paul and George were at the Institute and had nothing to do with Quarry Hill High School, and John was now at the Art College. They had a succession of names after that, often made up on the spur of the moment. One night they called themselves The Rainbows because they all turned up in different-colored shirts.

The group had made no real progress for about the year after George had joined it, as far as George himself can remember, though his guitar playing was improving all the time.

"I can't remember even getting paid in the first year I was with them. Perhaps just a few bob. We either got free Cokes or plates of beans; that was about all. The only times we got anywhere near real money was when we started entering for skiffle competitions. We'd get through the early rounds, keeping going to try and win something. But you never got paid for entering, just winning, and the rounds seemed to go on forever.

"It was pretty daft, of course, having no proper drummer and about eighteen guitarists. We mainly played at fellows' parties when I first joined. We'd go along with our guitars, uninvited, and get in."

While Mrs. Harrison was mad about George and his group, Mr. Harrison was very worried. He'd fought a losing battle over George's clothes and his long hair, mainly because Mrs. Harrison sided with George. "It's his own hair," I used to say. "Why should anyone tell you what to do with what's your own?"

"But I wanted him to stick it at school and get a good job," says Mr. Harrison. "I was very upset when I saw he was so keen on the group. I realized you had to be good in show business to get to the top and even better to stay there. I couldn't see how they were going to get anywhere. My other two boys were well set up, Harry as a fitter and Peter as a panel beater in a car factory. I wanted George to do as well.

"But George said he wanted to leave school. He didn't want to be any sort of pen-pusher. He wanted to work with his hands. He decided with his mother he wanted to leave, unknown to me. He never took his school certificate. He just left."

George started work in the summer of 1959, when he was sixteen.

"It became obvious I wasn't going to get any qualifications. The most I could have got, pushing it, would have been two O levels. But you need two O levels before they even let you dig shit. So what good would that have been?

"I stayed till the end of term, sagging off school most of the time to be with John at the Art College. Paul and I used to hang round there a lot.

"I hadn't a job for a long time when I left school. I hadn't a clue. My dad was all keen on the apprenticeship thing, so I tried the apprentice's exam for the Liverpool Corporation, but failed it. Eventually the Youth Employment Officer came up with a job of being a window dresser at Blacklers, the big department store. I went along, but it had gone. They offered me an apprenticeship as an electrician instead.

"I enjoyed it. It was better than school. And with winter coming on, it was nice to be in a big warm shop. We used to play darts most of the time. But I began to think at the time about emigrating to Australia. At least I tried to get my dad interested in us all going, as I was too young. Then I thought of Malta as I'd seen some travel brochures. Then I thought of Canada. I got the papers to fill in, but when I found my parents had to sign them for me, I didn't bother. I felt something would turn up."

Over at the McCartney household, widower Jim was struggling to bring up two teenage boys on the right lines. At least Paul was still at school, much to Jim's pleasure. But with spending all his spare time with John and George, messing around with a beat group, it didn't leave much time for schoolwork.

Paul had still managed to stay in 5B, which was looked upon as the main English and languages stream, but he didn't do very well in O levels. He didn't do as badly as John, who didn't pass any. Paul did manage to pass one, Art.

He then thought about leaving, but couldn't think of what job to do. His father was still keen for him to stay on. It seemed easier *not* to leave. School still gave him lots of time for playing. So he stayed on and went into the Remove form, as he hadn't enough O levels to get immediately into the Sixth. He sat O levels again and got four more this time and so went into the Sixth Form.

"School was still a complete drag, but there was an English master called Dusty Durband I liked, the only one I did. He was great. He liked modern poetry and used to tell us about Lady Chatterley, long before we'd heard of it, and 'The Miller's Tale.' He said they were considered dirty books, though they weren't."

This spark of interest kept him in the Sixth Form, although he did no work. Officially he was preparing two subjects, English and Art at A level or Advanced level, as officially he was going to go to a training college and become a teacher. Everybody knew he was more than capable of it. It kept Jim happy, anyway.

"I never thought much of the music Paul was interested in," says Jim. "That Bill Haley, I never liked him. There was no tune to it all. But one day I came home at five-thirty and heard them in the house playing. I realized then that they were getting good, not just bashing about. They were making some nice chords."

Jim then began to want to sit in with them, giving advice and hints about how *he* used to do it in the good old days of Jim Mac's Band. Why didn't they play some really *good* tunes? Like "Stairway to Paradise"? He'd always thought that was a really lovely number. He told them about how he used to run his band and how they should present their numbers.

They said no thanks, very much, just make some tea, eh, Dad. He said all right. But if they didn't like "Stairway to Paradise" how about some really jazzy numbers, like "When the Saints"? He could tell them a good way to do that. They said no, more firmly this time.

In the end, Jim restricted himself to making them food. He'd had to take up cooking, after a fashion, when his wife died. He found to his delight that although his own two, Paul and Michael, were very choosy about their food and were poor eaters—and when Paul was busy he wouldn't eat at all—John and George turned out to be gluttons who would eat anything at any time. "I used to work off all the stuff onto them that Paul and Michael had left. In the end I didn't have to disguise it but just say there was some leftovers here, would they like it. To this day I always have to make George some custard when he comes. He says my custard's the best in the world."

The group was improving, getting some primitive amplifiers together and creating more of a loud beat, compared with the soft patterings of skiffle, which had now died anyway. "But each year seemed five years at the time," says Paul. They were now mainly playing at workingmen's social clubs or church functions and had given up parties. They played at places like the Wilson Hall and the Finch Lane Bus Depot.

They went in for more and more competitions, like all the embryo groups. "There was this woman who played the spoons who kept on beating us," says Paul. "Then there was the Sunny Siders. This group had a great gimmick. They had a midget."

The members of the group were still constantly changing. As nobody knew them, they could turn up on dates with whomever they could get. "We had a bloke called Duff as pianist for some time, but his dad wouldn't let him stay out late. He'd be playing away one minute, and the next he would have disappeared, gone home in the middle of a number."

For their public performances, they were usually all dressed like Teddy-boy cowboys, with black-and-white cowboy shirts with white tassels from the top pockets and black bootlace ties. But they spent more time in George's or Paul's house than onstage. "We used to come back to our house and smoke tea in me dad's pipe," says Paul. "Sometimes we'd bring a girl home and sit and draw each other. But we were playing guitars most of the time and writing songs."

John and Paul wrote about a hundred songs together in that first year. Only one was ever used later, "Love Me Do." A lot of them were thrown out years later by mistake by Jane Asher when she was cleaning out Paul's cupboards.

"The first thing we did when we started a new one was write *Another original by John Lennon and Paul McCartney*."

They were both getting more adept at playing the guitars as well, thanks partly to watching the big stars of the day playing on TV. "I watched the Shadows backing Cliff Richard one night. I'd heard them play a very clever introduction to 'Move It' on the record, but could never work out how they did it. Then I saw them do it on TV. I rushed out of the house straight away, got on me bike, and raced up to John's with me guitar. 'I've got it,' I shouted. And we all got down to learning it right away. It gave us a little bit of flash to start off our numbers. I also got some good chords from listening to 'Blue Moon.' "

As they were always keen to enter any competition, however crummy, there was great excitement when the biggest competition organizer of the day arrived in Liverpool. The advertisement in the Liverpool *Echo* said that "Mr. Star-Maker, Carroll Levis" was due to pay a visit soon as part of his Carroll Levis Discoveries TV show. The show was going to be recorded in Manchester but he was to hold a local audition in Liverpool, at the Empire Theatre, to see which Liverpudlian talent was fit for the program itself in Manchester.

John, Paul, and George, like half the population of Liverpool—by that time almost half the teenage population of Liverpool was in groups—went along for the audition. They got through the audition and were invited to Manchester to do the show.

Mrs. Harrison remembers the excitement. "George was dead thrilled by this letter which had come through the post one day. I couldn't see what all the fuss was about. The letter was addressed to some group called The Moondogs."

The Moondogs was what they had become, just a name thought up on the spur of the moment for the Carroll Levis Show. They were in fact on the bill as Johnny and the Moondogs. All groups had a leader in those days, like Cliff Richard and the Shadows. So they had to have John's name in first. He was the leader anyway, if anyone was.

They did their bit in Manchester and got a reasonable amount of applause afterward. But the whole basis of the Carroll Levis show was that at the end each group comes on, does a few bars from its piece again, and the audience claps like mad, or otherwise. It is this final clap which is registered and the winners decided.

But Johnny and the Moondogs, being poor Liverpool lads, with no transport of any kind to get them back to Liverpool, couldn't wait. The show was running late and they were about to miss their last train back to Liverpool. They hadn't enough money for a night in a Manchester hotel. So when the time came for the final applause, they had gone. Naturally, they didn't win. But they weren't even spotted, or noticed, or given any encouragement by the talent spotters around. Neither was the Billy Fury to be. Nobody wanted him either.

For John, Paul, and George it was a big disappointment. Their first time within touching distance of the big-time professionals had come and gone.

Chapter 9: Stu and Scotland and the Silver Beatles

At the Art College John and Stuart were becoming even closer friends. Stu spent most of his time following the group round and watching them practice. He and John together managed to persuade a college committee to buy them a tape recorder, ostensibly for use by all students. John took it over for himself, to record his group playing, or just messing around, so that they could hear what they sounded like. They also got a public-address system bought for use at college dances. This ended up as part of the group's amplification equipment.

Stu was still as interested in art, despite spending so much time with John and his group. He entered some paintings for the John Moore Exhibition, one of the best exhibitions of its type, not just on Merseyside but throughout Britain. John Moore, a member of the wealthy Liverpool family which is connected with Littlewoods soccer pools, always awards substantial prizes for the best exhibits. Stuart Sutcliffe, although still a student, won a prize worth £60, a huge sum and a great honor for one so young.

John, his best friend and biggest influence, immediately saw a way of using the money in the best possible way. Stu had always been saying that he wished he could play an instrument and really be in their group, instead of just hanging around. John said now was his chance to join. With his £60 he could buy a bass guitar, which the group had always lacked. Then he could join. It didn't matter that he couldn't play. They would teach him.

Paul and George were equally keen on the idea, as they needed another member for the group and also a bass player. From what George remembers, Stu was offered an alternative—he could buy himself a bass and join or a set of drums. They needed both, they had three stars on guitars and no backing of any sort.

"Stu had no idea how to play it," says George. "We all showed him what we could, but he really picked it up by just coming round with us and playing onstage." In those early days, as can be seen from photographs, Stu usually had his back to the audience, just so that no one could see how very few chords he was playing. They were doing more and more engagements, but still as an amateur group, earning a few bob on the side, playing at workingmen's clubs and socials.

But as the beat-group boom took over Liverpool completely, with so many groups competing to play, there sprang up little teenage clubs which put on special beat shows. Sometimes these were simply coffee clubs, on the lines of the hundreds of coffee bars, serving espresso coffee amid lots of rubber plants and bamboo, which had sprung up all over the country. Only the Liverpool ones had live beat groups playing as well.

But the groups couldn't get into the sort of clubs, like the Cavern, which had always had live groups. They were only for jazz bands and jazz fans, a much higher art form, attracting a much higher class of following. The beat groups were all scruffy and amateur and Teddy-boyish. It was a real working-class art form, full of electricians and laborers. There was a strong tendency to look down upon all beat groups and the people who played in them. The best groups wanted to get into places like jazz clubs because unlike the night clubs, where the music was just a background noise, jazz clubs at least were places where you went mainly to listen to the music.

"We were always anti-jazz," says John. "I think it is shit music, even more stupid than rock and roll, followed by people like students in cheap pullovers. Jazz never gets anywhere, never does anything, it's always the same and all they do is drink pints of beer. We hated jazz particularly because in the early days they wouldn't let us play at clubs, as they only wanted jazz. We'd never get auditions because of the jazz bands."

They were now all trying to get wired up, with electric guitars using amps, which skiffle groups had never done. There were lots of other rock-type singers who had come along in Elvis' wake, like Little Richard and Jerry Lee Lewis.

But of course it was still in London that everything in Britain happened. Britain's first rock-and-roll singer who had any national success in Britain on the lines of the American stars was a cockney who made it in London through the London coffee bars—Tommy Steele. Then there was Cliff Richard, who at first modeled himself completely on Elvis. He became even more of a teenage heart-throb than Tommy Steele.

John, George, and Paul seem to have been unaware of Tommy Steele; at least they can't remember him making any impression on them. But they actively hated Cliff Richard and the Shadows. John says it was Cliff's sort of Christian image, even then, which also offended him, as at the time he was against all such images. But they also hated the sort of traditional pop ballads Cliff Richard went on to sing, on the same lines as Perry Como and Frankie Vaughan.

Paul, as the one who always tried to make things happen, was always prepared to play down their likes and dislikes and chat up anyone who looked like helping them. He was trying hard to get them some publicity in the local newspapers so someone like Larry Parnes might hear of them. He has a letter now which he wrote at the time to some journalist called Mr. Low they had met in a pub.

Dear Mr Low,

I am sorry about the time I have taken to write to you, but I hope I have not left it too late. Here are some details about the group.

It consists of four boys: Paul McCartney (guitar), John Lennon (guitar), Stuart Sutcliffe (bass) and George Harrison (another guitar) and is called . . .

This line-up may at first seem dull but it must be appreciated that as the boys have above average instrumental ability they achieve surprisingly varied effects. Their basic beat is off-beat, but this has recently tended to be accompanied by a faint on-beat; thus the overall sound is rather reminiscent of the four in the bar of traditional jazz. This could possibly be put down to the influence of Mr McCartney who led one of the top local jazz bands (Jim Mac's Jazz Band) in the 1920s.

Modern music, however, is the group's delight, and, as if to prove the point, John and Paul have written over fifty tunes, ballads and faster numbers, during the last three years. Some of these tunes are purely instrumental (such as "Looking Glass Catswalk" and "Winston's Walk") and others were composed with the modern audience in mind (tunes like "Thinking of Linking" "The One after 909," "Years Roll Along" and "Keep Looking That Way").

The group also derive a great deal of pleasure from re-arranging old favourites ("Ain't She Sweet," "You Were Meant For Me," "Home," "Moonglow," "You Are My Sunshine," and others).

Now for a few details about the boys themselves. John, who leads the group, attends the College of Art, and, as well as being an accomplished guitarist and banjo player, he is an experienced cartoonist. His many interests include painting, the theatre, poetry, and of course singing. He is 19 years old and is a founder member of the group.

Paul is 18 years old and is reading English Literature at Liverpool University. He, like the other boys, plays more than one instrument—his specialties being the piano and drums, plus, of course . . .

Dear Mr. Low,

I am sorry about the time I have taken to write to you, but I ~~still~~ hope I have not left it too late. Here are some details about the group.

It ~~is made up~~ consists of ~~four~~ four boys :- Paul (guitar) McCartney, John (guitar) Lennon, ~~and~~ Stuart (bass) Sutcliffe and George (another Harrison guitarist.) and is called the .... This line-up may at first seem rather dull, but it must be appreciated that as the boys all have above-average ~~playing~~ instrumental ability, ~~they~~ achieve ~~a surprising amount of~~ surprisingly varied effects. Their basic beat is the off-beat, but this has recently ~~been~~ ~~the~~ tended to be accompanied by a faint on-beat; thus the overall sound is ~~rather~~ reminiscent of the 4-in-the-bar beat of traditional Jazz. This could possibly be put down to the influence on the group of Mr. McCartney, who

Beat
Mr. Mac.
50 tunes
Billy Fury
Places
Competition.
Records.

led one of the top local jazz bands (Jim Mac's Jazz Band) in the 1920's.

Modern music is, however, the groups' delight, and, as if to prove the point, John and Paul have written over 50 tunes, ballads & faster numbers, during the last three years. Some of these tunes are purely instrumental (such as 'Looking Glass, Catswalk, and Winston's Walk') and others were composed with the modern audience in mind. (tunes like ' Thinking of Linking, The One after 909, Years Roll Along, and keep looking that way.) The group also derive a great deal of pleasure from re-arranging old favourites (Ain't She Sweet, You were meant for me, Home, Moonglow, You are my Sunshine, and others.) Now for a few details about the boys themselves.

John, who leads the group, attends the College of Art, and, as well as being an accomplished guitarist and banjo-player, he is an experienced cartoonist. His many interests include painting, the theatre, poetry, and, of course, singing. He is 18 years old and is a founder member of the group.

Paul is 18 years old, and is reading English Literature at Liverpool University. He, like the other boys, plays more than one instrument, his specialities being the piano + drums, plus, of course,

And there this highly colorful mixture of fact and fiction ends.

In 1959, because it looked once again as if they were about to get an important audition, they got a new name. They started seriously trying to think of what to call themselves, just as they'd done for the Carroll Levis audition.

This is when the idea of the Beatles came up for the first time. No one is definitely sure how it happened. Paul and George just remember John arriving with it one day.

They'd always been fans of Buddy Holly and the Crickets. They liked his music and also his name. They particularly liked the Crickets bit. It had a nice double meaning, one of them a purely English meaning which Americans couldn't have appreciated. They wished they'd thought of calling themselves the Crickets. Thinking of the name Crickets, John naturally thought of other insects with a name which could also be played around with. He'd filled books as a child with similar word play.

"I was sitting at home one day," says John. "Just thinking about what a good name the Crickets would be for an English group. The idea of beetles came into my head. I decided to spell it BEAtles to make it look like beat music, just as a joke."

That was the real and simple origin of their name, though for years afterward they made up different daft reasons each time anyone asked them. Usually they said a man with a magic carpet appeared at a window and told them.

Though they now had a name they at last liked, they weren't called the Beatles for a long time. They met a friend who ran another beat group, Casy Jones of Cass and the Casanovas, who asked them what their new name was. He said it was rotten. You had to have a long name for a group, he said, like his. Why didn't they call themselves Long John and the Silver Beatles? Beatles on its own, he said, was far too short and simple. They didn't think much of his idea either. But when this important audition came up and they were asked what they were calling themselves they said Silver Beatles, which was a name they stuck to for the rest of that year, 1959.

The important auditioner was none other than the famous Larry Parnes, the king of British rock and roll, who now had in his stable—apart from Tommy Steele and Billy Fury—people like Marty Wilde, Duffy Power, and Johnny Gentle. They'd heard about Larry Parnes coming to Liverpool while hanging around the Jackaranda, a club where most of the beat groups used to play. This was owned by a Liverpool Welshman called Alan Williams. He also ran the Blue Angel, the club in which the Larry Parnes audition was going to be held.

Not only did they arrive at the audition without a definite name (it was only when one of Larry Parnes' assistants asked them for a name that they came out with Silver Beatles), they also arrived without a drummer. A drummer they'd been using now and again had promised to turn up, but he didn't. Once again they were drummerless.

But a drummer, who was at the Blue Angel for the audition with another group, did them a favor and stood in with them. He was Johnny Hutch, looked upon as one of the top three drummers of the time in Liverpool. There is a photograph of the Silver Beatles taken at that audition. Johnny Hutch is sitting at the back looking very bored and superior. As usual, you can't see much of Stu. He has his back to Larry Parnes, trying to hide his fingerwork on the bass.

They passed the audition and got a job, which was to be a two-week tour of Scotland as the backing group to one of Larry Parnes' newest discoveries, Johnny Gentle. It was in no sense their tour. The Silver Beatles were to be very minor. But it was their first-ever proper engagement as professionals, and a real tour at that, however short and however third-rate.

George, who was then coming on for sixteen, took his two weeks' holiday so that he could go. Paul was about to sit his O levels, but he had no intention of missing the chance of a tour for something as trivial as his GCE. Ivan Vaughan, his friend at the Institute, remembers arguing with him and saying he was silly to go off and not do any work for his exams.

Paul somehow managed to convince his father that he'd been given two weeks' holiday from school. Paul said that the whole class had, as a two-week rest after all their hard work preparing for the exams. They'd been told to take things easy. He said he would be back just in time for the exams and the tour would be a good rest for his brain. No wonder he only passed in one subject.

They had to get yet another new drummer for this tour of Scotland. He was called Thomas Moore. They can't remember anything else about him, except that they went to his flat to get him and that he'd been living on the dole. Thomas Moore, apparently, was his real name.

But the Silver Beatles themselves, in this first flush of being pro, all wanted to change their names. That was the fashion. "It was exciting changing your name," says Paul. "It made it seem all real and professional. It sort of proved you did a real act if you had a stage name."

Paul turned himself into Paul Ramon. He can't remember where he got the Ramon bit from. "I must have heard it somewhere. I thought it sounded really glamorous, sort of Valentinoish." George became Carl Harrison after one of his heroes, Carl Perkins. Stu was still Stu. John can't remember what he called himself, if anything, but others remember him as Johnny Silver.

The tour of Scotland was to be in the far north, round little ballrooms on the northeast coast. Paul can remember Inverness and Nairn but no other names. "I can remember lying around on some sand dunes, but I don't know where." He sent back post cards to his father saying: "It's gear. I've been asked for my autograph."

They were all a bit jealous of the fact that George was getting on particularly well with the star of the tour, Johnny Gentle. He promised to give George a present after the tour, one of Eddie Cochrane's old shirts.

They were all thrilled to see their name, Silver Beatles, on posters, however small. They argued as usual among themselves, but most of all they picked on Stu, the new member of the group. John, George, and Paul had been with each other long enough to know that rows and arguments and criticism didn't mean much. If they did, you just argued back. But Stu, slight and sensitive, took it all to heart. They all ganged up and picked on him. They all say now that they regret being so cruel to him.

"We were terrible," says John. "We'd tell him he couldn't sit with us, or eat with us, or tell him to go away, and he did." At one hotel they stayed at, a variety show had just gone. "I think it was Jimmy Logan." In this show there was a dwarf. They somehow found out which bed he had slept in and said that would have to be Stu's. They certainly weren't going to sleep in it. So Stu had to. All very petty and childish, but hurtful if you took it seriously, as Stu did. "That was how he learned to be with us," says John. "Because that was what we were like."

After Scotland they didn't get much work, although they were now becoming more experienced. They were still not playing to the sort of people they were really aiming at. Any dates they got were still dances full of drunken Teds, workingmen on their night out, or sleazy clubs.

They got one date, not long after Scotland, at a strip club in Upper Parliament Street. They had to accompany Janice the stripper as she shed her clothes. "She handed us the music she wanted," says George. "It was something like the Gypsy Fire Dance. As we couldn't read music, it wasn't much use to us. We just played 'Ramrod,' then 'Moonglow' as I'd just learned it. We did quite a few nights with her."

They did manage a couple of dates at the Cavern Club in Mathew Street around the same time, but this was still a jazz stronghold. The Cavern didn't want really rock-and-roll groups. "We used to get little notes passed up to us telling us not to play rock and roll." They would introduce their next number as if it were a genuine jazz piece. "And now an old favorite by Leadbelly called 'Long Tall Sally.' " And they'd play a beat number, which wasn't liked by the management and didn't help them to get further dates.

But most of the time they didn't do much, except hang around each other's houses or when they had any money, the clubs. "Scotland had been our first glimpse of show business, a faint hope," says George. "It was a bit of come down being back in Liverpool. We were lucky to get more than two dates a week. We were making about fifteen bob a night, plus as much eggs on toast and Cokes we could take."

Chapter 10: The Casbah

One of the places they started going back to, for want of anything better, was the Casbah Club. They'd played there earlier in the year, before they'd gone to Scotland.

Mrs. Best, who founded the Casbah, is small, dark-haired, and very volatile. She comes from Delhi, India. She met her husband, Johnny Best, an ex-boxing promoter, in India during the war. She came back to Liverpool with him and eventually they bought a large fourteen-room Victorian house at number 8 Hayman's Green, in the good residential district of West Derby.

Pete Best, her elder son, was born in 1941. He went to Liverpool Collegiate, another of Liverpool's grammar schools. He passed five subjects at O level and went into the Sixth Form. His plan was to be a teacher.

Pete was handsome and well-built but rather shy, almost sullen-looking and uncommunicative, especially in comparison with his dynamic, energetic mother. When he began to bring friends back from school, she went to great lengths to encourage him. During the summer holidays of 1959, when Pete was about to go into his second year in the sixth, he and a gang of his friends asked his mother if instead of cluttering up all her rooms playing records they could clear out the huge cellar and use that. "The original idea was that it would be their den," she says. "That developed into the idea of making it into a coffee club just for teenagers. We decided to make it a private club, charging a membership fee of a shilling, just to keep out the Teds and roughs."

They decided to have in some of the beat groups which were springing up all over Liverpool. They knew there would be many who would jump at the chance. Mrs. Best, with her flair for running things and people, probably jumped at the chance as well.

The group they found was the Quarrymen. This came through a girl who knew one of the members of the Quarrymen and said how good they were. It wasn't John, Paul, or George she knew, but someone else who was playing the guitar for them at the time, Ken Brown. He was one of the many members of the Quarrymen who were always coming and going in those days. Ken Brown was the direct link with Mrs. Best's club, but George, through his own friends, had also heard about Pete Best and his mother starting a club.

When John, Paul, and George heard they were looking for a group, they all came round at once. They were immediately given paintbrushes and helped with the final week or so of cleaning and decorating the cellar. John brought his girl friend, Cynthia Powell, to help.

"I remember telling John," says Mrs. Best, "to put some undercoat on a wall. When I came back, he had finished painting but had done it all in gloss. He was so shortsighted he hadn't been able to tell the difference. I was in a panic that it would never dry in time."

Even up to the opening day, they hadn't decided on a name. "I went down one evening to see how they were getting on. It was so bloody mysterious, with little dark corners everywhere. It seemed Oriental. I thought of this picture I'd just seen with Hedy Lamarr and Charles Boyer, *Algiers* I think it was called, in which they go to the Casbah. So that was the name I chose, the Casbah Club. As I come from India, it seemed very apt."

It opened at the end of August 1959. There were nearly 300 there that first night. The Quarrymen got a great reception. The Casbah seemed launched for a long time. "I was very pleased," says Mrs. Best. "Not for myself of course, but for Peter. He had vague notions about going into show business and I thought this might be some sort of experience for him, helping with the club, in a small way. I thought it would make him less self-conscious, give him more confidence."

The club thrived. The price was a shilling to come in. Coffee and sweets were on sale and the Quarrymen to listen to. At weekends, there were crowds in the evening of up to 400. Very soon there was a membership of 3,000. A bouncer, Frank Garner, was hired to look after the door and keep out Teds.

All went well for a couple of months. Then a row developed over the Quarrymen. Their fee for playing was 15 shillings each a night. One night only John, Paul, and George played. Ken Brown was missing. "I paid the three of them fifteen shillings each, then I paid Ken Brown his fifteen bob when I saw him. They said he shouldn't have been paid at all as he hadn't been there. They said the fee for the group was really £3 for the evening. The three who had turned up should have got £3 between them, not fifteen bob each."

This is the basis of the disagreement as Mrs. Best and Pete Best remember it. The others can't. Anyway, after the row over the money, Ken Brown left them. Perhaps they'd just wanted to be rid of Ken Brown.

Pete Best had by this time started banging away at an old snare drum, seeing how well the Quarrymen were doing, but mainly just to amuse himself in odd moments at the club. When Ken Brown left, it was decided that he and Pete should form a new group. They got two others, Bill Barlow and Chas Newby, and called themselves the Blackjacks, aided and abetted by Mrs. Best.

"They were very good," says Mrs. Best. "I remember Rory Storme, who was very big in those days, issuing a challenge to see who could get the biggest crowd. Rory got 390 but the Blackjacks got 450, the most we ever had."

The Quarrymen began to move away to other and better engagements. They went to Scotland and became the Silver Beatles but did occasional return engagements at the Casbah, when nothing else turned up. The Blackjacks, with Pete Best on drums, became the Casbah's resident group. "I'd just started for a laugh," says Pete. "At first we were just making a noise."

But they got better during the following year. Pete decided he did want to go into show business. "I got fed up with school. I'd been thinking by then of going to a teachers' training college. My five O levels would have got me in. But I got fed up and just left before sitting A levels."

He left school in the summer term of 1960. The Casbah was still a big success and there was enough for him to do there, but then his group began to disintegrate. Ken Brown moved south with his family and the two others went away on courses connected with their full-time work. Pete had left school for a career in show business, but was now left with nothing to do. But in August 1960, five weeks after he'd left school, Paul McCartney rang him.

"Paul said had I still got any drums," says Pete. "I told him I'd just got a complete new kit. I was very proud of that. He said they'd got a job in Hamburg and was I interested in being their drummer? I said yes. I'd always liked them very much. They said I'd get £15 a week, which was a lot. Much better than going to a training college.

"I went down to Alan Williams' club, the Jackaranda. I met Stu for the first time. I had an audition. I blasted off a few numbers and they all said fine, you can come to Hamburg with us." The reasons how a small-time night-club owner in Liverpool came to be sending a pop group to Hamburg in 1960 are not completely clear.

As Mrs. Best had got in on the beat-group act at the coffee club end, Alan Williams, an experienced night-club man, was getting onto it slightly higher up the scale. He was not only putting on the groups in his own night clubs but finding them for other people and acting as a sort of agent-cum-manager for groups looking for work. He had helped the Beatles get their Larry Parnes audition, which had been held at one of his clubs.

The Beatles' money for their Scottish tour, though paid by Larry Parnes, had come through Alan Williams, who had acted for them in getting the tour.

In meeting up with Larry Parnes, keeping an eye on Merseyside groups for him, Williams had established contact with London, which no one in Liverpool had done till then. Apart from the Beatles, he had been involved in getting another Liverpool group a provincial tour with Larry Parnes. This was a group called Derry and the Seniors. There had been some argument over money with this group. They thought they hadn't got enough. They decided to come to London and find the person they thought hadn't paid them enough.

"They told me they were going to London to fill in this bloke," says George Harrison. "As far as I can remember, Alan Williams decided to go with them." In London, Alan Williams and Derry and the Seniors naturally ended up hanging around the Two Is coffee bar in Soho, then the center for British rock groups. Tommy Steele and Lionel Bart both started there.

While he was at the Two Is, he met a Hamburg night-club owner, Bruno Koschmeider, who was in London, attracted by the rock groups springing up in Britain. He was looking for a likely group to take back with him. Alan Williams suggested Derry and the Seniors. A contract was made and Derry and the Seniors went to Hamburg, the first Liverpool group to go there.

They went over well. Alan Williams was asked if he could find another one. He thought of the Beatles.

In the Harrison household there was no undue excitement—apart of course from George. But his mother at least never tried to stop his going. She was worried about him being only seventeen and going abroad for the first time, especially Hamburg. She'd heard things about Hamburg. "But it was what he wanted to do. They were going to get properly paid for once. I knew they were good and were bound to do well. All I'd heard up to till then was 'Heh, Mum, we've got a booking, lend's the bus fare, eh, and I'll pay you back when I'm famous.' "

So Mrs. Harrison got George ready. She made him promise to write and gave him a tin of homemade scones. George, despite his great youth, was at least a working man. But Paul and John were still ostensibly studying. Going to Hamburg was going to ruin their great careers once and for all.

Jim McCartney was naturally all against Paul going to Hamburg. Paul had just sat his A levels—Art and English—and they were all waiting to hear if he'd got through them so that they would definitely know if he'd got a place at a teachers' training college.

Michael McCartney, Paul's brother, says that Paul, as ever, arranged everything very cleverly. "Our kid was always very good at handling Dad, and getting his own way. I remember coming home from school with Paul the day he told me they'd been invited to Hamburg, just casually. I said, Wow! But he didn't know if he should, pretending he was all undecided. I said it was fantastic! He was going to be a big star, wow! He said, do you think Dad will let me? That was very smart. I was then on his side in persuading Dad. He let me get all excited, so that I was desperately wanting him to go."

Paul says that he was of course very excited. "It was £15 a week, wow. We hadn't seemed to have done anything for weeks, just hanging around. It was the long summer holidays and I didn't want to go back to school, or college. But there wasn't much alternative until suddenly Hamburg came up. That meant I definitely didn't need to go back to school. There was now something else to do."

There was still Jim to persuade. Paul got Alan Williams to come home to help soften up Jim. "Alan Williams never got our names right, though," says Paul. "He would call me John." However, Alan Williams managed to tell Jim how well organized it was all going to be and what a lovely respectable place Hamburg was. "I think, basically, Dad was quite pleased," says Michael, "though he said he wasn't at the time."

"What could I do?" says Jim. "I knew they were well liked at what they were doing. It was their first big engagement and they were determined to go. Paul was just eighteen. He'd just had four weeks of his school holidays. He went on a student passport. I gave him a pep talk, you know, about being a good lad. What else could I do?

"I was worried all the time that he wouldn't get enough to eat in Germany. He did send post cards, saying, 'I'm eating plenty. We had this that and the other this evening.' That satisfied me, I suppose."

Jim was slightly satisfied when, just after Paul had gone, the results of the GCE A levels came through. Paul had failed his English but passed in Art, which was quite good, all things considered. Though by that time even Jim realized it didn't matter any more.

But John's Aunt Mimi put up more of a fight. Since the days when she had banned Paul and George from coming to her house and John from playing his guitar at home, she'd also banned John from playing in a group. All the time since the Quarrymen had begun, almost five years previously, John had managed to lie to her most of the time about what he was doing. She had no idea how serious it had become. She knew he was still messing around writing silly songs and that, but she didn't know the extent of his interest.

She really thought he was sticking in at the Art College till one day someone told her how he was spending his lunch hours—playing in a group. She decided to go and investigate for herself, to see just what depth of depravity John had sunk to.

The lunchtime she decided to investigate turned out to be one of the days they were playing at the Cavern. They weren't a resident group there, as it was still basically a jazz club, but they were getting more dates all the time as the Cavern realized that the Beatles had created their own following, who always filled the club up when the Beatles played.

"I'd never heard of this awful place, the Cavern," says Mimi. "It took a long time to find. I just had to follow the crowds in the end. I went down some steps with them all and there was this chap, Rory McFall, taking money. I pushed him out of the way. 'You're getting no money out of me. I want John Lennon!'

"I pushed on in, but the noise was so deafening. It had this low ceiling which made it worse. He could hear me shouting for him, as he was used to the noise, but I could only see his lips moving. There was so much screaming I couldn't hear anything. But I couldn't move to get at him. The girls were jammed together, with their arms down by their sides, it was so packed.

"Try as I might, I just couldn't get near the stage. If I could, I would have pulled him off it. In the end, I just went and sat in one of the dressing rooms. Dressing room! Just a scruffy little cubicle. When he came off, with the girls still screaming, he couldn't see me at first. He's blind without his glasses. Then he put them on and saw me. 'What are you doing, Mimi!'

" 'Very nice, John,' I said, 'this is very nice.' "

Mimi made sure he went back to College that afternoon. But she couldn't stop him from playing, though she went on at him all the time to stick in at his studies, not this silly playing, so that he could get himself a proper job of work. "What do you mean?" John used to say. "I'm not a workingman and never will be. No matter what you do or say, I'll never end up with a nine-to-five job."

Then Hamburg came up. This was going to mean a proper severance, for a long time in a foreign country. Mimi remembers John trying to get her as excited as he was. "Mimi, isn't it marvelous," he told her. "I'm going to get £100 a week, isn't that marvelous!"

A slight exaggeration on the money, but still marvelous for five teenage lads. John, of course, jumped at the chance of having a good excuse to leave the College for good. He'd survived three years, just. Arthur Ballard, the lecturer who had most to do with him, saved him from being expelled several times. But John was now glad to get away, though he'd failed all exams and was leaving without any qualifications. He was also leaving Cyn.

"The group had started to get its own fans," says Cynthia. "I knew they had lots of girls hanging round them, but I never worried or got jealous. I seemed so much older than all the girls. I felt very secure.

"But I was much more worried about Hamburg. That seemed so far away and for such a long time. I knew the Liverpool girls, but I didn't know anything about the situation in Hamburg. Anything could happen to them in Hamburg."

Chapter 11: Hamburg

Hamburg is Germany's Liverpool. It is a large northern port. The inhabitants are rough and tough but underneath they can be soft and sentimental. The climate is wet and windy. They have the same sort of nasal accents, easily recognizable in each country. They even have the same latitude, 53 degrees North.

But Hamburg is twice the size of Liverpool and traditionally a much wickeder city. Hamburg crime and Hamburg sex life are known throughout Europe. The Reeperbahn, the main street in Hamburg's Soho, must have more strip clubs than any other street in the world.

When the Beatles arrived there in 1960, with George sweet seventeen and never been kissed, well hardly, Wicked Hamburg was at its wickedest. Hamburg, being a free port, had become a center for FLN gun-running during the Algerian crisis. This had brought in foreign gangsters and money. Then when the Berlin wall went up in August 1960, a lot of East German crooks and illegal immigrants headed for Hamburg rather than Berlin. The gang warfare which ensued centered round the clubs. Waiters were hired for their strength, rather than their waiting, to be ready to fight off the gangs from the next club.

Alan Williams brought the Beatles to Hamburg himself. He drove them in a mini-van, via Harwich and the Hook of Holland. The only thing John remembers about the journey is that he stopped off in Holland somewhere to do some shoplifting.

They were all very pleased with the attempts at stage dress—their very first; after all, they were now professionals—they were bringing with them. It consisted of little velvet jackets which Paul had got the man next door to him to make for him. They were intending to wear them with their usual Teddy-boy rig-out, tight black jeans, white shirt with black-ribbon tie, and winkle-pickers. They all still of course had their high, greased-back Tony Curtis hair style.

"Bruno Koschmeider, who owned a couple of Hamburg clubs, met us when we arrived," says Pete Best. "He took us round to the Kaiserkeller, where we expected we'd be playing. We met Howie Casey, another Liverpool group, who were already there. We liked the look of the place. We said when do we move in? He said we didn't. Then we were taken round to this other club, the Indra, that was much smaller. It was eleven thirty at night and there was just two people in the place.

"We were shown our dressing room at the club which turned out to be also the gents' toilet. We expected anyway we'd be living in a hotel, but instead we were taken round to this cinema, the Bambi, where he showed us our sleeping quarters. It was like the black hole of Calcutta. But being young and foolish, we didn't complain but just went straight to sleep. Next day, we set up our stuff at the Indra at seven o'clock. We started every night at seven—except Saturdays, when it was six."

The Indra, named after the German word for India, had a huge elephant outside across the street, the *Grosse Freiheit,* as its symbol. But inside it was small and pokey. None of them liked it, or sleeping in the Bambi cinema. "We would go to bed late," says John, "and be wakened up next day by the sound of the cinema show. They had to use the ordinary cinema lavatory for washing in. We'd try to get into the ladies' first, which was cleanest, but fat old German women would push past us.

"The cellar we slept in was smelly and like a bog.

"At first, we got a pretty cool reception. Then the manager said we should Mak Show, like the group down the road were doing, so we tried. We were a bit scared by it all at first, being in the middle of the tough-club land. But we felt cocky, being from Liverpool, at least believing the myth about Liverpool producing cocky people, so we tried to be it. The first Mak Show I did was to jump around in one number like Gene Vincent. Every number lasted twenty minutes, just to spin it out.

"We only once ever tried a German number, playing to the crowd. Paul learned 'Wooden Heart,' which was then very popular. We got better and got more confidence. We couldn't help it, with all the experience, playing all night long. It was handy them being foreign. We had to try even harder, put our heart and soul into it, to get ourselves over.

"Back home in Liverpool we'd only ever done hour-long sessions, so we just did our best numbers over and over again. In Hamburg we had to play for eight hours, so we really had to find a new way of playing. We played very loud in Hamburg—bang, bang all the time. The Germans loved it."

"Once the news got about that we were making show," says Pete, "the place started packing them in. We played seven nights a week. At first we played almost non-stop till twelve thirty, when it closed, but as we got better the crowds stayed till two most mornings. We saw lots of fights. Real hip ones, with people swinging from lights and jumping off tables like in film fights."

They actually used to beat on the stage with their feet, to add to the noise and also increase the beat. There is a suggestion that Pete Best hadn't fitted into their ways at the beginning, so they all had to pound out the rhythm as well, which was probably true. But Pete soon improved, as they all did.

The Making Show, as the Germans called it, was the vital thing. Although they were a rock group, they'd been pretty quiet in Liverpool. Now they were actively encouraged to let themselves go and make as much show onstage as possible, which of course was easy for John. He also started making a show all the time, much to the amusement of the local rockers they were getting among their fans. Stories about John are still told in Hamburg, a lot of them improving with age.

"It was hard work," says Pete, "but we were just five fellows having a good time. We did daft things all the time. John had a pair of Long John underpants, as it was getting very cold with winter drawing on. George bet him ten marks that he wouldn't go out, wearing them and nothing else. He went out in the street, just in his Long Johns, with sun specs on and reading a newspaper for five minutes. We watched him, killing ourselves laughing."

But after two months, the Indra was closed because of complaints from neighbors about noise, and they moved to the Kaiserkeller. "The stage at the Kaiserkeller was very old, more or less planks on orange boxes. We decided we'd go through it so they'd have to make a new one. We did go through in the end, by jumping around and making show, but they never got us a new one. We just played on an open stage.

"We got drunk a lot. You couldn't help it. They'd be sending us drinks up all the time so we naturally drank too much. We had a lot of girls. We soon realized they were easy to get. Girls are girls, fellers are fellers. Everything improved one hundred per cent. We'd been meek and mild musicians at first, now we became a powerhouse."

But at the Kaiserkeller they were working even harder than ever. The group which had been there in the first place had now gone back to Liverpool and been replaced by another Liverpool group, Rory Storme and the Hurricanes. They were officially booked to play six hours a night, but as there were now two groups in the same club, they did alternate hours through the night. Their time off was too short to do anything or go any-where, so they were in effect playing for a total of twelve hours at a time, which all of them tried, except Pete Best.

"Your voice began to hurt with the pain of singing," says John. "We learned from the Germans that you could stay awake by eating slim-ming pills, so we did that." The pills at first were pretty harmless, but they moved on to other ones, like Black Bombers and Purple Hearts, but they never appear to have been dependent on them or to have taken them to excess. But it was the beginning of an interest and a liking for drugs, however minor.

They never let the pills get out of control because they were genuinely taking them to keep awake, not for kicks. They wanted to keep awake because they were loving everything, playing the sort of stuff they wanted to, to wild Hamburg teenagers, for as long as they wanted.

The times they did get fed up, with living accommodations or with having to work so hard, were very few. Because they were so far from home, being fed up became meaningless. There was little they could do about it. If they hadn't been so far from home, of course, and in a for-eign country, they might have packed up many times and gone home to their mums. But they couldn't, stuck away in Hamburg, as they were spending all the money as quickly as they got it. It's surprising their health didn't suffer more. They never ate properly and hardly slept. "What with playing, drinking, and birds, how could we find time to sleep?" says John.

Pete, George and Paul knew a bit of German from their school-days, but John and Stu knew nothing. But they weren't interested in speaking German anyway. "We just used to shout in English at the Ger-mans," says John. "Call them Nazis and tell them to fuck off." The audi-ence just cheered even more. The audiences were so entranced by them, so devoted to them, that they became less scared of the waiters and the fights.

They saw the waiters taking money out of the pockets of drunks and as they were so hard up, John decided one night to try it himself. "We chose a British sailor to roll, as I thought I could chat him up in English, kid him on we could get him some birds. We got him drinking and drink-ing and he kept on asking where's the girls. We kept chatting him up, try-ing to find out where he kept his money. We just hit him twice in the end, then gave up. We never made it. We didn't want to hurt him."

The Beatles had lots of little arguments among themselves, but nothing serious. It was mainly Stu and Pete, the relatively new boys, being picked on by the rest. Stu took it to heart, but Pete didn't seem to notice. It all passed over his head. He can't himself remember being involved in any rows or anyone criticizing him or mocking him, though the others do.

But Stu and Pete were proving particularly popular with the audience. Stu wore his sun spectacles on stage and looked very defiant. Pete never smiled or jumped around the way John did, but simply looked sullen and menacing. Both of them were looked upon as James Dean figures by the audience, moody and magnificent. The others, particularly John, were the wild extrovert ones. "Paul was telling me the other day," says John, "that he and I used to have rows about who was the leader. I can't remember them. It had stopped mattering by then. I wasn't so determined to be the leader at all costs. If I did argue, it was just out of pride.

"All the arguments were just trivial, mainly because we were fucked and irritable with working so hard. We were just kids as well. George threw some food at me once onstage. We usually ate onstage as we were onstage so long. The waiters would send us up beer onstage as well as food, so now and again we'd end up getting pissed while we were playing. Anyway, this time George threw some food at me over something stupid. I said I would smash his face in for him. We had a shouting match onstage, but that was all. I never did anything."

They were in the main very friendly with each other and also very friendly with Rory Storme and his group, who were alternating with them at the Kaiserkeller. They knew Rory's group very well. It was better known at the time in Liverpool than theirs was. Rory had been offered the Hamburg trip before they had. Because he turned it down, as he had another engagement, they'd got it instead. There were other Liverpool groups doing better than the Beatles in those days, like Cas and the Casanovas. The Beatles, at the time they left Liverpool for Hamburg, were probably about third or fourth in the hierarchy of Liverpool beat groups.

"We all knew Rory, of course," says George. "He was the big star of Liverpool, very flash and wild on stage." George knew the group well because at one stage, before he joined the Beatles, he was thinking of joining them. "I'd met Rory through one of the blokes in his group, Johnny Guitar. I was trying to knock off Johnny Guitar's little sister at the time."

The drummer with Rory Storme's group spent a lot of his sitting-out time watching the Beatles and requesting songs from them. "I didn't like the look of Rory's drummer myself," says George. "He looked the nasty one, with his little gray streak of hair. But the nastier one turned out to be Ringo, the nicest of them all." Pete says that he remembered Ringo from the days he had played in the Casbah with Rory Storme, but the others didn't know him. It was a long time before they got to know him really well. But that was their first meeting with Ringo Starr.

Apart from this friendship with Ringo and the rest of Rory's group, they made no other friends. They hardly left the club and made no attempt to make any friends among the Germans. "They were all half-witted," says John.

And they made even less of an attempt to get to know any British people who came into the club. "When we could smell Senior Service in the audience," says John, "we knew there would be trouble before the night was out. You could tell British cigarettes straight away by the smell. After a few drinks, they'd start shouting, 'Up Liverpool' or 'Up Pompy.' Gangs of fucking British servicemen, trying to stir things up.

"You'd know that before the night was over they'd all be lying there half dead, after they'd tried to pick a fight with the waiters over the bill, or just over nothing. The waiters would get their flick knives out, or their truncheons. And that would be it. I've never seen such killers."

Chapter 12: Astrid and Klaus

It's not really surprising that they made so few German friends in Hamburg. The majority of respectable Hamburgers never go anywhere near the St. Pauli district, least of all the Reeperbahn.

But Klaus Voorman and Astrid Kichener did. Quite by chance they came across the Beatles. They became fans, the first intellectual fans the group had ever had. They saw in the Beatles qualities no one had ever seen before.

Klaus had been born in Berlin, the son of an eminent doctor. He arrived in Hamburg in 1956 to study at the Art School. He was training to be a commercial artist, but he also took up photography as a special subject, which is how he met Astrid, who became his girl friend.

Astrid comes from a good solid middle-class Hamburg family. She was specializing in photography. By 1960 they'd both left Art School. Klaus was working for local magazines (Hamburg is a big press center) doing advertising posters. Astrid was working as an assistant to a photographer. They'd been going out for about two years. Klaus had moved into a flat at the top of Astrid's house. One evening they had a slight row. Klaus decided to go off to the cinema on his own.

"I came out and was walking around. I was in the *Grosse Freiheit* when I heard a lot of noise coming from a basement. I went down to see what was going on." Klaus had never been to a club like it before. Not even students went into such clubs. They didn't want to get into any fights and, anyway, students were more interested in jazz than primitive rock and roll. Klaus was interested in jazz but not pop.

"It was a very rough scene down there. There were some real tough rockers, all in leather. But I was knocked out by the group onstage and the noise they were making. So very carefully I sat down to listen."

The Club was the Kaiserkeller, but it wasn't the Beatles onstage. It was Rory Storme's group, with Ringo on drums. But without realizing it

Klaus had sat down beside the other resident group. "I was staring at them because they looked so funny. They wore check jackets, black-and-white check. They looked so funny. The most ridiculous-looking of all—Stu, as I discovered later—had his hair piled back and high, long pointed shoes and sunglasses. Not really sunglasses, just those sun things you clip over ordinary glasses.

"They went onstage and I realized that they were the other group. They did 'Sweet Little Sixteen' with John singing it. They knocked me out even more than Rory did. I couldn't take my eyes off them. I wanted to speak to them, to get near them, but I didn't know how to. I was scared with all the rockers. I was embarrassed and felt out of it. But I stayed there all night. I couldn't get over how they played, how they played together so well, so powerful and so funny. And all the time they were jumping around. I gathered they kept it up for eight hours as well."

He got home in the early hours of the morning and told Astrid where he'd been. She was rather disgusted with him, spending an evening at a club in St. Pauli, of all places. He told her how marvelous this group was. But she wasn't interested. She refused to come back with him the next night. So he went alone.

This time he thought of a way of introducing himself to them, of getting to know them, or at least saying hello to them. He took with him a record cover he had designed for a single called "Walk Don't Run." He'd done one or two covers as a commercial artist, although most of his work had been for magazines. This was a vague rock-and-roll record, the German version of the John Barry Seven record. He thought the Beatles would be interested to see it.

He sat around for a long time, trying to get nearer and nearer. At last when the Beatles sat down for their rest turn, he approached John, who seemed to be the leader. In very halting, schoolboy English, Klaus showed him the record. It made little effect on John. "I just remember this bloke shoving a cover in my hand, I didn't know why," says John. "I said 'Lovely,' but made faces at the others behind his back and said, 'Who's this Kraut?'"

John didn't speak German and never tried to. Klaus says John then muttered something about Stu being the artist, and he'd better show the cover to him. Klaus started to move toward Stu but something happened and he couldn't get to him. So he just sat down again, feeling more scared and embarrassed, and listened to the music all night through again.

For the next night, his third visit, he did at last persuade Astrid, against her better wishes, to come with him, along with another friend, Jurgen Vollmer. "I was frightened when I arrived," says Astrid. "But I soon forgot all that, when I saw these five people. I can't explain how I felt. Something got me. I just couldn't believe it. I had always been fascinated in a way by Teddy boys. I'd liked the look of them in photographs and films. Suddenly there was five of them in front of me, with their hair all high and long sidies. I just sat there open-mouthed and couldn't move.

"The atmosphere around was pretty frightening. They were just the typical Reeperbahn crowd. Broken noses, Teddy boys, that sort of thing. *Schlägers* we would call them in German. Punchers, real toughs."

More and more of their student friends started to come when Klaus and Astrid began to rave about the group. Slowly the atmosphere of the Kaiserkeller began to change. They took over their own tables and part of the cellar. The students, with their smoother styles, their more mod clothes, began to affect and then dictate the atmosphere.

The rockers were still there, although not so predominant. "It became our scene," says Klaus. "There was no rivalry between us and the rockers. In fact I became friends with a few, though I'd never known any of them before, and never would have. There were funny little rocker girls I'd never come across before. When they danced they were like little mushrooms. They had short flared skirts with stiffened petticoats to make them stick out."

The Beatles began to spend most of their spare time sitting talking and drinking with Klaus, Astrid, and their friends. They couldn't speak German, but some of the students could understand a little English.

"We were suddenly getting a lot of arty types," says George. "Existentialists, the lot. They were really groovy, especially Astrid and Klaus."

"They were great," says Paul. "A change from the usual fat Germans. They were knocked out by Stu doing his James Dean bit."

" 'Exis,' that's what I called them," says John. "They were the first Germans I ever wanted to talk to."

"I couldn't understand John's accent," says Klaus. "But George used to speak very slowly to us and we could understand him. He looked so funny. He had big ears which stuck out, with his hair being short at the back and piled so high on top."

After about a week of going there every night Astrid at last got the courage, when the Beatles had by then become friendly, to ask if she could take their pictures. "We were getting on so well with them so I felt more protected. I realized that the Reeperbahn rockers all loved them, adored them. They would have killed for them." She managed to blurt out a couple of words, indicating that she wanted to take their photographs.

"They were made up. I could tell, though John made a few funny remarks. He was always saying terrible things about the Krauts in front of their faces. Not to me. But I felt he wasn't really like that anyway." But she wasn't really interested in John's reaction. As long as he agreed, that was enough. "I wanted to get to know Stu, that was the real reason. I'd fallen in love with him at first sight. It's true. It wasn't slushy romance and all that. I just had."

They all made a date to meet in the Reeperbahn next day. She took them to a fairground nearby and photographed them there, then she invited them home with her for tea. Pete Best refused, as he had something else to do. But the four others went with her. She gave them ham sandwiches. They were delighted. It was the first German home they'd been into. But not only was it the first German house they had been inside, they had never experienced rooms like Astrid's before. They'd never moved in any artistic, or even student, circles in Liverpool. Their own homes were the epitome of working-class convention.

The room Astrid gave them tea in was very dark and mysterious, as it is now, but in a different way. Then, after the first impression of darkness, all you could see were black and white. Everything, the walls, furniture, and carpets, was either black or white. She also had trees growing up the walls and across the ceiling and down the room. The room is in the back of the house, with a view over the backs of other houses, but the window was obscured and the only light came from candles. There was a black cloth hanging down one wall. One of them drew it aside to see what was behind it and found himself looking into a mirror. "It was my Jean Cocteau phase," says Astrid.

The tea was a little more prosaic—ham sandwiches. "Heh, look at these," said George. "Ham sarnies! I didn't know the Germans had ham sarnies." Which shows how much George had seen of German life, stuck for twelve hours at a time at the Kaiserkeller. Then Astrid drove them in her car back to the club for their night's work.

She began to bring her camera along all the time and took many photographs of them. They were the first professional photographs taken of the group and, for many years to come, by far the most artistic. By clever lighting she managed to take them half in the shadows. This gimmick of a half-shadow face was used and copied by others in photography for a long time to come. Astrid was the first to see their photogenic potential, a factor which was later absolutely invaluable in all promotions.

She took the boys out and around other parts of Hamburg to photograph them, lining them up once in the docks, then at a disused railway siding, to get unusual photographs. It takes good-quality printing and paper to get the best out of Astrid's photographs, to see how excellent they are, but even on newsprint they look dramatic and unusual. "They were great," says Paul. "Nobody could take our picture as well as Astrid."

She was trying all the time, in those early sessions, to get talking to Stu, trying to say to him she would like to take his photograph on his own. But she couldn't make him understand. He spoke no German. She spoke no English.

She got Klaus to start teaching her English. "He nearly went out of his mind trying to explain things to me. I just couldn't learn it."

They all came for a meal at her place practically every night after that first tea, she and Stu slowly making more and more progress. Then he started to come at other times on his own and they would sit together on her black bed, she struggling over words from a German-English dictionary and he with an English-German dictionary.

This was still only three weeks after first meeting, but she had got to know them all very well. "After Stu, I liked John and George best. Then I liked Pete Best. I liked him very much, but he was so very very shy. He could be funny, but I didn't have much contact with him. Even in those days, one tended to forget him. He was on his own, really.

"Paul I found hard to get close to. He was always friendly. He was by far the most popular with the fans. He always did the talking and announcing and the autograph bit. Most people among the fans looked upon him as the leader.

"John of course was the leader. He was far and away the strongest. I don't mean physically; as a personality.

"Stu was the most intelligent one. I think they all agreed on that. John did.

"George, we never thought about George's intelligence one way or another when we were talking about them. We knew he wasn't stupid, but he was just such a young lovely boy. He was so sweet and open about everything, like admiring the ham sarnies. He had a great following. Jurgen used to have a notice which said 'I love George.' He was one of the first to do that sort of thing.

"I got on like a house on fire with George. He'd never met anyone like me before and he showed it, so openly and sweetly. After all, he was only seventeen. There was me, the sort of intelligent girl he'd never come across before, with my own car, working as a photographer and wearing leather jackets. It was natural he should be very interested in me. I never fancied him or anything like that. It wasn't that sort of thing. I was five years older, so it didn't matter being open. We got on great."

In November 1960, only two months after their first meeting, Stu and Astrid got engaged. They put their money together and went out and bought the rings—one for each of them, in the German fashion. Then they drove in her car along the Elbe. "From when we first started being able to communicate with each other we intended to get married."

Stu was not yet nineteen, not much older really than George, but much more developed and mature in his thoughts. He knew a lot about art, had great talent, and had the same views on art and design as Astrid.

Stu was as passionately interested in art as he'd always been, though John had left it all behind, but he was also as passionate about the group. He could concentrate completely on whatever he was doing, put himself wholly into something.

One night he had a fight onstage with Paul that was an example of determination. Despite being much smaller and weaker than Paul, his anger was so intense that it gave him extra strength. "He could become really hysterical when he was angry," says Astrid. She remembers the fight vividly, but can't recall the details of what caused it. It was something to do with her, something Paul had said about her, but she doesn't know what or why.

The relationship between Paul and Stu, the petty jealousies and rows, is not too difficult to explain. In a way they were both competing for John's attention. Paul had had it for a couple of years, until Stu came along. Stu was obviously very talented, more mature, more in touch. Even Michael McCartney, Paul's younger brother, remembers beforehand in Liverpool that Paul was a bit jealous of Stu.

The relationship between five Teds from Liverpool and a group of intellectual Hamburg students is harder to explain. Back home in Liverpool they'd always despised any arty student type. The Hamburg ones were more genuine and less phoney, more mature and knowledgeable, than their Liverpool counterparts. They were highly fashionable in their clothes as well as in their thoughts. Klaus and Jurgen had their hair brushed forward in the French style, as it was called then. They knew all about books and art and other sorts of music.

The Beatles now had two devoted sets of followers, the rockers and the exis. Their original six-week contract was extended several times by popular demand. The exis had nicknames for them all—John was the Sidie Man, George the Beautiful One, and Paul the Little One.

The name Beatles in German had had everyone highly amused from the minute they arrived. "The Peedles" was how they pronounced it. This in German is also a small-boy vulgarity, meaning cock or John Thomas.

Christmas was approaching. They'd been in Hamburg nearly five months. They were scheming to get into an even bigger and better club, the Top Ten. They realized they were a success in the Kaiserkeller, but they wanted to branch out into a bigger club. They asked the manager of the Top Ten, Peter Eckhorn, for an audition. "They came to me," he said. "I liked them and offered them a contract." They fancied the Top Ten because it wasn't so rough. Then George was told he would have to leave the country.

"At all clubs," says George, "they used to read out a notice every night saying that all people under eighteen had to leave. Someone eventually realized I was only seventeen, without a work permit or a resident permit. So I had to leave. I had to go home on my own. I felt terrible."

Astrid and Stu drove him to the station, got him his ticket and a place on the train. "He was just standing there," says Astrid. "Little George, all lost. I gave him a big bag of sweets and some apples. He threw his arms round me and Stu, which was the sort of demonstrative thing they never did."

The other four had just moved to the Top Ten and had done only one night when more trouble struck them. "Paul and I," says Pete Best, "were just clearing out of the Bambi. John and Stu had already moved their things into the Top Ten. We were getting a light on to see what we were doing and we must have started a fire. It wasn't much, but the police threw us in jail for three hours and then said we were to be deported as well." Which left John and Stu.

"John appeared a day or so later at my house," says Astrid, "saying he was going home as well because his work permit had been taken away. He said he'd sold some of his clothes to buy his ticket home, but he wanted to borrow some more."

"It was terrible," says John. "Setting off home on me own. I had my amp on my back, scared stiff I was going to get it pinched. I hadn't paid for it. I was convinced I'd never find England." Then Stu was told that he would have to leave as well. The real reasons for all their deportations, apart from George obviously being illegally under age, were never really clear. Perhaps there was a bit of interclub rivalry.

Stu was the only one who came home in any style. He flew to Liverpool. He'd had a touch of tonsillitis. Astrid didn't want him to get worse on a long journey by land and sea, so she'd given him his air fare. The others dragged themselves back to Liverpool under their own steam.

What had been the greatest experience of their careers so far had ended in pathos and squalor.

They got home in ones and twos, broke and in tatters, dejected and dispirited. They didn't see each other or make any contact for some time. They even wondered if the Beatles would ever get going again.

Chapter 13: Liverpool—
Litherland and Cavern

John arrived back in Menlove Avenue from Hamburg in the middle of the night. He had to throw stones up at Mimi's bedroom window so she would get up and let him in.

"He had these awful cowboy boots on, up to here they were, all gold and silver. He just pushed past me and said, 'Pay that taxi, Mimi.' I shouted after him up the stairs, 'Where's your £100 a week, John?' "

"Just like you, Mimi," shouted John, "to go on about £100 a week when you know I'm tired."

"And you can get rid of those boots. You're not going out of this house in boots like that."

John went to bed and stayed at home for almost two weeks, not because of the awful boots but because there didn't seem much alternative. "We'd got back, but there didn't seem anything to do."

Cyn was naturally pleased to see him. "He'd written all the time he was away, of course."

"The sexiest letters this side of Henry Miller," says John. "Forty pages long, some of them. You haven't destroyed them, have you?"

George, who had reached home first, didn't know for some time that the others had eventually followed him. "I felt ashamed, after all the big talk when we set off for Hamburg. My dad gave me a lift to town one night and I had to borrow ten bob off him."

Paul was also hanging around at home, and soon had his father to contend with. Jim hadn't wanted him to leave school and go to Hamburg in the first place; now that he had, he said Paul should get a job and not just mess around doing nothing.

"Satan finds things for idle hands," Jim told Paul, with great originality, several times a day. Paul, never a rebel on principle and always willing to please, eventually gave in. "Dad went on and on so in the end I went down to the Labour Exchange. That seemed to be the scene. They fixed me up with a job as second man on a lorry. I'd been on the Post Office the Christmas before from school, so I thought I'd try something different.

"The firm was called Speedy Prompt Delivery—SPD. They did deliveries round the docks way. I got the early bus down to the docks and bought the *Daily Mirror,* trying to be a real working lad, though I was really just a college pudding. I used to sit on the back of the lorry and helped to carry parcels. I was so buggered sometimes I fell asleep on the lorry when we went to places like Chester. I was with them about two weeks and felt very worldly, having a job and a few quid in my pocket. But I got laid off. The Christmas period was over and there wasn't so much work.

"Dad started moaning again, the usual stuff about the group being all very well but I'd never make a living at it. I half agreed with him, but there was always somebody who said we were promising, some fans liked us and made us feel good.

"I got another job at Massey and Coggins, winding electrical coils. I had to wear a donkey jacket for that. A fellow called me Mantovani, with me long hair. I had to stand astride this winch and wind the coils. I was always breaking it. I did about a coil and a half in a day; some of the others could do eight, even fourteen. I wasn't much good. The tea breaks were great though, with jam butties and all the lads playing football on a sort of prison exercise yard.

"I'd actually gone, now it's all coming back to me, for a job brushing up the yard, which I thought would be all right. When the bloke noticed I had a few GCEs, he became suspicious, as if I might have a criminal record as well. Then he decided I was okay and gave me a better job, which was winding the coils. He said if I stuck in I'd be all right. I imagined myself as working my way up, being an executive one of these days, if I tried hard.

"I was getting £7 a week for winding coils and making the tea. The group had got going again but I didn't know if I wanted to go back full time. I stayed on at work, just going over the wall for lunchtime sessions or being off sick. But I left in the end. I was there about two months altogether. I quite enjoyed being a workingman. I met this bloke called Albert and had some good chats with him."

"I'll say this for Paul," says his father Jim. "He was always a tryer. He wasn't really interested in either job. It was just to oblige me."

They'd come back from Hamburg in early December 1960. In all, they were probably not more than two or three weeks without a date of any sort, then things started to happen. Their first date was at the Casbah,

Pete Best's mother's club. Pete got a great welcome back from his mother and from his friend Neil Aspinall.

Neil, who'd been a friend of Pete's for a couple of years, was actually living at the Casbah; at least he'd left home and taken a room in Mrs. Best's house. He hadn't gone to school with Pete but had been at the Institute, starting in the same form as Paul. He'd known George as well. They'd both been in trouble for smoking. But he hadn't been affected by the skiffle craze, though he'd supported the local groups. With a gang of his classmates he'd gone along to cheer the Beatles (or Moondogs) at the Empire in the early audition for the Carroll Levis Show.

Neil left the Institute with eight O levels and was training to be an accountant. He was getting two pounds ten a week, plus luncheon vouchers, and seemed all set for a professional career. Most of his nights at first were taken up with correspondence courses. "I hated taking abuse from some fellow 300 miles away. It was like sending it off to the moon, just to get shit on." When he started hanging around the Casbah his courses started to slip, especially when he moved in and lived there full time.

"Pete had written to me all the time he was in Hamburg," says Neil. "He said it was going great and they'd been asked to stay on another month, then another month, and another.

"Derry and the Seniors had come back from Hamburg first. Pete had sent them round to his mother's and she'd given them an evening at the Casbah. They were very much improved. They said wait till we hear the Beatles. When I heard that the Beatles were definitely coming home I wrote out lots of posters saying *Return of the Fabulous Beatles;* I put them up on walls and doors all over the place. I'd never seen them as a group, with Pete as a member. I didn't know how they'd changed in Hamburg. They might have been awful."

But, despite Neil's enthusiasm, it wasn't possible to put the Beatles on at the Casbah right away. Nobody seemed to know what the others were doing, or even if they were all back. "I didn't know for a week after John came back that he had to leave Hamburg as well," says Pete Best. "We didn't know for weeks what had happened to Stu, till well into January."

But their first post-Hamburg booking was at the Casbah and they did very well.

"They were great," says Neil. "They had improved enormously. They began to get other jobs and a big following. Frank Garner, the fellow on the door at the Casbah, started to drive them round in his van. I saw a lot of them from then on as the Casbah was the base for their amps and tackle. Rory Storme also came back from Hamburg and played at the Casbah. It was a big scene."

But their most important engagement after Hamburg took place on December 27, 1960, at Litherland Town Hall. If it is possible to say that any date was the watershed, this was it. All their development, all their new sounds and new songs, suddenly hit Liverpool that evening. From then on, as far as a devoted fanatical following was concerned, they never looked back.

They owe that engagement to Bob Wooller. In that same month he had become disk jockey at the Cavern Club. He is short and very neat but completely unfashionable in his dress, in fact more like a clerk than a disk jockey. He'd worked as clerk for British Railways until the skiffle era began. He wasn't involved in it himself, being by then almost thirty, but he was fascinated by its development. "It was amazing to see teenagers making their own music for the first time and becoming entertainers themselves."

He'd seen the Beatles at various little clubs. When he heard they were back from Hamburg he decided to help them. "They were really very sorry for themselves. I knew their capabilities, but they were really down at the time. George was very bitter about the way his Hamburg trip had ended."

He managed to get them the Litherland Town Hall date. This is a big hall which was used regularly twice a week for teenage dances. It was the biggest they'd played in up to then. Their loud, stomping, pounding Hamburg music caused literally a riot, the first they'd ever caused. They also get seven pounds ten each for the night, again the best they'd ever had.

"The kids went mad," says Pete Best. "Afterwards we found they'd been chalking on our van, the first time it had happened." They were billed for that evening as "The Beatles, Direct from Hamburg." A lot of the kids who rioted that night, and for many other nights, thought they must be German. When they signed autograph books and were heard to speak everyone said with surprise, "You speak good English."

"We probably looked German as well," says George. "At least we looked very different from all the other groups, with our leather trousers and cowboy boots. We looked funny and we played differently. We went down a bomb."

"It was that evening," says John, "that we really came out of our shell and let go as we'd played in Hamburg. We discovered we were quite famous. It was when we began to think for the first time that we were

good. Up to Hamburg we'd thought we were okay, but not good enough."
Not only had the Beatles changed, there had been important changes in
Britain while they'd been away. Every group was now trying like mad to
be like the Shadows.

Cliff Richard's personal success had led the Shadows, his backing
group of Jet Harris, Tony Meehan, Bruce Welch, and Hank Marvin, to
become successes in their own right. Their instrumental record "Apache"
had swept the country. Every group was copying their sober, terribly
neat stage dress of gray suits, matching ties, and highly polished shoes.
They did little dance steps, three one way and three the other. Everything
was neat, polished but restrained, in their appearance as well as in their
music.

The Beatles, on the other hand, played loud and wild and looked
scruffy and disorganized, like some aboriginal throwback. They had continued in the rock-and-roll style, which had been the fashion when they
left Liverpool but was now dying out, thanks to the Shadows. They'd
become even more rock-and-rollish if anything, adding extra pounding,
volume, and wild Mak Showing onstage. As well as other ingredients of
their own, they had created in effect their own new sound—a sound
light years away from that of the discreet Shadows. A sound you had to
run away and hide your ears from, or go as wild and ecstatic as the
people producing it.

"It was Hamburg that had done it," says John. "That's where we'd
really developed. To get the Germans going and keep it up for twelve
hours at a time, we'd really had to hammer. We would never have developed as much if we'd stayed at home. We had to try anything that came
into our heads in Hamburg. There was nobody to copy from. We played
what we liked best. And the Germans liked it, as long as it was loud.

"But it was only back in Liverpool that we realized the difference and
saw what had happened. Everyone else was playing Cliff Richard shit."
Trying to analyze the music the Beatles had suddenly found for themselves only leads to pretentiousness, as thousands later found, although
it didn't stop them doing it. You would have to have been there to have
heard what they were doing and to have felt the effects. Their own passion and personalities, which were contagious and affected the audience,
also helped. It was a new sound but it was being made by people who
were like the audience, natural, unaffected, unsmooth, un-tarted up, un-
show-business.

Bob Wooller, the Cavern disk jockey, was one of the first to rush into
print with his analysis. This appeared just six months later, in the summer of 1961, in a local Merseyside beat newspaper. It is summing up this

early 1961 period, when they first hit Liverpool after the Litherland Town Hall:

> Why do you think the Beatles are so popular? They resurrected original rock 'n' roll music, the origins of which are to be found in American Negro singers. They hit the scene when it had been emasculated by figures like Cliff Richard. Gone was the drive that inflamed emotions. The Beatles exploded on a jaded scene. The Beatles were the stuff that screams were made of. Here was the excitement, both physical and aural, that symbolised the rebellion of youth.
>
> Essentially a vocal act, hardly ever instrumental, they were independently minded, playing what they liked for kicks, kudos and cash. Privileged in having gained prestige and experience in Hamburg. Musically authoritative and physically magnetic, example the mean, moody magnificence of drummer Pete Best—a sort of teenage Jeff Chandler. A remarkable variety of talented voices but when speaking, possess the same naivete of tone. Rhythmic revolutionaries. An act which from beginning to end is a succession of climaxes. A personality cult. Seemingly unambitious, yet fluctuating between self-assured and the vulnerable. Truly a phenomenon—and also a predicament to promoters! Such are the fantastic Beatles. I don't think anything like them will happen again.

In the New Year of 1961, other large ballroom dates followed their Litherland Town Hall success. In most places the appearance ended in riots, especially when Paul sang "Long Tall Sally," a standard rock number but done with tremendous beat and excitement. They were beginning to realize the effect they could have on an audience and often made the most of it, until things got out of hand. Paul says that some of the early ballrooms were terrifying. "At the Grosvenor Ballroom in Wallasey there would be a hundred Wallasey lads all ready to fight a hundred lads from Secombe when things got going. They started one night before I realized what was happening and I tried to save my amp. An El Pico amp, it was my pride and joy at the time. One Ted grabbed me and said don't move, son, or you're fucking dead. The Hambledon Hall was another place there was often fights. They used fire extinguishers on each other one night there. When we played 'Hully Gully,' that used to be one of the tunes which ended in fighting."

Most of the ballrooms hired large numbers of bouncers to stop that sort of trouble. The bouncers also began to be used for another purpose.

"I remember one hall we were at," says John. "There were so many people that we told each other that there must be other managers around

The Cavern Club

offers congratulations and
best wishes to

The Beatles

on the release of their first recording
for Parlophone

Love me do/P.S. I love you

It is with pleasure that the Club
announces that **The Beatles** will
continue to be featured regularly

at **The Cavern**

10 Matthew Street
off North John Street
Liverpool 1

Telephone Central 1591

Ringo Starr

Paul McCartney

George Harrison

John Lennon

John, Paul and George met when at school in 1956 and have remained together ever since. They have played as a group with numerous names, various drummers and other augmentations. Their present drummer, Ringo Starr, has only recently joined the group but they have admired and known him since their schooldays.

Back in '56 they, in common with their contemporaries, were on a skiffle kick, wash board, banjo and the like. For four years they continued in varying forms to entertain in Liverpool clubs, pubs, Church halls and at fetes. They played for a time at a strip club in the heart of Liverpool's Chinatown.

During this period John left his school to study at the College of Art. During a vacation he worked for five weeks on a building site—with his earnings he bought his first electrified guitar. Paul was at school and attained five subjects in G.C.E. and then English Literature at advanced level. He speaks Spanish and German. George left his school to become an apprentice electrician. But from the beginning there was little doubt that to be successful making music and entertaining was the only goal for these three characters. They form essentially a vocal group but at the same time they comprise musicians of the first order. John plays rhythm guitar, George, lead and Paul, bass.

Early in 1960 Larry Parnes selected the group at an audition to back Johnny Gentle on a tour of Scotland. This was rough and hard stuff but it led to a beginning. Back in Liverpool they were offered a contract to play in Germany at a night club in Hamburg. At that stage once and for all they left their schools and jobs to accept the offer. In Hamburg they played many hours for few Marks but their music became formed and their sound was different.

Returning home in December 1960 they opened at The Beatles at a surburban Town Hall. The reception was rapturous—from there they went from strength to strength playing locally night after night. They were a dance promotor's dream.

In April 1961 they were invited to play again in Hamburg at another club offering better conditions. Their popularity in Germany is as phenomenal as in North West England. And once again on return to Liverpool they packed the halls.

In October 1961 their appeal was brought to the attention of Brian Epstein, director of NEMS (record stores). The Liverpool public clamoured for records by The Beatles and in an endeavour to assist and progress their professional interests Brian Epstein became their personal manager. In November they were voted Merseyside's most popular group by a huge majority of fans. The poll was organised by the local entertainments publication 'Mersey Beat'.

1962 has been an exciting and important year for The Beatles. They have spread their wings and their appearances in many different parts of the country have always effected the same result ... an invitation to return. They have made three broadcasts on the Light Programme in Peter Pilbeam's 'Teenagers' Turn'. Granada T.V. filmed the group at the Cavern Club, Liverpool. They play at the Cavern (in the heart of the city) sometimes as many as three times a week, often a mid-day session ... always it's a full house.

In May they were the principal attraction to open the fantastically successful Star-Club in Hamburg. Whilst they were away their manager took tapes to A. & R. Manager George Martin who subsequently signed them for Parlophone records. Both sides of their first single have been written by Paul and John. 'Love Me Do' was written in 1958 (in the skiffle days) and P.S. I Love You' was written whilst the group was playing in Germany at the Star-Club.

THE BEATLES

NEMS Enterprises present

LITTLE RICHARD AT THE TOWER

Friday 12 October 1962

1 The Mersey Beats

2 The Four Jays

3 Billy Kramer with the Coasters

4 The Big Three

5 Lee Curtis with the All Stars

6 THE BEATLES

7 LITTLE RICHARD

8 Pete Maclaine with the Dakotas

9 The Undertakers

10 Rory Storm and The Hurricanes

11 Gus Travis and the Midnighters

The groups will be introduced and the entire stage presentation by BOB WOOLER and we'd get a lot of work out of it. What we didn't know was that the management had laid on lots of bouncers to stop the other promoters getting near us. So nobody came to us, except this bloke from the management who said he liked us and would give us a long series of dates at £8 a night. It was a couple of quid more than we were getting anyway, so we were pleased."

They could have made a lot more money from 1961 onward because they were in demand and very gradually catching up on Rory Storme (Mr. Showmaker they called him) as Liverpool's leading group. But they didn't have a manager and they didn't really realize themselves what was happening to them.

"We could have asked for bigger money from then on," says George, "because we were getting big crowds everywhere. But it took us a while to realize how much better we'd become than the other groups. When we did, and saw that we were getting big crowds everywhere, we realized that part of the reason was that for the first time people were following us round, coming to see us personally, not just coming to dance."

Stu was by this time back from Hamburg and playing with the other four. They were still picking on him and Pete Best, but there were no fights, the way there had been in Hamburg. They used to fight over the best seat in the van after a show or fight for food. There was often an argument about who should drive, because it was thought that the driver always had the best seat, instead of being crammed in with all the gear.

"This sort of bickering was usually between me and George," says Paul, "as we were about the same age. John was older and the natural leader. George and I were very bitchy, arguing about who would drive. I'd rush to get the keys and get in the driving seat first. George would get in and say, 'Heh, I thought I was driving. You drove last night.' I would say, 'Well, you're not, are you?' "

Their successes at the various ballrooms around Merseyside naturally led them to being offered their own place, where they were the resident group, where their fans would always know where to expect them. This, thanks to Bob Wooller, was the Cavern Club. They'd outgrown the Casbah coffee club, which was away from the main center of Liverpool and very much a small local club anyway.

The Cavern had been for a long time the main club for live music in the center of Liverpool, but of course it had been purely for jazz. Even at the time of the article by Bob Wooller in the summer of 1961, the Cavern was still being advertised on another page of the same issue as a jazz club, although by then it had become dominated by beat groups, particularly the Beatles. The Cavern is at number 8 Mathew Street. This is a narrow lane in the center of Liverpool, just round the corner from Whitechapel where Nems, the leading record store, is situated. It's a couple of blocks away from the Liverpool *Echo* building and not far from the Pier Head.

Mathew Street is the fruit-market area. Most of the buildings in Mathew Street are fruit warehouses, so the street is always littered and untidy. Throughout the day and early morning there are lorries unloading. Day and night there is a pungent smell of fruit and vegetables. You go down seventeen steps to the Cavern. It's the basement of what was once a wine cellar. It still looks very much like a cellar, dark and poky, with high vaulted pillars. There appears to be no ventilation of any sort, even today when it has all been tarted up into a restaurant-night club.

Ray McFall, an ex-accountant, had taken over the Cavern in 1959 and ran it as a jazz club. Johnny Dankworth, Humphrey Lyttleton, Acker Bilk, Chris Barber all played there. But more and more days began to be given over to the growing beat groups.

From December 1960, when the Beatles returned from Hamburg, they played regularly at the Cavern, alternating at first with the Swinging Bluejeans, who'd been the resident semi-jazz group before them.

"From December 1960 to February 1962 I introduced the Beatles at the Cavern Club 292 times," says Bob Wooller. This not only shows how much Bob Wooller must have been impressed by them, to bother to count up the exact times, but also how hard they were working.

"We probably loved the Cavern best of anything," says George. "It was fantastic. We never lost our identification with the audience all the time. We never rehearsed anything, not like the other groups who kept on copying the Shadows. We were playing to our own fans who were like us. They would come in their lunchtimes to hear us and bring their sandwiches to eat instead of having lunch. We would do the same, eating our lunch while we played. The audience sat there and ate while we stood up there and ate as we played. We enjoyed it all and so did they. It was just spontaneous. Everything just happened."

"It was really a dump," says Mrs. Harrison. "There was no air at all. The walls ran with sweat all the time. The sweat used to drip off them or off the walls and onto the amps and short them. But they'd just carry on all the same, singing on their own. John used to shout out things at the audience. They all did. They'd tell them to shut up. But George never used to say anything or smile. I used to ask him why he didn't. He always looked so serious. Girls were always asking me why he looked so serious. He used to say, 'I'm the lead guitar. If the others make mistakes through larking around, no one notices, but I can't make mistakes.' He was always very serious about his music, and the money. He always wanted to know how much they were getting."

Mrs. Harrison, as ever, was one of their most devoted fans, following them everywhere. Not just following them, but taking relations and friends along as well. She was at the Cavern that time before they went to Hamburg when John's Aunt Mimi had stormed in, determined to pull John out by his ear.

"I saw her on the way out," says Mrs. Harrison. " 'Aren't they great,' I shouted at her. She turned to me and said she was glad someone thought so. I met Mimi a few times after that. She always used to say 'You thing. We'd all have had lovely peaceful lives but for you encouraging them.' "

Everyone who saw the group in their Cavern days remembers most of all their impromptu performances, what they did when the amps failed, or how they messed around between numbers. The Shadows had not only influenced how other groups played but also how they got themselves onto and off stage and how they introduced their numbers. Other groups, when anything went wrong, rushed to the wings, doing the big show-business bit, till someone mended the fuse. What the Beatles did was get everyone to sing "Coming Round the Mountain" or some such corny song.

The Cavern was witnessing the birth of some folk heroes, just by them happening and some people, just like themselves, happening to like them. It was unadulterated, unaffected, almost pure and innocent. Mrs. Harrison approved of it all. Mimi didn't. Jim McCartney was beginning to learn how to live with it.

He used to spend his lunch hours in the same sort of area as the Cavern, hanging around the Cotton Exchange pubs and cafés, chatting with prospective buyers. This makes his job sound grander than it was. He was still just an ordinary cotton salesman, earning under £10 a week and finding it difficult to make ends meet. Michael, Paul's brother, was by this time working, but not doing very well. He'd failed to get into the Art College, and after a series of dead-end jobs was training to be a hairdresser.

Jim often used to pop into the Cavern at lunchtime. "They should have paid you danger money to go down there. There was no ventilation and no proper light, just a few gas lamps. They liked it mysterious, I suppose. It reeked of perspiration. When Paul used to come home from the Cavern I would wring his shirt out in the sink and the sweat would pour out.

"The kids would be in a terrible state as well, fighting with each other to get near the front, or fainting with the excitement and the atmosphere.

I'd see Paul and the others on the stage, looking like something the cat brought home. I'd try to fight my way through the kids, but never make it, so I used to go to their little dressing-room place and wait for them to come offstage."

He wasn't waiting for their autograph, but because he had to see Paul to give him something. As Paul and Michael's only parent, cook, cleaner, and bottlewasher, he had to spend his lunch hour doing the shopping for the evening meal. "That's all I went to the Cavern for, to give Paul the sausages or chops or whatever it was. I'd be in a terrible rush and I'd just have time to fight off the fans and give Paul the meat.

" 'Now don't forget, son,' I'd say. 'Put this on regulo 250 on the electric oven when you get home.' "

Chapter 14: Marking Time— Liverpool and Hamburg

Their success as a local phenomenon was assured once the Cavern days arrived. After four or five years of messing around, they had at last built up an individual act and had acquired a devoted following.

But for the next year, throughout most of 1961, nothing really dramatic happened. They improved all the time and their following grew and became more fanatical. They visited Hamburg again, the first of several return visits, and their success there continued. But they now entered a trough of local success. They seemed destined to play forever in Liverpool or Hamburg. No one else was interested in them.

The second Hamburg trip began in April 1961, by which time George had become eighteen. Peter Eckhorn, manager of the Top Ten Club, and Astrid helped to get all the right work permits. Peter Eckhorn still has the contract. It said they would play every night from seven until two in the morning, except Saturdays when they would play till three. "After each hour of play there will be no less than a break of fifteen minutes," which was very civil of them.

The Top Ten was bigger and not as rough as the two other clubs they'd played in. It had better accommodation, decor, and audiences. There were even more exis in the audience shouting for them now, many of them photographers who would lie down in front, trying to get unusual angles of the Beatles onstage and shouting, "More sveat, pleese, more sveat."

Astrid met them at the train—they were doing it in a bit more style this time—wearing a complete leather trouser suit. Previously she'd just worn a leather jacket, which they'd all copied, wearing it with their jeans and cowboy boots. Stu got her to make a leather suit for him. The others copied, but got them done so cheaply that they split almost as soon as they put them on.

It was at this time that Astrid got around to telling Stu that she didn't like his greasy Teddy-boy hair style. She said he would suit the sort of style that Klaus and Jurgen had. After a lot of persuading, Stu let her do a special style for him. She brushed it all down, snipped bits off, and tidied it up.

Stu turned up at the Top Ten that evening with his hair in the new style, and the others collapsed on the floor with hysterics. Halfway through he gave up and combed his hair high. But thanks to Astrid, he tried it again the next night. He was ridiculed again, but the night after, George turned up with the same style. Then Paul had a go, though for a long time he was always changing it back to the old style as John hadn't yet made up his mind. Pete Best ignored the whole craze. But the Beatle hair style had been born.

Astrid went on to influence them in other ways, such as collarless suits. She'd made one for herself which Stu had admired, so she'd made one for him despite the jokes from the rest of them. "What are you doing with Mum's suit then, Stu?"

They got a bit wilder during this trip, turning to pep pills to keep them going during the all-night sessions—all except Pete Best. "But it never got out of control," says Astrid. "Neither did their drinking. They hardly drank at all, just now and again."

John was still doing a little bit of shoplifting, when the urge took him. Astrid says it was great, which is the phrase Pete Shotton, John's school friend, had used. "It's the way John was," says Astrid. "Everybody feels like doing things sometimes, but of course you don't. But John would suddenly rub his hands and say, 'I know, let's go shoplifting now.' It was all fun. You couldn't be shocked. The idea had suddenly come into his head, so he acted on it. He wouldn't do it again for weeks. Things don't go round in John's head first, the way they do with Paul."

John was still turning out his antireligious cartoons—drawing Christ on the cross with a pair of bedroom slippers at the bottom—and getting involved in other adolescent jokes. He put on a paper dog-collar once, cut himself a paper cross, and preached from a window of the club in a Peter Sellers Indian accent to the crowds below.

They made their first record during this trip, though they were simply backing Tony Sheridan, the singer from the Top Ten. "When the offer came," says John, "we thought it would be easy. The Germans had such shitty records. Ours was bound to be better. We did five of our own numbers, but they didn't like them. They preferred 'My Bonnie Lies over the Ocean.' "

Bert Kaempfert, the well-known German orchestra leader and A and R man, did the recording. On the records, backing Tony Sheridan, they were called The Beat Boys. It was thought the name Beatles was too confusing.

Only four of them were involved in this record. Pete Best was still there. He says he thought he was getting on well. He'd had a fight with Tony Sheridan, but that was all. But Stu Sutcliffe had left. "We were awful to him sometimes," says John. "Especially Paul, always picking on him. I used to explain afterwards to him that we didn't dislike him, really."

They still feel a bit guilty about how they treated Stu, but this wasn't the reason for his leaving. He'd decided to stay in Hamburg, marry Astrid, and go back to being an art student. He enrolled at the Art College, thanks to an eminent visiting professor, Eduardo Paulozzi, the Scots-born sculptor who even managed to get Stu a grant from the Hamburg authorities. Stu still liked the Beatles' music, but he felt he was better at art than on the bass guitar. Paul could obviously play it much better. It would be best for him to take over, which he did.

In July 1961 the four Beatles returned to Liverpool, leaving Stu in Hamburg. He did well at the Art College. "He had so much energy and was so very inventive," says Paulozzi. "The feeling of potential splashed out from him. He had the right kind of sensibility and arrogance to succeed."

The Beatles did a special welcome-home show when they arrived in Liverpool with another leading group they'd known for a long time, Gerry and the Pacemakers. They all played each other's instruments, or daft objects like paper and a comb. They billed themselves as the Beatmakers, an in-joke all the fans appreciated.

The Beatles were still lucky to be making £10 a week each, but the Liverpool beat cult had arrived. The most obvious sign of its existence was the birth of a newspaper completely devoted to the doings of beat groups. This was *Mersey Beat*, for which Bob Wooller wrote the article about the Beatles, referred to earlier. Its first issue came out on July 6, 1961. It contained gossip about the leading groups, such as Gerry and the Pacemakers and Rory Storme and the Hurricanes, the group in which Ringo Starr was on drums. These appear to have been the two main groups. The Beatles came after them in popularity, judging by the first issues. But the Beatles did provide the only bit of humor in the first issue, when John was asked to knock out a bit about their history:

BEING A SHORT DIVERSION ON THE DUBIOUS ORIGINS OF BEATLES
Translated from the John Lennon

Once upon a time there were three little boys called John, George and Paul, by name christened. They decided to get together because they were the getting together type. When they were together they wondered what for after all, what for? So all of a sudden they all grew guitars and formed a noise. Funnily enough, no one was interested, least of all the three little men. So-o-o-o on discovering a fourth little even littler man called Stuart Sutcliffe running about them they said, quote "Sonny get a bass guitar and you will be alright" and he did—but he wasn't alright because he couldn't play it. So they sat on him with comfort 'til he could play. Still there was no beat, and a kindly old aged man said, quote "Thou hast not drums!" We had no drums! they coffed. So a series of drums came and went and came.

Suddenly in Scotland, touring with Johnny Gentle, the group (called the Beatles) discovered they had not a very nice sound— because they had no amplifiers. They got some. Many people ask what are Beatles? Why Beatles? Uh, Beatles, how did the name arrive? So we will tell you. It came in a vision—a man appeared on a flaming pie and said unto them "From this day on you are Beatles with an A." Thank you, Mister Man, they said, thanking him.

And then a man with a beard cut off said—will you go to Germany (Hamburg) and play mighty rock for the peasants for money? And we said we would play mighty anything for money.

But before we could go we had to grow a drummer, so we grew one in West Derby in a club called Some Casbah and his trouble was Pete Best. We called "Hello, Pete, come off to Germany!" "Yes!" Zooooom. After a few months, Peter and Paul (who is called McArtrey, son of Jim McArtrey, his father) lit a Kino (cinema) and the German police said "Bad Beatles, you must go home and light your English cinemas." Zoooooom, half a group. But even before this, the Gestapo had taken my friend little George Harrison (of Speke) away because he was only twelve and too young to vote in Germany; but after two months in England he grew eighteen, and the Gestapoes said "you can come." So suddenly all back in Liverpool Village were many groups playing in grey suits and Jim said "Why have you no grey suits?" "We don't like them, Jim" we said speaking to Jim. After playing in the clubs a bit, everyone said "Go to Germany!" So we are. Zooooom. Stuart gone. Zoom zoom John (of Woolton) George (of Speke) Peter and Paul zoom zoom. All of them gone.

Thank you club members, from John and George (what are friends).

The jokes and the deliberate mistakes in John's article were reproduced many times in the next few years. The whole front page of the second issue of *Mersey Beat* was about their German recording contract. They used one of Astrid's photographs of them, one of the five of them taken in a railway siding in Hamburg. In the caption Paul is called Paul MacArthy. In the same issue there were some fashion notes by someone called Priscilla in which she said that "grey was now the colour for evening wear." This was Cilla Black, then a typist and part-time cloakroom girl and occasional singer at the Cavern.

The Beatles were by now the main group at the Cavern, but they were still using the Casbah Club, Pete Best's home, as their headquarters. Mrs. Best had branched out as a dance promoter, but the Casbah was still her main interest. Most of all she took an interest in the Beatles. "Most people referred to them as 'Pete Best and the Beatles,'" she says. Pete did take the main responsibility for their bookings, helped by his mother, and tried to organize them.

The Casbah became even more their center when Neil Aspinall, Pete's friend who was still living there, bought himself an old van for £80 and started driving the Beatles round Merseyside. He got five bob from each of them for each session. "The evenings became a real drag. I'd drive them somewhere, come home and do a bit of studying, then go back for them. I began to think, what am I doing? I was still getting only two pounds ten a week as an accountant, yet I could get £3 for three lunch hours at the Cavern. So in July I left work for good."

Neil had become their road manager, which he still is, though he hates the term. It was his job to pick up Pete and all their gear from the Casbah, then take them all to where they were playing. "They were beginning to cause riots everywhere," says Neil. "The kids would get going, then the Teds would try to wreck the place. John once got his finger broken in a fight in the bogs."

But despite their large fan following and the fact that some weeks they were earning up to £15 (out of which they now had to pay Neil), nothing was really happening. London seemed to be the only place where pop singers came from, or at least the only place where they could make their name.

Mersey Beat was doing them proud with lots of write-ups, and Pete Best was trying hard to organize them, but with being on the road so much they missed many bookings. They didn't seem to care about bookings anyway, mocking any promoters who were interested in them. Nobody asked to manage them. They weren't earning enough for the normal manager to want them, and anyway they weren't the sort of neat, clean, well-mannered blokes managements liked.

They spent most of their time between the lunch and evening sessions just walking round Liverpool, sitting in coffee bars or hanging around record shops, listening to records for nothing. They were always hard up. Danny English, the manager of the Old Dive, a pub near the Cavern (now knocked down), remembers them spinning out a glass of brown ale for hours. He told them one day that it was about time they bought the barmaid a drink.

"After a lot of discussion, they asked me what she was drinking. I said stout. They said how much was that. After more discussions they produced fourpenny halfpence each and bought her a Guinness."

Danny English tried to get another of his customers to help them. This was George Harrison, no relation to our George Harrison, who has written a column in the Liverpool *Echo* for what seems like centuries. But he didn't do anything. There were so many groups competing for his attention and the Beatles looked the scruffiest of them all.

They were all getting more and more depressed by their lack of progress. All the parents, except Mrs. Harrison and Mrs. Best, were on at their sons once again to give up and get proper jobs.

"I knew John would always be a bohemian," says Mimi. "But I wanted him to have some sort of job. Here he was at nearly twenty-one years old, having thrown away his chance at Art College, touting round stupid halls for £3 a night. Where was the point in that?"

When John was coming up for twenty-one, in September 1961, he got some money as a present from his aunt in Edinburgh and decided on the spur of the moment to go off with Paul to Paris. George and Pete Best were naturally very hurt at being left on their own. "We got fed up," says John. "We did have bookings, but we just broke them and went off."

In Paris they met Jurgen Vollmer, one of their Hamburg friends. It was during this Paris visit, which was mainly spent hanging around the clubs till their money ran out, that John finally brushed his hair forward.

"Jurgen had bell-bottom trousers as well," says John. "But we thought that would be considered too queer back in Liverpool. We didn't want to appear feminine or anything like that because our audience in Liverpool still had a lot of fellows. We were playing rock, dressed in leather, but Paul's ballads were bringing in more and more girls." John had learned from Stu that Jurgen was in Paris. Even though Stu had left them to study art in Hamburg, he and John sent long letters to each other. At first the

I remember a time when everyone
I loved hated me
because I hated them so bad.
so bad so fucking bad.
I remember a time when totally
buttons we a we high
when only shitting we dirty
and everything else clean
& beautiful

I can't remember anything
with out a salary
so deep that it hardly
becomes known to me
so deep that it tears
leave me special
of anyone STUPID!
& so ga ramble on
with a ? ? key having?

January 19__ Ave 17

early da Astrid

this letter ain't EASY
forting to sleep

STVAK
DOWN

How long can one go on writing
and writing, but you'd never doubt.
Really I know who I'm writing to
so why it's quite pointless I
usually write to and
forget about it all if
I put it into the past
of my almost secret self
in the head of someone
while a way to will enough
what I'll tell is going on
isn't turn off at least too
anyway I dunno care really
isn't it happen because when
I think about it, its so
blocky unimportant — but what
is important who ties the weight,
to seen that this letter is not
im-portant and so on
something anyway — er anyway
anyway — yeah !
I wonder what should I write

To be a creation or something I
bet its yeah,
& how are you today
Start each day anew an
etc — in life or quest — bowl stale,
great — wonderful as it was or
Is it just 2 thousand years
of nothing and continue on
an akward...
I think the is if
Goodbye I'm don't wait
end of (or what is it?)
well not because you
think you ought to
bable with you I feel like
so Goodbye goodbye Grandad
you sawn
the me write & hi neo

Anyway
BYE BYE
See you soon
'I don't know
when I shall start

letters were full of jokes and daft stories, the sort John had written as a child, when he did those little scrapbooks. "Uncle Norman has just driven up on his moustaches." "P.S. Mary Queen of Scots was a Nigger."

He passed on to Stu any good bits of news about the group's progress, such as a Beatle fan club at last being started in Liverpool (Rory Storme already had one). But the letters soon became full of disappointments and moans. "It's all a shitty deal. Something is going to happen, but where is it?"

John started writing more serious poetry, the sort he never showed Mimi, though they usually ended in obscenity or self-consciousness. He filled up his letters to Stu with them, when he could think of nothing else.

> I remember a time when
> Everyone I loved hated me
> Because I hated them.
> So what, so what, so
> Fucking what.
>
> I remember a time when
> Belly buttons were knee high
> When only shitting was
> Dirty and everything else
> Clean and beautiful.
>
> I can't remember anything
> without a sadness
> So deep that it hardly
> becomes known to me.
> So deep that its tears
> leave me a spectator
> of my own stupidity.
> And so I go rambling on
> With a hey nonny nonny no.

Stu in Hamburg was filling his letters up with the same sort of wailings and anguish, only his began to be much worse than John's. Stu wrote in his letters as if he was Jesus. John, thinking at first it was all a joke, pretended to be John the Baptist.

One day, toward the end of 1961, Stu collapsed at the Art College in Hamburg and was brought home. "He'd been getting a lot of headaches," says Astrid, "but we just put it down to working too hard at College."

Stu went back the next day, but in February 1962 it happened again. He collapsed, was brought back to Astrid's, and was taken to his room.

This time he stayed there. He wrote long thirty-page letters to John, did endless drawings and paintings, or just walked round and round his room. He had violent headaches and temper tantrums which made it difficult for Astrid and her mother to look after him. He did have medical treatment, but nothing seemed to help. "He came back from a specialist one day and said he didn't want a black coffin like everyone else. He'd just seen a white coffin in a window and he wanted that."

Stu died in April 1962 after a brain hemorrhage. "He lived so much in such a short time," says Klaus. "Every second of his short time he was doing something. He saw ten times more than other people. His imagination was fantastic. His death was a tragedy. He would have done so much." There is no doubt about Stu's artistic talent. Spok thought he was obviously destined to succeed. He'd won prizes in Liverpool at an early age. Since his death, his paintings have appeared in numerous exhibitions in Liverpool and London.

He had had a great influence on John and the rest of the Beatles, leading their fashion in hair, clothes, and in thoughts. "I looked up to Stu," says John. "I depended on him to tell me the truth, the way I do with Paul today. Stu would tell me if something was good and I'd believe him."

Even today, they still miss him. It's strange to think that by 1962, the one who was looked upon as the cleverest Beatle had died. The death of Stu was in a way a macabre climax to their year of apparently getting nowhere and feeling depressed. But back in Liverpool in the late autumn of 1961, just before Stu collapsed, the something John was looking for was at last about to happen.

It happened, to be precise, at three o'clock on the afternoon of October 28, 1961. A youth in a black leather jacket called Raymond Jones walked into the Nems record store in Whitechapel, Liverpool, and asked for a record called "My Bonnie" by a group called the Beatles. Brian Epstein, who was behind the counter, said he was terribly sorry. He'd never heard of that record, or of a group called the Beatles.

Chapter 15: Brian Epstein

The Epstein family fortunes were founded by Brian's grandfather Isaac, a Jewish refugee from Poland, who came to Liverpool at the turn of the century. He opened a furniture store, I. Epstein and Sons, in Walton Road, Liverpool. This in turn was taken over by his elder son Harry, Brian's father.

It is assumed by many people in Liverpool that the Epsteins have always owned Nems, North End Music Stores, the name which Brian later made famous locally, through the record shop. But Nems had been going long before the Epsteins made it so well known. Jim McCartney, Paul's father, remembers having a piano which came from Nems long before it was owned by the Epsteins.

The Epsteins didn't take over Nems until the 1930s. It was at the end of the block in Walton Road which contained I. Epstein and Sons, and they had always had an eye on it for expansion. Harry saw that its record and music business would fit easily into his furniture firm, but it was the site as much as anything he wanted when he eventually bought it.

Harry married into another Jewish furniture family even wealthier and more successful than the Epsteins, the Hymans from Sheffield. He married his wife Queenie in 1930 when she was eighteen and he was twenty-nine. Brian, their elder son, was born on September 19, 1934, in a private nursing home in Rodney Street, the Harley Street of Liverpool. Their second son, Clive, was born twenty-one months later.

With two sons, the fortunes of the Epstein furniture firm seemed assured for many decades to come. Shortly after Brian's birth Harry and Queenie moved into a large five-bedroom detached house in Childwall, one of Liverpool's most desirable residential areas. The Epsteins lived in this house, 197 Queen's Drive, for the next thirty years, until Clive left to get married. Today it is lived in by the Dean of Liverpool.

The Epsteins lived in some style up to the outbreak of the war. They had two live-in servants—a nanny for the boys and a cook-cum-general help. All that Mrs. Epstein can remember of Brian's babyhood is that he was the most beautiful child she'd ever seen. "As he began to walk and talk, he developed a very inquiring mind. He always wanted to know everything." Brian's earliest memories are of the great excitement of being taken through to visit his relations in Sheffield.

His first school of any sort was the Beechanhurst Kindergarten in Liverpool, where he hammered wooden shapes into a plywood board. In 1940, when he was six, Liverpool was under heavy bombing and the family was evacuated first of all to Prestatyn, in North Wales, then to Southport, where there was a large Jewish community. Brian was sent to Southport College, where he began his formal education, the beginning of a very long and very unhappy process.

"I was one of those out-of-sorts boys who never quite fit," so he recorded in his autobiography in 1964.* "I was ragged, nagged, and bullied by boys and masters. My parents must have despaired of me many times." In 1943 the family returned to Liverpool and Brian entered Liverpool College, a private fee-paying school. The following year, at the age of ten, Liverpool College expelled him.

"The official reason was for inattention and for being below standard. I'd been caught in a maths lesson doing drawings of girls. There were other crimes I was supposed to have committed. I'm sure my failings were many." He remembers arriving home and sitting on a sofa, with his father saying, "I just don't know what on earth we're going to do with you."

His mother thinks that in later years he tended to overestimate his own failings at school. She agrees he was hardly happy or successful at any of them, but she thinks it was often as much the fault of the school system as anything. "It was just after the war. Schools were hard to get into. There was none of the freedom they have today. They just threw you out if they didn't like you."

Brian himself thought that, apart from his own inability to fit in, there might also have been some anti-Semitism. "I do remember being called Jew or Yid. But it didn't seem to mean much more than the way a red-headed boy gets called Ginger."

After his expulsion from Liverpool College, his parents found him another local private school, but they kept him there for only a few weeks. They realized it was the sort of pseudo-posh school which took advantage of such parents, caring little for education but a lot for taking money from wealthy parents who couldn't get their kids in anywhere else. In the

* *A Cellarful of Noise,* Souvenir Press.

end they turned to their religion and found him a good Jewish prep school called Beaconsfield near Tunbridge Wells. Here he took up horseback riding, which he loved, and art, which was something he was encouraged to do for the first time.

At thirteen he took the common entrance exam. This is the examination needed to get into any of the good Headmasters' Conference private schools. He failed this miserably, but it didn't stop his parents still trying to get him into one of them. Rugby, Repton, and Clifton all turned him down. He went eventually to the sort of establishment that will take anybody, a very hearty outdoor one in the West Country. He was forced to play rugby. He was very unhappy.

But his father didn't give up trying, and in the autumn of 1948, just on Brian's fourteenth birthday, he got him into Wrekin College, a well-known and established private school in Shropshire. He didn't look forward to Wrekin; he'd eventually begun to settle down at the West Country school. He was getting on with his art and at last making a few friends. He wrote in a diary at the time: "Now for the Wrekin I hate. I am going there only because my parents want me to . . . it is a pity because it has been a great year for me. The birth of new ideas. A little more popularity."

A little later, just before his first day at Wrekin, he wrote: "Before going to Wrekin we spent the day in Sheffield. I expected to be taken to the Grand [Hotel]. But no." He eventually settled down at Wrekin; at least he found ways of putting the time in. His interest in art continued. He became top of the class in it and decided that he was going to be a dress designer. "I wrote to Dad that I wanted to be a dress designer, but he was against it. He said it wasn't the sort of thing for young men to do."

At the same time he developed an interest in acting. At home in Liverpool his mother took him to many plays. "I used to take him first of all to Fol de Rol sorts of things. Then later to improve his mind I took him to Peter Glanville. I also took him to hear the Liverpool Philharmonic."

Brian took a star part in the school's production of O'Neill's *Christopher Columbus*. "His daddy and I drove down to see it," says his mother. "We sat through it all and the headmaster came up and asked us afterwards if we'd liked Brian. We hadn't realized which one he was. He was just so good we hadn't recognized him."

Brian left Wrekin just before he was sixteen, without taking his school certificate. No one thought he could ever have passed it. His father was still against him becoming a dress designer, but Brian decided he wanted to leave school and get a job all the same. "After seven schools, all of them rotten, I'd had enough. I'd been thwarted in the only thing I wanted to do, so I just accepted anything. On September 10, 1950, very thin, pink-cheeked, curly-haired, and half-educated I reported for duty at the family store in Walton, Liverpool."

He started as a furniture salesman at £5 a week. The day after he joined he sold a twelve-pound dining table to a woman who had come into the shop to buy a mirror. He found he was a good salesman, and he enjoyed it. He also started taking an interest in the design and layout of the shop. His father had been naturally pleased that his elder son had at last decided to come into the business. Brian found, to his surprise, that it pleased him as well.

"Brian always had beautiful taste," says his mother. "And he was brought up among lovely furniture, which also helped." But Brian didn't think the store's window displays were all that lovely. He started experimenting, doing what was considered very daring things, such as putting chairs with their backs to the window. His father thought perhaps he was doings things a bit quicker than was necessary but didn't complain as he was so pleased that his son and heir was settling down well in the career he had chosen for him. As further experience he decided to send Brian to another firm, not connected with them, to do a six-month apprenticeship.

Brian spent the six months at The Times furniture store in Lord Street, Liverpool, still at £5 a week. He seems to have done well there too. When he left they presented him with a Parker pen and pencil set. (The pen was the one he loaned to Paul McCartney, a few years later, to sign his first contract.)

After the six months, he moved back to Walton. He began to take over the designing of the whole store. "I enjoyed it, especially trying new things. I enjoyed selling as well, watching people relax and show trust in me. It was pleasant to see the wary look dissolve and people begin to think there were good things ahead for them and I would be the provider."

He had a few rows with his grandfather Isaac over his plans for window-dressing. "He wanted all the windows jam-packed. I preferred very little in the window, perhaps just one chair. I was also crazy about contemporary furniture. It was just coming in and I wanted everybody to know about it. I think if you show the public something lovely, they'll accept it."

On December 9, 1952, in the midst of his brave new schemes for I. Epstein and Sons, he was called up for national service. If school horrified him, the thought of the Army was terrifying. "I'd been a poor schoolboy. I was sure I was going to make the lousiest soldier ever." He applied for the RAF and was made a clerk in the Royal Army Service Corps. He did his basic training at Aldershot.

"It was like prison and I did everything wrong. I turned right instead of left and when I was told to stand still I fell over." He managed to get through his square bashing, after a fashion, and even had the notion that he might be chosen to be on parade for the Coronation. The year was 1953. He thought the Coronation sounded glamorous and exciting and it would be nice to be part of it. But he wasn't chosen. Instead he went round the pubs and clubs and got drunk.

He was about the only ex-private-school boy in his draft group who didn't become an officer. But in his off-duty hours, dressed as always in impeccable taste and spending his time in smart West End clubs, he could easily have passed for one. After Aldershot, Brian managed to get assignment to Regent's Park Barracks in London, one of the most desirable postings for young officers around town. He had lots of relations in London and managed to get out and enjoy himself. He drove himself back one night in a large car, wearing a bowler hat, pin-striped suit, and carrying an umbrella over his arm.

As he entered the barracks, the guard saluted him, two soldiers confined to the guardhouse jerked their heads in an eyes right, and a clerk shouted, "Good night, Sir." But an officer inside wasn't so easily misled. "Private Epstein. You will report to the company office at ten hundred hours tomorrow morning, charged with impersonating an officer."

He was confined to barracks for some time. It wasn't his first offense. He'd been guilty of other minor insubordinations, or at least inabilities to do the right thing. "The Army was generally getting on my nerves. I really was becoming genuinely upset. It was getting me down so much that I reported to the barracks doctor, who referred me to a psychiatrist."

Several other psychiatrists were consulted and all agreed that Private Epstein wasn't one of nature's soldiers. They agreed that he was mentally and emotionally unsuited to military service. After twelve months, his national service only half completed, he was discharged on medical grounds. As is the way of the Army, they still gave him most impressive-sounding military references. It described him in glowing terms as a "sober, reliable and utterly trustworthy soldier."

Brian told the story of his Army debacle in very cheerful terms, almost hinting that he might have engineered his discharge. But there seems little doubt that he had been seriously disturbed by it all. He ran all the way to Euston and caught the first train to Liverpool. He went back to the family store and worked very hard. He began to take an increasing interest in the record side. He'd always been interested in music, classical records mainly but popular music as well. Edmundo Ros was one of his favorites at the time.

But he began to get even more interested in a new hobby, one he had been very fond of at school—acting. He was beginning to realize that perhaps he was more interested in artistic things than being a furniture salesman. He went to every production at the Liverpool Playhouse and began to spend more and more of his spare time either in amateur productions or in the company of professional actors from the Playhouse. He became very friendly with two in particular, Brian Bedford and Helen Lindsay.

One night in the Basnett Bar near the Playhouse, they were all set for a long evening talking and drinking, but he said he had to be home early. He had work to do in the evening. "You two are all right," he said. "But I'm a doomed middle-aged businessman."

They suggested that he too could be an actor. He had the interest, the right feelings, and they were sure the talent. Why didn't he apply for RADA? They would help him. So he applied for the Royal Academy of Dramatic Art. And he got in.

"I read two pieces for the Director, John Fernald. They were from Eliot's *Confidential Clerk* and from *Macbeth*. I got in without a full audition, for some reason. Perhaps the fact that I had no money problems helped." His father, naturally enough, wasn't particularly pleased. Acting was second only to dress designing in his list of unmanly jobs. But at twenty-two his son and heir went off again to interrupt his career. This time willingly, unlike the Army. Perhaps even forever.

He was in the same year at RADA as Susannah York and Joanna Dunham. Albert Finney and Peter O'Toole had just left. "I was doing reasonably well. John Fernald had great faith in me. But I began to loathe actors and all their social life. I hadn't enjoyed school. And here I was seven years later in another community life. I just didn't like it, or any of the people. I began to think it was too late. I was more a businessman after all."

From the day he had started RADA his father was always asking him when he was coming back to the business. Each holiday, as he was going back to RADA, he asked him to stay. During the summer vacation of 1957, before he began his fourth term, he asked Brian again over dinner at the Adelphi Hotel. This time Brian said yes.

His father had decided to open a new branch in Liverpool, this time in the city center, in Great Charlotte Street. This was as much to tempt Brian back to the firm as anything. "Everything my husband did was for the boys," says Mrs. Epstein. Clive, Brian's younger brother, was by this time also working in the firm.

Brian was put in charge of the record department with one assistant. Anne Shelton, the singer, opened the new store. On the first morning the record department took in £20. In Walton the record department took in £70 in a good week.

"Most record shops I'd ever been in were lousy. The minute a record became popular, it went out of stock. I aimed to have everything in stock, even the most way-out records. I did this by ordering in triplicate any record that anyone ever wanted. I reckoned that if one person asked for something, there must be others who would want it too. I even ordered three copies of the LP *The Birth of a Baby* just because one person had wanted it."

Every customer was encouraged to leave an order for a record if by chance it wasn't in. An immediate delivery was always promised. Brian worked out a simple but ingenious stock index whereby it could be seen immediately which record had sold out. This consisted of strings attached inside each folder. When any were dangling down, it could be seen immediately that more records were needed. This was checked constantly throughout the day and replacements put in or reordered immediately.

He also worked out his own top-twenty best-seller list of the pop records being sold in Nems. This was checked twice daily. Apart from being a good gimmick of interest to customers and an encouragement for them to buy certain records, it also showed him exactly which of the up-and-coming records should be ordered in bulk.

"I've never seen anybody work as hard before," says his mother. "He seemed to have found something which completely fulfilled him for the first time in his life."

Brian agreed. "I did work very hard. I don't think I worked physically harder in my life, before or after. I started at eight each day and didn't finish until well into the night. On Sundays I was in the store all day making orders." By 1959, two years after opening, Nems in Great Charlotte Street had an extensive pop and classical department covering two floors of the store. The staff had expanded from two to thirty. Business was going so well that it was decided to open another branch of Nems in Whitechapel, the heart of Liverpool's shopping center.

The new shop was opened by Anthony Newley. Brian had got in touch with him through a Decca sales contact. The crowds on the opening day in Central Liverpool were compared to the return of a triumphal cup-final team. Nobody in Liverpool had seen such a turnout for a pop singer until then. Things were a bit different a few years later.

Both shops thrived and expanded. By August 1961 Brian was boasting that the two Nems record shops in central Liverpool, those in White-chapel and Great Charlotte Street, contained "The finest record selections in the North." This boast appeared in an advertisement for Nems on August 31, 1961, in *Mersey Beat,* that same Merseyside pop-music news-paper which had begun the preceding month. Brian himself was not per-sonally a fan of pop music. His favorite composer at the time was Sibelius. But, as a smart businessman, he saw that *Mersey Beat* was thriving and a good advertising market.

In that same issue he started a column called "Record Releases." This was bylined "Brian Epstein of NEMS." He reviewed forthcoming rec-ords, light, jazz, and pop. In that first column he said "The Shadows' popularity seems to increase continually." That must have made the Beatles sick.

The column gave him free publicity for his shops and also helped him push certain records, but it was also smart of *Mersey Beat* to have got him. In the four years since he'd left RADA, fed up and disillusioned, he'd become about the leading personality in the record retailing business on Merseyside. His name and solid business background gave weight to *Mersey Beat.*

But very soon he was beginning to feel he had expanded as far as he could go. There weren't many fresh fields to conquer in Merseyside, at least in his line. By the autumn of 1961 the feeling of boredom and dis-satisfaction was coming on again. His mother remembers sensing it.

"He started taking up teaching himself foreign languages. He became very interested in Spain and Spanish. He also went back to amateur act-ing again."

His father was naturally worried that he would want to be off again, having built up two prosperous record stores. Brian himself remembered this feeling of wanting something new, of being bored and frustrated by business. But his three closest friends at the time don't remember him moaning about that, though they do recall him having other things which bothered him.

Once Whitechapel was established, he had begun to have more of a social life. He used to see a lot of Geoffrey Ellis, a boyhood friend who lived near him in Queen's Drive. He had also gone to a private school, Ellesmere College, and then on to Oxford, where he read law. Geoffrey says Brian was terribly shy and hesitant in his schooldays. But after Ox-ford, Geoffrey went to New York to work for an insurance firm, and they lost contact for a few years.

There was also a friend called Terry Doran, from a completely different background. He was an ex-secondary modern-school boy, now a car salesman, with a good line in Liverpool wit and mimicry. "I met Brian by chance one day in a Liverpool pub in 1959. I just fell in love with him from the beginning," Geoffrey and Terry were simply social friends, unconnected with his business, at least in those days. But his third friend, Peter Brown, was a friend in the same business. He eventually became Brian's closest friend of all.

Peter was born in Birkenhead, went to a Roman Catholic grammar school, got two O levels, worked in Henderson's, the Liverpool store, and then worked in Lewis's, where he became manager of the record department.

When Brian came to plan the opening of the new Nems store in Whitechapel, he asked Peter to take over as manager of Charlotte Street. Peter was getting £12 a week managing the record department at Lewis's. Brian offered him £16, plus commission, which he thought was enormous. "I soon learned all about Brian's highly efficient ordering systems. After closing time at six we had to do all the orders. It could take up from forty minutes to two hours."

Terry remembers being kept waiting while they were both doing orders. Brian would tell Terry to meet him after the shop closed. "I'd go for a drink and end up being there till closing time, still waiting for them."

There was a slight delay in opening Whitechapel and Peter found that for a few months Brian was still at Charlotte Street with him. "It was pretty difficult, officially being the manager, but having the boss still there running things. It was one long row. We were still as good social friends, but I think he was disappointed in me as a businessman. He was very fond of sending notes to all the staff, even though there were so few of us. His stock-control system really was marvelous. It assured that we were never out of stock of any best-selling record. EMI people used to tell us we were the largest sellers in the North."

Brian always maintained, quite wrongly, that girls didn't find him attractive. But it was about this time that he started going out with a girl from his record store, Rita Harris.

"It took him a long time to realize she had fallen in love with him," says Peter Brown. "We all used to go into Cheshire for a meal, Rita and Brian and me and perhaps one or two others." This was the most serious romance that Brian ever had with a girl, but it eventually amounted to nothing.

His love life always appears to have ended unhappily. He did have violent affairs with other people, but they rarely lasted long, which worried him a great deal. "He never really came to terms with himself sexually. He thought there was something wrong about it all. But he decided that was how he was and he never tried to go against his nature. But he sometimes almost had a self-destruction complex.

"He was really very lonely in Liverpool," says Peter. "He felt there were few places he could go and really enjoy himself. Our best nights out were in Manchester. Brian, Terry, and I used to drive through there most Saturday evenings.

"He had a phobia about his unhappy affairs and also another one, just slightly, about being Jewish. I think he imagined anti-Semitism sometimes when there wasn't any. Perhaps it wasn't awareness of his Jewishness. Perhaps it was just being part of an environment he didn't really care for—the sort of successful, provincial, furniture-shop Jewishness, when his real nature was towards the artistic and the aesthetic.

"But of course he could be a good businessman when he wanted to, saving pennies and being mean when he suddenly felt he had to. We had lots of rows over money. But it just happened now and again. He was mostly a very lavish spender."

It's easy to overstate the case about Brian's personality and interests at this stage in his career. His parents knew little of any worries. They certainly didn't see any effects of them, although his mother did remember him becoming restless once both Nems shops were thriving, and start looking for something new.

He went off in the autumn of 1961 for a five-week holiday in Spain, the longest he'd had. He took with him a slight feeling of frustration, in his personal life as well as in his business life. Nothing serious, perhaps. Just a feeling of unfulfillment. He'd been too busy really, building up Nems for the last four years, ever to become seriously worried by it all, the way he had done in the Army. One or two did consider him a poor little spoiled rich boy. But so far as most people could see, he was hard-working, charming and gay, with a family who loved him.

But he obviously felt he needed something new to fill his life, preferably something in some way artistic. RADA had been an outlet of a sort, the failure of which had stopped his artistic longings for a while. But there is nothing more insidiously frustrating than an artistic leaning when one's artistic tastes happen to be greater than one's artistic talents, or so it seems.

This was Brian Epstein on October 28, 1961. He was twenty-seven.

So far he had been a failed schoolboy, a successful furniture salesman, a failed soldier, a successful record salesman, a failed actor, a successful record-shop executive. When into the shop came a customer asking for the Beatles.

Chapter 16: Brian Signs the Beatles

The famous Epstein index system was beaten. All these lovely little bits of dangling string couldn't help. Brian Epstein had to admit that he'd heard neither of a record called "My Bonnie" nor a group called the Beatles.

It is strange in some ways that he hadn't heard of the Beatles. After all, he'd been advertising and writing a record column in *Mersey Beat* for several months. His eye must have passed over their name in articles many times. But his interest in *Mersey Beat* was purely professional, as a retailer taking space in order to sell records. He was only interested in those groups which had made records, because records were what he sold. None of the Liverpool groups being written about in *Mersey Beat* had made a record, so there was no reason for him to have taken any notice of them.

He was aware that there were flourishing beat groups and clubs in Liverpool. But he wasn't interested in them personally. At twenty-seven he was well out of the age range for the coffee bars and groups. He'd also been, for most of the preceding five years, a full-time businessman with little time for any sort of leisure activities apart from the theater.

But he was annoyed by his lack of knowledge of the new record he was being asked for. Surely if this group, wherever they came from, had produced a record, *he* must know about it. So when Raymond Jones made his request he promised to get it for him and wrote down on a pad: "My Bonnie. The Beatles. Check on Monday."

Raymond Jones had also mentioned that the Beatles' record came from Germany. That was something to go on. He telephoned a few agents who imported foreign records, but not one of them had the record in stock or had even imported it. "I might have stopped there, but for the rigid rule I'd laid down that no customer should ever be turned away.

"I was also intrigued to find out why a completely unknown disk had been asked for three times in two days. Because on Monday morning, before I'd started making inquiries, two girls came in and asked for the same record." He talked to various contacts around Liverpool and found to his amazement that not only were the Beatles a British and not a German group, but that they came from Liverpool.

He asked the girls in his store about the Beatles. They told him the Beatles were fabulous. Then he found to his surprise that they'd even been in his store. He must have seen them many an afternoon without knowing who they were. "One of the girls told me they were the boys I'd once been complaining about, hanging around the counters all day listening to records but not buying any. They were a scruffy crowd in leather. But they were supposed to be quite nice really, so all the girls told me, so I'd never actually asked them to leave. Anyway, they filled the shop up in the afternoon."

Brian decided to go along to the Cavern himself and get some details about the Beatles and their record. If there was such interest in them, especially being a local group, it might be worth his while to import some of their records himself, being a good businessman.

"But I wasn't a member of the Cavern and I was very shy about going along to a teenage club. I was frightened they might not let me in. So I asked *Mersey Beat* if they could help me. They rang up the Cavern and said who I was and could I come." His first visit was the lunchtime session of November 9, 1962. "It was dark, damp, and smelly and I regretted my decision immediately. The noise was deafening, loud amplifiers sending out mainly American hits. I remember as I listened to the records they were playing thinking that there might be some tie-up possible between the Cavern and my Top Twenty selection.

"Then the Beatles came on and I saw them for the first time. They were not very tidy and not very clean. They smoked as they played and they ate and talked and pretended to hit each other. They turned their backs on the audience and shouted at people and laughed at their private jokes. But there was quite clearly enormous excitement. They seemed to give off some sort of personal magnetism. I was fascinated by them."

It was John, the main shouter and jumper-about, who particularly fascinated him. This wasn't apparent at the time, as he didn't know which was which, but he realized it later. He couldn't keep his eyes off John.

But he hadn't come to watch. He'd come simply to do a bit of business. The Cavern disk jockey, Bob Wooller, announced over the microphone that Mr. Epstein of Nems was in the audience and would everybody give him a big hand. This helped when he at last managed to get within shouting distance of the Beatles themselves. "What brings Mr. Epstein here?" said George, slightly sarcastically. He explained that he'd had a request for their German disk but didn't know which company produced it. Could they help? George told him the company was called Polydor. George only very vaguely remembers talking to Brian that lunchtime. The other Beatles—John, Paul, and Pete Best—don't remember him at all this first visit.

Just for company, to hide his shyness among all the kids, on his frequent visits to the Cavern Brian began to take along one of his assistants from his store. This was Alistair Taylor, who worked on the counter at Nems but was also Brian's personal assistant. Like sending memos to his staff when he could have talked to them all in a telephone booth, Brian liked the executive image.

It took Brian some time to get his thoughts clear. "All I was interested in was selling records. But in a few weeks I'd found myself coming to the Cavern more and more often. I also found myself asking my record contacts what managing a group meant. How did one do it? What sort of contract one would have with a group, supposing, just supposing, one wanted to become a manager."

His contacts weren't all that expert on management problems. They were, naturally, mainly in the retail side of records, not the production. But during a trip down to London, purely on retail business, he talked more than usual to people like the general manager of His Master's Voice in Oxford Street and the manager at Keith Prowse's shop, picking up any tips he could. He also contacted the Deutsche Gramophone Company and ordered 200 copies of "My Bonnie." "I was so fascinated by the Beatles that I thought it was worth taking a chance on selling them all.

"I suppose it was all part of getting bored with simply selling records. I was looking for a new hobby. The Beatles at the same time, though I didn't know it and perhaps they didn't either, were also getting a bit bored with Liverpool. They were wanting to do something new. To expand and get on to something new.

"I began talking to them more at lunchtime sessions. 'You should have been here last night,' Paul said to me one day. 'We were signing autographs. I signed one on a girl's arm.' I always seemed to miss their greatest moments."

He also found out what their present situation was about a manager. He found that Alan Williams had been associated with them at one time and had been the one who had organized their trips to Hamburg. "I went to see him and he said, 'They're nice boys, but they'll let you down all the time.'"

On December 3, 1961, Brian invited them along for a chat in his office at the Whitechapel store. He told them it was just a chat, as he hadn't worked out everything in his mind. He'd seen a lot of them prior to that first proper meeting at his office, but the Beatles themselves had still scarcely taken him in. He was just a fringe figure. They have few real memories of him before that meeting. "He'd looked efficient and rich, that's all I remember," says John. George says he looked the executive type. Paul was impressed by his Zodiac car. They decided to give him a try.

For that first official meeting the Beatles decided to bring along Bob Wooller with them, just to show they weren't completely alone in the world. John introduced Bob Wooller as his dad. It was many months before Brian realized that Bob Wooller was not John's dad. It was even longer before he realized John didn't know who or where his dad was.

John and Bob Wooller arrived at the appointed time at four thirty. So did George and Pete Best. But there was no sign of Paul. After half an hour, during which Brian was becoming very irritated, he asked George to ring Paul. George returned from the phone to say that Paul was in the bath. "This is disgraceful," said Brian. "He's going to be very late." "Late," said George. "But very clean."

Paul arrived at last and they discussed the future of the Beatles. What they all wanted to do, what sort of terms they would like. Nobody knew what sort of contracts were arranged in such circumstances because no one had ever seen one. But of course, Brian made clear, this was just all an introductory chat, to see what was in their minds.

They all arranged to meet again the following Wednesday. By that time Brian had been to see a lawyer friend, Rex Makin. Brian was looking for enthusiasm as well as advice. "Oh, yes," he was told. "Another Epstein idea. How long before you lose interest in this one?"

They met again on the Wednesday and Brian this time said he definitely wanted to manage them. He said he'd want 25 per cent. They said why couldn't he take 20. He said he needed that extra 5 per cent as he would entail so many expenses in promoting them and working for them. He expected to lose money for many months to come. The contract was signed the following Sunday at the Casbah Club, Pete Best's home and the Beatles' headquarters. Each Beatle signature was signed in the presence of Alistair Taylor. Brian didn't sign. "That was a great boob," says Alistair. "I signed my name as a witness to Brian's signature. It made me look a right fool."

Brian never did sign the contract, either. "I had given my word about what I intended to do, and that was enough. I abided by the terms and no one ever worried about me not signing it."

He thinks the Beatles liked the idea of him managing them because they liked the look of him. "I had money, a car, a record shop. I think that helped. But they also liked me. I liked them because of this quality they had, a sort of presence. They were incredibly likable."

His parents sensed something was happening. They came back from a week in London and found him waiting for them. "Brian said he wanted us to listen to this record," says his mother. "It was 'My Bonnie.' He said take no notice of the singing, just the backing. He said they are going to be a big hit and I'm going to manage them." Before his father could interrupt, Brian added that of course it would just be a part-time interest, but he wouldn't mind if he took a little time off work? His father wasn't too thrilled. He realized that Brian once again had found something new, but at least this time it was in Liverpool.

Brian decided to start a new company to manage the Beatles and he called it Nems Enterprises, after the record stores. "That was a fortunate decision. I might easily have run them simply under the same company as Nems, without Enterprises. When we sold Nems, the record shops, years later, that could have been very complicated."

He asked his brother Clive to lend him some money in setting up Nems Enterprises. "This was partly because I needed more money, but partly because I was scheming to get Clive interested in perhaps helping me."

The Beatles' next (third) Hamburg trip was as good as fixed long before Brian Epstein came along. Not long after they'd left Hamburg, Peter Eckhorn of the Top Ten and several other club managers came across to Liverpool, scouting for talent.

They'd promised Peter Eckhorn they would come back to his club, but when he arrived in Liverpool to discuss details with them and see any other likely groups, he found they had now Brian Epstein as manager.

"Brian wanted a lot more money than I was offering," says Peter Eckhorn. "I tried Gerry and the Pacemakers, but I couldn't get them either." In the end, Peter Eckhorn returned to Hamburg with a drummer, which was all he could get. This drummer, Ringo Starr, was to back Tony Sheridan.

Eventually other Hamburg club owners came and offered better terms. Brian in the end accepted an offer from Manfred Weislieder, who was opening a brand-new club in Hamburg, the Star Club. This was to be bigger and better than any of the others. His offer for the Beatles was 400 marks each a week, about £40. The Top Ten offer had been around 300 marks a week.

These were very good terms, but months before that was settled, Brian was already holding out for better terms wherever they played locally in Liverpool. He made a rule, the minute he took them over, that they would never play for less than £15 a night. But Brian Epstein did his biggest and most immediate work in smartening up the Beatles, in their organization, in their appearance, and in their presentation.

Brian took over all the bookings from Pete Best and put them on a properly organized basis. He also made sure that each of them knew exactly where and when they were playing. "Brian put all our instructions down neatly on paper and it made it all seem real," says John. "We were just in a daydream till he came along. We'd no idea what we were doing, or where we'd agreed to be. Seeing our marching orders on paper made it all official."

Brian's instructions were all beautifully typed, usually on paper with his own crest on the top, a clever typographical sign made of his initials. He also added little homilies about looking smart, wearing the right clothes and not smoking, eating, or chewing during their performance. "Brian was trying to clean our image up," says John. "He said our look wasn't right. We'd never get past the door at a good place. We just used to dress how we liked, on and off stage. He talked us into the suit scene."

Brian also smartened up their onstage presentation, which up till then had been all ad-libbed. "He said we must work out a proper program, playing our best numbers each time, not just the ones we felt like playing," says Pete Best. "It was no use just laughing and joking with the kids at the front when there might be 700 or 800 at the back who had no idea what was happening. He made us work out a strict program, with no messing about."

Things have changed enormously since then and swung completely the other way. Later John regretted slightly their smartening up, because he knew it wasn't really them, or anyway really John. But he went along with it. He knew it was the only way, to join the suit set.

"It was natural we should put on our best show," says John, "for people like reporters, even the ones who were snooty, letting us know they were doing us a favor. We would play them along, agreeing with them, how kind they were to talk to us. We were very two-faced about it all. Trying to get publicity was just a game. We used to traipse round the offices of the local papers and the musical papers asking them to write about us because that was what you had to do."

Although they privately laughed at all the people who didn't want to know them, carefully sent them up, or even openly sent them up, they were still very hurt by all the prejudice against them.

"All we ever got in those days," says Paul, "was, 'Where are you from? Liverpool? You'll never do anything from there. Too far away. You'll have to be in London before you can do it. Nobody's ever done it from Liverpool.' That's all we ever heard for years." But Brian was going the right way about making them acceptable to the London sort of mind.

"But I didn't *change* them. I just projected what was there. What was there was this presence. Onstage they had this undefinable feeling. But it was being spoiled by smoking and eating and talking to the front few rows."

Brian had naturally been to see the Beatles' parents when he decided to become their manager. They were impressed by his manners and obvious wealth, unlike all the previous friends their sons had had.

Only Mimi, John's aunt, seems to have been at all hesitant, though Brian should have impressed her most of all, except that she wasn't impressed by anything to do with beat groups.

"I had misgivings when I first heard of Brian Epstein. Not against him personally. But he was so well off. It seemed just a novelty to him and it didn't really matter whether they sank or swum. If they hadn't made it, it wouldn't have made any difference to him. He wasn't depending on it, the way they were.

"I found Brian very charming. I always did. But this was the worry I had when he came along. I thought, that'll be it. He'll have finished with them in two months and gone on to something else. While John and the others won't ever have got started."

Chapter 17: Decca and Pete Best

Almost from the beginning, Brian Epstein started using his record contacts, exerting any pressures he could as the owner of the self-styled "finest record store in the North." And almost from the beginning it began to work. Decca said they were interested.

Brian's contacts with Decca had always been the best, though of course they were solely on the retail side. But by getting his credentials passed from department to department, he managed to land a promise that an A and R (Artists and Repertoire) man would come up to Liverpool to see what all the boasting was about. Mike Smith of Decca duly appeared toward the end of December 1961. Success at his first go. Brian was ecstatic. "What an occasion it was! An A and R manager at the Cavern."

Mike Smith was very impressed. He liked the sound of the Beatles and promised to arrange for them to come down to London and have an audition at the Decca Studios. This sort of audition, just to hear their sound and see how they would react to taping, doesn't mean all that much. But it did to Brian Epstein, to the Beatles, and to Liverpool. No one else had got as far as this.

The audition was arranged for January 1, 1962. Brian went down to London by train for the appointment. The Beatles—John, Paul, George, and Pete Best—were taken down by their road manager, Neil Aspinall, on New Year's Eve.

"I hired a bigger van specially. I'd never been anywhere near London before. It took ten hours and we got lost in the snow somewhere near Wolverhampton. We got to London about ten o'clock at night and found our hotel, the Royal, off Russell Square. Then we went for a drink. We tried to get a meal in some place in the Charing Cross Road. We all went in, a right gang of scruffs we were, and sat down. It said six bob for soup and we said, you're kidding. The bloke said we'd have to go. So we had to.

130

"We went to Trafalgar Square and saw all the New Year's Eve drunks falling in the fountain. Then we met two blokes in Shaftesbury Avenue who were stoned, though we didn't know it. They had some pot, but we'd never seen that either. We were too green. When they heard we had a van they asked if they could smoke it there. We said no, no, no! We were dead scared."

Brian was first at Decca Studios next morning, bang on time. "Mike Smith was late and I was pretty annoyed. Not because we were anxious to tape our songs, but because we felt we were being treated as people who didn't matter."

At last they were told it was their turn. They got out their old, battered amplifiers and were immediately told to put them away. "They didn't want our tackle," says Neil. "We had to use theirs. We needn't have dragged our amps all the way from Liverpool."

They got going and George sang, in a very clipped voice, "The Sheik of Araby." Paul sang, rather nervously, "Red Sails in the Sunset" and "Like Dreamers Do." They didn't try any of their own compositions, although they had scores they could have done. Brian advised them to stick to standards.

"They were pretty frightened," says Neil. "Paul couldn't sing one song. He was too nervous and his voice started cracking up. They were all worried about the red light on. I asked if it could be put off, but we were told people might come in if it was off. You what? we said. We didn't know what all that meant." They finished doing the tapes about two o'clock and everyone seemed very pleased.

"Mike Smith said the tapes were terrific," says Pete Best. "We thought we were in. Brian took us all out for dinner that night at some place in Swiss Cottage. He ordered wine, but it never turned up for some reason."

The weeks passed and nothing happened. They continued playing their local dates on Merseyside, but all the time expecting Decca to whisk them to the big time. Then in March, after a lot of pestering, Brian heard from Dick Rowe, Mike Smith's boss at Decca, that they had decided not to record the Beatles. "He told me they didn't like the sound. Groups of guitars were on the way out. I told him I was completely confident that these boys were going to be bigger than Elvis Presley."

It was suggested to him that as he had a good record business in Liverpool he should stick to it. It was also hinted that there were other ways of having a record made—for a payment of £100, for example, he could hire a studio and an A and R man. He contemplated this for a day or so. But he was still being treated in such an offhand manner that he decided it was a complete waste of money.

"I think Decca expected us to be all polished," says John. "We were just doing a demo. They should have seen our potential. I think a lot of halfwits were looking after it." After that began a long and dispiriting trail round all the other major recording companies. In turn, Pye and EMI turned them down. Other smaller companies also said no.

"I was the last to hear about being turned down by Decca," says Pete Best. "John, Paul, and George heard long before me. They just let it slip out one day, that they'd known for weeks. Why didn't you tell me? They said they didn't want to dishearten me." The others veered between being disheartened and an illogical optimism that something would turn up in the end.

"We did have a few little fights with Brian," says John. "We used to say he was doing nothing and we were doing all the work. We were just saying it, really. We knew how hard he was working. It was Us against Them. We used to wait for Brian at Lime Street to hear his news," says Paul. "He'd ring us up and we'd think perhaps he'd have something for us. He'd come off the train with his brief case full of papers and we'd go for a coffee in the Punch and Judy and hear how Pye or Philips or whoever it was had turned us down."

"But we still used to send up the idea of getting to the top," says George. "When things were a real drag and nothing happening, we used to go through this routine: John would shout, 'Where are we going, fellas?' We'd shout back, 'To the Top, Johnny!' Then he would shout, 'What Top?' 'To the Toppermost of the Poppermost, Johnny!' "

Alistair Taylor, Brian's assistant at Nems, says that Brian was often near tears with the trail round the record companies. "He was bringing all the pressures he could, but there are always 10,000 groups, bringing all the pressures they can. He was getting nowhere."

In December 1961 *Mersey Beat* ran a popularity poll. John and Paul still have copies of that issue lying around their homes, all with the entry forms cut out. They filled in dozens in assumed names, all putting the Beatles first and Gerry and the Pacemakers last. They were genuinely worried he would win. All the groups were voting for themselves, of course, so any cheating canceled itself out. In fact, the Beatles were out-and-out winners.

Brian made the most of the award. For a performance on March 24, 1962, they were billed in big capitals as MERSEY BEAT POLL WINNERS! POLYDOR RECORDING ARTISTS! PRIOR TO EUROPEAN TOUR! The actual concert was held at Barnston Women's Institute, which is rather small beer after such a buildup.

The European tour they were billed as being prior to was of course

The HESWALL JAZZ CLUB
******* ******

present their ★ ★ ★

★ALL★STAR★BILL

 Starring

THE BEATLES

★ Mersey Beat Poll Winners!
★ Polydor Recording Artists!
★ Prior to European Tour!

★ *plus*

The Pasadena Jazzmen

Firm Favourites !

plus ★

'Top Twenty' Records

at Barnston Women's Institute
on Saturday March 24th, 1962
7-30 p.m. —— 11-15 p.m.

7/6   ADMISSION   **7/6**
Strictly by TICKETS ONLY

F. W. COOPER SEAVIEW PRESS, 368, BOROUGH ROAD, BIRKENHEAD.

their third visit to Hamburg. This took place just a week later, in April 1962. They arrived at Hamburg by plane. This was the very first time they'd traveled by plane. "Brian made us do it," says Pete Best. "We were all dead chuffed."

They were to play this time at the Star Club, the biggest Hamburg club of its type. "It even had proper curtains on stage," says George. Astrid, still in mourning for Stu, didn't come to their concerts at first, but the Beatles went out of their way to go and get her, give her presents, and cheer her up. She says that any slight feelings she might have had that they could be cruel disappeared forever. "I'd never realized they could be so kind."

Meanwhile, back in Britain, Brian was working on a last attempt to get someone interested in the Beatles. He decided he would spend one further outlay of money. He'd been taking tapes to all the record companies, some of them ones they'd originally made at the Decca audition back in January. He decided it would be more impressive and much handier for carrying round and letting people hear if he had the tapes made into a record.

His father by this time was becoming more and more annoyed at all the time he was wasting on the Beatles. "I told my father I wanted to take my tapes to London for an all-out, all-or-failure attack. He agreed, providing it was only for a day or two."

Brian made for the HMV record center in Oxford Street. This is just a normal retail shop, though very large and part of the vast EMI empire. Brian talked to a contact there and asked him how he could get his tapes turned into a disk.

"The technician who recorded the tape told me it wasn't at all bad. He said he'd have a word with a music publisher upstairs, Syd Coleman. Coleman was very excited and said he'd like to publish them and that he would speak to a friend of his at Parlophone, George Martin." An appointment was made to meet George Martin next day at EMI. Parlophone is part of EMI, the parent company which had already turned the Beatles down.

"George Martin listened to the record and said he liked Paul's voice and George's guitar playing. Those were the two things he particularly said. Paul was singing 'Hello Little Girl,' which he liked very much, and 'Till There Was You.'"

George Martin discussed it all very slowly and calmly and at last said it was very "interesting." Yes, and he thought they were interesting enough to give them an audition. This was May 1962. The Beatles were still in Hamburg. Brian rushed out of EMI and sent them cables with the good news.

"We were all still in bed," says Pete Best. "Whoever was first up always went for the post. George was first up this day and got the telegram: CONGRATULATIONS BOYS. EMI REQUEST RECORDING SESSION. PLEASE REHEARSE NEW MATERIAL.

"We felt terrific. John and Paul started composing straight away— and they produced 'Love Me Do.' Brian came out to see us and negotiated a new contract—£85 a week each, I think we got then. He heard us play 'Love Me Do.' "

Klaus says he was disappointed by Brian Epstein when he arrived in Hamburg. "I didn't like the look of him. He was very shy, not at all powerful, the way I had expected. I was a bit depressed. I had this idea in my head of the manager they were bound to get. He would be the top man in the business, absolutely dynamic, not a shy novice."

But the Beatles were very pleased with themselves. Klaus remembers their delight at the EMI news, how they went off to show their contracts to the Polydor people, who'd only made them the backing group, not the stars.

"I went to the seaside one day with Paul and George and George was discussing money. He said he felt he was going to make a lot of it. He was going to buy a house and a swimming pool, then he'd buy a bus for his father, as he was a bus driver."

They came back from Hamburg at the beginning of June 1962. On June 6 they did their audition before George Martin at the EMI studios in St. John's Wood. Brian, efficient as ever, had sent on in advance to George Martin a neatly typed list, on his specially crested notepaper, of the suggested numbers they would like to play for Mr. Martin, if of course Mr. Martin agreed. The list included some original compositions—"Love Me Do," "P.S. I Love You," "Ask Me Why," and "Hello Little Girl." But the main suggestions were songs like "Besame Mucho."

George Martin listened carefully to everything and said very nice. He liked them. It was nice to see the boys in person at last, having heard so much about them from Brian. Very nice. He'd let them know. That was it. They weren't deflated, or anything as bad as that. But they'd expected a more definite reaction. They traveled back to Liverpool the next day and went into a hectic circuit of one-night stands around Liverpool which Brian had fixed up while they'd been in Hamburg. Their first date was a welcome-home night at the Cavern on Saturday, June 9, and then on the Monday a BBC radio show in Manchester which Brian had managed to fix. After that they were fully booked up as far ahead as July with odd bookings after that until the end of September.

These bookings included the Cavern, of course, plus the Casbah, New Brighton Tower, the Northwich Memorial Hall, Majestic Ballroom Birkenhead, Plaza Ballroom St. Helens, Hulme Hall Golf Club, and the Automatic Telephone Company's Royal Iris River Cruise.

Brian as usual sent each of them typed out notes with full details of all their dates and notes, usually in capital letters, on how they should deport themselves:

> Friday 29th June 1962—
>
> TOWER BALLROOM, NEW BRIGHTON
>
> Neil will call for you between 6:45 and 7:00 P.M. in order to arrive at the Tower at 7:30 P.M. This is a Leach night for which he has given you excellent publicity as stars of the Bill. With this point in mind and the fact that he has been fairly co-operative over several matters recently I would like you to give him one of your great performances. And as it's the night before Sam's wedding! It should be a big audience which will be mainly paying to see The Beatles. Programme, continuity, suits, white shirts, ties, etc., etc.
>
> One hour spot.
>
> N.B.   In the attached copy of "Mersey Beat" the name "THE BEATLES" on a rough count has been mentioned 15 times. On the 10 pages of "Mersey Beat" "THE BEATLES" appears on 6 pages. There has been a lot of publicity and there will be more and in this connection it will be of vital importance to live up to the publicity. Note that on ALL the above engagements, during the performances, smoking, eating, chewing and drinking is STRICTLY PROHIBITED, *prohibited.*

Brian was trying all this time to get them dates farther afield than Merseyside, but with little luck. He did during that summer manage to get them a date in Peterborough, but it was a complete failure. Nobody knew them and nobody liked them. "The audience sat on their hands," says Arthur Howes, the promoter who put them on.

All this time they were waiting anxiously to hear from George Martin. He'd said he'd let them know when they could come down and do a proper recording.

Brian eventually heard from George Martin at the end of July. He wanted them to sign a contract with Parlophone records. He was now trying to think of what songs they might record. Brian, as well as John, Paul, and George, was ecstatic.

They didn't tell Pete Best.

"We were playing on the Wednesday evening, August fifteenth, at the Cavern," says Pete Best. "We were due to go the next evening to Chester and I was supposed to be taking John. As we were leaving the Cavern, I asked John what time he wanted me to pick him up for Chester. He said, oh no, he would go on his own. I said, what's up? But he was off. His face looked scared. Then Brian rang, asking to see me and Neil at his office next morning.

"Neil drove me down the next day. Brian looked very shaky, not his usual happy self. He always showed his feelings and it was obvious there was something up. He was fidgeting all the time.

"He said 'I've got some bad news for you. The boys want you out and Ringo in.' It was a complete bombshell. I was stunned. I couldn't say anything for two minutes.

"I started asking him why and I couldn't get any definite reasons. He said George Martin wasn't too pleased with my playing. He said the boys thought I didn't fit in. But there didn't seem anything definite. At last I said if that's the way it is, then that's it. I went out and told Neil who was waiting outside. I must have looked white. I told him I'd been booted out after two years with them. I didn't know why. I said I couldn't get a direct answer.

"Brian came out and spoke to both of us. He asked me if I could stay on till the end of the week, playing on Thursday and Friday, till Ringo could come. I said yeh.

"I just walked around, had a few pints. I didn't tell anyone what had happened. I don't know how the news came out. I didn't tell anyone."

The news did get out, almost immediately, and there was pandemonium in Liverpool. *Mersey Beat* splashed it on their August 23 issue: MERSEY BEAT EXCLUSIVE. BEATLES CHANGE DRUMMER. They didn't give any reasons. They said it was all amicable. But they finished the story by saying that the Beatles were flying to London on September 4 for a recording session at EMI.

Pete Best fans, who were as numerous at least as Paul McCartney's fans, were furious. Their idol had been chucked out just at the Beatles' moment of glory. They paraded through the streets, hung around Nems with placards, picketed outside the Cavern, and shouted slogans at all concerts. John, Paul, and George were attacked by Pete Best fans but Brian Epstein became their number-one enemy.

"The sacking of Pete Best left me in an appalling position. This was the first real problem I'd had. Overnight I became the most disliked man on the beat scene. For two nights I didn't dare go near the Cavern because of the crowds shouting 'Pete Forever, Ringo Never,' or 'Pete Is Best.' I couldn't stay away for long, so Ray McFall laid on a bodyguard for me."

Pete Best fans tried to get at the Beatles to hit or scratch them, while John, Paul, and George fans tried to keep them off. In all the fights many girls got hurt, but only George of the Beatles was injured. He got a black eye.

There were scores of rumors round Liverpool. Mal Evans, then a bouncer at the Cavern, says he heard people saying it was because Pete wouldn't smile. Others said it was because he wouldn't change his hair style. There seems little doubt that Brian didn't want to do it.

"I knew how popular Pete was. He was incredibly good-looking, with a big following. I had got on well with him. In fact, he'd been the first one I'd got to know. I thought the way through was through Pete because he was the easiest to get to know, the simplest.

"So I was very upset when the three of them came to me one night and said they didn't want him. They wanted Pete out and Ringo in. It had been on the cards for a long time, but I'd hoped it wouldn't happen." Because Brian was so loath to do it, he dragged in other excuses, like George Martin not liking his drumming, which was half true, but not a main reason for the sacking.

"I did offer to keep Pete on in another group. I was a bit annoyed he didn't turn up at Chester in the evening, when he said he would. I expected him. I hadn't realized he couldn't face meeting the boys again."

"How could I?" says Pete. "What was the point, as they didn't want me any more? I just sat at home for two weeks. Not knowing what to do. Birds came to the door all the time. They were camping in the garden and shouting for me."

Neil thinks it was George who was most to blame. He thinks John really was fairly close to Pete, and Paul, being as popular with the fans as Pete, would never have done anything like that, as he might have been suspected. Neil says they all agreed to it, but it was George who gave Brian the final push as George was the one who was the biggest admirer of Ringo. George's punch in the eye, says Neil, proves that theory.

Mrs. Best has the simplest theory of all. "Pete's beat had made them. They were jealous and they wanted him out. Pete hadn't realized what a following he had till he left. He was always so very shy and quiet, never shot his mouth off, like some people I could mention.

"He'd been their manager before Brian arrived, did the bookings and collected the money. I'd looked upon them as friends. I'd helped them so much, got them bookings, lending them money. I fed them when they were hungry. I was far more interested in them than their own parents."

There is some justification for a little of Mrs. Best's anger. The sacking of Pete Best is one of the few murky incidents in the Beatles' history. There was something sneaky about the way it was done. Admittedly, most people would have done the same and got the manager to do the dirty work. But all of them, especially John, had always been so honest and truthful with everyone.

It's also true what Mrs. Best says about Pete having served them well for so long. But it's not true, and far from it, that they were simply producing the Pete Best sound, although Pete's drumming played a part in their success.

"When we came back from Germany," says Pete, "I was playing using my bass drum very loud and laying down a very solid beat. This was unheard of at the time in Liverpool as all the groups were playing the Shadows style. Even Ringo in Rory Storme's group copied our beat and it wasn't long before most drummers in Liverpool were playing the same style. This way of drumming had a great deal to do with the big sound we were producing."

The others say that the main reason for keeping Pete so long was not his sound but that their permanent problem for so long had been a drummer. They wanted any good drummer because the lack of one had hindered their progress. When a reasonable one came along, they stuck to him. Not necessarily because he was great, but because they knew what it was like not having one.

"But if I wasn't that great, why was I kept on for two and a half years? When we first returned to Liverpool, why didn't they get another drummer then? There was plenty of them. Why wasn't Ringo asked then, instead of two years later on the eve of success?"

What makes or doesn't make a good drummer is hard to define, but as personality there is some evidence to suggest that Pete had not fitted in, as Astrid and Klaus had noticed in Hamburg, although Pete himself seems to have been unaware of it. Stu, unlike Pete, had realized from the beginning when he was being got at. Pete presumed he was a proper part of the group, after so long, and was naturally very surprised when the end came.

But for the sake of Pete's career, whatever happened to the Beatles afterward, the handling and especially the announcing of the sacking might have been done more neatly and cleanly. He could have been fixed up with a job in another group before the news was announced. It is easy of course to say all this now. Nobody knew how well the

Beatles were going to do and what Pete was going to miss. The Beatles themselves did feel a bit guilty, but they say that it was a joint decision, not George's. They'd never felt that Pete was one of them and it was only a matter of time.

"We were cowards when we sacked him," says John. "We made Brian do it. But if we'd told Pete to his face, that would have been much nastier than getting Brian to do it. It would probably have ended in a fight if we'd told him."

Pete left and lost his chance of show-business fame. But the affair had one happy outcome for the Beatles. Ringo Starr.

Chapter 18: Ringo

Richard Starkey, Ringo, is the oldest of the Beatles. He would have been called Parkin today if his grandfather hadn't decided to change his name. When his grandfather's mother remarried and changed her name from Parkin to Starkey, Ringo's grandfather also changed his name to Starkey. This caused great confusion when at one time Ringo tried to trace his family back. The name Starkey is originally supposed to have come from the Shetland Islands.

Ringo's mother, Elsie Gleave, married his father, Richard Starkey, in 1936. They met when they were both working at the same Liverpool bakery. She is short, stocky, and blonde and looks today very much like Mrs. Harrison.

When they got married they moved in with the Starkeys, Ringo's father's parents, in the Dingle. After Scotland Road, the Dingle is known as the roughest area of Liverpool. It is in the center, not far from the docks, far less salubrious than the slightly more airy new suburbs where John, Paul, and George were all brought up.

"There's a lot of tenements in the Dingle," says Ringo. "A lot of people in little boxes all trying to get out. You'd say you were from the Dingle and other people in Liverpool would say to you, oh aye, the Peanut Gang. This was a gang that got involved in a lot of stabbings at one time."

Elsie and Richard Starkey got themselves a little house of their own just before Ringo was born. This was not in a tenement but in Madryn Street, a dismal row of low two-story terrace houses. Their house was bigger than most, three up and three down, as opposed to the usual two rooms up and two rooms down. Their rent in 1940 was 14/10 a week.

"We've always been just ordinary, poor working class on both sides of the family," says Ringo, "though there's a rumor in the family that me grandmother was fairly well off. She had chromium railings round her house. Well, they were very shiny anyway. Perhaps I just made that up. You know what it's like, you dream things, or your mother tells you things so you often come to believe you actually saw them.

"But me mother's mother really was very poor. She had fourteen kids." Ringo was born just after midnight on the morning of July 7, 1940, at number 9 Madryn Street. He was a week late. He was delivered by forceps and weighed ten pounds. He arrived with his eyes open and looking all around the place. His mother told all the neighbors that she was sure he must have been here before.

His mother Elsie was then twenty-six and his father Richard twenty-eight. They christened their first—and only—baby Richard. It is a working-class tradition always to call the first son after the father. They also called him Ritchie, just as his father was called and just as they are both called by their families today. Nanny Starkey, Ringo's grandmother, was present at the birth. Mrs. Starkey, Ringo's mother, remembers lying in bed, still recovering from the birth, when she heard the first sirens of the war. The bombing of Liverpool had begun.

They hadn't yet got round to installing shelters in the Dingle. When the first really serious bombing raids occurred a few weeks later, the Starkeys, along with two neighbors who'd been in chatting in the house, all rushed to take shelter in the coal hole under the stairs. Ritchie started screaming. His mother discovered that in the rush and crush she had put him over her shoulder upside down. She put him the right way up and he slept right through the raid. This was another story which she soon told the neighbors, and still does.

When Ritchie was just over three years old, his parents parted. Except on three occasions later, Ritchie has never seen his father since.

There was none of the drama or hysteria of John's parents when Ritchie's parted. Naturally, neither of them wants to discuss it. It appears to have been settled quietly. Elsie took the baby and they were eventually divorced.

Ringo and his mother stayed on alone in Madryn Street for some time, but the rent soon became too expensive and they moved around the corner to number 10 Admiral Grove. This house has only four rooms, two up and two down. The rent in 1940 was ten shillings a week.

Ringo's earliest memory dates from this move. He thinks he must have been about five at the time. "All I can remember is sitting on the back flap of the removal van taking our things round to Admiral Grove." He has no memory of his parents' parting. The three occasions he remembers meeting his father was twice as a very young child, and once later as an early teenager.

"He came once to see me in hospital with a little notebook and asked me what I wanted. Then I saw him once later at me Grandma Starkey's. He offered me money, but I wouldn't speak to him. I suppose me mother filled me up with all the things about him. But I suppose if it had been the other way round, if I'd gone with me dad, I'd have thought the opposite."

It seems likely that Ringo saw more of his father as a child, after they'd parted, than he remembers, as he spent a lot of time at his Grandma Starkey's. It was some time before his father, still working in a bakery, moved away from Liverpool and remarried.

His mother doesn't remember Ringo being upset in any way by the parting or even later asking any questions about what had happened. "Sometimes he used to wish there was more than just the two of us. When it was raining he used to look out of the window and say, 'I wish I had brothers and sisters. There's nobody to talk to when it's raining.'"

Ritchie went to Sunday school at four and primary school at five. This was St. Silas's Junior School, just 300 yards from his home. It is a faded red Victorian building, one of the National Schools, erected in 1870.

She got a maintenance allowance from the father of thirty bob a week, but this wasn't enough to live on so she had to go out to work. She'd done lots of different jobs before her marriage, including working as a barmaid, so she went back to that. She'd always enjoyed it, being jolly and sociable and fond of company, and the hours suited her.

She went back to work again as a barmaid before Ringo started school, doing mornings and lunchtimes for 18 shillings a week, leaving Ringo with Grandma Starkey or neighbors. "I never thought of putting Ritchie away in a home. He was my child. With the bar job, I was just able to manage. There was a lot of work to be done in bars, with the war on."

At six years of age, after hardly a year at school, Ritchie developed appendicitis. The appendix burst, and peritonitis set in. He was taken to Myrtle Street Children's Hospital and had two operations.

"I remember being taken bad and going out of the house on a stretcher to the ambulance. In hospital this nurse started smashing me stomach. That's how it felt, anyway. She probably just touched it. I was wheeled in for the operation and I asked for a cup of tea. They said not before the operation, but I'd get one when I came round. I went into a coma and didn't come round for ten weeks."

He was in hospital in all for just over twelve months. He was on the way to recovering at one stage but fell out of his cot while he was stretching out for a present during a birthday party.

Parents were not allowed to visit their children. It was thought it might disturb them too much. But Ritchie was so seriously ill at one time that they let his mother peep at him in his cot, late at night, when she'd finished working in the bar.

He came out when he was seven and went back to St. Silas's. He was never very quick at lessons, but with the year in hospital he was completely behind and unable to read or write. Without Marie Maguire he thinks he might never ever have learned.

Marie was four years older than Ritchie. Her mother and Ritchie's mother were lifelong friends. They went out together and left Marie in charge of Ritchie.

"I was very bossy with him," she says, "being four years older. He was so much part of our family that people used to come and knock at our door and say 'Your Ritchie's doing so and so.' When he had meals with us and we were having scouse I always had to pick the onions out for him. He hates onions. I was always cursing him.

"My very first memory of him was when he must have been about three. There was a terrible thunderstorm and I looked across to his house and I saw him and his mother both huddling in the hall.

"I started teaching him to read and write when he came out of hospital. He wasn't stupid. He'd just missed a lot. We had it properly organized. Twice a week I used to give him lessons and his mother would give me pocket money for doing it. I bought Chambers Primary Readers and we used to sit up at his kitchen table and read them.

"I would look after him on Saturday nights at our house while our mothers were out. They would leave us bottles of lemonade and sweets. We used to play with chemistry sets or at school, or just crazy games. He once took his shirt off and I painted all his back with paints. Sounds very primitive, now I think about it. At Christmas time he always bought me a bottle of scent from Woolworth's. But he would no sooner give it to me than he'd want me to empty it so he could have the fancy bottle back. He once brought his girl friend to see me. He insisted she was called Jellatine.

"I always liked him. He was just so happy and easy-going, just like his mother. He had lovely big blue eyes. I never ever noticed he had a big nose. It wasn't till the press pointed it out later that I realized he had."

"My Grandmother Gleave, my mother's mother, lived on her own, but she had this friend called Mr. Lester who used to come and play the mouth organ to her. They were both about sixty. 'Oh aye,' we used to say. 'We know what you're up to, playing the mouth organ to her in the dark.' But she wouldn't marry him. In the end Mr. Lester went off and married someone else.

"I used to love going to my Grandad Starkey's when he'd lost a lot of money on the horses. He'd go off his head. They were a great couple. They used to have real fights. He was a boilerman at the docks, a real tough docker, but he used to make me lovely things. He once made me a big train with real fire inside. It caused a riot going down our street. I used to boil apples inside it."

Ringo has no memories of St. Silas's primary school. He just remembers playing truant or holding up kids in the playground and taking pennies off them. "We used to steal bits and pieces from Woolworth's. Just silly plastic things which you could slip in your pocket." Another time his Aunt Nancy found a pearl necklace missing. Ritchie turned up outside a pub in Park Street offering it for sale for six shillings.

At eleven years Ringo went to Dingle Vale Secondary Modern School. He didn't sit the Eleven Plus. He failed the Review, an exam to see if you were good enough to sit the Eleven Plus.

"He liked it in spasms," says his mother. "Then he'd play truant. He and some others would hang around outside before school till the final bell went and they just wouldn't go in. They'd maintain they'd been locked out. They would go and spend the afternoon playing in Sefton Park."

When Ritchie was just over eleven his mother started going out with a Liverpool Corporation painter and decorator called Harry Graves. He was a Londoner, from the Romford area. He'd been ill and his doctor had suggested a change of air. For some inexplicable reason, he decided to try the Liverpool air. He still can't remember why. He met Elsie through mutual friends, the Maguires. He got on well with Ritchie from the beginning. They went together to the pictures two or three times a week.

"I told Ritchie that Harry wanted to marry me. If he'd said no, I wouldn't have done it. But he said, 'You get married, Mum. I won't always be little. You don't want to end up like me grandma.' " She was the one who hadn't married Mr. Lester and his mouth organ.

Harry Graves and Elsie Starkey were married on April 17, 1953, when Ritchie was coming up for thirteen. She stopped work soon after. Harry says that he and Ritchie have never had a wrong word between them. Elsie says he was awful. When she used to tell her husband that Ritchie had been giving her cheek he just used to smile and do nothing.

At thirteen Ritchie suffered his second major illness. He got a cold, which turned to pleurisy, which turned to effusion on the lung. He went into Myrtle Street again and then the Hezzle Children's Hospital.

While Ritchie was in hospital, Tom Whittaker, then manager of Arsenal, happened to be in Liverpool. Harry wrote to him, saying what a nice gesture it would be if he could visit one of his keenest young supporters who was lying ill in hospital. Mr. Whittaker couldn't make it, but he did write back a nice letter which Ritchie treasured very much, so Harry says. Ritchie himself can't remember anything at all about any letter, or ever being in The Arsenal Supporters Club.

But Ringo has good memories of Harry himself, right from the beginning. "He used to bring me lots of Yankee comics. He was great. In fact I used to take his side if he and me mum had any rows. I just thought she was being bossy and felt sorry for Harry. I learned gentleness from Harry. There's never any need for violence."

Ringo was in hospital almost two years this time, from the age of thirteen to fifteen. "I was given lots of things to keep my mind occupied, like knitting. I made a big island out of papier-mâché and a farm full of animals. I had a fight in the hospital with another lad. He went berserk and brought a huge tray down on me, just missed smashing me fingers."

He came out of hospital at fifteen, which meant that he'd officially finished his school days, though he'd hardly been at school. He had to go back to Dingle Vale Secondary Modern for a report, so that he could use it as a reference for a job. He says that nobody could remember him, he'd been away so long. Then he went back home, where he had to stay recuperating till he was well enough to start thinking about taking jobs. His mother was very worried about what sort of job he could get. She knew he wasn't strong enough to lift anything heavy and he hadn't had the education to do anything too clever.

Through the Youth Employment Officer he eventually secured a job as a messenger boy for British Railways at fifty bob a week.

"I went for me uniform, but all they gave me was the hat. I thought, what a lousy job. You have to be there twenty years before you get the full uniform. I left after six weeks. It wasn't just not getting the uniform. You have to pass a medical exam and I failed. Then I spent six weeks on board a boat going back and forward to North Wales as a barman. I went to an all-night party and got drunk and went straight on to work. I gave cheek to the boss and he said, get your cards, son."

After that he got a job at H. Hunt and Son through friends of Harry's. "I went as a joiner. But all I did for two months was go out on bike taking orders. I'd by this time turned seventeen and was getting fed up

HALF YEARLY REPORT.

Name. *Richard* *Starkey* Class. *2C* House. *Gibraltar*

Term. *Xmas 1952* Class Position. 23/34 Times Absent. 3.4.

Punctuality.... *A*.. General Appearance.... *A*.. Conduct.... *A*...

A:- V.Good; B:- Good; C:- Average or Fair; D:- Weak; E:- V.Weak.

Subject.	Class Mark.	Class Pos'n.	General Standard.	Class, Teacher's Remarks.
Arithmetic.	47	8	D	
English.	35	32	D	
History.	69	15	*creditable*	*A quiet thoughtful type, although working rather slowly. Academic work will no doubt improve in time as he is trying to do his best. Helpful & willing.*
Geography.	44	31	*Satisfactory*	
Social Studies.				
Science.	36	13	*Fair*	
Geometry.	49	17		
Art.		*C*		
Music.				
Woodwork.		*C*	*Tries*	
Metalwork.		*C*	*Tries*	
Pottery.				
Weaving.				
Printing.				
Drama.		*A*	*Takes a real interest and has done very well.*	
Gardening.		*C*		
P.T.		*D*	*Needs much more confidence.*	

Signed: ..... *S. Roberts* ......
Class Master.

Signed: ....
headmaster.

I have examined the Report for ....
upon the work of my son.

Signed: ....
(Parent or Guardian.)

with not starting my apprenticeship as a joiner. So I went to see them and they said there were no vacancies as a joiner, would I like to be a fitter, so I said okay. It was a trade. Everyone always said, if you've got a trade, you'll be okay." Nobody else thought he was necessarily going to be okay. He was small, weak-looking, and undernourished with very, very little schooling.

"He'd had a difficult childhood," says Marie Maguire, the girl who'd taught him to read, "with a broken home and two long illnesses. I just hoped he'd be happy. Not successful or anything. Just happy."

The two long illnesses must have had a big effect on him, making it very difficult to adjust to school and to work and to ordinary life. Today he can't remember any of his schoolmaster's names, but he does remember two of the nurses who looked after him—Sister Clark and Nurse Edgington.

But he himself never remembers being unhappy. He thinks he had a good childhood.

It was ironic that when he went back to Dingle Vale Secondary Modern for a reference no one could remember him, but a few years later during an open house they brought out a desk which Ringo Starr was supposed to have sat at and charged people sixpence a time to sit in it and have their photographs taken.

Chapter 19: Ringo with the Beatles

Ringo showed no musical interest and learned no instrument as a boy. "We did have a ward band in the hospital. There were four kids on cymbals and two on triangles. I would never play unless I had a drum."

It was when he started to work as an apprentice fitter that the skiffle craze arrived. He helped to form a group called the Eddie Clayton Skiffle which played to the rest of the apprentices in the dinner hour. His first set of drums was bought by his father for him when he was down home in Romford. They cost £10. "I brought them up from London in the guard's van," says Harry. "I was waiting for a taxi home at Lyme Street when I saw Joe Loss walking over. I thought, if he asks me if I can play them, I'll have to say no. But he walked right past me."

His first new set of drums cost £100. He went to his grandad for the £50 deposit.

"If his grandad even refused him a shilling, he'd do a war dance," says his mother. "This time his grandad came to see me. 'Hey, do you know what that bloody noddler of yours wants?' He always called him the Noddler. But he gave him the money. Ritchie paid it back faithfully, a pound a week out of wages."

His mother was a bit worried about the group taking up too much of his time, as he was supposed to be going to classes at Riverdale Technical College, catching up on some of the schooling he'd missed.

But Harry, his stepfather, was quite interested in the skiffle group. It gave the boy an interest. One night Harry met a bloke in a bar who said he was in a band. The man agreed to give Ringo a go and Harry made a date for him. Ringo went along and came back furious. It turned out to be a prize silver band. They gave him a huge drum, strapped it on his front, then made him march along the street going bang, bang in time to a military march.

Not that he was doing much better in the Eddie Clayton group. Not that there was an Eddie Clayton, come to that. Eddie Miles, who was really the leader of the group, had changed his name for professional purposes to Eddie Clayton the minute the group had begun. Just as Paul, George, and John had changed their names when they went to Scotland.

But eventually, going through the same skiffle competitions and parties and little dance halls which the rest of the Beatles did, Ringo joined Rory Storme's group. When they were offered a season at Butlin's, Ringo had to make the decision whether to leave work. He was then twenty, with just one more year of his apprenticeship to go. "Everybody said I shouldn't leave, and I suppose they were right. But I just felt I wanted to. I was getting by then £6 a week at Hunt's, and about £8 by playing at nights. Butlin's was offering me £20 a week in all, £16 when they took off the money for the chalet."

Rory's was by that time Liverpool's leading group and doing very well. But the offer of a thirteen-week season at Butlin's was their big break. They decided to change their names. "We were going to make our names, so we thought we'd better have good ones. Rory Storme had already changed his name twice. He's really Alan Caldwell, then he became Jet Storme, then Rory Storme."

Ringo's popularity as the drummer of the leading group can be seen from his twenty-first birthday party, held at his home in Admiral Grove. All the leading groups of the day came to the party, including Gerry and the Pacemakers, the Big Three, and Cilla Black. The Beatles didn't come. Ringo didn't know them. They were from another part of Liverpool and just another struggling group.

The living room at Admiral Grove is tiny, just ten feet by twelve feet, but somehow they got sixty people in for the party. They know the number because Ringo lined them up afterward for a picture on the brick rubble heap opposite the house.

Elsie, Ringo's mum, had known Cilla Black for a long time, as a local lass called Cilla White. For over a year she'd been coming to Mrs. Starkey's, with a friend, every Wednesday after work. Cilla had her tea and then did Elsie's hair for her.

Ringo's thirteen-week season at Butlin's led to other engagements. They did a tour of United States air bases in France but Ringo says this was terrible. "The French don't like the British; at least I didn't like them."

Rory's group was doing so well that when the first offer came to go to Hamburg they couldn't make it. But they went later, joining the Beatles at the Kaiserkeller, which was where they met for the first time.

Ringo has a slight memory of catching sight of them once before, in Liverpool. He looked into the Jackaranda Club one day and saw them teaching Stu how to play the bass. Ringo's group was the big time in those days, and still was when they arrived in Hamburg.

Ringo did a few stand-in engagements with them in Hamburg and used to sit around with them between numbers. He came back to Liverpool with Rory, then returned to Hamburg on his own, accompanying Tony Sheridan. During this spell in Hamburg he seriously considered staying on for good. He was offered his own flat, a car, and £30 a week to stay for a year. But he decided to come back to Liverpool and Rory Storme again for another season at Butlin's. This was when he was asked to join the Beatles. John told him on the phone that he would have to brush his hair down, but he could keep his sidies.

Ringo had to put up with a lot of shouts and threatening letters from Pete Best fans. "The birds loved Pete. Me, I was just a skinny, bearded scruff. Brian didn't really want me either. He thought I didn't have .the personality. And why get a bad-looking cat when you can get a good-looking one?"

It was the money that made Ringo decide. "I got another offer at the same time, from King Size Taylor and the Dominoes. He offered £20 a week. The Beatles offered £25, so I took them."

As with all of them, and as with everyone in life, their paths might not have crossed. Much earlier Ringo was on the point of emigrating to the United States. He and a friend were looking through some records one day and read "Lightning Hopkins comes from Houston, Texas." They went to the U.S. consul in Liverpool and said they wanted to go to Houston, Texas. He said they had to have a job first. Ringo picked one in a factory. "Then the really big forms arrived, all about was your grandfather's Great Dane a Commie. I couldn't understand them. If I had, I would definitely have gone."

With Ringo fitting in as a personality and as a drummer, the Beatles were now the indisputable top group in Liverpool. They had a gentleman-manager and had at last made contact with London. But their success, however local, was beginning to split up some of the old loyalties which Ringo particularly had been very fond of.

"There were so many groups in Liverpool at one time that we often used to play just for each other, sitting in on each other's sessions, or just listening. It was a community on its own, just made up of groups. All going to the same places, playing for each other. It was all nice. Then when the record companies came up and started signing groups, it wasn't so friendly. Some made it and others didn't.

"You'd meet someone you'd known and he'd say, 'Fine man, just crazy. Just did a recording, but they're not releasing it. They said I'm too much like Ray Charles.'

"It broke all the community up. People started hating each other. I stopped going to the old places. But it was one of the great times of my life, those early days in Liverpool. Like at my twenty-first birthday party, they were all there."

They were waiting now to hear a definite date from George Martin about their recording debut. In the meantime, other things in Liverpool fell into place. Brian at last decided that running two record stores and a beat group was too much, which is what his father had been saying for a long time. He decided to give up day-to-day work at the Whitechapel store and moved Peter Brown across from Charlotte Street as manager. He concentrated on Nems Enterprises, popping down now and again to see how Peter was getting on. This led to rows, as Brian couldn't bear to see his lovely arrangements being changed. Peter was fired, after a furious row, but was reinstated.

But Brian never had any rows with any of the Beatles. The nearest was an incident with Paul. They all came round to pick him up one night but Paul was in the bath and refused to come out. "I shouted to them to wait, I'd just be a few minutes. But when I got out, they'd all driven off with Brian. So I said, fuck them, temperamental fool that I was. If they can't be arsed awaiting for me, I can't be arsed going after them. So I sat down and watched telly."

The real reason was that Paul had got it into his head that he should revolt. "I'd always been the keeny, the one who was always eager, chatting up managements and making announcements. Perhaps I was being big-headed at first, or perhaps I was better at doing it than the others. Anyway, it always seemed to be me."

It led to an argument between Paul and Brian, but nothing serious. Paul was soon back to being the keeny. "It had sometimes worried me that perhaps I was false in always making an effort. But I realized that I was being more false by *not* making the effort."

He and John were still as keen as ever about writing songs, turning out "Another Lennon-McCartney original" all the time. But Mimi still thought it wasn't serious. "I always expected John to come home one day and say he wasn't doing the group any more: 'It bores me to death.'

"I was the last to realize they were doing well. Little girls started to come to the door and ask if John was in. I'd say, why? They'd say they just wanted to see John. I couldn't understand it. They were such little girls. I knew his only serious girl friend had ever been Cyn."

In the summer of 1962 Cyn found that she was pregnant. "I didn't know if John would want to get married. I didn't want to tie him down."

"I was a bit shocked when she told me," says John. "But I said yes. We'll have to get married. I didn't fight it."

They were married on August 23, 1962, at Mount Pleasant Register Office in Liverpool. "I went in the day before to tell Mimi. I said Cyn was having a baby, we were getting married tomorrow, did she want to come? She just let out a groan."

No parents were at the wedding, which sounds similar to his own parents' wedding, twenty-four years previously. John, Paul, and George all wore black. "There was a drill going on all the time outside," says John. "I couldn't hear a word the bloke was saying. Then we went across the road and had a chicken dinner. I can't remember any presents. We never went in for them."

They tried to keep the marriage secret from Beatle fans, but one of the tea ladies from the Cavern saw them coming out of the register office and the news leaked out, though they denied it. "I thought it would be goodbye to the group, getting married, because everybody said it would be. We went mad keeping it secret. None of us ever took any girls to the Cavern as we thought we would lose fans, which turned out to be a farce in the end. But I did feel embarrassed being married. Walking about, married. It was like walking about with odd socks on, your fly open."

Cynthia was all for keeping their marriage quiet. "It was bad enough John being recognized and chased everywhere. I didn't want that to happen to me." The girl fans had grown to enormous proportions by this time, fanatically following them everywhere and screaming at the slightest excuse. Yet no one outside Liverpool had heard of the Beatles. Even in Liverpool, it had all happened with no publicity and promotion. The fans had discovered the Beatles by themselves.

Maureen Cox was one of these fans. She and a friend ran after Ringo in the street one day, just after he'd joined the Beatles. He was getting out of his car. His little gray streak at the front of his hair gave him away. She got his autograph and wrote down his car number on her exercise book. She was on her way to night class as a hairdresser at the time, having just left school. "I can remember his car number to this day— NWM 466."

Today, Maureen Cox is Ringo's wife. But it was Paul she first kissed, slightly to her embarrassment now.

She was in the Cavern one evening with a friend and the friend bet her that she wouldn't go and kiss Paul. "I said to her that it was she who was scared to do it. She said I was scared. So just for a bet, I fought my way to the band room and kissed Paul when he came out. My friend was so annoyed and jealous that she started crying. But it was really Ritchie I liked best. I'd just kissed Paul for a dare. So I waited till Ritchie came out and kissed him as well."

Ringo has no memory of being kissed by Maureen or of giving her his autograph. "That was the scene at the time, getting kissed. It had progressed from getting a Beatle's autograph to touching one, then kissing one. You'd be trying to get to the band room and you'd suddenly have some girl's arm flung round you. I probably thought Maureen was some fly pecking me."

But three weeks later at the Cavern he asked Maureen to dance. He took her home afterward, but he had to take her friend home as well. This went on for several weeks. Maureen says she didn't like to tell her friend she was in the way. "I felt a bit scared."

From then on, Maureen hardly missed a Cavern session. This was when she realized just how fanatical many fans were. "They used to hang round the Cavern all day long, just on the off chance of seeing them. They'd come out of the lunchtime session and just stand outside all afternoon, queuing up for the evening. Ritchie and I once went past at midnight and they were already queuing up for the next day. We bought them some pies. They were knocked out.

"The object was to get as near the front row as possible, so that they could see the Beatles, and be seen. I never joined the queue till about two or three hours before the Cavern opened. It frightened me. There would be fights and rows among the girls. When the doors opened the first ones would tear in, knocking each other over.

"They'd keep their rollers in and jeans on for the first groups. Then when it got near the time for the Beatles to come on, if there was a gang of four say, they would go off in turns to the lavatory with their little cases to get changed and made up. So when the Beatles came on they'd all look smashing, as if they'd just arrived.

"I suppose it was partly sex and partly the music. That was the attraction. They were obviously dying to be noticed and get to know one of them. But no, it was really just everything about being there. It was terrible, the mad screams when they came on. They went potty."

When Maureen did go out with Ringo, she had to keep completely in the background. "I might have been killed otherwise. The other girls were not friendly at all. They wanted to stab me in the back. It was part of their image, that they weren't married and so each girl thought she might have a chance. None of them were supposed to have steadies. A few eventually found out, of course. They used to come into the hair-dresser's where I was working. I couldn't do anything about that. I would have to do their hair. Then they would threaten me—'If you see that Ringo Starr again you're for it.' When I went outside they'd push me. I used to get threatening phone calls—my brother's going to get you, they used to say.

"They were playing at the Locarno once. Just before they'd finished, Ritchie told me to go outside and sit in the car and wait for him so no one would see me. I was sitting in the car when this girl came up. She must have followed me. She said, 'Are you going out with Ringo?' I said, 'No, oh no, not me. He's just a friend of my brother's.' 'Liar,' she said, 'I just saw you talking to him.' I'd forgotten to wind the window up. Before I could do anything, she had her hand through the window and scratched me down my face. She started screaming and shouting some very select language at me. I thought this is it. I'm going to get stabbed. I just got the window up in time. If I hadn't, she would have opened the door and killed me."

PART 2: LONDON AND THE WORLD

Chapter 20: George Martin and Dick James

George Martin always seems light years away from the Beatles in class, tastes, and background. He is tall and handsome in a matinee idol sort of way, with a studied prep-school master manner and a clipped BBC accent. But his early background at least was as humble and working-class as the Beatles.

He was born in 1926 in Muswell Hill, North London, the son of a carpenter. He went first to a Jesuit college in Stamford Hill; then the family moved to Kent and he went to Bromley County School. There was no musical tradition in the family and he had no musical training as a young boy, but he taught himself to play the piano by ear and by the age of sixteen he was running his own school dance band.

During the war he served in the Fleet Air Arm, finishing with the rank of lieutenant. He was demobilized in 1947 and found himself with nothing to do. Thanks to someone who'd heard him play the piano in wartime concerts, he tried for the Guildhall School of Music. He spent three years there, taking up the oboe as a second instrument. After he graduated, he free-lanced for a while as an oboist but never rose above pit orchestra work or Sunday afternoon playing with bands in London parks. He got the sack from that eventually for not being good enough.

Late in 1950 a proper job presented itself, as an assistant A and R man at Parlophone, one of EMI's smaller companies, though he didn't know what EMI meant at the time. Although it was his Guildhall classical training which had got him the job, he was expected to help with jazz and light music as well as classical. The range was wide at Parlophone but in the main unexciting. "Parlophone was the poor relation in those days, compared with the EMI big boys, HMV, and Columbia. We were still recording on wax when I joined in 1950."

Parlophone had been bought just before the war from Germany. It had done little since being taken over and a lot of people inside, according to George Martin, expected it not to last very much longer. Its familiar symbol £, in the shape of the pound-sterling sign, has no connection with the millions of pounds it has made since. It comes from the initial of the founder's surname, Carl Lindberg, plus a fancy stroke in the middle, on the lines of a continental figure seven.

His salary at EMI was very modest. To eke it out he still played occasional Sunday-afternoon concerts in the parks, when he could get them, and arranged some school orchestral recitals. George Martin found himself doing more and more of the popular records. Two of his earliest stars were Bob and Alf Pearson, who used to sing songs about "My Brother and I." He also recorded The Five Smith Brothers and the Scottish country dance band, Jimmy Shand and his Band. He recorded their "Blue Bell Polka," still a good-selling recording. He also moved into jazz, recording Johnny Dankworth and Humphrey Lyttleton.

LPs were a great innovation in the early 1950s, though they now seem to have been with us forever. "EMI were very late getting on to them, not until 1954. I don't know why it took us so long. Decca had them about 1952. It meant we had a lot of leeway to catch up."

In the early 1950s, producing records in Britain was a very routine, traditional business. It was just like bringing out a regular monthly magazine. Each month a company like Parlophone would bring out around ten new records, all planned about two months ahead, which they called their monthly supplements. They were always very strictly and fairly balanced. Out of the ten new records two would be classical, two jazz, two dance music—the Victor Sylvester sort of dance music— two would be male vocal, and two would be female vocal. There was no such category as pop. "We never talked about pop, just classical, jazz, dance, and vocal."

Out of all these categories, Parlophone had very few of the leading lights. Victor Sylvester, for example, was with Columbia, one of EMI's more successful offshoots. The main money-spinning singers came from America. Parlophone had none of them.

But slowly George Martin managed to create a little niche for himself by creating a stream of comedy records, which no one in the record business said would ever sell. One of his earliest comedy records was Peter Ustinov's *Phoney Folklore Mock Mozart.*

George Martin did most of the best comedy records, such as Peter Sellers, Flanders and Swann, and later on Beyond the Fringe, recording them in Cambridge before they came to the West End. Then skiffle and rock arrived, transforming the whole teenage pop-music scene. British stars and groups at last started to make hit records, though still nothing on the scale of the American groups. But poor old Parlophone was left farther behind, despite George Martin's comedy numbers.

"Everybody seemed to find a group or a singer except Parlophone. I toured the London coffee bars looking for talent." He turned down the chance of signing Timmy Hicks, or Tommy Steele as he became, because he thought he was just another Elvis copy.

"I envied so much HMV and Columbia with their American stars or other companies with British stars like Cliff Richard. In a way that is so easy, once you have a singer or a group which you know the public likes. All you have to do then is find them another song. With comedy, you start each time completely from scratch."

As skiffle and rock revealed a huge new teenage market and as record charts and records sales became increasingly important, Parlophone, the company which many people didn't think had much life left anyway, got even farther behind.

By May 1962, unbeknown to Brian Epstein and the Beatles, Parlophone was desperately waiting for the Beatles to turn up. The great George Martin, whose every cough and comment they tried to analyze, was far from being great. Judy Lockhart-Smith, then George Martin's secretary and now his wife, remembers being very impressed by Brian Epstein. "He had a very nice coat on and was well-mannered and well-spoken, not the usual sort of Charing Cross Road manager."

George was also favorably impressed. "But I wasn't particularly knocked out by what he played me. I didn't think a great deal of the songs or the singers. But I did think they produced an interesting sound. I said I'd give them a recording test." Brian went away ecstatic, but to George it was just another would-be recording group. He was so keen to find a good new group he was giving tests to a great many.

"I just really wanted to see what his group looked like, to see how they would react to a studio. Voices can sound completely different in a proper studio. Nine out of ten groups fail to be any good when it comes to a recording test.

"I was originally thinking of using them as a backing group with a name lead singer, like Cliff Richard and the Shadows. I desperately wanted my own Cliff. That was how my mind was working at the beginning, looking for the possibilities of one of them being the lead singer. When I met them, I soon realized that would never work."

George met them for the first time on June 6, 1962. He gave them their recording test at EMI's number-three studio in St. John's Wood.

"I found them very attractive people. I liked being with them, which was funny, I suppose, as they were so insignificant and I was so sig-

nificant. It shouldn't really have mattered to me whether they liked me
or not, but I was pleased they seemed to. I discovered that John was a
fan of the Peter Sellers and his Goon records I'd produced."

George chose only three or four numbers from Brian's list, including
"Love Me Do" and "PS I Love You." George says he thinks it must
only have been an early version of "Love Me Do" because the songs
themselves didn't knock him out. But he again liked their sound, and
their personalities. "I was impressed by them as people. I thought, I
can't lose anything if I sign them up, although I had no idea what to do
with them or which songs they could record."

He was still busy with other records, much more important to him at
the time, such as an LP of The Establishment, London's first but short-
lived satirical night club. He was also taking his time over fixing a date
for the Beatles because he still wasn't sure what he would let them
record, whether he could chance them doing something of their own or
get a song writer to do one for them.

At long last, on September 11, 1962, he brought them down to London to record their first British record, "Love Me Do," with "PS I Love
You" on the B side.

"I chose 'Love Me Do' as the best of the bunch in the end. It was
John's harmonica which gave it its appeal."

George Martin had heard that Pete Best had gone and they'd got a
new drummer. But he wasn't taking any chances. He decided to hire a
really experienced session drummer called Andy White and have him all
ready, just in case.

Before they started the session, George Martin explained to them
what he was trying to do. "Let me know if there's anything you don't
like," said George Martin.

"Well, for a start," said George Harrison, "I don't like your tie."
This was a half-serious joke, and has been recalled many times since,
but it didn't go down all that well with George Martin. It was in fact a
brand-new tie he was particularly proud of. It was black with red horses
on it and came from Liberty's. But everyone laughed, and the session
proceeded.

It was the first-ever recording session for Ringo and he was far from
confident. He would have been even more scared if he had realized from
the beginning, which he didn't, that another drummer was hanging
around, waiting. They went into their first number, "Love Me Do,"
which in all took about seventeen takes before George Martin was happy.

"I didn't rate Ringo very highly," says George Martin. "He couldn't
do a roll—and still can't—though he's improved a lot since. Andy was

the kind of drummer I needed. Ringo was only used to ballrooms. It was obviously best to use someone with experience."

"I was nervous and terrified of the studio," says Ringo. "When we came back later to do the B side, I found that George Martin had got another drummer sitting in my place. It was terrible. I'd been asked to join the Beatles, but now it looked as if I was only going to be good enough to do ballrooms with them, but not good enough for records.

"They started 'PS I Love You.' The other bloke played the drums and I was given the maracas. I thought, that's the end. They're doing a Pete Best on me. They then decided to record the other side again, the one on which I'd played the drums originally. I was given the tambourine this time.

"I was shattered. What a drag. How phoney the whole record business was, I thought. Just what I'd heard about. Getting other musicians to make your records for you in the studios. If I was going to be no use for records, I might as well leave. But nobody said anything. What could the others say, or me? We were just lads, being pushed around. You know what I mean. They were so big, the London record company and all that. We just did what we were told.

"When the record came out as a single, my name was on 'PS I Love You,' but I was only playing the maracas, the other bloke was on drums. But luckily for me, they decided to stick to the first version of 'Love Me Do,' the one in which I'm playing drums, so that was okay.

"Love Me Do," their first record, was released on October 4, 1962. They were by that time back in Liverpool, trailing round the local halls again, but waiting for their record to astound the world. Nothing happened.

The Beatles' Liverpool fans very faithfully bought the record in great numbers, but of course sales in a provincial town don't have much effect on the charts. They also wrote in hordes to all the request programs. The first play of it was on Radio Luxembourg. Mrs. Harrison, George's mother, sat up for hours one night because George said they might be on. She got fed up waiting and went to bed, only to be wakened by George screaming that they were on. With his shouting he woke Mr. Harrison, who was very angry as he had to be up early for the first shift on the buses.

"The first time I heard 'Love Me Do' on the radio," says George, "I went shivery all over. I listened to some of the lead guitar work and couldn't believe it. But the most important thing in our lives was to get into the Top Twenty." They eventually crept into the charts at Number 49, in the *New Record Mirror*. The next week it started showing up in another pop newspaper, the *New Musical Express,* where it got to 27. It stayed there for some time.

On the strength of having a record, Brian managed to secure them their first TV show, though it was just in the North. This was on Granada's *People and Places* from Manchester.

But they were then due to go back to Hamburg, another appearance at the Star Club which they had contracted to make before their record had been made. They thought that being out of the country, unable to get in any live plugs on the radio or TV, their record would go straight down.

They went off, on their fourth visit to Hamburg. Their record slowly kept creeping up, which gave them an excuse each time for wild celebrations. The highest "Love Me Do" ever got was to number 17.

George Martin, meanwhile, was pleased but not overexcited by "Love Me Do." "I didn't think it was all that brilliant, but I was very thrilled by the reaction to the Beatles and their sound. The problem now was to get a follow-up record for them."

He found a song he was sure was going to be a hit called "How Do You Do It." He sent it to the Beatles who didn't like it. George Martin said he did. He was the boss. He wanted them to record it. So they had to. They did, but still said they didn't like it and didn't want it produced. It was a brave, or perhaps simply naïve, show of stubbornness for a group of young, inexperienced provincials who couldn't even read or write music to tell the highly knowledgeable and powerful George Martin that they knew better than he did.

"I told them they were turning down a hit. It was their funeral, but if they were going to be so obstinate, then they had better produce something better themselves. They were very self-opinionated in those days. They haven't changed one bit. They did produce something better, 'Please Please Me,' which knocked me out."

But he was right about "How Do You Do It." He eventually gave that instead to another group, Gerry and the Pacemakers, whom Brian had signed up. Gerry got to number one with "How Do You Do It."

The Beatles' second record, "Please Please Me," was recorded on November 26, 1962, but not released until January 1963. They came back from Hamburg to do it, then went off again, this time just for a couple of weeks, for their fifth and final session in the Hamburg clubs.

At the end of the year, the *New Musical Express* did its usual popularity poll. The Springfields were voted top of the Vocal Group Department with 21,843 votes. The Beatles were way, way down with 3906 votes, presumably all from Liverpool. But they were in. They existed, though there was still little sign that they might be the group which George Martin and Parlophone so desperately needed.

George Martin leads on to Dick James, the other important figure who joined the Beatles at this time, and is still there.

Dick James is the only traditional show-business man who has ever got into the Beatles' circle, either professionally or as a friend. Not long after, when they started to be successful, they began to bring down their own buddies and helpers from Liverpool. Nobody else got in after that.

Dick James has always been around in the business. He's from the sort of London Jewish background where you grow up with all the agents and bandleaders of the future, the boys who will always help you. Dick James has a lot of schmaltz, but it's all genuine. He's a sort of cuddly, boy's own Tin Pan Alley man. They all love Dick James. They tease him about loving ballads. They know that a good corny When I'm Sixty-Four song is going to make Dick James very happy. Dick James is very happy anyway. He's probably the luckiest man in their whole circle. From being a one-man music publisher when he met them he now runs a large music corporation. He's a millionaire, not just thanks to them, but to his own hard work.

He was born Richard Leon Vapnick in 1920 in the East End of London. His father, a butcher, came from Poland in 1910, just around the time the Epstein family came from Poland.

At seventeen he was a professional singer, appearing with Al Berlin (now an agent) and his band at the Cricklewood Palais. During the war he was in the Medical Corps, not doing anything medical, but playing in the Medical Corps Band. This was when he learned to read music, which was very lucky. In 1945 he joined Geraldo, who immediately changed his name to Dick James. After that, for many years, he appeared with most of the big bands of the time and then went on to become a solo singer. "I never got to the pinnacle. Nobody ever got hysterical when I came on, the way they did with Donald Peers and David Whitfield."

But he made a good living. He also did a lot of records, though nothing startling. His first was in 1942, during an Army leave, when he did a singalong with Primo Scala's Accordion Band. He was with Decca for a while but didn't make much money for them. In 1952 he ended up with Parlophone. They had a bright-looking young A and R man called George Martin who was willing to work hard on any popular singer. In 1955, under George Martin, Dick James did his best-ever record and the only one he is now remembered by. This was "Robin Hood," the theme song for the TV series. It got to number nine in the charts, the highest either had ever done. It led to Dick James' own fifteen-minute spot on Radio Luxembourg, produced by another bright young man called Philip Jones.

But despite the success of "Robin Hood," Dick James knew there wasn't much future for him as a singer, not the way the business was going, with rock and skiffle and all these young lads coming on. "I felt there was going to be a revolution and I was in the wrong place at the wrong time." He was still in his early thirties, but he'd been wearing a toupee for some years. "Just for stage work, of course. Not in my private life. That would have been cheating."

He continued singing until 1959, but by then only part time and only in the London area, as he wanted to be near his wife and son. As a sideline he'd taken up music publishing. He became an unpaid assistant to Sid Bron, father of the actress Eleanor Bron. (She appeared in the Beatles' second film, *Help!*)

In September 1961 he opened his own music-publishing firm in two rooms in Charing Cross Road. He had the company going by the summer of 1962, but hadn't discovered any hits. Through contacts, the son of a friend came to see him one day with a song he hadn't managed to sell to any other music publisher. This song was called "How Do You Do It." Dick James rushed round to George Martin, his old friend at Parlophone. The reason George Martin was so keen to get the Beatles to record this song now becomes clearer.

"I told George it was brilliant. He said it might do for this new group he'd got, from Liverpool. 'Liverpool?' I said. 'You're joking. So what's from Liverpool?' "

George Martin knew it was a good commercial song, and persuaded Dick James to let him keep it for a while. Dick was very excited, convinced at last he'd got the hit he was waiting for. But in November 1962, George rang Dick to tell him that the Beatles had written their own follow-up song, "Please Please Me," which he said was excellent.

That seemed to be it as far as Dick James was concerned. But George Martin said he had Brian Epstein in his office. He didn't know anyone in London; perhaps Dick could help him. On the phone Dick James said he would. He also asked if he could publish "Please Please Me," as George had said it was so excellent.

Brian had already arranged to see another music publisher first thing in the morning, but he told Dick James he would come to him afterward and see what he thought. "I was in my office at ten thirty next morning when Brian walked in, half an hour earlier than arranged. He said he'd been to this other music publisher. He'd waited twenty-five minutes but only an office boy turned up. So he said I could have first option instead. He played it to me and I said it was the most exciting song I'd heard for years. Could I have it?"

Brian Epstein was fresh out of Liverpool, but he wasn't all that green. He said that if Dick James could get them some promotion, he could have the song. Dick James, though much smaller than even Brian Epstein realized at the time, picked up the phone and rang one of his old contacts. This was Philip Jones, who'd produced his old Radio Luxembourg singsongs. He had just taken over a new TV pop program, *Thank Your Lucky Stars.*

"Over the phone, there and then, I fixed it up. I played 'Please Please Me' to Philip and he said he liked it. He'd fit them into a show." In five minutes, Dick James had arranged the Beatles' first London TV appearance. Brian Epstein was naturally very much impressed. Over lunch, Dick James became the Beatles' music publisher. A music publisher can do pretty well if he has the right composers writing for him. All copyright fees are shared fifty-fifty between publisher and composer.

Dick James in many ways had made a wrong choice, way back in the fifties, when he'd decided to try to be a music publisher rather than a singer. He might have been safer as an agent, which was something else he thought of at the time. Music publishers had for decades existed on the sales of sheet music. Once the record boom started and people stopped playing the piano at home, sheet music had had its day. But by meeting the Beatles, Dick James' day was just about to begin.

Chapter 21: Touring

The Beatles began 1963 with one record out and another one about to be released. They'd found George Martin and Dick James. They were lined up to appear on their first London television program. But they were still completely unknown. Brian Epstein was finding it very hard to get them any publicity, nationally or locally.

He was still trying the Liverpool *Echo*'s George Harrison, but with no success. He also wrote again to Disker, the Liverpool *Echo*'s record critic. He'd first written to Disker back in 1962 and been surprised to get a letter back from Decca in London, not from Liverpool, from someone called Tony Barrow.

Tony Barrow had become Disker in 1953 when he was seventeen and still at school in Crosby near Liverpool. He kept it up while he was at Durham University and later when he joined Decca, writing sleeve notes for them. He still is Disker today, though he's also the Beatles' senior press officer.

When Brian wrote to him the first time it had looked as if Decca had liked the audition and was going to record them. Tony Barrow had written a little paragraph to this effect the first time the Beatles were mentioned in print. When it all fell through, Tony Barrow wasn't so keen to write about them again. But when "Love Me Do," their first record, was out, he wrote about the Beatles again in his Disker column.

Brian came to London more often once his group had a record out. He met Tony Barrow and asked him for advice on getting publicity. "Brian didn't know how you promoted a record, so I put him in touch with the trade press. Then he said he hadn't got a press officer. He'd just been sending round duplicated handouts on his own. He asked if I could help. So sitting in my office at Decca, I wrote out the very first official press release from the Beatles."

He hadn't actually met them and he couldn't use his own name or phone number, as he was with Decca. He also didn't have a mailing list. "I took out a publicity man I'd met. It was a one-and-ninepenny lunch at the BBC canteen. He agreed to share his mailing list and addresses." This publicist was Andrew Oldham, who later became one of Brian Epstein's assistants and later the manager of the Rolling Stones.

At the same time, EMI also did a handout to go with their first record, but this was a rewrite of Brian's duplicated letter, which he'd based on fan-club literature. It said that John's favorite color was black, he liked curry and Carl Perkins, hated thick heads and traditional jazz. Under the heading marked *Type of car* he put "Bus." All of them, according to this handout, had the same ambition—to make a lot of money and retire. This was the wrong ambition, judging by the usual handouts of the time. Their ambition should have been to be all-round entertainers.

Tony Barrow left Decca and began working for Nems full time on May 1, 1963, from a one-room office in Monmouth Street, Brian Epstein's first London office. For six months he sent out innumerable press releases, most of which were ignored.

The music papers did write about the Beatles' records when they came out, especially "Please Please Me," which was eventually released on January 12. It got to number one on February 16 and they covered it well, but the national papers still completely ignored the group.

The first, and for six months the only, general feature in any sort of national paper was in the London *Evening Standard* in February 1963 by Maureen Cleave. "Please Please Me" still hadn't got to number one and they were still largely unknown, even to the record business. But Miss Cleave had heard about their following in Liverpool through a Liverpool friend. She said in her article how their Liverpool fans had forced Granada TV to film them but were now worried that the Beatles might leave Liverpool. She described how funny and natural they were. She also drew attention, for the first time in any paper, to their hair. She described it as "French hair style" with the fringe brushed forward. This was the correct general term for it at the time, as it had originated on the Continent. But very soon no one referred to it as French but as the Beatle style.

"I could never get any feature writers or news reporters interested in the Beatles," says Tony Barrow. "It wasn't till October 1963 that it all happened.

"I would love to say that it was my brilliant handouts which built the Beatles, but they didn't. The press was very very late catching on. Kids everywhere were starting to go wild about them, not just in Liverpool.

But nobody seemed to notice. They'd got to the top of the Hit Parade with their second record, but the nationals still couldn't see them as a news or feature story. To this day, I don't know why the press was so late."

The simple explanation is that as it had never happened before in Britain, the British press had no way of recognizing it. They had to wait until it jumped out and hit them over the head.

Though they were being ignored nationally, the Beatles were at last getting good coverage in Liverpool. On January 5, 1963, Disker gave a long review to their forthcoming second record, "Please Please Me"— without mentioning that he also worked part time as the Beatles' PR man.

The famous George Harrison was also lumbering onto the bandwagon. In his "Over the Mersey Wall" column on February 21, he gave a plug for the TV appearance they were about to make on *Thank Your Lucky Stars*. He said this had been recorded before "Please Please Me" had got to number one. He also wondered, in his column, if they were going to be a one-hit group or not.

But a couple of months later there was no holding him. It was his turn to boast that his name was the same as the really famous George Harrison. He said he'd been getting masses of birthday cards addressed to *George Harrison, Liverpool*. He was even getting requests for locks of his hair, the earliest sign of the fans' craze for getting bits of the Beatles. He only wished he had some hair for himself, never mind to give away.

People in Liverpool called Lennon, McCartney, Harrison, and Starkey were also beginning to be pestered, with strange girls ringing them up all night long. But the big result of getting into the Top Twenty was not the Liverpool *Echo* writing about them but getting a national tour. This didn't mean big success, because all packaged tours which go round on one-night stands have big and small stars. But getting onto this circuit was vital to them at this stage. They needed to break out of Merseyside and become exposed nationally to see if they could have the same sort of effects on strangers as on the Liverpool fans they'd grown up with. Doing a big tour was also the steadiest way of plugging a record, by playing it live all over the country.

The first tour, in February 1963, was Helen Shapiro's. She was the star of the show. She'd caused a sensation a couple of years previously by becoming the first of the very young teenage girl singing stars.

Arthur Howes, the promoter, was already a success in his field. He'd promoted all the Cliff Richard tours. But by spotting the Beatles very early on, before they'd got to number one, he became the promoter of all their British tours except one.

Brian had been trying to contact Arthur Howes for a long time, once he'd been given his name as the promoter of the Cliff Richard tours. He was surprised, when he eventually got his home number, to find he lived in Peterborough. This was back in 1962, while Brian was still trailing round the record companies.

"One Saturday afternoon I got a telephone call at home in Peterborough. Someone saying he was called Brian Epstein was ringing from Liverpool. He said he had a great group, was there anything I could fit them into? He told me their names, Beatles, and I laughed. Oh, God, here we go again, I thought. Another group with a funny name. But I've never turned down a group without first hearing them. I said there was a show in Peterborough they could join. Just a two-shot at the Embassy Theatre in Frank Ifield's show." He didn't give them a fee, just their expenses from Liverpool.

Their night at the Embassy, Peterborough, was their first night in a theater outside Merseyside. It was a complete failure. This was the night the audience "sat on their hands." "It was a Frank Ifield show, so I suppose it wasn't so surprising. They loved him so much that the show was good enough to take ten minutes of a bad group."

But Arthur Howes liked the look of the Beatles. He put them on at another theater near Peterborough. Again they were a failure. All the same, Arthur Howes put them under contract. This didn't mean much, but it committed the Beatles to him, if he wanted them. "I still liked them as people and I saw Brian as a great businessman. I was very impressed by him."

By early 1963, when they had a record out, he took up his contract with them and decided to give them a spot on his Helen Shapiro tour. They still hadn't got to number one when they set off in February 1963. They were just another group, filling up the bill. "They took six months to happen, as far as I was concerned. My concern is strictly box office. If they don't work, there's no income. There's no romance for a promoter. Just hard work."

"Touring was a relief," says John, "just to get out of Liverpool and break new ground. We were beginning to feel stale and cramped. We were always getting the pack-ups. We'd get tired of one stage and be deciding to pack up when another stage would come on. We'd outlived the Hamburg stage and wanted to pack that up. We hated going back to Hamburg those last two times. We'd had all that scene."

"It was a big thrill," says Ringo, "going with Helen Shapiro and playing in real theaters. We'd done the Empire once in Liverpool, when

Brian put on a show just to get us on somewhere. We were third on the bill. Some cockney manager of one of the so-called stars had a hassle with us. He didn't want us to be on the show at all.

"But touring properly round theaters was great. We didn't know anything about things like make-up, because we'd never done proper stage shows. It was a long time before we had a go at that. I think it was watching Frank Ifield. His eyes looked amazing. We thought we'd try it ourselves. We pranced on like Red Indians, covered in the stuff."

They caused no sensation at the beginning of the Helen Shapiro tour. It wasn't till later, when their second record became top, that they started getting a big reaction.

"Helen was the star," says Ringo. "She had the telly in her dressing room and we didn't have one. We had to ask her if we could watch hers. We weren't getting packed houses, but we were on the boards, man."

John remembers there was a bit of screaming in Glasgow. He says they always screamed there. They liked rock and roll long after everyone else had progressed to liking the Shadows. The Beatles were still basically a rock-and-roll group. "Twist and Shout," which they started putting into their act at this stage, was perhaps the most out-and-out wild rock-and-roll style they ever sang. "We always got screams in Scotland. I suppose they haven't got much else to do up there."

Although he was on the boards, Ringo for a long time was still a bit worried about fitting in with the others. "When we got to hotels I wondered who I'd be with. I didn't know what to do. They all knew each other so well. What usually happened was that John shared with George and I shared with Paul. It was always okay, of course."

John can't remember any town or place from any tour they ever did. "We never knew where we were. It was all the same."

Ringo's only specific memory of that first Helen Shapiro tour was being thrown out of a ball. "It was in Carlisle, I think. There was a hunt ball on in the hotel we were staying in and we thought we'd look in. It was full of soft people, all stoned out of their heads. They chucked us out because we were so scruffy, which we were."

When "Please Please Me" got to number one, they began to become better known to the pop fans. Toward the end they were getting as much applause as Helen Shapiro, the star of the show, which led to a slightly strained relationship.

After the tour, with a number one behind them, Arthur Howes immediately sent them on another one. This started in March 1963. The stars of this show were Chris Montez and Tommy Roe. The Beatles were third on the bill. Their reception on this tour increased all the time.

They were now becoming well known in the pop world. Their appearance on *Thank Your Lucky Stars* helped their record. They were asked to write songs for other people. They did one for Helen Shapiro.

Cliff Richard's new song "Summer Holiday" soon toppled "Please Please Me" from the top. But Gerry and the Pacemakers, with the song the Beatles had turned down, "How Do You Do It," soon became number one. By March 1963, the Liverpool Sound was a phrase people in the pop business had started to use.

The success of "Please Please Me" led in April 1963 to the Beatles' first LP, which had the same name. It included both sides of their first two records plus "Twist and Shout," "A Taste of Honey," and others. This album remained in the LP charts for six months.

In April 1963 they also brought out their third single, "From Me to You." This reached number one, like "Please Please Me," and was awarded a silver disk.

Brian was still signing up other Liverpool artists. He took over Billy Kramer, put a J in the middle of his name, and gave him a new backing group, the Dakotas from Manchester. John and Paul wrote a song for him, "Do You Want to Know a Secret." It became number one.

Already, even as early as April 1963, when their third record "From Me to You" came out, people were comparing their records and saying they'd gone off. Disk jockey Keith Fordyce wrote that the "singing and harmonizing are good and there's plenty of sparkle. The lyric is commercial, but I don't rate the tune as being anything as good as on the last two disks by this group." John and Paul had composed this song while on a coach during the Helen Shapiro tour. They were writing simple and uncomplicated lyrics, as they'd always done, going in for easy audience-identifying words like *me* and *you* in the titles.

They were signed up for another national tour in May, this time with Roy Orbison. This was the only British tour which Arthur Howes didn't do. He didn't have a tour going out at the time, but Brian thought they should keep touring and cash in on their record fame.

Before they went off, they had a short holiday in Teneriffe in the Canary Islands. This was at the holiday home of Klaus' father; Klaus was their Hamburg friend, whom they had still kept in contact with. Paul was nearly killed on this holiday when he swam out too far and got swept out to sea.

Whenever they could, during these tours or in any breaks, they all went home to Liverpool. "We went around boasting," says Ringo. "Professional group, you know. Most groups were still going out to ordinary jobs."

John felt slightly embarrassed and somehow self-conscious being back in Liverpool, despite their success. "We couldn't say it, but we didn't really like going back to Liverpool. Being local heroes made us nervous. When we did shows there they were always full of people we knew. We felt embarrassed in our suits and being very clean. We were worried that friends might think we'd sold out. Which we had, in a way."

During their third tour, with Roy Orbison in May 1963, they started causing riots, though not the sort which made any national papers. This was their first tour as the stars of the show and they were beginning to have everywhere the sort of reaction they'd had in the Cavern in Liverpool.

Although Brian had made them more show-business and polished, so John thought anyway, they were still larking around on stage, singing corny songs if anything went wrong, and making funny introductions. "And now for a song by that Red-hot Gospel-singing Mama, Victor Sylvester." In any interviews they managed to get with the pop-music writers, they were much the same. Maureen Cleave had said in her *Evening Standard* piece that it was like living it up with four Marx Brothers.

It was on this tour with Roy Orbison that a black market started in tickets. Jellybeans were thrown at them on stage—after George had been foolish enough to say he liked them—and they were mobbed in the theater, at their hotel, and everywhere they went.

Roy Orbison got equal billing with the Beatles, but he was the second-last act on the bill, with the Beatles following him as the main stars of the show. "It was terrible following him," says Ringo. "He'd slay them and they'd scream for more. In Glasgow we were all backstage, listening to the tremendous applause he was getting.

"He was just doing it by his voice. Just standing there singing, not moving or anything. He was knocking them out. As it got near our turn, we would hide behind the curtain, whispering to each other—guess who's next folks, it's your favorite rave. But once we got on the stage, it was always okay."

It wasn't okay for Neil Aspinall, their road manager, once the touring days began. It hadn't been so bad in Liverpool, round and round the same old places. But now it was a new road, a new hotel, a new theater and new problems every day.

"There was always trouble with the mikes on every tour," says John. "No theater ever got it how we liked it. Even rehearsing in the afternoon first and telling them how we wanted it, it still wouldn't be right. They'd either be in the wrong position or not loud enough. They would just set it up as they would for amateur talent night. Perhaps we had a chip about them not taking our music seriously. It drove us mad. Brian would sit up in the control room and we'd shout at him. He'd signal back that that was all they could do."

They used to shout most of all at Neil. It was one of his jobs to get them and their gear everywhere at the right time and help set it up. As the fans started mobbing, endangering them physically as well as trying to steal bits of equipment, it became more and more impossible for Neil to do everything. "In five weeks of touring I lost three stone in weight. No one will believe it, but it was true. I went down from eleven stone to eight stone. I just didn't eat or sleep for five weeks. There was no time."

So Malcolm Evans, the bouncer from the Cavern, was taken on. He joined Neil as road manager and continued throughout their touring days. They are both still with the Beatles today, as their closest companions and friends.

Neil is thin, highly intelligent, quietly efficient but with very strong opinions and by no means a yes man. He looks a bit like George. Mal is big and hefty, open-hearted, good-natured, and easygoing. Neil gave up a career in accounting to join the Beatles. Mal's job was less imposing, but he was completely settled into it.

Mal had been working for eleven years as a telecommunications engineer when the Beatles came along and changed his life. He was twenty-seven when it happened, married with one child, paying up the mortgage on a terrace house in Allerton Road, Liverpool, the proud owner of his first car and a good salary of £15 a week. He had absolute security, paid holidays, and a pension when he retired. He looked obviously set for life.

One day in 1962 he came out of work at the Post Office and decided not to walk around the Pier Head, which is where he usually went for a walk in his lunch hours. "I saw this little street called Mathew Street that I'd never noticed before. I walked down it and came to this club, the Cavern Club. I'd never been inside a club before. I heard this music coming, real rock it sounded, a bit like Elvis. So I paid me shilling and went in." He went in so often after that it was suggested if he became a bouncer, guarding the door, he could get in for nothing.

He'd been part-time bouncing for about three months when in the summer of 1963 Brian asked him to give up the Post Office and be their second road manager. Mal's job, during all the years of touring, was to drive the van containing the equipment to the next theater, set it up, and test it in time for their coming on. Afterward, he packed it all up safely and looked after it till the next stop. Neil looked after the Beatles personally.

During his first week with the Beatles Mal estimates he was sacked six times. "I'd never seen a drum kit close up before. I didn't understand any of it. Neil helped me the first couple of days, but the first day I was on my own was terrible. It was a huge stage and my mind went a blank. I didn't know where to put anything. I asked a drummer from another group to help me. I didn't realize each drummer likes his cymbals at a special height. He did them his own way, but they were useless for Ringo.

"The worst of all was at the Finsbury Empire in London when I lost John's guitar. It was one he'd had for years as well. It just disappeared. 'Where's my Jumbo,' he said. I didn't know. It's still a mystery today. I fairly got it that day.

"It was great meeting all the people I'd seen on TV. I was really starstruck. I still am. I soon realized of course that people were being nice to me, trying to get to know me, just to use me to get to the Beatles. I soon got to spot them a mile off."

"It was okay for him," says Neil. "Going out in front getting the instruments ready. Dead popular he was. As they cheered and shouted at him he talked to them and made jokes. He didn't have to physically fight them off, once it started."

"My ideas about the fellows soon changed," says Mal. "Up to then, they'd been four beautiful people. I'd looked upon them as gods. I soon found out they were just ordinary blokes, not made of platinum. I got some bellyaching and I couldn't answer back. I just had to put up with it." The worst part of all touring, they both say, was in the dressing room before a show, when it was full inside with reporters, police, and theater staff, while outside fans were trying to break in. "I had to look after all that," says Neil, "until we got a press man ourselves. And I was supposed to get food.

"When things got too much, if someone was going on a bit, John or one of them would shout 'Cripples, Neil.' This meant get rid of somebody. It originally had just meant cripples, but it came to mean anyone who was in the way.

"We always got masses of cripples, even from the first tours. They would be in the dressing room when we arrived at the theater. The management would let them in, thinking we'd love to see them, as we were supposed to be such lovely blokes. It was terrible. You couldn't move for them. What could you do? They wouldn't be able to move themselves so Mal or I usually had to carry them out. Mal got a claw stuck round his neck one night.

John

John, aged nine

John at the age of eight with his mother Julia

Fred Lennon, John's father

John's Aunt Mimi, who brought him up from the age of three

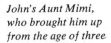

On the back of this self-photo taken in Germany, John wrote, "Come-hither-type look. I love you. XXX" and sent it to Mimi

Paul

*Paul (left), aged seven,
with his mother and brother Michael*

Paul, aged nine

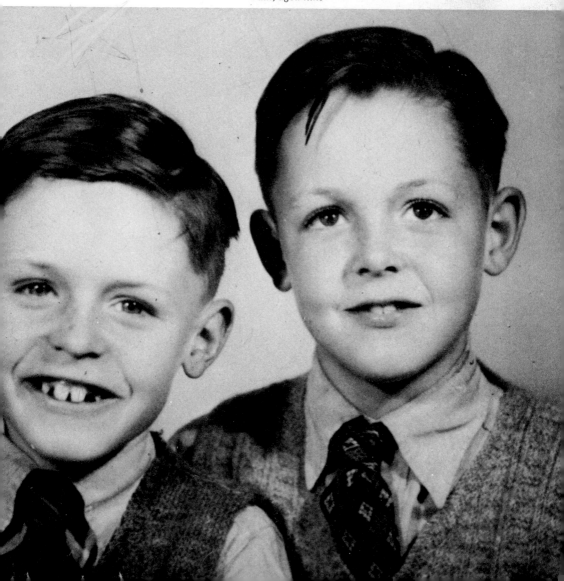

The McCartney family in 1967: Michael, Angela (Paul's stepmother),
Paul, Jim (Paul's father)

George

George, aged five

The Harrison family:
George, aged eight, in the middle,
with his parents, Harold and Louise, beside him.
Behind, his brothers, Harold and Peter

George, aged fifteen,
at his first dance

Ringo

Ringo, aged seven, with his mother Elsie

Ringo's father, Richard Starkey

*Ringo, right, aged sixteen,
in his first job,
as a barman on a ferryboat*

*Ringo's mother Elsie
and his stepfather Harry Graves*

Ringo

The earliest known picture of the Beatles as a group, then called the Quarrymen, taken in 1956 at a Liverpool church-hall dance. On the left, wearing a jacket, is Paul, with John singing at the microphone. George joined them over a year later. Ringo didn't join till 1962

The Beatles, then called the Silver Beatles, in 1960, auditioning before Larry Parnes. The audition led to their first fully professional engagement — a two-week tour as a backing group round the north of Scotland. Left is Stu Sutcliffe, who had just joined the group. At the time he could hardly play the bass guitar, which is why he is trying to keep his back to the audience. John, Paul, and George are in the foreground. The drummer, looking very bored, is Johnny Hutch, who stood in at the last moment, as they arrived without a drummer

UGO HAAS
HANNOVER

20

Astrid Kirchherr

Paul, John, and George, in German Leather with cowboy overtones, on a roof in Hamburg, 1961

George, Stu Sutcliffe, and John, Hamburg, 1960

*Astrid Kirchherr (left), the Beatles' Hamburg friend,
photographer, and creator of their hair style.
With her is Stu Sutcliffe, the Beatles' bass guitarist,
to whom she was engaged*

The Beatles, back in Liverpool from Hamburg with their new hair style, are rated the most popular group in Merseyside by the readers of Mersey Beat, *a local pop newspaper which had just begun. Despite such fame, Paul's surname is misspelled*

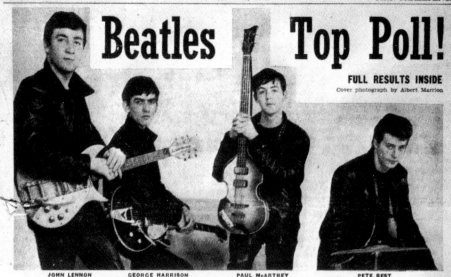

MERSEYSIDE'S OWN ENTERTAINMENTS PAPER

MERSEY BEAT

CRANES
The name for
Records. Amplifiers
Transistor Radios
Also Pianos
and Organs

HANOVER STREET, LIVERPOOL 1
Telephone: ROYal 4714

N E M S
WHITECHAPEL AND GREAT
CHARLOTTE STREET
*THE FINEST RECORD SELEC-
TIONS IN THE NORTH*
Open until 6-0 p.m. each day
(Thursday and Saturday 6-30 p.m.)

Vol. 1 No. 13   JANUARY 4-18, 1962   Price **THREEPENCE**

Beatles Top Poll!

FULL RESULTS INSIDE
Cover photograph by Albert Marrion

JOHN LENNON   GEORGE HARRISON   PAUL McARTREY   PETE BEST

Touring: from 1963 to 1966 their arrival and departure from London Airport became a familiar photograph in British newspapers. Here, in 1965, they are leaving for the Bahamas. Looking rather nervous in the right-hand corner is Brian Epstein

Celebration dinner at the George V Hotel in Paris in January 1963 of the news that "I Want to Hold Your Hand" had become Number One in the U.S.A. Left to right: Judy Lockhart-Smith (now Mrs. George Martin), Ringo, George, Paul, John, and George Martin. Brian Epstein is wearing a chamber pot.

The Beatles on stage, guarded by the police, in August 1966 in Chicago

Express

The changing face
of the Beatles,
as seen through
their official
hand-out photographs

1963

1965

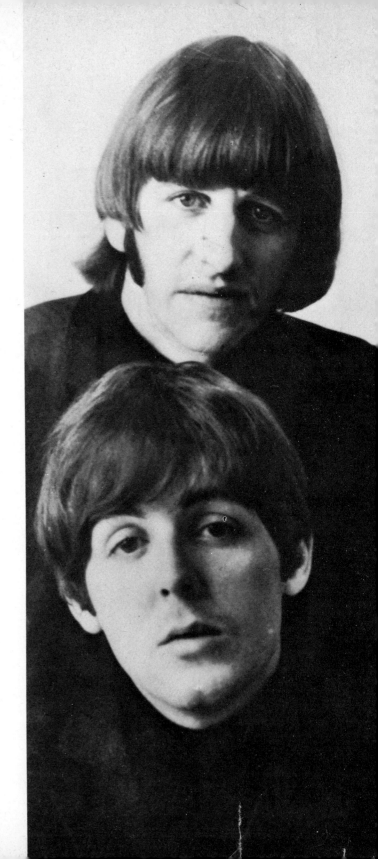

1967

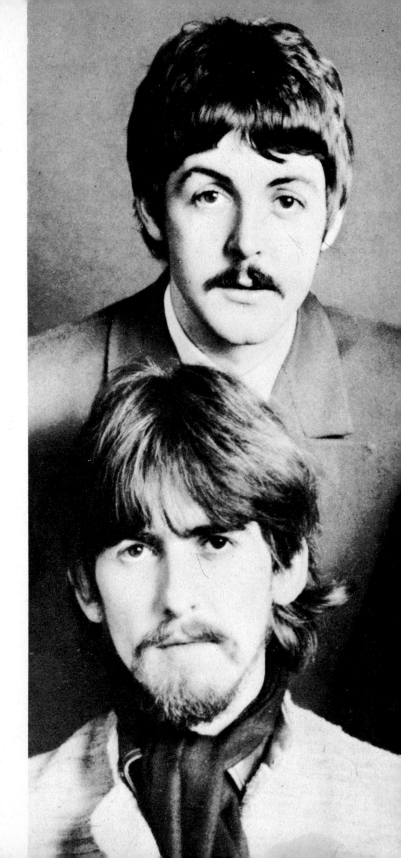

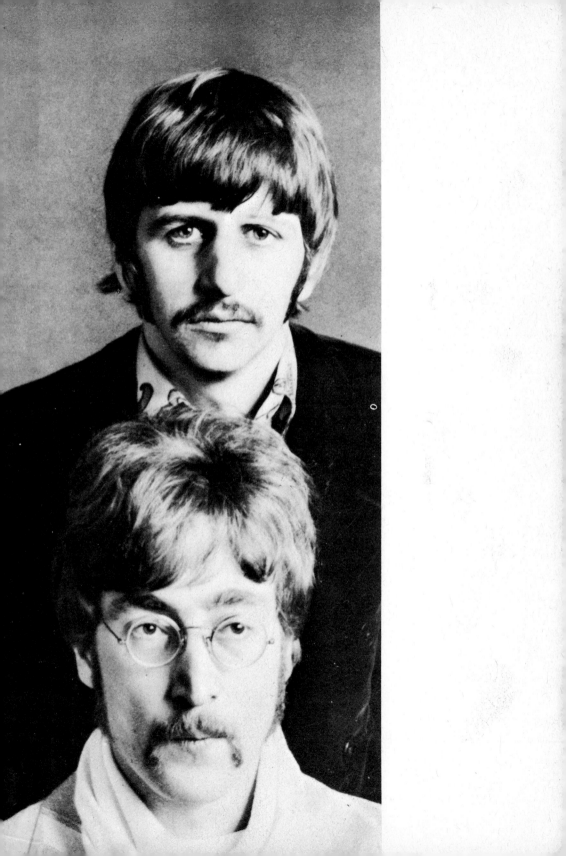

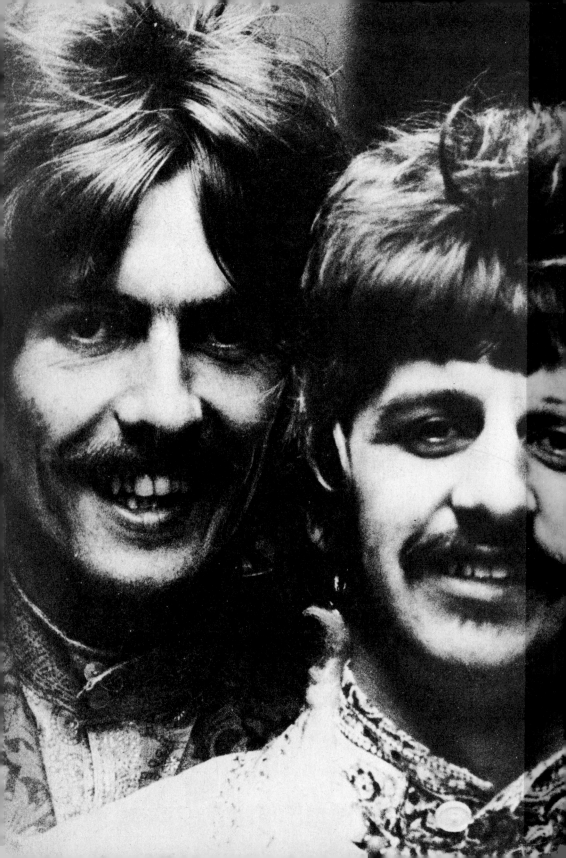

1968

The Beatles at home
with their families in 1968,
taken by ace photographer
Ringo Starr.

Pattie and George Harrison

Ringo Starr

The John Lennons: Julian, Cynthia, and John

Ringo Starr

Paul McCartney and Jane Asher

The Beatles—1976–1977

Paul on stage, 1977

Paul and Linda, 1977

Linda, Paul and baby James, October 1977

Linda McCartney

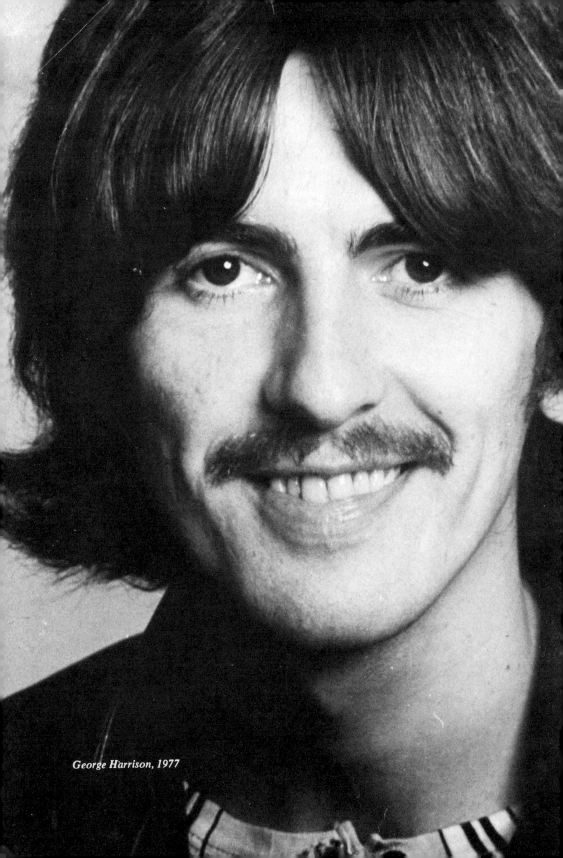

George Harrison, 1977

George

John Lennon and Yoko Ono, August 1976, New York

John

Ringo

"As the Beatles' following got bigger, we got more and more. The image of the Beatles was so good and nice, for some reason. They thought we'd *want* to see them, or we'd be disappointed."

Some even thought that being in the presence of the Beatles might miraculously cure them. It was one aspect of their adulation which never made the papers. Pictures of cripples being carried out of their dressing room would have been too much. Riots were starting on these early tours, as they traveled up and down the country, but they were still completely a Liverpool group, doing shows round their old Merseyside haunts between tours. They didn't do their last performance at the Cavern until August 23, 1963.

John was home in Liverpool for the birth of his son Julian—named after his mother Julia. When he visited Cyn at Sefton General Hospital he had to wear a disguise so no one would see him. This was still April 1963. They were household names in Liverpool, but unknown elsewhere. "A few did recognize me. 'Dere's one of dem,' I heard someone shout, and I had to run for it." A few days after the birth, John went on holiday to Spain with Brian.

Cyn moved out of the little flat they'd had in the center of Liverpool and moved in with Mimi in Menlove Avenue. "When I was pushing Julian in his pram round Woolton people would come up to me and say are you Cynthia Lennon. I'd say no."

They were all still Liverpool-based by June 1963 when it was Paul's twenty-first birthday. All the fans knew, of course, so he couldn't have a party at his home in Forthlin Avenue. Instead he had it at his Aunt Jinny's, one of the two aunts who had helped a lot when his mother died.

This was a huge drunken noisy orgy, with all the other groups playing, as at Ringo's party and as at all their welcome-homes from Hamburg. The Fourmost, who had also been signed on by Brian, played; so did the Scaffold, the Liverpool group which had just gotten going. This consisted of Roger McGough, the Liverpool poet; John Gorman, a comedian actor and boutique owner; and Michael McGear, formerly Michael McCartney, Paul's brother.

Michael was still working as a hairdresser, but had started appearing with the Scaffold in his spare time. Once Paul became famous in Liverpool, Michael had changed his name for any acting work, in case anyone felt he was cashing in. He also refused to sing.

During this party, John picked a fight with a local disk jockey who had done a lot before Brian to get them bookings.

"I smashed him up," says John. "I broke his bloody ribs for him. I was pissed at the time. He'd called me a queer. He sued me afterwards, for thumping him. I paid him two hundred pounds to settle it. That was probably the last real fight I've ever had."

The end of an era, in many ways. It was the beginning of the end of John's violently aggressive, chip-on-the-shoulder attitude to life and everyone. And it was the beginning of the end of the whole Liverpool stage; their touring was at last receiving national attention.

Back in London in August they produced their fourth single, "She Loves You." This was the start of *yeh yeh* and the beginning of national fame. Liverpool was now where they had come from.

Chapter 22: Beatlemania

Beatlemania descended on the British Isles in October 1963, just as the Christine Keeler–Profumo scandal fizzled out.

It didn't lift for three years, by which time it had spread and had covered the whole world. There was perpetual screaming and *yeh-yeh*ing for three years, one long continuous succession of hysterical teenagers of every class' and color, shouting uncontrollably, not one of whom could hear what was going on for the noise of each other. Each of them emotionally, mentally, or sexually excited, foaming at the mouth, bursting into tears, hurling themselves like lemmings in the direction of the Beatles or just simply fainting.

Throughout the whole of the three years it was happening somewhere in the world. Each country witnessed the same scenes of mass emotion, scenes which had never been thought possible before and which are unlikely to be ever seen again. Writing about it now makes it all sound like fiction. It is impossible to exaggerate Beatlemania because Beatlemania was in itself an exaggeration. No words can fully describe those scenes, although every major newspaper in the world has miles of words and pictures in its clipping library, giving blow-by-blow accounts of what happened when the Beatles descended on their part of the globe.

Once it had stopped, by 1967, and everyone was either overcome by exhaustion or boredom, it was difficult to believe it had all happened. Could everyone have been so mad? It wasn't just teenagers; people of all ages and all intellects had succumbed, though perhaps not all as hysterically as the teenagers.

World leaders and famous personages, who'd often started by warning or criticizing, fell over each other to drag in references to the Beatles, to show that they were in touch, to let people see that they also knew that a phenomenon of mass communication had occurred.

It occurred suddenly and dramatically in Britain in October 1963 and Brian Epstein said he wasn't prepared for it.

He was prepared for success, because they were already having it. What he meant was that he wasn't prepared for hysteria.

"She Loves You," which had come out at the end of August, also went to number one, following the pattern of their previous two singles. As early as June, even before it had a title, thousands of fans had already ordered the next Beatle single. The day before it was on sale, there were 500,000 advance orders for it.

By September the Beatles had reached a unique position in Britain. They had the top-selling LP record, "Please Please Me." They had the top-selling EP record, "Twist and Shout." They had the top-selling single, "She Loves You."

But it wasn't until the night of October 13, 1963, that the Beatles stopped being simply an interesting pop-music story and became front-page hard news in every national newspaper. This was the night they topped the bill at the London Palladium on a show which was televised as "Sunday Night at the London Palladium." An estimated audience of fifteen million viewers watched them that night.

Argyll Street, where the Palladium is situated (and where today Nems has offices) was besieged by fans all day long. Newspapermen started arriving once the stories of the crowds got round. The stage door was blocked by fans, mountains of presents, and piles of telegrams. Inside it was almost impossible to rehearse for the continual screams of the thousands of fans chanting outside in the streets.

Other TV companies turned up, from the news departments, to record the crowd scenes, even though the show was being broadcast by a rival network. The police, taken completely by surprise, were unable to control most of the crowd. It was decided that the Beatles' getaway car should be stationed at the front doors, as everyone expected them to leave afterward by the stage door. Their car by this time was a chauffeur-driven Austin Princess. Neil's old van had long since been discarded once the hit records started appearing.

The police, thinking they were clever, moved the car slightly away from the front door, trying to conceal it. Which meant that when the Beatles did appear, shepherded by Neil, they had to search wildly for the car, then make a dash of fifty yards, almost being killed by the mobs in the process.

The front page of every newspaper next day had long news stories and large pictures of the hysterical crowd scenes. The stories weren't about how well or how badly the group had played their songs, but simply about the chaos they had caused.

"From that day on," says Tony Barrow, the press officer, "everything changed. My job was never the same again. From spending six months ringing up newspapers and getting no, I now had every national reporter and feature writer chasing *me*." His job from then on became to select, along with Brian and other press officers who were later used, journalists who were allowed to interview the Beatles. They never had to ask anyone again to do anything. His job, as far as the Beatles were concerned, was simply to become an information officer. The Queen's so-called press officer is in effect an information officer. He never rings people. He is there to answer questions, or in most cases, not answer questions. The Beatles' press officers—there was eventually one who went on tour and one, Tony Barrow, in London—from then on assumed the same sort of functions.

"Even before that, I'd never been in any sense a publicist, the way most groups have publicists, thinking up publicity stunts. I didn't know about that, as I'd never been one. Brian anyway would have been against any stunts. We never used any and we never had to."

The following Wednesday Bernard Delfont announced the names for what is looked upon by most British show-business people as the biggest show of the year—the Royal Variety Performance. "That was an even greater honor than the Palladium," said Brian.

Brian might have thought so, being naturally impressed by them appearing before Royalty, but the Beatles themselves, not being nature's royalists, were more impressed by the bill—Marlene Dietrich and Maurice Chevalier.

The Beatles were back on tour when this news broke. They were still doing tour after tour and still in some cases doing ballroom dates. They were actually in Liverpool, about to appear at a Southport ballroom, when the news came out. All the national newspapers sent reporters and photographers across from their Manchester offices to get the Beatles' reactions to the news. They were obviously hoping for some satirical remarks about the Royal Family, but to Brian's relief, there were none. The Royal Variety Show was planned for November 4. Before that they continued touring in Britain and for the first time abroad, to Sweden.

In Britain each one-night stand resulted in the same hysterical crowd scenes. Everyday the newspaper had almost word-for-word the same front-page news stories, only the name of the town was different.

Even in smallish towns, like Carlisle, where earlier in the year they'd had trouble at a local hotel, the crowds were huge. On the night of October 24, over 600 teenagers waited all night long in Warwick Road, Carlisle, as they queued to buy tickets the next day at the ABC Cinema, where the Beatles were to appear. Most of them brought sleeping bags and slept. Some had been there for as long as thirty-six hours. When the box office opened and the line moved forward, shop windows were smashed and nine people were taken to the hospital. In bigger towns like Newcastle and Leicester the all-night queues were bigger, 4000 and 3000 respectively.

The Swedish tour, their first foreign trip since Hamburg, was a direct result of their records' sales. "She Loves You" soon reached the million figure in Britain, for which it got a gold disk, but it was also selling well in Europe, which British pop stars' records had rarely done before.

The Swedish tour lasted only five days, from the twenty-fourth of October to the twenty-ninth. This tour, day by day, made the British papers at home as well as the Swedish press and television. At a concert in Stockholm, forty policemen, with batons at the ready, stood guarding the stage to stop fans climbing on. Outside there were more police with police dogs, trying to control the fans who couldn't get in. The fans did eventually break through the barrier of police and get onto the stage. George was knocked over, but the police managed to restore order before he was trodden on.

Swedish fans were already affecting Beatle hairstyles and clothes, as British fans had also started to do. In Sweden the hair style was known as the Hamlet style. The Beatles themselves date the beginning of Beatlemania from a week or so later than Tony Barrow first put it. They first realized their massive popularity on October thirty-first, when they arrived back at London Airport from Sweden.

They had of course been aware of the chaos at the London Palladium two weeks previously, and all the other riots up and down the country. But this had been going on, building up all the time but less publicized, since their Cavern days. They had gotten into a pattern on tour of having to be smuggled in and out of theaters. They were trying to escape it, rather than face up to it and risk being killed.

But when they arrived back at London Airport their popularity suddenly hit them. It was their first triumphal arrival from anywhere since the Cavern welcome-homes. Thousands of screaming fans had been choking London Airport for hours. In the chaos of surrounding their arrival the car containing the Prime Minister, Sir Alec Douglas-Home, was held up. Miss World, who was also passing through London Airport at the time, was completely ignored. The airport scenes became familiar pictures for the next three years.

The Royal Variety Performance, on November 4, was held at the Prince of Wales' Theatre. The audience wasn't as big as the Palladium show but in theory much more select as the seats were about four times the normal price. It was a charity show, full of show-business establishment, minor society and rag-trade moguls, all hoping for a glimpse of the Royals. On this occasion they were the Queen Mother, Princess Margaret, and Lord Snowdon. It's said to be a difficult audience to play to. There is the nauseating tradition of the audience craning to see what effect each act is having in the royal box before they also clap or laugh.

Paul got a laugh all round from the beginning. The Beatles came on immediately after Sophie Tucker. Paul said how pleased they were to be following their favorite American group. Musically, they did their usual act—causing hysterics just by announcing they were going to sing "She Loves You." Then they did "Till There Was You" and "Twist and Shout."

For one number John asked the audience to clap their hands in time. Nodding toward the royal box, he added: "Those upstairs, just rattle your jewelry."

This joke was on every front page the next day, everyone loving the implied, though very slight, joke at the Royals' expense. All completely harmless, of course. But it was looked upon as being rather cheeky, though of course lovable, because the Beatles had become so lovable. It led the way in later years for other comedians and comperes to try to get in their Royal joke.

The Queen Mother, in talking to them afterward, showed that she was well aware of what they did. She even made her own joky remark, though it probably wasn't meant to be joky. She asked them where they were appearing next and they said Slough. "Oh," said the Queen Mother, "that's near us."

The show was televised the following Sunday and had an audience of twenty-six million. The front-page stories about Beatles' concerts became monotonously the same. Even papers like the *Daily Telegraph,* which up to then had considered itself too staid to cover pop stories (they now religiously publish the top ten each week) gave columns to every riot. For a long time, however, they still referred in their reports, as in one about a Newcastle concert on October 28, to "teenagers fighting to get tickets for the Beatles 'pop' group. . . ." They still felt it necessary to explain who the Beatles were.

There were questions in Parliament about the thousands of extra policemen all around the country who were being made to do extra, and dangerous, duty because of the Beatles. One MP suggested that the police should withdraw and see what happened. Luckily, no one took that suggestion seriously. On November the first they began another tour, this time billed simply as the Beatles Show. There was no other joint star, as there had been with Roy Orbison, because none was needed.

In the program for this show, which toured until December 13, there were several advertisements for Beatle products. A firm in Peckham was offering Beatles Sweaters "designed specially for Beatle people by a leading British manufacturer with a top quality two-tone Beatle badge." All for 35 shillings each.

Manufacturers all over the country were by this time competing to get a concession to use the word *Beatle* on their products. Beatles jackets—the collarless ones, usually in corduroy, first worn by Stu in Hamburg—were on sale everywhere as early as September 1963.

Beatle wigs started appearing. A factory in Bethnal Green was working night and day to keep up with the demand. It had orders from Eton College and from Buckingham Palace. Most teenage boys were growing their own Beatle-length hair. From November on there was a continuous stream of newspaper stories about schoolboys being sent home from school because of their long hair and of apprentices not being allowed into factories.

The *Daily Telegraph,* on November second, produced the first leader criticizing the Beatles hysteria. It said the mass hysteria was simply filling empty heads, just as Hitler had done. The *Daily Mirror* jumped to the Beatles' defense. "You have to be a real sour square not to love the nutty, noisy, happy handsome Beatles." The paper complimented the Beatles for not relying "on off-color jokes about homos for their fun."

They were attacked and then defended in the Church Assembly, the annual meeting of leaders of the Church of England. One bishop said they were a "psychopathetic group" and that one week of their wages could build a cathedral in Africa. But another speaker said he was a fan and that it was all healthy fun.

The *Daily Mirror* was about the first paper to drag out a tame psychologist to try to explain what was happening, a practice which kept tame psychologists all over the world, most of all in America, in easy money for the next three years. This psychologist said the Beatles were "relieving a sexual urge." Doctors later testified to say that girls had had orgasms during their concerts.

In Plymouth, on November 14, hoses had to be turned on screaming fans to control them. There was greater panic at Portsmouth because Paul had slight flu and the group had to miss a concert. Every paper gave hour-by-hour bulletins on his condition. In Birmingham on November 11 they managed to escape the crowds disguised as policemen. On November 18 a Church of England vicar got a lot of space in the papers when he asked the Beatles to tape him "Oh Come All Ye Faithful, Yeh, Yeh," for Christmas.

EMI sales were shooting up. When the story came out about Decca and all the other companies having turned them down it was compared with 20th Century-Fox turning down *Gone with the Wind.*

At the end of November they brought out their fifth single, "I Want to Hold Your Hand." This went direct to number one. It had advance orders in Britain of one million. Their second LP came out a few days before, *With the Beatles.* This had the stark but very arty photograph on the cover showing their four heads and shoulders, dressed in black turtleneck sweaters. Their faces were cleverly lit so that one side was in the shade, as Astrid had done in Hamburg. When this LP was announced, at the beginning of November, it had immediate advance orders of 250,000. It was noted at the time that this was the best advance for an LP record anywhere in the world. The best Elvis Presley had done was 200,000 for his "Blue Hawaii" album.

Every big bylined feature writer was competing for an interview, waiting for hours and hours outside their dressing room, hoping for a word. Donald Zec of the *Daily Mirror* was one of the first to do a large interview with them, right at the beginning of their nationally famous days, on September 10. In describing their hair style, which journalists still felt they had to do, he said it was a Stone-Age cut.

By December 1963, the staid Sunday papers had got in on the act, doing long and very solemn investigations of the phenomenon, also dragging out their own psychologists, but using even longer words. The *Observer* used a picture of a guitar-shaped Cycladic fertility goddess from Amorgos that it said "dates the potency of the guitar as a sex symbol to about 4,800 years before the Beatle era." The *Sunday Times* commented on how they had enlarged the English language, bringing Liverpool words like *gear* (meaning good or great) into general usage. This rather put the Conservative politician Edward Heath in his place. Earlier he had criticized the Beatles by saying their language was "unrecognizable as the Queen's English." But Mr. Heath redeemed himself slightly later when he was reported as asking "who could have forecast only a year ago that the Beatles would prove the salvation of the corduroy industry?"

Even the *Daily Worker,* the British Communist Party newspaper, was getting its comment in. "The Mersey Sound is the voice of 80,000 crumbling houses and 30,000 people on the dole."

By early December seven of their records, singles as well as EPs, were in the Top Twenty. On December 11 they went on the TV program *Juke Box Jury,* the four of them taking over the complete jury, and gave the show the highest rating it had ever had.

A film deal was announced. Walter Shenson and George Ornstein, in association with United Artists, said they were going to star the Beatles in their first film, with a script by the Liverpool playwright Alun Owen. Brian Epstein was in on this deal, making sure that the Beatles were to take a large percentage. He was by now doing the same with their tours, once it was obvious that their name alone was enough to guarantee a full house everywhere. The Beatles Tour, which had begun in November, this time was "presented by Arthur Howes, by arrangement with Brian Epstein." Brian was making sure they were being involved in all the enormous profits which were being made and were putting aside their share of it each time.

In October Brian had moved his own office to London, joining Tony Barrow and the growing number of secretaries and assistants.

The fan club was also growing to huge proportions and was completely unable to cope with the thousands of application forms pouring in. There were many stories in the newspapers about poor fans not having their letters answered for months, but the deluge was just too much. By the end of the year the official fan club had almost eighty thousand paid-up members, compared with a couple of thousand at the beginning of the year.

BBC TV, like all other media, desperate for any sort of Beatle story, even when the Beatles themselves wouldn't be interviewed, did a half show from the Northern Area convention of the Beatles Fan Club from the Liverpool Empire.

At Christmastime the Beatles did a Christmas show, along with other Brian Epstein artists—Cilla Black, Billy J. Kramer, Tommy Quickly, and the Fourmost. It opened in Bradford, then Liverpool, then came to London at the Finsbury Park Empire, which was where Mal lost John's favorite guitar. The intellectual following was now in full cry. The prestigious papers were giving the group as much space as the tabloids. Paul and John were commissioned to write the music for a ballet, *Mods and Rockers.*

Brian worried at first about his own name and personality becoming famous, but eventually he couldn't help it. He realized that it made things easier for him to get things done if he was known by name almost as much as the Beatles.

"What I was worried about was all of us becoming over exposed. At first sight the endless discussion in the newspapers of the Beatles' habits, clothes, and views was exciting. They liked it at first and so did I. It was good for business. But finally it became an anxiety. How much could they maintain public interest without rationing either personal appearances or newspaper coverage? By a stringent watch on their bookings and press contacts we just averted saturation point. But it was very close. Other artists have been destroyed by this very thing."

At the time, judging by the newspaper and TV reports, it looked as though there was no control at all. Every paper every day had something on them. In one week five national newspapers were serializing their life story, most of it taken from the old handouts. Everyone remotely connected with the Beatles got himself into the newspaper. Almost anyone with any opinion on them, for or against, was guaranteed to be reported. Several papers said that Brian Epstein was the Svengali. He'd cleverly created and promoted them. Brian always denied this.

"In all our handouts," says Tony Barrow, "and in all our press dealings. Brian only stressed what was good about them. He never created any nonexistent good points.

"The Beatles were four local lads from down the street, the sort you might have seen at the local church hall. This was the essence of their personal communication with the public. This was the appeal. People identified with them from the beginning. Brian realized this and never tried to hide it."

But Brian did of course create a smooth machinery, organized their lives meticulously, never let people down—which they had always done when they were on their own. But the big attraction was the Beatles themselves. Every reporter knew that every interview would be different and funny. Ringo turned out to be just as funny as the rest of them. He was asked why he had so many rings on his fingers. He said it was because he couldn't get them all through his nose.

John, today, says they were really putting-on the press. He despised many newspapers because for long, he says, they had refused to accept them as anything more than ordinary.

"We were funny at press conferences because it was all a joke. They'd ask joke questions so you'd give joke answers. But we weren't really funny at all. It was just fifth-form humor, the sort of you laugh at at school. They were putrid. If there were any good questions, about our music, we took them seriously. Our image was only a teeny part of us. It was created by the press and by us. It had to be wrong because you can't put over how you really are. Newspapers always get things wrong. Even when bits were true it was always old. New images would catch on just as we were leaving them."

In just twelve months from the release of the first record, they had become an established part of the British way of life. Dora Bryan did a record about them at Christmas 1963, "All I Want for Christmas Is a Beatle." That even got into the hit parade. There was by now nobody else on the hit parade scene, unless you counted the other Liverpool groups, all of whom Brian Epstein managed and all of whom were being recorded by George Martin.

In 1963, out of the fifty-two weeks in the year a record produced by George Martin was at the top of the British Hit Parade for thirty-seven weeks. This is an achievement no one has ever equaled, or is likely to.

The *New Musical Express,* in its end-of-the-year charts, made the Beatles the world's top group. They polled 14,666 votes. The American group, the Everly Brothers, was runner-up with 3,232 votes. In the "British Vocal Section," the section they had been near the bottom of the year before, they polled 18,623 votes. The second group, the Searchers, were miles away with only 2,169 votes. The two highest-selling singles of the year were "She Loves You" with 1.3 million and "I Want to Hold Your Hand" with 1.25 million. Cliff Richard with "Bachelor Boy" was a long way down in third place.

The *Times* musical critic, William Mann, did a long and serious review of their music in which he said John Lennon and Paul McCartney were "the outstanding English composers of 1963."

"I think I'll invite them down for the weekend, just to see what kind of fellas they are," said Viscount Montgomery.

On December 29 in the *Sunday Times,* Richard Buckle, in reviewing John and Paul's music for the ballet *Mods and Rockers,* said they were "the greatest composers since Beethoven."

Chapter 23: U.S.A.

Sandi Stewart is an ordinary American Beatle fan, not silly, not half-witted, just nice and sensible. She was living with her parents in a wealthy middle-class small town in New Hampshire at the end of 1963. She was fifteen and in the ninth grade.

"I was going to the supermarket in the car with my mother one day, in our Jaguar, that's what we had at the time, though that's not important. Over the car radio came 'I Want to Hold Your Hand.' It was the first time I'd ever heard of the Beatles. I went, Wow! What a strange sound. I just couldn't get over it. No tune had ever affected me as much.

"I found a lot of the girls at school had also heard it and felt the same. I remember walking down the street with two of my friends and discussing them. We all said how ugly they looked in their photographs, especially with no collars on their jackets. The music was great, but we thought, they did look ugly.

"Then slowly we changed our minds. I became really interested in pop music, which I'd never been before. I knew about everything they did. I read everything about them. I grew my hair long, because I read they said they liked girls with long hair.

"At the beginning I loved Paul most of all. He was so beautiful. I couldn't pinpoint it. He just seemed very beautiful. I didn't like George, for some reason. I drew in a werewolf's fangs on his face because I didn't like him. I suppose the Beatles were outlets for love and hate. I eventually did like George a bit more.

"Then I went more on John instead of Paul. He seemed so intelligent and witty. His body was very sexy. He became the one I loved passionately. I became obsessed about John. I dreamed about him all the time. We'd compare dreams at school. Tell each other what we did with our favorite Beatle. I knew when I was depressed I could start a dream about John, by lying there thinking about him, then falling asleep.

189

Those dreams were absolutely beautiful. We did a lot of things together, John and I. He made love to me and I'd tell my friends next day. They weren't all sexual, but a lot were. They were so real.

"I talked and thought about them nonstop. My father was always telling me I'd get over them. I'd shout Never, Never, Never!

"It was funny though. Even though I loved John so much, it didn't stop me chasing other boys at school. That was sort of different. But John was the most important person in my life. I read all the fan mags and listened to Murray the K all the time. He was the disk jockey who was the sort-of Beatles expert.

"I got so desperate about John that I wrote a letter to Cynthia. I was very nice in the letter. I just told her I was very sorry, but I loved her husband. I never got a reply. I got all their records and had their photographs all over my bedroom. When I saw a photograph of them in half shadows my friends and I all went into town and got our photographs taken the same way.

"When absolutely nothing else in life was good, I'd go to my room and have the Beatles, especially my darling John. They all furnished something I desperately needed. The sort of rich community I lived in in New Hampshire gave me nothing. I didn't like school and I didn't like home. They gave me something to live for when everything was black and depressing.

"When I heard they were coming to Carnegie Hall in New York, I planned with two of my school friends to go and see them. We pleaded and pleaded, as we weren't allowed to go to New York on our own. No teenage girl is, from our sort of homes. We said it could be our special birthday treat, or we'd run away. . . ."

This Carnegie Hall concert was to be promoted by Sid Bernstein, a short, tubby ex-Columbia University student, ex-ballroom manager, ex-promoter who had become an agent with General Artists Corporation, one of the biggest agencies in America. Throughout his attempts to break into showbusiness big time he'd kept up his academic interests.

For ten years he'd gone to evening classes, specializing in English government. "I remember going to hear your Harold Laski give a lecture. He was one of the finest speakers I ever heard. After Churchill, of course." Bernstein's interest in English government led him to read the British newspapers. In mid-1963, something caught his attention. "I kept on reading about these Beatles. I was supposed to be specializing in teenage music at GAC, yet I'd never heard of them. Nobody in the business bothered about the English scene."

He took out subscriptions to all the English newspapers and decided to ring Brian Epstein. After a lot of difficulty, he got his home number in Liverpool. He said who he was and Brian had never heard of him. He asked him if he'd like his Beatles to appear at Carnegie Hall, though he hadn't actually got Carnegie Hall. "Brian said when and I said what about February 12. I chose this day because it was Lincoln's birthday and I knew I'd be able to get it. I offered him $6500 for two shows." Brian didn't say yes immediately. It took some time to work out, although the dates sounded fine as he'd already fixed up two Ed Sullivan shows, on February 9 and 16.

Sid Bernstein was made, just by getting in first as the New York promoter. He soon left agency work and branched out on his own with a partner. He promoted all the Beatles' New York shows except one. His story, of getting in first, could be duplicated all over the States, and all over the world.

But it wasn't all Sid Bernstein's doing, as far as New York was concerned. Brian had been working on launching the Beatles in America from the summer of 1963. But he wasn't sure if the Beatles were ready, because at first they had been a failure in the States. In the first half of 1963 they'd had two records out in the States, each by a different record company, and they'd gotten nowhere. Once their success in Britain was assured, Brian went over to New York with Billy J. Kramer in November 1963, the month President Kennedy was assassinated.

"I wanted to find out why the biggest thing in British pop that anyone had ever known hadn't happened in America. It was like the early days in London in 1962. I started going the rounds of recording firms and television people." During this trip he met his old friend Geoffrey Ellis, who'd lived beside him in Liverpool but had gone to Oxford and then into insurance in New York.

"I'd vaguely heard Brian was involved with some sort of beat group, but I didn't believe it. It sounded a lot of rubbish, not something shy little Brian would get mixed up in.

"I was walking down Broadway with Brian and Billy J. Kramer. We got to Times Square and Billy wanted to buy an awful shirt they have in those awful shops round there. Brian said no, he couldn't. He said, 'It's not your image, Billy.' That was the first time I realized that Brian was seriously in all this and that he had changed."

Brian arranged for Capitol Records to record the Beatles this time. Capitol, although a subsidiary of EMI, hadn't been very keen on the Beatles at first which was why the two other American companies had issued them, though with little success.

Brian got an appointment with Ed Sullivan, whose TV show is the biggest of its kind in the United States. His talent scouts had already passed on the word about the Beatles' success in Britain. After a lot of discussion, Ed Sullivan agreed to book the Beatles for two of his shows.

Brian insisted that they should get top billing on both shows. "This was contested vaguely by Ed Sullivan. He saw the coming importance of the Beatles, but he rejected my view that they were going to be the biggest thing in the world. He agreed in the end, but his producer later told me that Sullivan had said it was ridiculous to give a British group top billing when a British group had never made it big in the States before."

The Beatles themselves were very nervous at the idea of America. George had been there for a short holiday earlier in 1963. He said the natives were quite human and he thought they might be all right. He'd been to see his sister Louise, who by this time had married an American and had emigrated from Liverpool to St. Louis. Like her mother, Mrs. Harrison, she was a devoted Beatle fan and rang up her local radio stations, requesting Beatle numbers.

But John was worried because no British groups or singers had ever got through in America before. "Cliff went there and died. He was fourteenth on the bill with Frankie Avalon." George said he'd seen Cliff's film *Summer Holiday* reduced to the second feature in a drive-in in St. Louis.

In January 1963 "I Want to Hold Your Hand" entered the U.S. charts at 83. In Britain it was at last knocked from the top, after two months, by what many people thought was going to be the new sensation —Dave Clark Five and "Glad All Over."

The London papers went to town on the story, glad of a local pop story for a change, after all the Liverpool successes. The *Daily Express* had a front-page headline which said TOTTENHAM SOUND HAS CRUSHED THE BEATLES.

The cartoonists, after almost six months of having to think up Liverpool jokes, jumped at the idea of the Beatles being finished. Vicky in the London *Evening Standard* had the Cabinet in Beatle haircuts with the Prime Minister saying to them: "How can I say you're with it, with old-fashioned haircuts like that?" For a while the Beatles themselves were worried. "We couldn't help it," says John. "Everyone was telling us Dave Clark is coming, you've had it now. It worried us, but just for a minute, the way we'd worried in Liverpool that Gerry would beat us in the *Mersey Beat* poll."

Before America, Brian had arranged the Beatles' second continental trip. This was three weeks in France, playing at the Olympia in Paris, starting on January 15. Several thousand fans saw the three Beatles off from London Airport. Ringo had been delayed by fog in Liverpool and followed later. When he left London Airport he held up a sign saying *TLES* after the initials *BEA* on the plane. Osbert Lancaster in his *Daily Express* cartoon had Napoleon with a Beatles haircut.

The first concert at the Olympia was not a success, the first poor reception, in Beatle terms, they'd had in almost a year of touring. There was a fist fight involving photographers, French policemen, and Brian Sommerville, the Beatles' new publicity man who was now responsible for handling the press on tour. They did get a bit of clapping and John replied *"Mersey beaucoup."*

BBC interviewer in Paris: How important is it for you to succeed here?

Paul: It is important to succeed anywhere.

BBC: The French have not made up their minds about the Beatles. What do you think of them?

John: Oh, we like the Beatles. They're gear.

In America, in its second week, "I Want to Hold Your Hand" got to 42. Norman Weiss from GAC in New York came to see Brian, made final the Carnegie Hall deal, and arranged to become the Beatles' agents in America from then on.

In London, the *Daily Mail,* in its report from Vincent Mulchrone (who was with the Beatles), said: "If Paris and the Beatles are going to have an affair, it's getting off to a slow start. Either the Champs-Élysées was not in mobbing mood today, or Beatlemania is still, like Britain's entry into the Common Market, a problem the French prefer to put off for a while."

The Beatles were in their suite at the George V hotel in Paris when the news came through that "I Want to Hold Your Hand" had got to number one in America. George Martin was with them, having come across to listen to their new songs. They had all had a big dinner to celebrate. Brian was photographed eating his dinner with a chamber pot on his head.

American reporters and TV interviewers started arriving in hordes. Paris shops stocked up with Beatle wigs. "She Loves You," having lingered nowhere in the American Hit Parade, suddenly started climbing after "I Want to Hold Your Hand." In the LP charts, "Please Please Me" was just about to get to the top.

The American press, like the English press the previous year, were arriving late but in deadly earnest. "Tell me about your hair-do," asked an American reporter.

"You mean hair-don'ts," said John.

"We were coming out of a swimming baths in Liverpool," said George. "And liked the way it looked."

Sheilah Graham, the syndicated columnist, arrived and asked them which one was which. *Life* came out with a six-page story on the Beatles.

To capitalize on all the free press publicity and the success of their records, Brian persuaded Capitol Records to spend fifty thousand dollars on what they called a "crash publicity program." Five million *The Beatles Are Coming* posters were plastered throughout the States, every disk jockey got a copy of every Beatles record brought out in Britain; Capitol gave out a million copies of a four-page newspaper on the Beatles and photographed its top executives wearing Beatle wigs.

"There was a lot of hype," said Voyle Gilmore, vice-president of Capitol Records. "But all the hype in the world isn't going to sell a bad product."

The Ed Sullivan Show couldn't cope with the demand for tickets—50,000 applied for 728 seats Sid Bernstein could have sold tickets for Carnegie Hall at twice the price. "Even Mrs. Nelson Rockefeller couldn't buy a ticket. I had to give her mine." Brian was offered another New York date, this time at Madison Square Garden, at double the fee for Carnegie Hall, but it was too late to fit in.

As the Beatles left London Airport, on Pan Am flight 101 on February 7, 1964, station WMCA in New York made the first of a series of announcements. "It is now 6:30 A.M. Beatle time. They left London thirty minutes ago. They're out over the Atlantic Ocean heading for New York. The temperature is 32 Beatle degrees." On the plane the Beatles were nervous. They hadn't heard details of all the promotion that was being done, but they had read reports of people criticizing them and saying they were ugly.

Cyn was on the plane with John, the first and only time she went on tour with them. The unfamous George Harrison was there from the Liverpool *Echo*. He thought he'd retired from national news for good when he left London for Liverpool. Now he was setting off on his first of four coast-to-coast trips with a group he'd once refused to write about. George Harrison the journalist says they were all very dubious about what sort of reception they would get. "They all said to me, 'America's got everything, George, so why should they want us?'" People always call George by his Christian name in his stories.

George Harrison, the famous one, said he was ill with flu. "I was worrying about my hair as well. I'd washed it but when it had dried it had gone up a bit."

"We did all feel a bit sick that first time," says Ringo. "We always did, though we never showed it, before anything big. We'd felt a bit sick before the Palladium show. Going to the States was a big step. People said just because we were popular in Britain, why should we be there?"

Neil and Mal were busy on the plane, forging Beatle signatures on photographs to give to any fans. Brian was also busy. Several British businessmen, having failed to get a second with him in London, had decided that 3000 feet above the Atlantic was the best place to get him. They sent little notes to Brian, asking if he would endorse their products. They were all politely refused.

But all the doubts were swept away the minute they saw Kennedy Airport when they landed at one thirty-five in the afternoon. More than 10,000 screaming teenagers were choking the airport. They were all singing "We Love You Beatles, Oh Yes We Do," a song, or at least doggerel, peculiar to American Beatle fans. Capitol was still pursuing its crash publicity, handing each person who got off the plane a Beatle Kit complete with wig, autographed photo, and a button saying *I Like the Beatles*.

They were led eventually to the airport press lounge and faced the biggest press conference they'd ever had. John shouted at them all to shurrup and everyone applauded him.

"Will you sing something for us?"

"We need money first," said John.

"How do you account for your success?"

"We have a press agent."

"What is your ambition?"

"To come to America."

"Do you hope to get haircuts?"

"We had one yesterday."

"Do you hope to take anything home with you?"

"The Rockefeller Center."

"Are you part of a social rebellion against the older generation?"

"It's a dirty lie."

"What about the movement in Detroit to stamp out Beatles?"

"We have a campaign to stamp out Detroit."

"What do you think of Beethoven?"

"I love him," said Ringo. "Especially his poems."

It was chaos at the Plaza Hotel, a hotel that prides itself on its discreet exclusiveness and hadn't checked the professions of the five English businessmen who'd booked some months ago. When a Plaza executive saw his hotel besieged by thousands of screaming teenagers he went on radio and offered the Beatles to any New York hotel who wanted them.

Not that the Beatles were grateful. "What made you pick the Plaza?" a reporter asked George. "I didn't. Our manager did. All I can tell you is that I do not like the food."

George was by this time ill in bed and it appeared he would miss the Ed Sullivan Show. Neil stood in for the rehearsal but George managed the show, filled with dope. The screams echoed across America. The show had a record audience of 73 million. In New York, during the show, not one hubcap from a car was stolen. Throughout America not one major crime was committed by a teenager.

Elvis Presley sent them a congratulatory telegram. Next morning the *Herald Tribune* said they were "75 per cent publicity, 20 per cent haircut and 5 per cent lilting lament." The *Daily News* said: "The Presleyan gyrations and caterwauling were but lukewarm dandelion tea compared to the 100-proof elixir served up by the Beatles." Every paper gave them huge coverage. The analyses were long and complicated. There was another huge press conference. "Do you have a leading lady for your film yet?" "We're trying for the Queen," said George. "She sells."

Billy Graham said he'd broken his strict rule and watched television on the Sabbath, just to see them. "They're a passing phase," he said. "All are symptoms of the uncertainty of the times and the confusion about us." Then the group set off by train for Washington.

"What happened in the States was just like Britain," says Ringo, "only ten times bigger, so I suppose it wasn't like Britain at all. That first Washington crowd was 20,000. We'd only been used to 2000 at home." The Coliseum, where the Washington concert was held, their first one on American soil, is normally used as a boxing ring or baseball field. The Beatles were put on a revolving stage, so the whole audience could see. It meant they were hit from all angles all the time by jellybeans.

"It was terrible," says George. "They hurt. They don't have soft jelly babies in America but hard jellybeans like bullets. Some newspaper had dug out the old joke which we'd forgotten about, when John had once said I'd eaten all his jelly babies. Everywhere we went I got them thrown at me."

Sir Alec Douglas-Home, the British Prime Minister, was due to arrive in Washington the same day. He put his arrival back to the day after, to avoid the Beatle chaos.

That evening they accepted their first and last Embassy invitation. They'd already turned down dinner with Lady Dixon, wife of the British Ambassador in Paris. "We always tried to get out of those crap things," says George. "But that time we got caught. They were always full of snobby people who really loathe our type, but want to see us because we're rich and famous. It's all hypocrisy. They were just trying to get publicity for the Embassy."

Reports of what exactly happened at the Embassy party vary in detail but it started off amicably enough.

"Hello, John," said Sir David Ormsby-Gore (now Lord Harlech) when they arrived.

"I'm not John," said John. "I'm Charlie. That's John."

"Hello, John," said the Ambassador to George.

"I'm not John," said George. "I'm Frank. That's John."

"Oh dear," said the Ambassador.

Several elderly ladies, with glasses of drink in their hands, accosted the Beatles and demanded autographs. Officious junior officials started pushing them around, insisting they speak to people and give autographs. "Sign this," one said to John, who refused. "You'll sign this and like it." Then a young lady guest walked up to Ringo, removed a pair of nail scissors from her purse and started snipping off locks of his hair. John left early, but the others stayed on and saw it out. The Ambassador and his wife said how sorry they were.

Even Brian's charm hadn't managed to calm things down. "Both the Ambassador and his wife were extremely nice," he said later. "But as is so often the way, their friends and guests were not quite as pleasant. The Beatles loathed that reception. Since then they have refused every invitation of that type."

Sir Alec Douglas-Home at last arrived to meet President Johnson. "I liked your advance party," said the President. "But don't you feel they need haircuts?"

The group started back for New York and their Carnegie Hall concert under the usual barrage of press, TV, and fans. The American wheeler-dealers were now out in strength trying to get contracts for Beatles products, at any price. It was estimated in 1964 that $50 million of Beatle goods would be sold in the States. Several unauthorized tape recorded interviews, which no one realized had been done, were brought out as LP records, billed heavily under the Beatles name, much to Brian's annoyance.

More than 6000 were in the audience for each of the two Carnegie Hall Concerts. Sid Bernstein had to turn down David Niven and Shirley MacLaine. Hysterical screams greeted and accompanied the Beatles' two appearances, each only twenty-five minutes long, so the papers reported next day.

Sandi Stewart, the fifteen-year-old fan from New Hampshire, made it, but she didn't think the screams were all that great. She says she heard them much greater at later concerts. "That first concert wasn't all that wild, I mean there wasn't much screaming, nothing like later concerts which were completely wild. I remember being very annoyed with George that first concert, perhaps that was why I didn't like him. He seemed to be standing in the way of Ringo and we couldn't see him. We all shouted at him to get out of the way and let us see Ringo.

"You really do believe they can see you, just you alone, when they're up on the stage. That's why you scream, so they'll notice you. I always felt John could see me. It was like a dream. Just me and John together and no one else.

"Even when you're screaming, you can still hear. All the reporters in the papers always said you couldn't hear anything with all the noise, but you could, even when you were screaming. Their sexy movements made you scream even louder. They were being sexy with you personally. It was an outlet. But I don't think many girls got sexually excited, not at concerts anyway. I didn't myself."

The Beatles then went from New York by plane down to Miami. The pilot wore a Beatle wig. They met Cassius Clay, who said he was the greatest but they were the most beautiful. It was getting near February 25, George's twenty-first birthday. Even though Sandi Stewart didn't like George so much, she still decided to send him a present. "We found out he was staying at the Deauville Hotel in Miami. We sent a registered parcel, figuring that was very clever as he'd have to sign for it and we'd get his autograph. But we didn't.

"It didn't really matter. John was the one I was in love with. I gave him three whole years of my life from then on."

Chapter 24: Britain and Back to the U.S.A.

Back in Liverpool, the Beatles' old schools were getting some strange requests. Teenagers from all over the world were writing for any old desks belonging to the Beatles, or old caps or exercise books. There were soon scores of signed exercise books in circulation, far more than the boys ever had.

"We were getting these very funny letters from girls, mainly in America," says Mr. Pobjoy of the Liverpool Institute. "Asking if our boys would write to them. I thought they were howlingly funny. I decided to tell the boys, for their amusement as well as mine, so I used to read them in the hall after morning prayers. The boys enjoyed them so much that they were convinced for a long time that I was making them all up. I gather that quite a few boys in the end did write to the wretched girls."

The Beatles' parents were also being contacted by a lot of American fans, some of them turning up on their doorsteps, having forced their parents to stop off from London or Paris on their European grand tours to fit in the Dingle and Woolton.

"I'd usually ask the ones who'd come a long way if they'd like some tea," said Jim McCartney. "When they said yes, I'd say there's the kitchen. They'd go in and start screaming and shouting because they'd recognize the kitchen from photographs. They knew more about me than I did myself. Fans would make very good detectives."

On George's twenty-first birthday, Mrs. Harrison was unable to find room in her house for all the cards and presents. Special mail vans had to cope with all the post.

Like the others, Elsie and Harry, Ringo's parents, began to find themselves surrounded, barricaded in their own homes, while fans stole bits of the door or chalked on the walls. "The first time I really noticed how well they were known," says Elsie, "was when we woke up one morning to find a busload of fans knocking at the front door. It was seven o'clock on a Sunday morning. They'd traveled overnight from London. Well, what could I do. I fetched them all in and gave them tea and biscuits. I thought it was marvelous. All that way, just for our Ritchie. They never ate anything. They just wrapped them up to take back as souvenirs.

"They used to climb over the backyard wall, or sleep in the street for days. They were physical wrecks, most of them, but they were just too excited to rest or eat. They'd ask which is his chair? I'd say, sit on them all, love, he has. They always wanted to go up and see his bed as well. They'd lie on it, moaning."

Cyn and Julian had by this time moved out of Mimi's and into a place of their own. She was still avoiding the press as much as possible. "A gang of reporters trailed me round for days, when they found out who I was. They cornered me one day when I was visiting my mother in Hoylake. This reporter chased me all over the place and besieged me in a shop. I managed to dart out the back of it and into a fruit shop next door where I hid for half an hour till he'd gone."

The Beatles came back from America to the usual hysterical scenes. The Prime Minister, Sir Alec Douglas-Home, called them "our best exports" and "a useful contribution to the balance of payments." Mr. Wilson, leader of the Labour Party and a Liverpool MP, didn't like the inference that a fourteenth earl should be trying to cash in. "The Tories are trying to make the Beatles their secret weapon," he said.

They were invited to dinner by the Master and dons of Brasenose College, Oxford, where they asked for jam sandwiches. A Roman Catholic bishop called them a "menace," but Prince Philip met them and thought them good chaps. He had a chat with John about books. They met Mr. Wilson at last, at a Variety Club presentation, and called him Mr. Dobson.

John's first book came out in March. It was called *In His Own Write,* a title suggested by Paul. They discarded another idea, *In His Own Write and Draw,* because most people would miss the pun. Most literary experts and most publishers said it was a stunt which would fail; how could a beat group player write anything that was any good? It went to the top of the best-seller list, beating James Bond. The *Times Literary Supplement* said: "It is worth the attention of anyone who fears for the impoverishment of the English language and the British imagination." John was invited to be guest of honor at Foyle's literary lunch. He didn't speak, and got a few boos for not doing so, but Brian Epstein did.

On March 24 their sixth single, "Can't Buy Me Love," came out.

John and Paul had written it on the way to Miami in February. It went straight to number one. It also went immediately to number one in America. In Britain and America, before it had come out, the advance sales were 3 million, a world record. At one time the group had the top six records on the United States Hit Parade.

Ringo was elected a vice-president of Leeds University in preference to a former Lord Chief Justice. Madame Tussaud's put wax effigies of all four Beatles on display. Paul Johnson in the *New Statesman* did an article headed "The Menace of Beatlism." A writer in the *Sunday Telegraph* said that the group would break up because eventually they would all get married and "the chance of four random women liking one another or even being able to get on with one another will be small indeed."

In March the Beatles started shooting their first film. It wasn't called *A Hard Day's Night* until it was almost finished and Ringo came out with the phrase.

Paul was by this time going out with Jane Asher, daughter of a Harley Street doctor and a professor of music. On the first day of the film, George met Pattie Boyd. Like Jane Asher, she is a girl with a South-of-England middle-class background, completely different from the girls in the other two Beatles' lives. Pattie was working as a model, mainly in magazines. But she did a TV commercial for Smith's Crisps which was very successful. This was directed by Dick Lester, which was how she came to be auditioned for a part in the Beatles' film, despite her not being an actress.

"I met them and they said hello. I couldn't believe it. They were so like how I'd imagined them to be. They were just like pictures of themselves coming to life. George hardly said hello. But the others came and chatted with us.

"When we started filming, I could feel George looking at me and I was a bit embarrassed. Ringo seemed the nicest and easiest to talk to, and so did Paul. But I was terrified of John. After that first day's shooting, I asked them all for their autograph, except John. I was too scared.

"When I was asking George for his, I said could he sign it for my two sisters as well. He signed his name and put two kisses each for them, but under mine he put seven kisses. I thought he must like me a little. He came into our carriage later and talked to Pru and me. She was the other schoolgirl in the film. Then he called me out into the corridor on my own. He said would I go out with him that night. I said, sorry, no."

She said no because she already had a steady boy friend. She'd gone out with him for two years. The following Tuesday George asked her out again, by which time she'd decided her boy friend wasn't so steady. She told him it was all off. After that she went out almost every night with George. "I took him to Mummy's, then he took me to see this house in Esher he was interested in. I thought it was lovely.

"The next weekend was Easter. I went with George, along with John and Cynthia, to Ireland by a private plane for the weekend. It was a dead secret very few people knew, but it got out and there were hordes of press men at the hotel.

"This was my first experience of that sort of thing. The manager tapped their phones and we could hear them sending back the most awful things to Fleet Street. When we went out, they all followed us with cameras.

"It was impossible to get out. In the end Cyn and I had to dress as maids. They took us out a back way, put us in a laundry basket, and we were driven to the airport in a laundry van." Naturally, with all the publicity and gossip interest in her, she was offered even more modeling jobs. "I took a lot, the ones I fancied, but George said I shouldn't. He didn't like it. They were just wanting me for the wrong reasons."

Coming into it all so late, she was more worried by the crowds and press interest than the others. She was also very worried by all the threatening letters, and even physical attacks, which all the girl friends and wives got from girl fans. "The letters upset me a lot. They were really nasty and said awful things, especially from the States. I used to worry that perhaps I was nasty. They always said they were really George's girl friend, I'd better leave him alone or they'd get me."

They moved into George's new house in Esher together. "We lived together for about a year before we got married. My mother knew, but she never mentioned it."

In the summer of 1964, the tours started again. They went to Europe first of all, starting with Denmark. In Amsterdam, Holland, a crowd of 100,000 turned up in the streets to see them. Then they went to Hong Kong, and then to Australia and New Zealand.

Although the American tours had, and always will have, the most publicity associated with the Beatles—because they were beating the Americans at what the Americans had always been leading the world in —the biggest crowd which ever turned out to watch the Beatles was in Adelaide in June 1964. This was a crowd which thronged the streets of Adelaide simply to watch the Beatles arrive. Every newspaper that day put the figure at over 300,000. Numbers like this never turned out to see them in New York, or even in Liverpool on their triumphal return there the following month.

Back in London on July 6, *A Hard Day's Night* had its premiere in front of Princess Margaret and Lord Snowdon. The LP of the film score came out the following month. On August 19, 1964, the Beatles left for their first major American tour. The trip in February had been a short two-week trip with only a couple of concerts and TV shows.

This tour, in August and September, covered in all 32 days. It was the longest, and most exhausting tour they ever did. They traveled in all 22,441 miles, spending a total of sixty hours, twenty-five minutes flying. They visited 24 cities in the United States and Canada. They gave a total of 30 performances, plus one charity show. "During that American tour," says Mal, the read manager, "each of us lost one and half stone in sweat."

Norman Weiss of GAC, their American agent, spent six months planning this tour. "It took about as much planning as the invasion of Normandy. Millions and millions of dollars must have changed hands. It would be impossible to work out what it all cost, from the Beatles' fees down to all the hot dogs sold and films used up. "We could have made a lot more money than we did. They could easily have charged three times the price and still sold out, but Brian said it was unfair to the fans. We had it written into all contracts, stating what the prices had to be. We dictated all the contracts, made the terms ourselves. Every promoter agreed, thankful to be putting them on.

"The Beatles and Elvis are both in show business. After that, any comparison is just a joke. No one, before or since, has had the crowds the Beatles had."

Records were broken everywhere, but to the Beatles themselves it all became meaningless. It was just like it had been yesterday. Even the questions were always the same, what did they think had caused their success and when did they think the bubble would burst? They almost got to screaming point with the endless repetition. They fled to a remote country town for a day's rest and the locals very kindly kept out of the way. But as they were boarding their plane to take off again, the sheriff and other town dignitaries could be seen coming across the tarmac toward them. Derek Taylor, the Beatles' press officer, was sent out to see what they wanted. They said they wanted autographs and photographs standing with the Beatles, which was the least they could do, as they'd been so kind and left them alone.

"I went back on to the plane to ask the boys," says Derek. "Paul was sitting beside the window, looking at them. He was smiling like mad at them, and nodding his head wildly up and down, but he was saying to me, 'Get out there quick. Tell them *we* want to go out and meet them, but *you* won't let us because we're too tired. Go on."

George Harrison, the Liverpool *Echo* one, even became numb by it all. "But I'll never forget this big noise from Kansas City coming to see Brian when we were in San Francisco. Kansas City wasn't on the tour. He was a millionaire, the owner of the local football club or something. He said he'd promised Kansas City that he would get the Beatles for them.

Brian said no. They couldn't fit it in. This bloke said would $100,000 change their mind. Brian said he'd go and ask the boys. They were all sitting playing cards and hardly looked up. Brian told them about the offer of $100,000, which was £30,000 in anybody's money. They said it's up to you, Brian, and went on playing.

"Brian went back and told the man he was terribly sorry. They couldn't give up a day off. He said he'd promised Kansas City and he couldn't go back without them. He tore up the check for $100,000. Then he wrote out one for $150,000. This was the biggest fee ever offered to any artist in America. He was offering them £50,000 for 35 minutes. Brian could see the prestige value of beating all American artists would be fantastic, so he said all right. The Beatles didn't look up when Brian told them.

"So the bloke went home, dead happy. But he knew he couldn't possibly make any money. The ground wasn't big enough to get back anything like he'd had to pay, but he'd kept his promise to Kansas City."

The pillowslips on which they slept in their Kansas City hotel were later sold to two Chicago businessmen for $1000. They cut them into 160,000 one-inch squares, mounted them on certificates saying whose bed it had come from, and sold them at one dollar each. A New York syndicate reportedly offered Brian $10,000,000 for the Beatles, but he turned them down.

During all the shouting and screaming and boasting of their record-breaking tours in Britain and America, the Beatles were crouching somewhere inside the giant piece of machinery which was transporting them round and round the world. They'd retreated inside it in 1963, forced by all the pressures, and remained there, hermetically sealed, as if on a desert island, from all life and reality.

They were trapped in their dressing room during a performance. There was the mad dash, guarded by hordes of police and bodyguards, to the hotel. There they stayed, with the outside world locked out, till the time came for the next move. They never went out in the street, to a restaurant or for a walk. Neil and Mal serviced them, bringing sandwiches, ciggies, and drinks. Out of jealousy, and sometimes out of fear of being left unprotected, they wouldn't let Mal or Neil go out either. So they all sat in their hotel bedrooms, smoking, playing cards, playing their guitars, putting in the hours. Earning £1000 or £10,000 or £100,000 for one-night stands was meaningless. Being rich and powerful and famous enough to enter any door was pointless. They were trapped.

For a long time, of course, there was great excitement. They had waited so long for this. Seven years they'd been playing together and getting nowhere, which at least meant they were up to all the one-night stands, physically and emotionally. Even the one-night stands weren't as strenuous as the Hamburg clubs, where they'd really learned to churn it out endlessly.

So many stages came one after the other so quickly that they never got bored or complained about the slowness, at least for some time. They all remember the excitement of going from one peak to another. Getting a record in the charts, then one at number one, then another, then TV shows, the Palladium, the Royal Variety tours, and then America.

Although John, Paul, and George were not taken in or affected by all the publicity, they considered themselves good. They knew their music was good and were annoyed when anyone didn't take it seriously. Because they knew what they could do they didn't for one minute consider, as so many people did, that they would just disappear. They knew that at last they were in and couldn't see any reason why they shouldn't stay in. This probably explains part of their attitude to the press. They didn't feel grateful or in any way humble. They didn't care about being rude because they didn't consider they owed anything to anybody.

Only Ringo was in any way rubbing his eyes about it all. It had all suddenly happened to him. He joined them, then immediately they were off and away.

"None of us ever worried about things like the future. I've always just taken chances myself and been lucky. I was luck to get an apprenticeship when I did. I was lucky giving it up when I did, yet never being out of work. I've always had a few bob in my pocket.

"But I always thought that it was bound to come to an end sometime.

"There were good nights and bad nights on the tours," says Ringo. "But they were really all the same. The only fun part was the hotels in the evening, smoking pot and that."

Chapter 25: The End of Touring

Throughout the next two years, 1965 and 1966, the Beatles' life was dominated by touring, which really meant no life at all.

They averaged three long tours a year—one British, one American, and one other foreign tour, taking in several countries. They produced around three singles a year and one LP. They also aimed to do one film a year, but after their second film (*Help!* in 1965) they came to a halt. It wasn't until the end of this two-year grind that their lives and their work began to settle down into new patterns.

The details of all their tours are in newspaper files somewhere for anyone mad enough to want to look them up. The Beatles certainly can't remember. As always, they can only remember the laughs, such as their MBE.

On June 12, 1965, it was announced that the Beatles were to be made Members of the Order of the British Empire. There were immediate protests, from members of the House of Lords to ancient wartime fire watchers who felt their MBE had been cheapened. A retired Colonel said he wasn't going to give the Labour Party a £11,000 bequest after all, or his 12 military medals. MBE medals were sent back from all over the world.

Brian was very much pleased about the honor. He said later he never had any doubt that the Beatles would accept it, but John says he seriously thought about saying no. Today his MBE sits on the TV in Mimi's bungalow.

"We thought getting the MBE was as funny as everybody else thought it was. Why? What for? We didn't believe it. It was a part we didn't want. We all met and agreed it was daft. What do you think, we all said. Let's not. Then it all just seemed part of the game we'd agreed to play, like getting the Ivor Novello awards. We'd nothing to lose, except that bit of you which said you didn't believe in it. We agreed in order to annoy even more the people who were annoyed, like John Gordon. We were just getting at the people who believe in such things.

"All we did when we were waiting in the Palace was giggle. We collapsed, the whole thing was so funny. There was this Guardsman telling us how to march, how many steps, and how to curtsey when we met the Queen. We knew in our hearts she was just some woman, yet we were going through it all. We'd agreed to it.

"I really think the Queen believes in it all. She must. I don't believe in John Lennon, Beatle, being any different from anyone else, because I know he's not. I'm just a feller. But I'm sure the Queen must think she's different.

"I always hated all the social things. All the horrible events and presentations we had to go to. All false. You could see right through them all and all the people there. I despised them. Perhaps it was partly from class. No, it wasn't. It was because they really *were* all false."

Some of the 1965–1966 tours have to be mentioned, if only as a brief record, especially the two other American tours. The third American tour began on August 13, 1965. It was decided to keep it to half the length of the previous one as that had been too exhausting. This tour covered 17 days and was insured for a million pounds, which was what the last tour had taken. It made even more money than the previous one, though it was half the length, because they concentrated on baseball grounds which they had pioneered the time before.

The biggest event of this tour of America was on August 23, 1965. This was when they played at the Shea Stadium, New York. "Over 55,000 people saw that show," says Sid Bernstein. "We took in $304,-000, the greatest gross ever in the history of show business." This is still a world record. It wasn't beaten during their subsequent American tour. Out of the $304,000 the Beatles got $160,000. More than $30,000 went on the rent of the stadium for the night. There were 130 police on duty, which cost $14,000. Insurance came to $11,000. After advertising, publicity, and other expenses, Sid Bernstein's profit on the evening came to $7,000.

"I could still do it again today. The Beatles are as popular in the United States as they ever were. I've offered them one million dollars for two shows at Shea Stadium. That offer still stands. It would have to be exclusive in the U.S.A. One million dollars. That's my offer."

Exactly a year later, in August 1966, the Beatles did their fourth and final American tour. This was again a short one, but it made the most money of all. Nat Weiss, who had been appointed head of Nemperor

Help me if you can I'm feeling down
And I do appreciate you being round
Help me get my feet back on the ground
Won't you please help me

When I was younger so much younger than I am today
I never needed anybody's help in anyway
But now these days are gone And I'm not so self assured
Now I find I've changed my mind
And opened up the doors.

Help I need someone
... And I just need love
Help You know I need someone
Help me

Artists, helped to organize it. He had been practicing in New York as a divorce attorney for fifteen years when he met Brian Epstein socially, and through him became interested in pop music. In June 1966 Brian decided to bring all the Nems bits and pieces in America under one office. Nemperor was named after the cable address of Nems.

It was during this tour that John's remark about Jesus Christ hit America. He had originally said that the Beatles "were now more popular than Christ" several months previously in a Maureen Cleave interview in the *Evening Standard*. No one had objected or remarked on it publicly. But when it was reproduced and went round America, out of context, it caused a furor.

"A friend rang me to say they were burning Beatle records in Nashville, Tennessee," says Nat Weiss. "I rang Brian and said I thought it serious enough to warrant his arrival in New York."

Brian was very worried, as the Ku Klux Klan came out and Beatle effigies were burned throughout the Bible Belt. He considered canceling several appearances, even though it would have meant paying back one million dollars. "I didn't want any chance of the boys being harmed, whatever the cost." But the promoters and mayors and local officials said there would be much more trouble from fans if any concerts were canceled. A slight retraction was put out from John, saying he hadn't meant it, and the tour went off. The concerts in the Bible Belt were the best of all.

Other foreign tours during these two years included France, Italy, Spain, and Germany (a huge welcome in Hamburg). From Germany, in June 1966, they flew to Tokyo for their one and only Japanese series of concerts. The Japanese Beatle fans turned out to be the most knowledgeable of all, judging by the program they produced for the concerts. This was the most lavish and exhaustive program for any of their concerts anywhere. It contained, among other academic information, the title of every song they'd ever sung up to that time and its chart position. Nobody in London had ever worked it out in such detail. Brian kept a copy of it in his desk as a work of reference.

From Japan, they returned home via Manila, and wished they hadn't. This visit resulted in the first and only scene of real violence throughout their touring career. All those times they'd nearly been killed in Britain and America were due to overaffection. In Manila they were kicked and punched by the crowds and the police. This was the result of a supposed act of discourtesy toward the President's wife. She expected them to turn up at the Palace after she had invited them. They said they'd never been invited. The President's wife was deeply hurt.

In Britain, Beatlemania hardly abated. The switchboard at University College Hospital was jammed when Ringo had his tonsils out. Hourly bulletins were issued. Thousands of fans wrote asking for his old tonsils. Ringo announced that no one was getting them. They were to be burned.

In October 1965, the Queen and Prince Philip were on tour in Canada. One of the biggest stories of the tour in the British press was when Prince Philip was quoted as saying that the Beatles were "on the wane." This got headlines everywhere. The London *Evening Standard* did a poll to find out if it was true; five out of seven said it wasn't true. A couple of days later Brian Epstein got a personal telegram from Prince Philip in which he explained that what he'd really said was "I think the Beatles are away."

This shows that famous personages were still coming out with Beatle references and were very much worried if they came out wrong. But more than that, it shows there was now a bit of wishful thinking around. Everybody was sure the Beatles must be on the wane. They couldn't possibly keep the same pace up.

But they were waxing as strongly as ever. After each wave of bubble-pricking, they brought out yet another record which went straight to number one. In December 1965, when "Day Tripper" came out and went direct to number one, it was their tenth consecutive record which had become number one on the British charts.

That same month, December 1965, they started what was to become, although no one said so at the time, their last British tour. They did one concert after that, on May 1, 1966, at Wembley, which is the last live concert the Beatles have done in Britain. At long last, one of their singles didn't reach number one. This was "Paperback Writer," in June 1966. Even more surprisingly, because it was much better, "Penny Lane" and "Strawberry Fields," in February 1967, didn't get to number one either. Perhaps by that time the fans knew they were never going to see the Beatles singing in the flesh again.

Their last live appearance anywhere in the world was at the end of their American tour, on August 29, 1966. "During that last show in San Francisco," says Nat Weiss, "Brian was very sad and almost pathetic. It was the first time I'd ever seen him pathetic. He suddenly said, 'What do I do now? What happens to my life? That's it. Should I go back to school and learn something else?'

"He was obviously greatly saddened. Then he took hold of himself and said no. He *would* carry on and do something."

There was no denial or confirmation about giving up touring when they came back to England. This led to some confusion, and rumors began spreading that they were splitting up. The fan club and *Beatles Monthly* were swamped by letters from fans. Mrs. Harrison, George's mother, got so fed up answering the same query that she had several hundred copies of a letter duplicated, saying they were *not* splitting. They were very busy doing a long-playing record which would keep them going all over Christmas. "So I think this proves that they have no plans what-so-ever for parting company. All my best wishes. Louise Harrison. (Mrs)"

They had decided for some time to stop touring, but it was difficult, because of contractual arrangements, to say so straight away. Arthur Howes, for example, had been hoping for another British tour. British fans had felt out of it for a long time. Since their first number-one days, they had been seen live by far more people in the States, on their four tours before huge open-air audiences, than on their seven tours round the smaller British halls and theaters.

There was no definite agreement with Arthur Howes which they had to get out of, just the natural expectation which he had that they'd go on for a bit longer.

"In this field," Howes says, "I look upon the life of an artist as five years. I know, because that's how it always happens. After five years, their generation has grown up and there are new artists with new audiences. The Beatles are different. The Beatles will last for ever. They've no need to worry. But I did, when they stopped touring in 1965. They didn't even do three years of touring."

In Britain a full house at the biggest theaters in Manchester, Birmingham, or Glasgow is only around the 2500 mark. The biggest theater in Britain of the type used for packaged shows is the Hammersmith Odeon, which seats 4000. Even ten full houses in Hammersmith still wouldn't equal a full house at Shea Stadium, which attracted 55,000 for the Beatles' first concert.

Because of the high percentage the Beatles took—50 per cent in the end—and also because they toured for such a comparatively short time, Mr. Howes made more from touring Cliff Richard than he made from the Beatles. Between October 1958 and February 1963, Cliff Richard did eleven tours with Arthur Howes. Between February 1963 and December 1965, the Beatles did seven tours, six of them with Arthur Howes.

"The biggest thing the Beatles did was to open up the American market to all British artists. Nobody had ever been able to get in before the Beatles. They alone did it. I had brought over lots of American stars, but nobody had gone over there. They just weren't interested. By opening up the States, the Beatles made an enormous amount of money for this country."

Once it was made clear to Arthur Howes and to various other people that touring was over, the Beatles let it be known publicly. One of the reasons given was that their music had developed so much, using full orchestras and electronic devices, that they couldn't possibly perform it onstage any more.

This is true to a great extent. But the real reason was that for a long, long time they had hated what they were doing. They disliked dragging around the world, appearing publicly in a glass box like a peep show. They disliked performing onstage in the same old way. They thought it was a farce, a mockery. Neil and Mal, their road managers, disliked the tensions, the panic and the chaos of it all.

"Open-air concerts in the States were terrible," says Mal. "We were in this baseball field once. There they were, stuck out on their own in the middle of the field with 30,000 kids screaming and waiting to hear them. I said to the promoter, where's the outlet, chief? He said, 'What? They play guitars, don't they?' He hadn't realized they used *electric* guitars. We had a right panic getting electricians to lay on wires in time.

"When it looked like rain in the open air I used to be scared stiff. Rain on the wires and everybody would have been blown up, yet if they'd stopped the show, the kids would have stampeded."

"We learned always to go on at the very last minute, if not later," says Neil. "If we went too early they just got mobbed on the way from the dressing room. But if they had to run like mad after they were supposed to be on, people would get out of the way and let them through. We did this with our first Ed Sullivan show in New York. He was sweating like a pig, convinced we were going to be late. It was a live show as well. He blamed me for it all, for just doing it."

"Touring was dangerous sometimes," says Ringo, "but we never thought about it. A plane did catch fire once in Texas and scared everyone. We flew from Liverpool to London once with a window open. We were a bit worried when our death was predicted on a plane in the States. That wasn't nice."

This was by a woman who had predicted President Kennedy's death. Some of the other acts refused to go on the Beatles' plane. Mal wrote his last letter to his wife, Lil, convinced he was going to die.

"There was one near escape at the Cow Palace in the States. The crowds surged forwards and got on the limousine we were supposed to be in. They got on top and squashed the roof in. We could have been killed, but we were safe in an ambulance with seven sailors, for some reason. That's how they were smuggling us that time.

"It was just one long hustle. You'd have a hustle with the police, then the theater people, then the hotel people. We always thought we were safe when we got into our hotel rooms, but we'd have to contend with the hotel staff as well, wanting autographs. You could see them thinking why not, what's the matter with you, you've only worked half an hour today. But we'd probably traveled 2000 miles since the last half hour and not eaten or slept properly for two weeks.

"The American police could be as bad as anybody, demanding autographs. I caught one once going through our pockets."

George says that as early as the first big American tour they were all beginning to dislike it. Even making the tours shorter didn't make them any more enjoyable.

"It was like the end of a cycle. In Hamburg we had played for up to eight hours at a stretch, loving it all, getting to know each other and what we could do. It was a real freak-out in those days; the things we did were really wild.

"Back in Liverpool we were doing shorter hours, but it was still as enjoyable. We were part of the audience. We lived our lives with them. We never rehearsed an act. We had to get more polished eventually, but the Cavern was fantastic. It was so spontaneous, all jokes and laughs. It was so intimate.

"Then came touring, which was great at first, doing an even shorter, more polished act and working out new songs. But it got played out. We got in a rut, going round the world. It was a different audience each day, but we were doing the same things. There was no satisfaction in it. Nobody could hear. It was just a bloody big row. We got worse as musicians, playing the same old junk every day. There was no satisfaction at all."

"It was wrecking our playing," says Ringo. "The noise of the people just drowned anything. Eventually I just used to play the off beat, instead of a constant beat. I couldn't hear myself half the time, even on the amps, with all the noise.

"We'd get put in silly positions in the halls so we'd be too far away from each other. Onstage we used to play things faster than on the records, mainly because we couldn't hear what we were doing. I used to come in at the wrong time sometimes because I'd no idea where we were at. We just used to mime half the time to the songs, especially if your throat was feeling rough.

"No one eventually enjoyed touring. You can't really. Once you've got to manufacture it, it doesn't work. You've got to give to receive. Some nights we'd feel it had been terrible. We didn't give anything. That was when we decided we should give it up, before others started disliking it as well."

"When we were away from it for a while," says John, "it was like the school holidays. You hadn't done any work for a bit and you'd just remember the laughs. You'd quite look forwards to it again. Until you got back and were fed up.

"It's like the Army, whatever the Army's like. One big sameness which you have to go through. One big mess. I can't remember any tours. We've had enough of performing forever. I can't imagine any reason which would make us do any sort of tour ever again."

Paul says they would do a live stage show if they could think of a way of doing a stage show which was completely different. But nobody can think of a new way. It looks as if Sid Bernstein will be keeping his million dollars.

It was a brave step, in some ways, to give up doing what had made their name. Very few people, certainly in show business, have given up at the height of their adulation. People often say they intend to give up the public before the public gives up them, but they usually do it too late.

The Beatles had no hesitation. They saw it as the end of Chapter One. Being naïve and simple, they did it without knowing what Chapter Two was going to be. All they knew was that it didn't include the drag of touring and the discomfort of Beatlemania.

Chapter 26: The Death of Brian Epstein

It was the end of a chapter when the Beatles stopped touring, as Brian Epstein had realized that time in San Francisco. But Brian was resolved, so he told Nat Weiss, to go on and do something else. Which he did, for a time.

Nems Enterprises had grown into a huge organization, handling many other artists apart from the Beatles—Cilla Black, Gerry and the Pacemakers, and many others. They moved into the agency business, they took on a theater—The Saville—as well as continuing and expanding as artists' managers.

Although his staff had grown so much since the Liverpool days, the more important personnel were still old friends and contacts from Liverpool. Alistair Taylor, Brian's assistant on the counter at Nems who had signed the original contract with the Beatles, rejoined the firm in 1963, after a spell with Pye records. More important, Geoffrey Ellis and Peter Brown, his two oldest Liverpool friends, also joined Nems in London.

Geoffrey Ellis, the ex-Oxford insurance man in New York, saw a lot of Brian on his American trips and was eventually persuaded to join Nems in London. His legal knowledge was invaluable in dealing with all contracts. He joined Nems in October 1964 as senior executive, becoming a director the following year.

Peter Brown didn't leave Nems in Liverpool until mid-1965. He had had nothing to do with the Beatle business until then, continuing simply to manage the record store in Whitechapel, which Brian had given up. But in June 1964, Harry Epstein, Brian's father, decided to sell most of his shops, although his other son Clive stayed on as managing director.

Peter Brown stayed on as well for a while, but didn't see eye to eye with the new owners. Brian offered him a job instead in Nems Enterprises in London. "I was a bit worried at first, working so closely with

Brian again, that it might lead to rows as it had done before. But it worked very well." He became Brian's personal assistant, taking over from Wendy Hanson.

In early 1967 Brian bought a country home in Sussex which Peter found for him. This was a large, historic country mansion at Kingsley Hill near Heathfield. It cost £25,000.

He also took on a personal secretary, Joanne Newfield, a niece of Joe Loss. She worked from an office at the top of his London house in Chapel Street, Belgravia. This was necessary as he did so much of his work at home.

This was the setting then of the life of Brian Epstein in the summer of 1967. He was thirty-two, rich, good-looking, charming, popular, and gay. He was a household name, known for spotting talent, associated by everyone with the success of the Beatles. He had many other artists and many other interests, particularly the Saville. His ventures there were getting a lot of attention from the press.

He was completely happy and fulfilled, as far the public could see. According to the *Financial Times* in the summer of 1967, they worked out that he was worth seven million pounds. The true figure turned out to be a great deal less, but Brian Epstein was rich enough not to have any money worries for the rest of his life.

Mrs. Queenie Epstein, Brian's mother, arrived in London on August 14, 1967, to spend ten days with her elder son at his Belgravia home. She returned to Liverpool on Thursday, August 24.

She was in rather a distressed state when she arrived. Her husband Harry had died the preceding month, which had upset Brian a great deal as well. Brian went out of his way to make her stay as happy and pleasant as possible. He was organizing a flat for her in Knightsbridge, as it had been decided she should now move to London from Liverpool. He wanted her to be as near him as possible.

Brian altered his normal daily habits to suit and please his mother. Instead of rising very late and going to bed very late, which had become his habit, he managed to be awake and ready each morning when his mother came into his bedroom to draw his curtains. About ten o'clock, he and his mother had breakfast together in his bedroom. She then saw him off bright and early to his office in Mayfair, which was something else which hadn't been his normal habit for a long time.

Throughout the ten days of his mother's stay he went into his office every morning and worked there all day. He came home, at a normal coming-home-from-the-office time, and had a meal with his mother.

Then they'd watch color TV together, have a cup of cocoa, and go to bed, always well before midnight.

Both Joanne and Peter Brown say he didn't dislike doing all this. He obviously preferred his usual habits, but he knew it gave his mother pleasure. He loved her and knew that she loved him, so he wanted her to enjoy her stay.

"I went to visit her after she'd been there five days, on the afternoon of Friday, August 18. We had tea and talked about Brian's childhood. They were obviously very close and affectionate. Brian showed me out. He talked about his forthcoming visit to the United States and Canada. He was going to appear on a big TV spectacular, as the MC, which he was obviously looking forward to. We made arrangements for me to spend the weekend with him in Sussex on his return."

His mother left the following Thursday for Liverpool. On Thursday evening he had his first night out for almost two weeks, but this was just a quiet dinner with Simon Napier-Bell at Carrier's Restaurant in Islington. What he was looking forward to most of all was the long August bank holiday weekend at his country house. He invited Simon Napier-Bell, but he said no as he had to go to Ireland.

"Brian left on Friday about three thirty," says Joanne. "He was all smiling and happy. He told me to have a lovely weekend and he'd see me on Tuesday. I watched him drive off with the roof of his Bentley down, waving at me."

She knew that his two oldest and closest friends and colleagues, Peter Brown and Geoffrey Ellis, were also due to go down to Sussex for the weekend with Brian. She heard from Peter later in the afternoon that he would be setting off much later than he'd intended. She realized that Brian would therefore be down there for a few hours on his own. She hoped Peter wouldn't be too late for dinner.

"I did get there in time for dinner," says Peter Brown. "We had a very good meal, just the three of us, with a bottle of wine and a couple of ports afterwards. I was supposed to be bringing some other people down with me, but at the last moment they hadn't turned up. Brian was very disappointed by this. It was his first weekend off for a bit and he was looking forward to enjoying himself, meeting a few new people. He didn't really fancy just spending it with his two oldest and very familiar friends."

Brian rang a few numbers in London, trying to contact people, but it was a Friday night before a long August bank holiday weekend and no one was available. Around ten o'clock, Brian decided to go back to London instead.

This wasn't such a strange decision as it might appear. It was typical of him to suddenly change his mind. He often walked out of his own parties in the middle, parties which he'd spent weeks preparing. As far as Brian was concerned, the weekend in Sussex was going to be boring, after looking forward to it for so long. London seemed the only place to find some excitement.

"I walked with him to the car," says Peter Brown. "I said he was soft going back to London at this time. He said I hadn't to worry. He'd be all right. He was slightly drunk, with the big meal, but nothing much. He said don't worry. He'd be back in the morning before I was up."

Not long after Brian left, a party of visitors did arrive by cab from London, in answer to one of his calls. But it was too late, he'd gone, though Peter Brown half thought he'd perhaps only gone for a drive round the local countryside and would soon return. But by twelve thirty, when he hadn't, Peter Brown started ringing Chapel Street to see if he had arrived. Antonio answered the telephone. He and his wife Maria were Brian's Spanish butler and housekeeper at Chapel Street. Antonio said Brian had returned. He buzzed Brian's intercom in his bedroom to say Mr. Ellis was on the phone, but he got no reply. Geoffrey and Peter weren't worried. They were satisfied Brian had arrived safely and was now, presumably, asleep.

Peter Brown and Geoffrey Ellis rose late the next morning, Saturday, in Sussex. Brian hadn't reappeared, but they didn't really expect him to. They didn't bother to ring him, assuming he was still sleeping. But Brian himself rang Peter about five o'clock on the Saturday afternoon.

"He was very apologetic for not having come back in the morning, as he'd said he would. He said he'd been sleeping all day and was still feeling drowsy. I said he'd better not drive back. If he got the train down to Lewes I'd meet him there. He agreed that was best, but he was still too dopey to start off. He was always drowsy when he woke up after taking sleeping pills. He said he'd ring back later, when he felt more like it, so I'd know when he was starting off. That was how we left it." But Brian didn't ring back.

By Sunday lunchtime at Chapel Street, when Brian hadn't wakened, Antonio and his wife Maria began to get worried. It wasn't unusual for him to be still sleeping at lunch time, but he hadn't been out of his bedroom, as far as they knew, since he'd returned from Sussex on the Friday evening. His Bentley stayed in the same position all weekend, because they specially noticed it. They also never heard him moving about, apart from breakfast on Saturday, which they say they would have done, if he'd got up or gone out after that. At twelve thirty they tried to ring Peter

Brown at Sussex to tell him their worries, but he was out at the pub. So they rang Joanne at her home in Edgware.

"Maria spoke to me and sounded very worried. She said Brian had been in his bedroom for so long, which was very unusual. I was very worried. I phoned Peter but couldn't get him. So I rang Alistair Taylor and told him. I said I was driving across to Brian's and I'd meet him there. I tried to contact Brian's doctor, but he was in Spain; then I got my car out."

Peter and Geoffrey got back from the pub just before two o'clock to find the housekeeper had several messages for them.

"I rang Chapel Street," says Peter, "and spoke to Antonio, who told me they were all very worried about Brian. He said Joanne and Alistair were on their way across. I told him there was nothing at all to worry about. I assumed Brian must have gone out on Saturday night and was sleeping late. I said they were all just panicking. I told him to stop Alistair coming if he could."

Joanne arrived at Chapel Street. She found Antonio and Maria still very agitated, despite Peter's reassurances. She rang Peter. He told her there was still no need to panic, but perhaps she should ring his doctor and get him to come round, just in case.

When the doctor came she rang Peter Brown again. Peter held on on the telephone, waiting to hear what the doctor had to say.

"The doctor and I went in," says Joanne. "The room was dark and I saw Brian, lying on the bed. He was on his side with his back to us. The doctor pushed me out of the room. I came out and told Maria and Antonio that it was all right, Brian was just asleep.

"Then John, the doctor, came out, all white and shaken, and said Brian was dead. He went to pick up Peter's phone to tell him."

"He couldn't get any words out," said Peter. "So I knew what happened." Peter and Geoffrey immediately contacted the Beatles in Bangor, then got into their car and came up to London. In an hour from the body being found, the *Daily Express* was ringing to ask if it was true that Brian Epstein was dead. They were told it wasn't true.

The next day it was on the front page of every paper. The *Times* obituary was across three columns at the top of the page. The man in the street seemed to think it was suicide. It is always comforting for those who have never had wealth, fame, or power to believe that those who have are of course not *really* happy.

Brian Epstein could be very happy and he could be very unhappy. His unhappiness hadn't been caused by the Beatles or even by success.

"In Liverpool, he always had depressions," says Peter Brown. "Not as bad or as long as later, but they were there, long before the Beatles came along."

The causes and origins of his mental state at the time of his death had been with him throughout his life. But it was during the year leading up to his death in August 1967 that many things came to a head.

"When he was in a depressed state," says Joanne, "it would just take a little thing to finally knock him out. There was once when he was trying to contact Nat Weiss, who was over in London from New York. He went round to the Grosvenor House hotel to see him, but couldn't find him. He came back furious and started ringing the hotel. For some reason I gave him the wrong number—I gave him MAY 6363 instead of GRO 8363. So he was getting nowhere. When I discovered my mistake, he was terribly angry."

Peter Brown says one of the troubles was that Brian was a perfectionist. If anything went wrong, or people interfered or spoiled perfect plans, it could throw him completely. He was so meticulous, exact, and organized himself. Those early memos to the Beatles, telling them which ballroom to be at and not to swear on stage, were models of efficiency.

As Nems grew larger and Brian had to delegate, more things were bound to be not to his liking—especially as he had the habit of appointing people out of a sudden feeling, rather than because of their knowledge and experience. But he always tried to keep his main artists to himself; he was completely possessive about the Beatles, and even disliked secretaries becoming too familiar with them. It was only in the last few months before his death that he let Peter Brown, his personal assistant, have any personal dealing with them.

Since early 1967 he had given up most of the daily responsibility for the running of Nems, apart from the Beatles. He brought in Robert Stigwood, an Australian, to be co-managing director. It was he who ran Nems from day to day, along with the other directors, Vic Lewis, Geoffrey Ellis, and his brother Clive Epstein.

The withdrawal from Nems came not long after the Beatles stopped touring. Apart from the Saville theater, which was never a success financially, nothing took the place in his affections of the Beatles. But he was still looking for something, as he'd been looking for something when he'd gone off to join RADA, then later when he left everything to manage the Beatles. It was the old creative urge coming out again. There is nothing more tormenting than an unfulfilled creative desire, to yearn with little possibility of satisfaction. This is what happened with Brian, with his love affairs, and with most of his pleasures.

There did come a chance to be creative when John Fernald, the ex-boss of RADA, who had taken Brian in as a student and whom Brian took on later to work at the Saville, fell ill during rehearsals of the play *A Smashing Day* and Brian took over.

"He'd been ill at the time, recovering from jaundice, but he threw himself into rehearsals completely," says Joanne. "I don't think I ever saw him as happy in all the three years I worked with him. He stayed up all night with the cast, waiting for the reviews, and adored every minute of it." But the play soon closed.

The urge to be creative never found another outlet. He didn't know what he was looking for, and nothing presented itself the way the Beatles had done. Instead it turned him more and more against a strictly business life. This was one of the reasons he withdrew so much from Nems.

"He didn't really like being a businessman," says Joanne. "He didn't like business meetings. He so wanted to be a creator. He used to cancel even the most important meetings. Sometimes I had to say he was ill or had an urgent conference. The real reason was that he was still in bed, having been awake with insomnia all night. It was awful. He would leave me notes telling me which meetings I had to get him out of. I had to cancel Bernard Delfont four times in one week. I don't know what he must have thought."

But there were several things which gave him great pleasure. He loved Kingsley Hill, his house in Sussex. He also loved bullfighting, dating from his early holidays in Spain. He once backed a fight and was financing a film about bullfighting at the time of his death. Other things he took up were more occasional whims, like drugs and gambling. He did take LSD several times, when he had heard from the Beatles the effects it had had on them, but on not more than a handful of occasions. He seems to have given it up about the same time as the Beatles—which was well before his death.

He had spasms of gambling. He enjoyed it and was successful. Joanne often found a note waiting for her when she arrived in the morning "with a big pile of money, perhaps around £300, which he'd won the night before. He would say in his note that I had to go and bank his happiness." Peter Brown, who often went with him, says he was a good gambler because he knew when to stop. "This was because he wasn't really carried away by it. The whole point of gambling was somewhere to go very late at night and to meet people."

Apart from the Beatles and Cilla Black, none of his artists lasted as big stars and many of them soon faded away completely. Quite a few of them naturally resented his overattention to the Beatles and then, as he drew out of Nems, his complete lack of work on their behalf. Brian regretted this as much as anyone. It would make him feel very guilty. "He believed in so many of them, really," says Joanne. "He honestly did. He would promise them great things, absolutely sincerely. They'd go away, feeling hopeful again. In a few months they'd be back, accusing him of having let them down."

But the only really important row he had with any of his artists was ironically not with any of the ones who were doing badly but with Cilla Black, his most successful single star.

She had felt for a long time that she wasn't getting the personal attention she'd had from Brian in the past and which she felt she deserved. At the beginning of the summer of 1967, she decided she'd had enough. Brian had gone off somewhere again, leaving her. He seemed to care only for the Beatles. So that was that. She was leaving him. As Brian was away, Peter Brown was the first to hear the news of her decision. He knew how badly it would affect Brian and he was worried about telling him. He consulted Brian's doctor for advice, who told him to do it slowly and carefully. When Brian heard, he made the mistake of allowing others to go and try to pacify her first, but they eventually met in Chapel Street. After several hours of discussions with Cilla and then agreements, it was all patched up. They became friendlier than they'd ever been and remained so, up to his death. Cilla realized she would never have left Brian anyway.

There were never any rows with any of the Beatles. He loved them all as much as ever, and they loved him. But with the end of touring, their main point of contact ceased to exist.

They still saw a lot of each other. Any business decision came through his hands. But at the end of 1966, when the touring had to stop, their concern was with themselves, working out what sort of life they would lead, what they would do with themselves, what was the point of it all. This was when the drugs and the religion started to enter their lives. They almost became hermits for several months, seeing only each other.

Brian went his own way, a way which had always been completely different in so many respects to theirs. If he hadn't become their manager, it is unlikely they would ever have been friends. He was of a different age, class, and background, with different attitudes and most of all different pleasures. But his life for five years had been his work for them. When that finished, the Beatles had each other and their wives. He was alone, obsessed by himself, worrying about his worries, worries he hadn't had much time to think about for five years.

The Beatles had no idea how he was leading his last year, how he had become increasingly dependent on pills as his worries, real and imagined, took over and obsessed him. They were amazed to hear, a long time after his death, that he'd hardly been at his office for so many months and had rarely been up and out in daylight. They knew nothing either of his personal affairs. They had heard he'd been mildly depressed early in 1967, but thought he'd got over it. When he was with them, he was certainly always happy. This was true. His greatest pleasure was to be with them. He loved doing anything for them.

"He had Pattie and me for a week's holiday in the south of France in 1966," says George. "When we arrived, he had every little thing worked out, each meal, each visit, each place we would go to for the whole week. A private plane arrived one day, which he'd organized to take us to a bullfight.

"He was always like this. He so wanted to please people that he worked everything out, down to the last detail." When he had a dinner party, he went to great lengths to know each person's favorite cigarettes and would have them all laid out by their plate at the table.

Pattie says she did once hear from Joanne about the amount of pills Brian was taking. "I said why couldn't she or Peter stop him, but she said they couldn't. I said to George that he should speak to Brian himself, but he said it wouldn't do any good."

Brian had at first been attracted most of all to John, from those early days in the Cavern. John was the only one he'd ever spent a holiday with alone—that time they went to Spain together, leaving Cyn in Liverpool. His relationship with Paul was the most subtle and complicated, at least Brian felt it was. He felt he had to overcompensate toward Paul. He admitted it himself once. "I think Paul thinks I'm closer to John than I am with him. It's not really true. It was earlier on, but now I love them all equally." He always gave Paul particularly lavish presents. They never gave him any.

"Paul was the only one who ever gave him any little worries," says Joanne, "when he rang up to complain about something, or ask things. The others might ask exactly the same, but he always worried more about pleasing Paul. He could be upset by talking to Paul on the phone, but never by any of the others."

This was probably because in 1967 Paul, for the first time, had become interested in business affairs. Formerly George had been the only one to cross-examine Brian on contracts, or how much they were getting and couldn't he do better. But George, when his interest in religion arrived, stopped worrying completely about materialistic things.

Brian was always involved, but now and again didn't like the way they were doing things, such as the complicated—legally, economically, and artistically—cover for Sergeant Pepper.

During the spring of 1967, when he was visiting New York, Nat Weiss says that Brian got a premonition he was going to die. At Kennedy Airport, he became convinced his plane was going to crash over the Atlantic. Just before takeoff, he wrote a note on a scrap of paper which he said Nat Weiss had to give to the Beatles as his last wish. The note, which Nat Weiss still has, reads, "Brown paper bags for Sergeant Pepper."

As he didn't crash, the Beatles never found out how much he was against their Sergeant Pepper cover, just as they never found out so many things about his last year. A Westminster coroner's court on September 8, 1967, pronounced that Brian Epstein's death was accidental. He had died from the cumulative effect of bromide in a drug he had been taking for some time. The drug was Carbitral. The level of bromide in him was only a "low fatal level," but he had taken repeated "incautious self overdoses" which had a cumulative effect enough to kill him.

His body showed there had been no one immense dose, but a series of large ones. The court was told he took drugs, in the form of sleeping tablets, as he suffered from perpetual insomnia. In his body were found an antidepressant drug and barbiturate, as well as bromide. The police reported that in his house they had found seventeen bottles of tablets of some sort, seven by his bedside, eight in the bathroom, and two in a brief case.

Medical experts said that the amount of bromide he had been taking would have made him drowsy and could also have made him careless and injudicious. He had died from an accidental overdose. There is not the slightest reason to doubt it. The medical evidence showed conclusively he had been dosing himself up for three days. With suicide, the practice is to take one large dose.

It's highly unlikely he would have deliberately committed suicide, not at that time, with his mother already recently bereaved. One or two small facts are still not known, but there were no rows or specific reasons for depression, as far as is known. It was just an escalating depression as he thought his longed-for weekend would turn out boring.

The memorial service for Brian Epstein was held at the New London Synagogue, Abbey Road, St. John's Wood on October 17, 1967.

It was an apt setting, just a few yards away from EMI's studios, where all the Beatles' records up to Brian's death had been recorded, and just round the corner from Paul's house in Cavendish Avenue.

It was also not far away from St. John's Wood Underground station which contains the nearest public telephones to Paul's house. Brian used these phones twice in his life. The first time was in 1962 when he rushed out of the EMI studios to cable the Beatles in Hamburg with some good news of their first record. The other time was five years later, just before his death. He'd been round to Paul's house but couldn't get in. Paul had been bothered by fans all day and had stopped answering the door. Brian had been forced to find a phone box and ring up Paul and tell him who it was before he was allowed in. Brian always thought this story was very symbolic.

George, when he heard of Brian's death, says it struck him like an old-fashioned film. "You know, where they turn over the last page of one section to show you they've come to the end of it before going on to the next. That was what Brian's death was like. The end of a chapter."

Chapter 27: 1967: The Beatles as a Group: From Drugs to Maharishi

When the touring was over, the Beatles had no idea what was going to be in the next chapter. They'd had ten years—from 1956 to 1966—of not just living a communal life but communally living the same life. They were still each other's greatest friends and they were still going to record together, but as individuals they felt it was time to look for a separate identity.

George was off first. The month after they stopped touring, September 1966, he went to India with his wife. For the first time he had found a serious interest not shared by the others.

John accepted a film part, in *How I Won the War*. He had always liked Dick Lester, though he hadn't particularly enjoyed doing the two Beatle films. He said it felt like being an extra, but he still thought that perhaps acting was the new thing he was looking for.

Ringo, the most home-and-family-minded of them all, started to expand his family and his home. Paul was the only one who felt out of it. He envied George. He wished he had something like Indian music to occupy himself. He did a bit of painting and decorated pieces of furniture, but without much interest. He tried hard to think about God, but nothing came. So he decided to do the music for a film, *The Family Way,* to see if he enjoyed writing film music, but he didn't. After that he went off on a long trip across Africa.

George's passion grew, but John soon found that he didn't like acting and he didn't like actors. He and Paul were both searching again. They had no intention of retiring from life as twenty-five-year-old millionaires, but they'd missed out on so much formal discipline and knowledge, the sort a university might have given them, that they didn't know where to begin. Materially and emotionally they were a hundred years old, but intellectually they were still in many ways adolescents. Not that they wanted anyone to teach them anything, which is where drugs came in. Through drugs they found out about themselves, by themselves.

They'd taken pep pills of varying strengths ever since their Hamburg days. They'd had occasional marijuana cigarettes as other people have a drink. None of them drink, apart from wine with a meal now and then. George and John were introduced to LSD through a dental friend in 1965 without realizing they had been given it. "It was as if I'd never tasted, talked, seen, thought or heard properly before," says George. "For the first time in my life I wasn't conscious of ego."

Taking drugs didn't stop their music. Now that they were all back together again, having found that things like acting didn't work, they began work on their most ambitious album so far, one which showed many traces of their interest in drugs. This was *Sergeant Pepper's Lonely Hearts Club Band.*

Now that they were back together, they had all started work again. During this session they also got the idea for a television film. They'd been putting off doing their third film for a year, at the same time they were putting off other things they didn't care for, like touring and appearing. Many scripts had been written, then rejected, the last being by the late Joe Orton. (Orton was an intense Beatle fan. "A Day in the Life" was played at his funeral.) They were slowly coming around to the idea of writing a script themselves.

They decided to do their own TV show, an hour-long color film. This would give them a chance to see if they could make their own film and also let themselves be seen by their fans. Paul thought of the idea in April, flying home from visiting Jane on her twenty-first birthday in the States, where she was on tour with the Old Vic. He thought they would all get onto a bus and just see what happened. It would be Magical, so they could do what they wanted. And Mysterious, as no one would know where they were going or what they were going to do.

That was as far as he got then. The others agreed on it, but no further work was done on it for almost six months.

George by this time was well immersed in Indian music, which also shows in *Sergeant Pepper.* But he'd also become very knowledgeable about Indian religion. His wife Pattie was with him in all this. In fact, it was she who first had any contact with the Maharishi.

Pattie says that their interest in religion had started by chance during their trip to India in September 1966. This had been simply to study Indian music, which again had started by chance. During the film *Help* there is a scene in which there are lots of unusual instruments. George, bored by the filming, had amused himself by trying to play one of them, which turned out to be a sitar. He kept on trying, long after the film was over.

"Those five weeks we spent in India were when we first started to pick up the feeling," says Pattie. "We had really gone so that George could study the sitar under Ravi Shankar. We met Ravi's guru, his spiritual guide. You can't be in India without being aware of everything. We went to a meeting at Benares, the Holy City on the Ganges. Millions of people had come for a big festival which went on for three days. We stood in a little compound and watched it all. It was all like a Biblical film. We felt like men just arrived from outer space.

"The King of Benares came into the center of the multitude riding on an elephant. He knelt down and said his prayers. The sun was going down behind him and he was just a dark silhouette.

"I know it all sounds very romantic, talking about it. But it had a great effect on us. It obviously meant so much to all these millions. The process was beginning, without our knowing it."

Back home, apart from continuing to study the sitar, George and Pattie started reading books about Indian religion. In February 1967 she became a member of the Spiritual Regeneration Movement—on her own, not with George.

"I'd been trying to teach myself meditation from books, but only really half doing it. One day a girl friend told me about transcendental meditation. I went along with her to a lecture given at the Caxton Hall. Maharishi himself wasn't there. It was just someone else talking about his work. I joined the movement, but I found the lecture very dull and all rather obvious.

"But I got all the movement's literature from them so I knew all about their summer conference at Bangor and what it was going to be about. I said yes, long before George and the others heard about it. I'd booked up weeks before."

George, in the meantime, was reading book after book. When he'd inwardly digested bits of them, he'd pass them on in little globules to Paul, John, and Ringo when they met during work on *Sergeant Pepper*. They were all very excited. It was impossible to speak to any of them at this time without their launching into a long spiritual diatribe. Most of it had been picked up from George, although they soon began to read for themselves.

George was not only passing on what he'd read, he was also looking round the world desperately for someone, some wise learned man, to tell him what he would do next. Someone to explain it all properly to him and put him on the right track. His trip to California in the summer of

1967, to have a look at the hippies, was partly in the hope that they might help him spiritually. But he decided they were all phoney—though that didn't stop the hippies making George and the other Beatles *their* spiritual leaders.

George even trailed down to a deserted part of Cornwall and spent several nights climbing up a high hill with a local guru. He was going to reveal all to George, but nothing happened. Many other experts, Indian and Western, came George's way, in books or in person, but not one seemed to him to be the right one until Maharishi.

It is important to stress that all of them were already very knowledgeable long before Maharishi came along. He didn't convert them, or reach out and direct them, or even tell them much they didn't know. He chanced upon their lives just at a time when they were looking for him.

All this spiritual groping didn't stop them from doing their normal Beatle work. They did a song, "All You Need Is Love," in July 1967 for a world-wide program, *Our World,* which was seen live by more than 150 million people.

The group's spiritual awakening did have one concrete effect. By August 1967 they had given up drugs. By actively thinking, reading, and discussing spiritual matters, they decided that artificial stimulants like drugs were no real help. It was better to get there without them. They don't regret having been on drugs. They see it as a stage in experimentation. They say it was useful for them at the time but is no more. It was nothing to do with Maharishi that they gave up drugs; they had already done so on their own. He simply confirmed and gave more lucid reasons for their decision.

It was ironic that all the acres of heavy print from leader writers and doctors, warning about drugs—after Paul and then Brian admitted they'd had LSD—had been ignored but spiritualism had worked.

In mid-August 1967 it was suddenly advertised in several newspapers that Maharishi was in London and would be giving a public lecture. "This seems to have been a sudden decision," says Pattie. "It wasn't in any of our literature that he was in London or even coming to our Bangor conference. When I heard, I said to George, 'Look, we've got to go.'" But by this time George had already heard from other people that Maharishi was in town. He contacted the other Beatles and said they must all go to his lecture at the Hilton Hotel. This was on Thursday evening, August 24, 1967. Afterward, Maharishi invited them to join his movement's summer conference at Bangor on Saturday. They said yes.

They told Brian Epstein about Maharishi and his transcendental meditation movement and how impressed they were by it all. Brian said he was interested. He might come up later during the conference, which was scheduled to last ten days. But he was more concerned with having an exciting August bank holiday weekend at his country home with a few new friends.

The news leaked out that the Beatles were going to Bangor with the Maharishi. What they thought was going to be a private spiritual experience developed into a carnival. It was almost like their touring days again, which they thought they'd given up forever a year ago.

Euston Station was crowded, with thousands of sightseers and press to watch the Beatles off on what the *Daily Mirror* called next day, a "Mystical Special," or the 3:05 local train to Bangor, North Wales. There was such chaos that Cynthia Lennon was left behind on the platform, unable to get through the crowds to join John. A policeman forcibly held her back, thinking she was a fan.

On the train, jammed tight in a first-class compartment, were John, Paul, George and Pattie, and Ringo, plus Mick Jagger, Marianne Faithfull, and Jennie Boyd, Pattie's sister.

Ringo was a late starter. His wife Maureen had just had their second child and was still in hospital. It wasn't clear if he would join them. "I rang Maureen in hospital. She said I had to go. I couldn't miss this."

Pattie was clutching a bag of apples and Marianne Faithfull was holding a Victor Value carrier bag. George lit incense. The blinds were pulled down in an attempt to shut out the press and others who choked the corridors. The train left a few minutes late. John said his wife was missing. An inspector said they'd hang on, which is the sort of thing British Rail would only do for the Queen, but they had to set off in the end without Cyn.

The decision to go had been very sudden. Brian Epstein knew about it but wasn't involved in any way. Even the ever-present Mal and Neil hadn't been brought along. For five years they'd never gone anywhere without Brian Epstein or someone looking after them. "It's like going somewhere without your trousers on," said John.

They sat tight for several hours, scared to go to the lavatory in case they got mobbed. They had no idea what had happened to their luggage. No one seemed to have any money. The Beatles, like the royal family, don't carry money. But they were all on a magical mystery tour, and they were all very excited. They wondered what Maharishi would tell them. John said perhaps he might just turn out to be another version of what they already knew, but on a different label. "You know, like some are on EMI and some on Decca."

George said, very seriously, he didn't think so. He was sure this was going to be it. But they were very happy and joky about it all, especially John, Paul, and Ringo. Mick Jagger sat very quiet and serious. John said he hoped it would save him having to work as a Beatle, if the Maharishi told him to go off and sit in a cave in India for the rest of his life. "But he won't, I bet. He'll just say go away and write 'Lucy in the Sky with Diamonds.' "

In another compartment the Maharishi was sitting cross-legged on a white sheet laid out on the seat by his followers. He bounced up and down when he laughed, which was most of the time. He admitted he'd never heard any Beatle music in his life. He had been told they were very famous, and so was Mick Jagger, but he got very confused about him being a Rolling Stone. He didn't know what that meant.

The Beatles were eventually ushered into his compartment. He laughed a great deal and told them very simply what was in store for them. He illustrated his talk by taking a flower in his hand and saying it was really all sap. Even the petals were an illusion, just like life.

He said that transcendental meditation, which he would indoctrinate them into at Bangor, was simply a method of quickly and easily reaching a spiritual state. His meditations, once learned, need only be practiced for half an hour every morning. That would be enough for the day. He said it was like a bank. You didn't need to carry money around with you if you had a bank, you just need to pop in now and again to get what you wanted.

"What if you're greedy?" said John. "And have another half hour's meditation after lunch, then slip in another half hour after tea?" Everybody laughed. The Maharishi nearly bounced his head against the ceiling this time.

The Beatles adjourned for tea while the girls and Mick Jagger had a turn with the Maharishi. The attendant roped off part of the dining room for them, but a few people managed to break through for autographs. "What you going to Bangor for?" asked two teenage boys, unable to believe that anyone would want to go to Bangor, least of all the Beatles. "Are you playing there?"

"That's right," said Ringo. "On the Pier Head at 8:30 Second house. See you." At Flint Station Ringo said that Flint had been the farthest he'd ever cycled on his bike from the Dingle.

Bangor was pandemonium. The whole town, unused to such arrivals, had turned out. The Beatles considered going on to the next station, then getting a taxi back. But Maharishi said if they stayed beside him they'd be all right. On the platform, rather lost and bemused among all the screaming kids, was a handful of Maharishi's followers waiting to welcome him to the conference. They were rather gentle middle-aged ladies, each earnestly clutching a flower ready to hand to him. They were bowled aside by the crowds screaming at the Beatles.

Bangor, a small seaside town on the north coast of Wales, is a university town, part of the University of Wales. It also has a large training college, which was where the conference was being held. More than 300 meditators were already in residence, all of an age and class similar to that of the nice ladies on the platform and all unaware of the Beatles' arrival.

Maharishi himself seemed to be enjoying all the commotion and excitement. He was very kind and considerate to all the press and TV men. He very smartly agreed with them to have a press conference after he'd spoken privately to the conference members.

Maharishi philosophy, very simply, is that life consists of spiritual as well as materialistic values. He is not in favor of becoming a spiritual recluse, cutting oneself off from the world. But he says that without spiritual consciousness it is impossible to lead a full life or fully enjoy materialism. In a way, it is a simple blend of Eastern mysticism and Western materialism. You don't have to give up money or even the pleasures of the flesh, within reason, to become one of his followers, but you have to learn his methods of spiritual realization. This helps you to transcend yourself, but not to leave an ordinary life.

At his private meeting Maharishi asked his 300 followers how they were getting on in their meditations. One man asked if it was possible still to hear motor cars during meditation. The press conference afterward was confused and unsatisfactory. The press, mainly local stringers of national papers, had little idea what was going on. They thought the Beatles must be involved in some publicity stunt. They couldn't believe they were serious about Maharishi, whoever he was. They were belligerent in their questions, almost as if they expected the Beatles to admit they were just doing it all for a laugh. The Beatles were cheered loudly by the congregation when they made it clear, at the expense of the press's ignorance, that they were very serious indeed.

John found a reporter's notes afterward in one of the college's telephone booths. It had the heading "Paul, George, Ringo, John Lennon, and Jagger" plus details of what each had been wearing. "You've taken over from me," said John to Mick Jagger, pointing out to him how the reporter had named each of them. "I just used to be called Lennon when I was wicked. Now I'm John Lennon. I haven't yet reached the next stage of just being John. You're still Jagger."

By midday on Sunday they all had been indoctrinated. They were all resting, after their mental efforts, when the news of Brian Epstein's death came through. Maharishi saw them all again, to help and comfort them, to cheer them up and explain how little death meant. Then they all went back to London by car, missing the rest of the conference.

They were due originally to go to India to be with the Maharishi in September 1967, but it was put back until 1968 for various reasons, such as the Magical Mystery Tour. They and Nems were a bit perturbed by the way various bodies, saying they were doing public relations work for the Maharishi, suddenly sprouted up and tried to get the Beatles to give a press conference. They were even talking of selling press and TV rights to cover the Beatles' trip to India and setting up an official press office long before the Beatles had made up their minds when to go.

An Indian official arrived, sent by the Indian government, and went to Nems saying he had organized visits for them to six Indian states and that he was going to arrange for them to meet Mrs. Gandhi, the Prime Minister of India. Any sort of publicity for their religion or anything else is the last thing the Beatles ever wanted.

There has always been a certain element, very often governmental, who try to turn the Beatles' presence or interest to their own advantage. The same sort of thing happened with Greece, around the same time in 1967. The Beatles were thinking of buying a Greek island. They had seen it during a cruising holiday, and even had the money organized. This was very difficult at the time because of the currency restrictions, but the Treasury gave them special dispensation—through Mr. Callaghan personally—to take the money out of the country.

It was agreed that as they'd brought so many millions into the country they should be allowed to buy an island refuge. The price was agreed upon. They didn't care about the military regime which had just taken over in Greece or appearing to condone it. But on one trip to Greece they were asked by an official if they would be kind enough to look at a very quiet little village. When they got there, they found hordes of press and TV people. It had all been organized by the tourist people, who used the Beatles as propaganda. Other government officials started asking them to come to Athens. They decided to forget about Greece.

It might seem slightly far-fetched that governments should wish to court four members of a beat group. Many said the Labour government did, by giving them an MBE. But it has always happened, since the beginning, from trying to get them to go to embassy or government parties to state visits. Most governments see the Beatles as a way of giving themselves a young identity and keeping in with the young voters.

But all the wheeling-dealing that went on around the Maharishi didn't put them off him. Most of it had nothing to do with Maharishi anyway, although his natural enthusiasm to spread the word led him to be talked into lots of things by press and PR men. But the Beatles did want to help if possible. George and John even went on the David Frost TV show, the first time they agreed to talk on any television program for over two years.

The year 1967, the year of LSD and Maharishi, turned out to be the Beatles' most creative year so far. In the first six months they wrote and recorded even more new songs (sixteen in all) than in the first six months of 1963. This equaled what they'd done in the whole of 1966, which shows how much they gained from giving up touring.

Later in 1967, in November, they also did another single, "Hello, Goodbye," then the *Magical Mystery Tour* in December, their hour-long color-TV film. They spent more time on making the film than in doing the songs for it.

They'd done no work on the film from April, when they thought of the idea and recorded the title song, until September, when they started shooting. They set off for Devon in a bus with forty-three people on board, none of them, including the Beatles, knowing what would happen. They had no script, apart from Paul's sketch of a clock face on which he'd scribbled where the songs would go.

They did two weeks of shooting in all, some of it in semi-chaos. They'd blithely expected to do a week in the studios at Shepperton after Devon, thinking you could just turn up. Instead they had to use an airfield in Kent.

The main work was done at the editing stage, which took eleven weeks in all—eleven times as long as they'd expected. Paul, as with the shooting, was the main inspiration. He directed every minute of the editing. The others were there most of the time, usually having a singsong with a drunken street singer who wandered into the cutting rooms.

They disregarded all the rules and conventions in making this film, but just bashed on, unworried by their lack of film knowledge and experience. It was a completely new medium for them but, most of all, for the first time ever, they were doing something on their own, with no Brian Epstein to stage manage things or George Martin to lend his accumulated wisdom.

The film was shown at Christmastime 1967 in Britain on the BBC. It was also seen in most countries in Europe, South America, Australia, and Japan.

The lack of plot and experienced direction did show, and it was savagely criticized by most of the British television critics. The *Daily*

Express called it "blatant rubbish" and "tasteless nonsense." The pre-publicity had made most people forget it was an experiment and they possibly expected too much. It was the first time the Beatles had been criticized in five years. Most critics made the most of it.

Long before it was out, the Beatles had almost forgotten it, having learned their lessons, though Paul perhaps was still hoping it would be liked. But they'd gained enough to make them feel confident enough to have a go at a full-length feature film. Apart from the TV film, it had been a good year. *Sergeant Pepper* particularly was looked upon as their biggest advance so far. The *Times* music critic, William Mann, took thirty inches to say it was more genuinely creative than anything else in pop music.

The year had begun with the Beatles searching as individuals and ended with them as a group once more. But their searching meant that as individuals they'd begun to put their own minds and own homes into some sort of order.

PART 3: 1968

Chapter 28: Friends and Parents

There are no blue plaques on the Beatle birthplaces in Liverpool today, though they all get thousands of fans trekking to look at them every year.

There is only one Beatle parent left living in Liverpool, but Liverpool does have an ex-Beatle, Pete Best. He is married and has two children, lives with his in-laws, and works in a bakery, slicing bread, for £18 a week. He worked in groups until 1965, in Germany and in America, being billed everywhere he went as the ex-Beatle, though he tried to stop it. In 1965 he gave up show business for good. He did nothing for a year, became almost a recluse, refusing to see people. He turned down large sums for his life story from magazines all round the world. His memories of Hamburg, especially of the girls, drink, and pills, could have been very lucrative.

"What good would that have done, apart from the money? It would just have seemed like sour grapes. I just wanted to try and get a life of my own, but it took a long time. What I dreaded most was people's cruelty. When I met people, I knew what they were going to say or think. I was the bloke that was no good. It was the sort of psychological knowledge which got me down. People were rude and said awful things to me."

He has lost a bit of heart. He looked very tired, almost pathetic, slumped in front of the TV at his mother's home. He has a Beatle hair style at last, but he was still wearing a leather jacket and jeans, as they'd all done in their Hamburg days. Mrs. Best has given up all show business work, but she's as forceful as ever. She still maintains the Beatles chucked Pete Best because they were jealous of him. Pete says he knew all the time that they were good and obviously going to be successful. "That was what was really disappointing, knowing what I was going to miss. I did regret everything at first. When they kicked me in the teeth I did wish I'd never set eyes on them. I'd have just had an ordinary job, perhaps teaching, and never known all this anxiety.

"But not now. I'm glad really. I've got a lot of happy memories. I had some great times. I'm grateful for them. Then the Day of Judgment came."

In Hamburg the clubs are still full of British groups, but Klaus is no longer there. He's joined a British group, Manfred Mann. His fascination for the Beatles led him to follow them back to England and to join a group, even though he could play no musical instrument. He is still very friendly with them. George composed one of his songs in Klaus' house. Klaus also does a bit of drawing—he did the cover for the Beatles' LP "Revolver."

Astrid is still in Hamburg, but she's no longer a photographer. She says she got sickened by the press and refused all offers for her memories of the Beatles. Her last job was serving in a bar in one of Hamburg's small but strange night clubs. She is married to Gibson Kemp, a Liverpool-born ex-beat-group player. At one time he played in a trio with Klaus. Astrid still has Stu's room almost as it was. It is very dark and eerie. The candles are still burning.

Fred Lennon had no contact with John, or even bothered to go and see him or inquire about him, from 1945, when John was five, until 1964. Fred was then washing dishes at a hotel in Esher. "One day the washing-up woman said to me, 'If that's not your son, Freddy, then I don't know what.' She said there was a boy in this group with the same name as me and the same sort of voice, though he didn't sing as well as me. I'd never heard of them."

John must have passed the hotel where his dad was washing dishes many times, without knowing it, going back and forth to his home in Weybridge.

When Fred realized it was his son, he was immediately appearing in all the newspapers, giving interviews. Fred says of course he didn't seek publicity. It just happened. It also just happened that *Tit Bits* paid him £40 for his life story and that he made a record. He says that singing on this record didn't make him any money. "I lost, if anything. They made me get my teeth seen to. It cost £109. I'm still paying it up, £10 a month."

He had a twenty-minute meeting with John and then was shown out. He tried to see him again, by just arriving at his house one day, but had the door slammed in his face. Some papers made out that he was a drunkard, which he's not. He's surprisingly small, but almost dapper. He has thick graying hair which is swept back lushly at the sides like an ex-theatrical's. He's fifty-five but very cheerful and young-looking. "I can still get the girls, you know. Mainly teenagers as well. If they think I'm smashing, I must be okay. I know John has a horror of old age. But tell him this from me. I'm younger than he is."

He watches John's progress very carefully. "He's only let me down twice. Once was accepting that MBE. I wouldn't have done it. Royalty can't buy me. The other time was not speaking at the Foyles' literary lunch. I would definitely have given them a speech, and a song too." He would like to meet John properly. "Just to let him see what sort of bloke I *really* am." And he wouldn't say no to any help. "If John happened to offer it."

Mimi today lives alone in a luxury bungalow near Bournemouth with her cat Tim, a stray which John brought home many years ago. The house is very white and sunny with a magnificent setting, right beside the sea. It has its own little harbor and steps at the bottom of her garden leading down to the sea. It cost £20,000.

The front and the back of the house are completely unoverlooked. Only in the summer, when steamers go up and down across Poole Bay, can she be in any way interrupted. As they go past the house, she can hear a megaphone on board announcing: "And that is John Lennon's house with the striped blinds. That will be Mimi sitting there." The first time she heard it, she was so furious that she ran down to the bottom of the garden, stood on her sea steps, and shouted "Shut up!" Everybody on the boat just laughed.

Apart from that, her life is fairly uninterrupted. A few lamps from the front of the house have been stolen by fans. Now and again she's seen them snapping photographs of her and the house, but nothing much. She says she keeps her telephone number and address very secret. Every taxi driver in Bournemouth seemed to know them.

Most of the furniture is reproduction antique. It all looks very new, but most of it was brought from her old home in Liverpool. She did have some nice things there, she says. When a reporter came to see her once in her old house in Liverpool, he looked round at everything and said how nice it all was. "Wasn't John good to buy it all for her?" She threw him out immediately.

There are lots of books around, mainly classics and biographies. She'd just been reading *Max* by Lord David Cecil. She doesn't care for novels.

On the TV set she has John's MBE medal, though she is a bit worried some people might think it a slight on Royalty. John had arrived one day and pinned it on her, saying she deserved it more than him. She has a picture of John beside the medal, not a well-known one, but one sent from a fan in Liverpool. There is also a picture on another wall of Julian. In the hall and walls of the bedrooms she has some of their gold disks, although not as many as the other parents. She also has a large plaque which John presented her. Engraved on it is the phrase she used at him almost every day of his adolescent life: "The guitar's all right, but you'll never earn your living with it."

She had no strong desire to leave her house in Liverpool. "I said why should I? I was very happy. It was a very comfortable house. I'd spent hundreds on it. But John went on at me for about two years, then he said okay, stay. Then he started again, when other parents had moved into their new houses. 'You silly little sausage,' I said to him. 'There's no need to lift me out of the mire.'

"I was staying in London with him after the premiere of the first film. He came down to breakfast and said, 'Okay, I'm going to find you a house. Where would you like it?'

"I said Bournemouth, just for something to say. He picked up the phone and called Anthony, his chauffeur. He told him to get the maps out for Bournemouth, we're leaving now.

"Well, I thought, it would be a run. We came down and got a list of houses from Rumsey's. We went round a lot, but I wanted one by the sea and there wasn't one. So I thought, that'll be it, now we can go home. Then the man suddenly remembered one that had just come up.

"The people were still living in it and I didn't want to go in, especially the way John was dressed. He had old jeans with holes in them and an old suede jacket I'd bought him years ago which was miles too small for him. He had a silly yachting cap on as well. I said we shouldn't go in, the house was far too smart just to land on them like this. John told me it was just a tuppenny ha'penny little bourgeoise home. If I wasn't careful, I'd get a mind to match.

"He marched in and said how do you do, mind if I look round? The man and his wife just gaped at him. I sort of had a look at the woodwork, which looked to me as if it needed painting.

"John was more interested in finding out if the house could be overlooked, or if anyone else could build near it. Just shows you how his mind worked. I was worrying about things that didn't matter. I could see them looking at him and beginning to tell who he was. I said I'd just go and sit outside in the car. He said, 'Do you like it, Mimi? If you don't, I'll have it.' So he rang his accountant and bought it."

Mimi moved in in October 1965. She sold her old house in Liverpool for £6000, a good price, though, as she says, it was a good house in a good area. The Bournemouth house is still in John's name, but it is Mimi's for as long as she wants it. He pays all the bills. He told her just to spend her £6000, but she told him not to be so stupid.

"It's lovely down here. I had always vaguely thought of moving to the south coast when George retired. I haven't felt a winter since I arrived. I haven't made many friends. I've had drinks with people, but that's about all. I've never tended to make friends outside the family. I do a lot of walking and reading. The days are too short, really."

All the Beatle parents have had their material lives completely changed by their sons and all of them have reacted to it in slightly different ways. But Mimi is probably the only one whose relationship has not really changed. She still in many ways treats John as she's always done, whereas with the others there is a hint of hero worship, almost reverence. Mimi still criticizes John's clothes and how he looks, as she did when he was a teenager. She tells him when he's looking fat and not to spend too much. "He's too soft over money. He's an easy touch. Generous beyond belief. I'm always telling him." The other parents never voice any criticism of their sons.

Mimi even doesn't care for the way John speaks. She says he won't speak properly, never finishing sentences. "John's always been a bad speaker. And he's getting worse all the time. I often can't understand what he's talking about. His mind's jumping all over the place."

She doesn't see him very regularly, but he always sends her funny letters when he's abroad, with a little drawing on the envelope, specially for her. She keeps them all carefully arranged in a bureau. When John visits her he rakes through all her belongings, just to see what she's been doing while he's been away. She still has the old childhood books he used to write. She reads them now and again.

"It's just the same stuff that he's had published. Just his scribble, as I call it, which he's been doing for years. I think the first book was better, but I still burst out laughing at some of his poems." Her way of life isn't all that different, despite the luxury of her setting. She just eats the same and does the same things. She likes the new house, but says she would readily give up everything, her house and all their success, just to have John as her little boy again.

"I'd give up £2 million to be back again. It's very selfish, I know.

I always think of him as a little boy. I know it's stupid. But nothing could compensate for the pleasure he gave me as a boy." She obviously would like to see him a lot more, but would never in any way let this be known, or hang onto him at all. "It's not his fault I'm a widow. There's nothing worse for a boy to feel than that his mother's hanging onto him. He's got his own wife and family to think about. He knows I'm here. He comes to see me as often as he can. He sat up on the roof for four days in the summer. I ran up and down getting drinks for him. He never shows much emotion. He finds it hard to say sorry.

"But one night he said that even if he didn't come down to see me every day, or every month, he always thought about me at some time every day, wherever he was. That meant a great deal to me."

The happiest day in Jim McCartney's life, he says, occurred in 1964, when Paul told him he could give up work. Unlike some of the other parents, he needed no second telling. He was sixty-two at the time, with another three years before retiring. He'd worked for the same cotton firm since he'd been fourteen and he'd had enough. His wage, despite all his years and his experience, was only £10 a week. The recession in the cotton trade had made his last years very uncomfortable. For years he'd had the fear that they would pay him off anyway in favor of a younger man.

Paul found him a house, an £8750 detached house in the Wirral in Cheshire. About a year after that, Jim found himself a new wife, after almost ten years of being a widower. He'd met Angela only three times when he asked her to marry him. She was a widow, a good few years younger than himself, with a daughter, Ruth, aged five. She'd been living in one room in Kirby since her husband had been killed in a road accident. "We were two lonely people."

They are obviously very happy. He dotes on Ruth, a highly intelligent young lady who thinks the girls in her school who try to chat her up about her famous stepbrother are really rather silly. Angie is very bouncy, witty, and high-spirited. She runs the large house with great efficiency and drives his car, as Jim can't. She's given him a second youth. He now wears very fashionable, clinging polo-neck sweaters and well-tapered trousers, the type he used to shout at Paul for wearing not so long ago.

Michael, Paul's brother, is also still living at home and his friends are always dropping in; this also keeps the house very young and lively.

"I've just taken Mike up a lilo and three sheets of carbon paper," says Angie.

"That's very sanitary of you," said Jim.

"He now wants some more three-pound bags of flour. He's dropping the flour onto a breadboard and tape-recording it. A gear bedroom, but what a mess. What do you think he's after?"

"The sound of three-pound bags of flour dropping onto a breadboard," said Jim.

Another £8000 was spent on the house after Paul had bought it, putting in central heating and completely furnishing and decorating it. The house has large grounds with a view at the back towards the Dee estuary. Despite the newness of all the fittings, it has a homely, lived-in feeling. They're not scared to enjoy all the new luxury. "I do miss Liverpool and some of my old friends, but not all that much. I was getting a bit fed up with people saying, 'You must be very proud, what's it like?' That's all they ever asked, over and over again. I've cut myself off from people like that. But close friends and relations I often ring up and ask to come out here."

He's on Christian-names terms with his doctor—even using his pet name. He always calls him Pip. Not in an affected, putting-it-on way, but perfectly naturally. He gets out the whisky the minute Pip calls. And not blended whisky either. A very exclusive malt.

He has two part-time gardeners, but he looks after his vines in the large heated greenhouse himself. He's laid down lots of wine and always has a plentiful supply of all drinks. He gets books out of the library on ornithology and knows exactly which birds are in his garden. He's also an expert on squirrels.

Apart from his slight Liverpool accent, to see his life, his clothes, and his pleasures, it's impossible to imagine he's spent all his life in a council house earning less than £10 a week. Most of all when you see him at a race course. That's when he really looks one of nature's gents. Leaving work, getting the house, and most of all getting married again have all made him very happy. But his next biggest kick came on his sixty-second birthday. It was the same night, the sixth of July 1964, of the premiere of the Beatles' first film.

"We all went to the Dorchester afterwards. Princess Margaret was there. I could see Paul signaling to somebody and he was handed a parcel. He gave it to me and said, 'Here you are; all the best, Dad.'

"I opened it and it was a picture of a horse. I said, 'Very nice,' but I was thinking, what the hell do I want with a picture of a horse? Paul must have seen my face. He said, 'It's not just a picture. I've bought the bloody horse. It's yours and it's running at Chester on Saturday.' "

The horse, Drake's Drum, a well-known gelding, cost £1050. Paul also pays for its training fees, which come to around £60 a month. In the 1966 season, it won over £3000 in prize money, including a £1000 race at Newbury and the race before the Grand National.

Jim wants for nothing now. Like all the Beatle parents, he has an account from which he can take anything he likes. He doesn't go in for any ostentation, but he seems to enjoy and savor the middle-class life even more than the others.

"The change was a bit sudden, coming as it did when I was sixty-two. It took a while to get used to it. Now I've taken to it like a duck to water. I haven't started saying *glaas* or *baath,* but I'm enjoying everything. It's as if I've always been used to it."

Paul has always been very close to his brother, in age and in taste, more than George has been to his brothers, which made it worse for Michael. "I suppose I couldn't help being affected by our kid. He's always had success. He was the first boy, the best-looking one, the one who got all the girls and then all the fame."

He has always been asked for his autograph around Liverpool, being Paul's brother. He resolutely signs *Michael McGear,* much to their disappointment. He usually also denies any relationship. "No, love, wish I was his brother. I'd be in the money then, wouldn't I?"

He's now making Michael McGear more well-known, though it's taken a long time and long spells out of work. He became Michael McGear when he joined the Scaffold group in 1962. They started off well, with a twenty-seven-week TV series, then nothing much happened, apart from local theater shows, until 1967, when they got a record "Thank U Very Much" in the Top Ten. This has led to other shows and records. He is a good singer and he can compose, but he's always played that down, preferring to try something different, like acting in revues.

"I don't want to be famous, just a success at my job, as long as I'm making it on my own. What I always worried about was being like Sean Connery's brother, or Tommy Steele's brother, just trying to follow in their brothers' footsteps."

The Harrisons now live just outside Warrington. They moved from Liverpool in 1965 when Mr. Harrison stopped being a bus driver. Warrington isn't the sort of place Liverpool people usually move to when they make good. They prefer to move across the water, to the posh part of Cheshire, as Jim McCartney has done. Warrington is fifteen miles from Liverpool and about the same from Manchester, one of Lancashire's endless industrial towns where on the sunniest day the prevailing color is always gray.

The Harrisons, however, don't live in Warrington itself but in a village called Appleton, three or four miles out. Despite being in an industrial area, their house is in a forgotten rural oasis, surrounded completely by fields with no other houses in sight. Of all the parents' houses, the Harrisons' is the most isolated and the hardest to find.

It's a large L-shaped bungalow, with three acres of garden which until fairly recently was a farmer's field. They're busy planting trees and bushes. A gardener works two days a week knocking it into shape. They call it a bungalow, but it does have one upstairs room. They call it a room, but it is in fact thirty-two feet long, stretching the length of the house. They use it for parties or cinema shows.

The house cost George £10,000. With all the additions and improvements, such as a new open-plan staircase and a sun room, it's easily worth £20,000. The same house in Bournemouth, near Mimi, would probably fetch £40,000.

Inside it is full of brand-new contemporary but expensive furniture, deep-pile light-colored carpets and bright knickknacks from all over the world. Most of these presents from around the world have been sent not from their son, as in the other parents' homes, but personally to the Harrisons from fans. And unlike the other homes, you aren't too dazzled by the number of golden and silver disks inscribed to the Beatles. Their walls are instead hung with presentations inscribed to Harold and Louise Harrison.

On one wall is an enormous gold plaque with the inscription: *Presented to Harold and Louise Harrison for the time and effort they have shown towards Beatle people everywhere. United Beatles Fans. Pomona, California, 1965.*

The other Beatle parents think that Mrs. Harrison must be a little bit daft, at least they can't understand why she spends so much of her time being so kind to fans when she doesn't have to. Mrs. Harrison just happens to be fanatical about fans. She's a fans' fan. Every spare minute of the day she's answering fan letters. Most evenings she sits up till two o'clock, writing away. She personally writes 200 letters a week. Not notes but proper letters of about two pages each. This is apart from signing and sending photographs. Their stamp bill is enormous.

"I've always personally answered all letters, except from obvious cranks. If it's in a foreign language, like Spanish say, I read through it carefully and pick out words like *admiro*. I can roughly tell what it's about so I send them a signed photograph." Mrs. Harrison travels through to the Fan Club HQ in Liverpool each month to pick up a new load of photographs. They get through 2000 a month.

"From the beginning I used to get such lovely letters from fans when I'd answered their letters, usually from the fan's mum. 'Dear Mrs. Harrison: You'll never realize what your letter has meant. After years of writing to phoney fan club addresses and never hearing anything back, a personal letter from George's mum! My daughter went through the roof.' So you see, I just have to go on.

"Of course, at one time it was just physically impossible to answer all letters. In 1963 and 1964, we were getting four hundred fifty a day from all over the world. On George's twenty-first birthday we had 30,000 cards and scores of screaming fans. They had to put a policeman on duty outside. He couldn't get over the kids kissing the doorknob. 'Have you got to put up with this all the time?' the policeman said. 'I'd go mad.' For years the post office always sent a special van with our mail, but things have settled down a lot now. I find 200 letters a week enough to cope with, if I don't slack."

Fans she has corresponded with have a habit of suddenly turning up. She'd just had a family of Americans who had come specially to see her. "They were doing Europe and the Holy City in a fortnight. They were missing out Britain, but they decided to fly from Paris to Manchester, then get a taxi from Manchester, just to see us. It's a good job we were in."

Mrs. Harrison has always been a keen letter writer, long before George became a Beatle. She's got two pen pals she's corresponded with thirty years. She got their names through the *Woman's Companion*. One lives in Barnsley.

The other pen pal lives in Australia. With both these pen pals, she's swapped all family gossip since 1936. When the Beatles went to Australia, pictures of George as a little boy started appearing in the Australian press. Nobody could work out where they had come from. George himself had never seen them before. It was Mrs. Harrison's pen pal, who had dug out the snaps she'd been sent many years ago.

"People always think we must be different now, because of George. We went to a fan's wedding the other day, and people said 'How can you enjoy yourselves with the likes of us?' They expect us to wear mink all the time. They *want* you to be different, I don't know why. When Harry was still working, people used to say to him, don't tell me *you're* still working. Now that he's not, they're sure we must be different. You can't win."

Mr. Harrison gave up working in 1965 after thirty-one years on the buses. "I was driving the big 500. That's the limited-stop bus that goes right across Liverpool, very quick, you can't afford to be caught in any traffic. 'How much are you getting for driving that 500?' George said to me one day. 'Ten pound two shillings,' I said. He said was that a day. I said no, a week. He said what a bloody liberty. 'I'll give you three times that to do nothing. It'll put another ten years on your life.'"

Mr. Harrison is as keen as his wife is on being kind to fans. He and his wife enjoy the public side of being a Beatle parent more than any of the other parents.

Every summer they both open garden fetes up and down the country, usually Roman Catholic Church ones. Mrs. Harrison doesn't go to church, but as she was born a Catholic she thinks she should help them if she can.

"We've been as far south as Salisbury. What was that place north of London, Harry? Oh flippin' heck. I've forgotten. Harpenden, that was it. They advertised us in the local paper that we were going to open their fete. They usually do that.

"We judge beauty contests as well. We've done it for spastics, blind people as well as churches. I don't care what it's for, really. I usually say when I'm making my little opening speech that I'm quite pleased to be here to help them. I say how George and the boys wish to be remembered to them and send their best wishes. Then we get besieged when we go round the stalls. We enjoy it. Well, anything to help."

Ringo's real father, who is also called Ritchie Starkey, has seen very little of Ringo since he separated from his mother when Ringo was five years old.

As far as Ringo can recall, after his early childhood he has only ever seen his father once. This was in 1962, before he was with the Beatles and still with Rory Storme's group.

"He happened to be at the Starkeys one day when I called," says Ringo. "I wasn't so childish by that time and didn't feel anything against him. He said to me, 'I see you've got a car.' I'd just got the Zodiac. I said, 'Do you want to come outside and have a look at it?' He said yes. So we went out and had a look at my car. And that was all. I haven't seen him since or had any contact."

His father later moved away from Liverpool. He now lives in Crewe where he works as a confectioner in a bakery. He also has a part-time job as window cleaner. He has remarried but has no children. Ringo is his only son and Ringo's children his only grandchildren. He collects their photographs, tearing them out of newspapers every time they appear. He doesn't feel any envy at what his son has done, although he wishes his father had been alive as he was always so fond of Little Ritchie. He is referred to in his family as Big Ritchie and Ringo as Little Ritchie.

Since Ringo's earliest days of fame he has remained hidden from any publicity and from Ringo, which is highly commendable. On the occasions when people have noticed his name and asked if he was any connection he has said he was an uncle. But he does admit he would like to set his eyes on his son again. "But I'm slow. I want kicking to do anything." He gets annoyed when now and again Harry Graves, Ringo's stepfather, through no fault of his own, appears in the papers simply as "Ringo's father." He would like to correct it, but on the other hand he doesn't want the press to find out who he is and where he lives. He has no wish to get involved in Ringo's fame.

Like Ringo, he's quiet and self-deprecating. He has many of Ringo's features, particularly the nose. And like Ringo, he hates onions, which is strange, considering they have not spent their lives together.

Ringo's mother Elsie and his stepfather, Harry Graves, now live in a luxury Ideal Home Exhibition bungalow in a very select part of Woolton in Liverpool. It cost £8000. Marie McGuire, Ringo's childhood girl friend from the Dingle, helped his parents find it. It's not far from the part of Woolton, the best part, where the Epsteins used to live. Elsie and Harry are the only Beatle parents still living in Liverpool.

The bungalow is set well back from the road in almost an acre of land and is surrounded by lush lawns and rose bushes. It's in the sort of posh suburban neighborhood where all the houses look as if they're uninhabited exhibition models, unlike the Dingle where you can't get moving for human beings hanging out of windows or congregating on doorsteps.

Inside, it is all lushly furnished, in good-taste middle-class style, all bought by Ringo. There are three golden disks and two silver disks of Beatle records on the wall, all expensively framed. Over the TV is a wedding picture of Ritchie and Maureen and one of the children.

"Looking back," says Elsie, "I think the biggest thrill was going down to the Palladium that first time. Sitting in the audience and listening to all the London people cheering. 'Course, the two film premieres were nice. And the civic reception in Liverpool. They were all lovely. Everything was.

"I will say this, he's never got big-headed. He's never changed his life. Maureen's very quiet, very natural."

"I think I preferred their earlier music best," says Harry. "The rock-and-roll stuff. But they've got to change, haven't they? You've got to in this business. You've got to listen to their tunes properly now, more than once."

Ringo's parents were the last of the parents to be moved into a new house. "I always said I'd never ever move. I liked my neighbors so much down the Dingle. Even when the boys became famous, the neighbors never changed towards us. We never felt out of place.

"But the fans became too much. I couldn't stand it in the end. But it's not so bad now, especially here. It's still very difficult for the boys, though. I've seen Ritchie sit in here till it's dark because he's scared to go out in the light. Not being able to go out in the light. Isn't it terrible! But you can't have everything, can you?

"I thought I'd get more privacy up here. I've always hated any publicity, reporters coming to see me, people asking me to go places, open things. Up here it really is quiet. Nobody knows our phone number up here."

All the parents dislike the press, even the Harrisons. None of them ever give interviews. They wouldn't like to say anything which would annoy their sons in any way. Elsie and Harry most of all. Ringo had to ring up and tell his mother to think hard of any awful things about him.

While the Harrisons love being nice to fans, Jim McCartney loves all the new good things in life and Mimi loves her dream world of John as a little boy, Elsie and Harry in some ways haven't yet come to terms with it all. It's almost as if they can't believe it. They still tend to think twice about doing anything, although they do enjoy themselves. Harry gave up painting and decorating for Liverpool Corporation in 1965 at the age of fifty-one.

"I could have gone on another fourteen years if I'd wanted to. The Corporation were very good. They were almost as proud of the boys as I am. I had to take jokes, of course. '*You* don't have to queue up for your wages, do you!' That sort of thing. Ritchie was at me for a long time to retire, but I didn't think I should. Then one day one of his mates saw me up a forty-foot ladder in the snow painting a council house, and he forced me to give up.

"Time does drag by a bit. I've decorated the house. I might do it again now, or get somebody to do it, now we can afford it. I've had to get used to a new sort of life. But I think I'm settling to it now. I've always got the garden. Or little inside jobs."

In the evenings they watch the TV, play bingo, or go to dinner dances. Dinner dances are new things for them and they go a lot. They've made friends with several business people in the area who take them to their works dances. It usually comes out who they are and they have to sign autographs. Harry quite likes it, but Elsie doesn't.

"When I was down at Romford recently, seeing my relations," says Harry, "I went to a school do with my nephew. They had a sort of concert. It came out who I was, you know how it is, and I ended up signing about 300 autographs. I never saw the concert yet." Harry has always done a bit of singing, in pubs, usually imitating Billy Daniels. Since the Beatles, he always puts in a few of their numbers.

"It rained for three days the other week and we just sat here, looking out at the rain. Just to give myself something to do, I thought I'd write a few songs. Do you want to see them? Here's one, 'They sit all day, thinking alone, Waiting for a ring on the telephone.' I've done about five songs now. I sent them to Ritchie, hoping he might put some music to them. It's all they need, just a bit of nice music to go with them. But he sent them back. He says he can only play one instrument, so he couldn't do any music. Well, it's something to do, isn't it?

"It's funny, after all these years, not wanting for money. After all the years of pushing along. We still go second class on trains. You get just as good a seat.

"We do miss our old friends, but we often go and see them. Sometimes I go round the Corporation sites, if I'm passing. I look up at the lads and they all shout down at me. 'That's how it goes, lads,' I shout back. 'Keep the brush going.' "

"It's all out of this world, isn't it?" says Elsie. "There's not much more they can do. They've done everything. The last five years has been like a fairy story. But I still worry about him, about his health, after all he went through. I know he's a man, with little children of his own, but I still worry."

Chapter 29: The Beatles' Empire

After the death of Brian Epstein, there was some reorganization of Nems in London. Until then it had still been an expanding business—as managers, agents, and theater owners. The decision then had to be made whether to go on or to stop short and consolidate what they had. With the death of Brian, even though he had not done as much personally in the last year as before, the figurehead of the firm had gone. Brian had been the main talent spotter. He had created everything in the first place.

His mother, Mrs. Queenie Epstein, inherited the bulk of his fortune while his younger brother Clive took over as chairman; Clive had always had shares in Nems Enterprises, from those very early Liverpool days. Of 10,000 one-pound shares in Nems Enterprises, Brian had owned 7000, Clive 2000, and the Beatles 250 each.

But Clive had continued in the television business and had done little on the show business side of Nems. He has many of Brian's good looks, and many of his mannerisms—his habit of looking slightly away while talking to you—but he is strikingly fair-haired while Brian was dark-haired.

Unlike Brian, Clive has always led a much quieter and less exhausting life, professionally and privately. He likes to spend as much time as possible with his wife and two children.

Robert Stigwood left the firm soon after Clive took over, which in one way solved the problem of whether to expand as a management. Stigwood had been brought in to do just this—to use his flair to find new groups and promote them. He left, taking with him the groups he'd brought.

Nems Enterprises is now basically a management-and-agency organization whose managing director is Vic Lewis. Geoffrey Ellis, Brian's old friend, is still there as a director. A lot of the Beatles' interest and money now goes into Apple rather than Nems. Apple is the company they themselves have set up and which they alone control. It was being started, thanks mainly to Paul, before Brian died, but only began to be properly organized in 1968.

Peter Brown, Brian's closest friend and personal assistant, has taken over most of the personal handling of the Beatles, although it was stipulated by Clive Epstein that the Beatles were free to decide all their own affairs from then on; he and Nems would not try to take Brian's place in that respect. This is what the Beatles now do: they run themselves. But Peter is their link with Nems and with the outside world. Anybody wanting them, if not fobbed off immediately, has to go through Peter. He does all the arranging and fixing that they want him to do. He has an unlisted phone, his Beatles phone, the number of which only they know.

Tony Barrow is still the Beatles' senior press officer, although he also heads his own independent PR organization—Tony Barrow International. He is still writing "Disker" for the Liverpool *Echo*. He also does a lot of work coordinating the Fan Club, whose secretary is still Freda Kelly. It cost a total of seven and six a year to be in the Fan Club, for which members get a regular bulletin and a Christmas present. There has always been a special Christmas record, made by the Beatles, exclusively for the Fan Club. They usually do little sketches and sing a few corny songs, as in their old Cavern days. The membership of the Fan Club is now just over 40,000. In 1965 at its height it had twice that number. There are 40 regional secretaries, all voluntary, and 40 overseas branches.

The Fan Club runs at a loss and always has. The cost of sending out 40,000 bulletins and posters several times a year alone uses up most of the subscriptions. On top of that there is the cost of the contents— the special "Sergeant Pepper" color photo that everyone got cost £700 —plus the salaries of the two full-time Fan Club officials.

The *Beatles Monthly* makes a good profit. This is separate from the Fan Club, though most Fan Club members buy it, and a lot more besides. It costs two shillings a month and has a sale in Britain of 80,000. In America it comes as a supplement in *Datebook* magazine. It has been going since August 1963 and is the longest-running fan magazine in Britain. It is not produced by Nems but by a firm called Beat Publications, who pay for the privilege. Instead of taking a lot of the profits out of it, Nems insists on its quality being maintained by having, for example, many full-color pictures. It is an excellent publication. The best photographs of the Beatles appear in it, much better than any that appear in newspapers.

Very few new people have moved into the Beatles' magic circle. Professionally they are still associated with the people who first gave them their chance when they arrived in London in 1962.

Outside Nems, their most important professional adviser and friend is George Martin. But in five years his position has almost been reversed. In 1962 he was the god-figure from Parlophone, the great A and R man upon whom everything depended. Today, they depend on nobody.

George Martin left EMI in August 1965 after fifteen long years. During this time he saw Parlophone saved and the profits of EMI itself soar to immense heights.

"I never made any money out of the Beatles' successes. I just got my same EMI salary, which I would have done anyway, as I was under contract. I never participated at all in their huge profits. I'm glad of this because I've always been able to speak freely. No one could say I rode on the backs of the Beatles.

"But at EMI everyone always thought I *must* be in on their profits somehow, through one of their many companies. And the Beatles always thought I must be okay, because EMI must be looking after me."

During the first phenomenal year of Beatlemania, 1963, Martin must have been the only person at all connected with the Beatles who did not make a lot of money because of them. Dick James, their music publisher, certainly did.

In 1963 George Martin was responsible for more number-one records than any other record producer in the history of British pop music, which admittedly hasn't a very long history. Most of his successes, during his 37 weeks with the Number One, were by the Beatles. But he was also responsible for all the hit records by Cilla Black, Gerry and the Pacemakers, Billy J. Kramer, Matt Monro, and others.

In 1964 his salary did go up to £3000, but this was as part of his contract with EMI, made before the Beatles came along. He started negotiating for some sort of incentive scheme. "I thought the person doing all the hard work should be entitled to some recompense. But EMI were very unhappy about this."

So he decided to leave, which didn't make EMI any happier either, because he took two other A and R men with him—John Burgess and Ron Richards. Along with a fourth, Peter Sullivan from Decca, they began their own company, Associated Independent Recordings, AIR for short.

It was a big chance to take at the time, as everyone told them. It was going against the traditional pattern of the record industry. Independent

A and R men just need one flop to fold completely, whereas a big record company, with a huge staff, can afford lots of flops.

But the biggest chance George Martin was taking was whether or not he could retain the Beatles. Legally, their contract was still with EMI. George Martin was simply EMI's staff A and R man employed on Beatles records. If he was no longer on their staff and became a freelance, EMI need no longer give him any more work at all—unless of course the Beatles particularly requested him to be their A and R man.

"I didn't consult the boys about leaving. I just took the chance that they still wanted me." Which they did. And EMI agreed. EMI still produce Beatles records, but George now looks after them, not as EMI man but as a freelance. They have to pay him for his services, very highly. "I suppose now I am earning more than the managing director of EMI records."

Today AIR has, in its own little way, transformed the British record industry. Many of the best and most creative brains have opted out of the big corporations, selling back their services for double and treble what they got before.

In early 1967, AIR produced such artists as the Beatles, Cilla Black, Gerry and the Pacemakers, Shirley Bassey, Adam Faith, Lulu, Tom Jones, Manfred Mann, and many others.

George Martin, with his 23 Gold Disks behind him, has at last got few financial worries. He now lives in style in a large, brand-new luxury town house near Hyde Park and has a country cottage in Wiltshire. He and his wife Judy have a baby daughter called Lucy, no connection with "Lucy in the Sky." She has a full-time nanny to look after her.

Martin is trying to cut down more and get on with his own composing, which slightly amuses the Beatles, as they tend to think that only young people can write pop music. He has done several film scores on his own and did most of the knocking together of Paul's score for the film *The Family Way*. He composed the BBC's Radio One signature tune and has contracts to do more film music.

If the Beatles' plan, through Apple, to have their own recording studios and A and R men ever gets properly organized, this might in some ways affect George Martin's position. But whatever happens, his own company's success seems solid enough. They have an interest in Playtape, a system which he says will one day replace phonograph records completely.

Musically, George Martin now tends to keep in the wings when the Beatles are doing their records, as we shall see in the chapter on their music. They have now grown so sure of themselves as composers and even as arrangers that they make jokes about Big George.

Dick James, the Beatles' music publisher, has no such ambivalent position. His relationship with them is purely business, though they are very fond of him.

Dick James is on paper a millionaire, though not simply thanks to the Beatles, but to the fact that he built up his firm so well and attracted many other artists.

Today, his one-room-office days are far behind. He has his own posh block of offices in New Oxford Street—Dick James House, no less. The ground floor also contains a branch of the Midland Bank. Very handy. From this building Northern Songs, Dick James Music, and many other companies operate. He now has a staff of 32 people and 6000 square feet of office space on four floors.

Dick James still has a lot to do for the Beatles, plugging and selling their records. He says no one is so good that the release and promotion of their work doesn't need to be properly worked out. But his main job is collecting their royalties. It's up to him to fight for good terms, even though many percentages are laid down by agreements in the trade.

But when they brought out their *Magical Mystery Tour* records in a unique package of two extended players inside a book, he had to do a lot of haggling with EMI over what the royalties would be for that. This entailed endless discussions over fractions of a farthing. Multiplied by millions, fractions of a farthing matter.

Dick James has also branched out, as most of the old sheet-music people have had to. He now does every aspect of record work, even hiring recording studios and producing his own records, then leasing them to the big companies to sell.

The Beatles' personal buddies are all Liverpool lads like themselves. Many people have appeared or been connected with them at different stages of their lives, but only one or two have retained links. Alex Mordes, the electronics expert; Robert Fraser, the art-gallery owner; and Victor Spinetti, the actor who was in their film *Help!* are still friends, but most people are dropped completely once any contract is finished, such as the making of a film or a record. Even when they're looking for someone new to do something, they tend to dig out an even older mate from the past, such as Pete Shotton.

Pete Shotton was John's best friend from the age of about three. Thev were the bad lads at Quarry Bank together. But Pete went into the police force from school and lost contact with John. He gave up the police after three years, realizing that it was completely against his nature, and drifted into a series of dead-end jobs, such as looking after a café that went bust.

In 1965, when Pete had no job and no money, he met John again by chance in Liverpool. John said he would back Pete in any enterprise he wanted to start. "I was on holiday in Hampshire when I noticed this supermarket on Hayling Island. I liked the look of it. So John bought it for me to run. It cost £20,000."

On the face of it, John was taking a big chance, investing so much money in Pete, with no proof of his competence, more the opposite if anything. But Pete managed the supermarket for almost two years very successfully, making good profits. He increased its value and expanded it to include a men's wear department.

"If John hadn't come along then, I might have ended up a crook. This is what John says he might have ended up himself. I had no money at all. I was getting into lots of shady deals and meeting bad people through the cafés."

In the autumn of 1967, John asked Pete to leave the supermarket in Hayling Island—Pete's mother took it over as manager—and come up to London to work for Apple. He opened the first Apple Boutique in Baker Street and is still there as manager. He's now married with one son and almost as close to John as he was in their schooldays.

Terry Doran, another Liverpool friend, is also employed by Apple. He runs their music-publishing department. Terry was originally in Brian's Liverpool circle, but got to know the others from the earliest days. When their success started, Brian set Terry up with his own car firm—he'd originally been a car salesman in Liverpool. This was called Brydor Cars (after Brian and Doran). It sold cars to the Beatles, among others, but eventually closed.

Alistair Taylor, who was at Nems in Liverpool and in London and witnessed the original Beatles' contract, is now also working for Apple.

John's other childhood friend, Ivan Vaughan, is not employed by the Beatles in any way, but he is still a close friend. He went to school with Paul and it was he who introduced Paul to John and his Quarrymen skiffle group. He is now training to be an educational psychiatrist.

The Beatles' two closest, ever-present, and most important helpers and buddies are Neil and Mal. Neil (or Nell) Aspinall was their first road manager. Mal Evans joined them later, after a spot of bouncing at the

Cavern Club. Both, alone, were their road managers during all their big tours round the world.

Even in those days, they didn't like the term *road manager*. They did anything and everything. Now that they don't tour, it is even less applicable. Their relationship with the Beatles is very subtle, almost medieval. They are paid retainers, they do humble fetching and carrying, yet there is no master-servant relationship. They're just mates, who happen to get paid for being mates whenever or wherever any Beatle decides he wants a mate.

Mal is big and well built, very bland and good-natured, solid and sensible. Neil is smaller, slender, clever, and outspoken. He would obviously be prepared to give it all up any time and just leave, if there was ever a serious disagreement. He does say no if he doesn't want to do something, though he could only think of one time when he said he didn't want to go anywhere. This was when John said he would be coming with him to Spain for the filming of *How I Won the War*. In the end, Neil gave in and went, hanging around the set for days, so that John would have someone to talk to afterward apart from the actors, with whom they didn't have much in common.

Mal, on the other hand, with his years of doing a regular job, sees everything as part of his job and has no complaints about anything he has to do.

"In America we were constantly being asked, 'What will you do when the bubble bursts?' " says Neil. "It never worried me then and still doesn't. I'll be doing something else, that's all. I've no idea what I'm going to do for the rest of my life. It never worries me."

When the touring came to an end in 1966, they had a less strenuous life. But during recordings or TV or film work, Mal and Neil still go back to the old routine, getting the Beatles to and from the studios and making sure the instruments and equipment are ready.

They both follow Beatle fashion, growing mustaches and long sideburns when the others did, or wearing long neckerchiefs. They are completely part of the group. They look and talk the same.

When the Beatles are not recording, Mal and Neil's life is much more irregular—with long periods of doing nothing—but they are always expected to be on call. "We're supposed to take alternate weeks, but we just both always seem to be around."

When any of the Beatles individually has to go somewhere on his own, Mal or Neil accompanies him. Neil went with John on his film. Mal went with Paul to the United States to see Jane and with Ringo to Rome for his film. In February 1968 he was the one who went with them to India to see Maharishi. Neil went out later, taking messages and papers to sign.

They also do a lot of work liaisoning between the Beatles and Nems or Dick James, especially Neil. It's his job to make sure the words of a song are written down correctly and get sent to Dick James. They also help out sometimes by actually playing maracas, triangles, or anything else. John often asks Neil for ideas for the last lines of songs. They both appeared in *Magical Mystery Tour*. Mal was one of the five magicians.

Neil is a bachelor and lives in a large luxury flat in a new block of flats in Sloane Street, opposite the Carlton Towers Hotel. He spends some of his spare time painting, a hobby he shares with the Beatles. He has a piano in his flat, though he can't play, with a piano exercise book opened at the second lesson.

For a long time, Neil was slightly underused—after all he has more O levels than the rest of them put together—just because the Beatles valued him so much at what he was doing already. But since 1968 he has been Director of Apple Corps, the central organization, run by the Beatles, which looks after all their Apple branches. He has a large plush office in Wigmore Street, where he sits in executive style.

Mal, who is married with two children, shared Neil's flat for a long time when they first all moved to London, commuting to Liverpool when possible. In 1967 he bought a house at Sunbury and moved in with his family. He chose the house to be within reasonable distance of the homes of John, Ringo, and George. He also now has an executive position, as manager of Apple Records.

What Mal and Neil have never been able to understand is the marvelous image the Beatles have always had. "It wasn't really Brian's doing," says Neil. "He did make them smarter, put them in suits and got organized. But they've always come across as being so good and kind and nice, when they're not particularly, not more than other people. I think people *wanted* them to be like that. Fans made up the image for themselves. I don't know why. That's just what the fans wanted.

"They're now appearing to the public more like they really were before Brian came along, all individuals, doing and saying what they like.

"The public still think they're as nice, but perhaps they're a bit 'eccentric' now, that's all. It's strange, isn't it, how people take to an image?' "

"I'm always being asked which Beatle I like best," says Mal. "I usually say whichever one has just been nice to me."

Chapter 30: The Beatles and Their Music

It has all been a continual development. Now and again the Beatles appeared to be marking time, but not for long; then they were off and away again. They are always too bored by what they have just done to ever consider repeating it, however successful.

But with each new step they have laced the progressive with the traditional, like "Eleanor Rigby" and "Yellow Submarine," or "Hello Goodbye" and "I Am the Walrus."

There are many recognizable steps, if you like looking for recognizable steps. The first rock-and-roll stage was finished around the spring of 1964, after "Can't Buy Me Love." The end of the simple beat-group lineups came in August 1965 with "Yesterday" and the introduction of new instruments. The really serious experimentation started in August 1966 with the last track on "Revolver" and was continued in *Sergeant Pepper*.

Even apparent anomalies can be explained, like "All You Need Is Love." This came out in mid-1967 but at first sight seemed to fit more into the 1963–1964 period. But it wasn't, because it was satirical, poking fun at themselves—a stage the Beatles didn't reach in their music until 1967.

But trying to explain it all, slicing it up into nice pieces, is for the musicologists. It's not just Mr. Mann of the London *Times* who's gone to town on each stage in the group's career. Serious American musical criticism could fill a book, and probably has.

The simplest way to look at how they make their music, rather than trying to analyze it, is to split it into the touring days and the post-touring days.

John and Paul had had more than six years together, writing and throwing away their music, by the time they started seriously recording in 1963. In those pre-1963 years they wrote hundreds of songs, most of them now forgotten or lost. Paul still has an exercise book full, but they don't show much. The words are of the simple "Love Me Do," "You Know I Love You" pattern and the music consists of a few *do re mis.* Only they could work out at the time how the tune was supposed to go. They've forgotten now.

It was more vanity, or frustrated professionalism on Paul's part, that made them write them down—all as "Lennon-McCartney originals." They knew them all anyway, from playing them hundreds of times in the Cavern. Once "Love Me Do"—a very old one, from the Quarrymen skiffle days—was recorded, they could have used their old songs, but they didn't. They'd done so many already that it was comparatively easy for them to think up new ones for their next records.

In those days, Paul and John composed by playing together on their guitars, just to see what came, either in hotels or on the road. "I Want to Hold Your Hand" was written on a bus in Yorkshire. Each tried out his own chords and own bits and pieces, following his own thoughts, until one liked something the other was doing. They then joined in, pushing it forward, then back for the other to have a go.

They deny today that they were deliberately concentrating on simple emotive words like *I* and *me* and *you.* That was just how it happened. They think the words of "Love Me Do" are just as philosophical or poetic as, say, "Eleanor Rigby."

But their songs were simpler in those days. The Beatles were simpler lads, writing songs simply to play to screaming fans on one-night stands and wanting a simple and immediate reaction. The songs were written, worked out, and perfected on tour. By the time they got into the recording studio they knew them backward.

"We were held back in our development," says George, "by having to go onstage all the time and do it, with the same old guitars, drums, and bass. We just had to stick to the basic instruments.

"For a long time we didn't know what else you could do. We were just lads down from the North being allowed to make music in the big EMI studios. It was all done very quickly in one go on one track, as 'Love Me Do' was. We used to do 'Love Me Do' better on stage than we did on the records."

Their first LP, "Please Please Me," took just one day to record and cost £400. *Sergeant Pepper* took four months and cost £25,000.

Today, since they have stopped touring, their recording sessions are long and highly complicated.

"Now that we only play in the studios, and not anywhere else," says

George, "we haven't got a clue about what we're going to do. We have to start from scratch, thrashing it out in the studio, doing it the hard way. If Paul has written a song, he comes into the studio with it in his head. It's very hard for him to give it to us and for us to get it. When we suggest something, it might not be what he wants because he hasn't got it in his head. So it takes a long time. Nobody knows what the tunes sound like till we've recorded them, then listen to them afterwards."

Nobody knows, either, exactly how tunes come into their heads in the first place. They don't know, or can't remember, how and why they did something. Cross-examining them, unless the song is very recent, is impossible because it's all gone. The only way is to be there, except that with this method you still can't see into their heads; you only know what comes out.

"A Little Help from My Friends"

In mid-March 1967 they were getting toward the end of the *Sergeant Pepper* album. They were halfway through a song for Ringo, a Ringo sort of song, which they'd begun the day before.

At two o'clock in the afternoon John arrived at Paul's house in St. John's Wood. They both went up to Paul's workroom at the top of the house. It is a narrow, rectangular room, full of stereophonic equipment and amplifiers. There is a large triptych of Jane Asher on the wall and a large silver piece of sculpture by Paulozzi, shaped like a fireplace with Dalek heads on top.

John started playing his guitar and Paul started banging on his piano. For a couple of hours they both banged away. Each seemed to be in a trance until the other came up with something good, then he would pluck it out of a mass of noises and try it himself. They'd already established the tune the previous afternoon, a gentle lilting tune, and its name, "A Little Help from My Friends." Now they were trying to polish up the melody and think of some words to go with it.

"*Are you afraid when you turn out the light,*" sang John. Paul sang it after him and nodded that it was good. John said they could use that idea for all the verses, if they could think of some more questions on those lines.

"*Do you believe in love at first sight,*" sang John. "No," he said, stopping singing. "It hasn't got the right number of syllables. What do you think? Can we split it up and have a pause to give it an extra syllable?"

YESTERDAY

Yesterday, all my troubles seemed so far away,
now it looks as though they're here to stay
    oh I believe in yesterday.

Suddenly, I'm not half the man I used to be
There's a shadow hanging over me
Yesterday came suddenly.

middle &
—   Why she had to go, I don't know
    she wouldn't say,
I said something wrong. now I long
    for yesterday.....

Yesterday, love was such an easy game to
       play
Now I need a place to hide away
oh I believe in yesterday

I WANNA HOLD YOUR HAND

Oh yea I'll tell you somethin
I think you'll understand
When I say that somethin
I wanna hold your hand

Repeat twice

Oh Please Say to me
You'll let me be you man
And please say to me
you'll let me hold your hand

And when I touch you
I feel happy inside
It's such a feelin
that my love
— I can't hide
I can't hide

Oh you got that somethin
I think you understand
When I feel that somethin
I wanna hold your hand

John then sang the line, breaking it in the middle: *"Do you believe—ugh—in love at first sight."*

"How about," said Paul, *"Do you believe in a love at first sight."*

John sang it over and accepted it. In singing it, he added the next line, *"Yes, I'm certain it happens all the time."*

They both then sang the two lines to themselves, *la-la*-ing all the other lines. Apart from this, all they had was the chorus: *"I'll get by with a little help from my friends."* John found himself singing *"Would you believe,"* which he thought was better.

Then they changed the order, singing the two lines *"Would you believe in a love at first sight/Yes I'm certain it happens all the time"* before going on to *"Are you afraid when you turn out the light,"* but they still had to *la-la* the fourth line, which they couldn't think of.

It was now about five o'clock. Cynthia, John's wife, arrived wearing sunglasses, accompanied by Terry Doran, one of their (and Brian Epstein's) old Liverpool friends. John and Paul kept on playing. Cyn picked up a paperback book and started reading. Terry produced a magazine about horoscopes. John and Paul were singing their three lines over and over again, searching for a fourth.

"What's a rhyme for time?" said John. *"Yes, I'm certain it happens all the time.* It's got to rhyme with that line."

"How about 'I just feel fine,' " suggested Cyn.

"No," said John. "You never use the word just. It's meaningless. It's a fill-in word."

John sang *"I know it's mine,"* but nobody took much notice. It didn't make much sense, coming after "Are you afraid when you turn out the light." Somebody said it sounded obscene.

Terry asked me what my birthday was. I said January seventh. Paul stopped playing, although it had looked as if he was completely concentrating on the song, and said, "Heh, that's our kid's birthday as well." He listened while Terry read out the horoscope. Then he went back to doodling on the piano.

In the middle of the doodling, Paul suddenly started to play "Can't Buy Me Love." John joined in, singing it very loud, laughing and shouting. Then Paul began another song on the piano, "Tequila." They both joined in again, shouting and laughing even louder. Terry and Cyn went on reading.

"Remember in Germany?" said John. "We used to shout out anything."

They played the song again. This time John shouted out different things in each pause in the music. "Knickers" and "Duke of Edinburgh" and "tit" and "Hitler."

They both stopped all the shouting and larking around as suddenly as they'd begun it. They went back, very quietly, to the song they were supposed to be working on. *"What do you see when you turn out the light,"* sang John, trying slightly new words to their existing line, leaving out "afraid." Then he followed it with another line, *"I can't tell you, but I know it's mine."* By slightly rewording it, he'd made it fit in.

Paul said yes, that would do. He wrote down the finished four lines on a sheet of exercise paper propped up in front of him on his piano. They now had one whole verse, as well as the chorus. Paul got up and wandered round the room. John moved to the piano.

"How about a piece of amazing cake from Basingstoke?" said Paul, taking down a piece of rock-hard cake from a shelf. "It'll do for a trifle," said John. Paul made a face. Terry and Cynthia were still quietly reading.

Paul got a sitar from a corner and sat down and started to tune it, shushing John to keep quiet for a minute. John sat still at the piano, looking blankly out of the window. Outside in the front courtyard of Paul's house, the eyes and foreheads of six girls could just be seen peering over the front wall. Then they dropped, exhausted, on to the pavement beyond. A few minutes later they appeared again, hanging on till their strength gave way. John peered vacantly into space through his round wire spectacles. Then he began to play a hymn on the piano, singing words he was making up as he went along.

"Backs to the wall, if you want to see His face."

Then he seemed to jump in the air and started banging out a hearty Rugby song. "Let's write a Rugby song, eh?" No one listened to him.

Paul had got his sitar tuned and was playing some chords on it, the same ones over and over again. He got up again and wandered round the room. John picked up the sitar this time, but he couldn't get comfortable with it. Paul told him that he had to sit on the floor with his legs crossed and place it in the bowl of his foot. Paul said that George did it that way; it felt uncomfortable at first, but after a few centuries you got used to it. John tried it, gave up, and placed the sitar against a chair.

"Heh," said John to Terry, "did you get to the place?"

"Yeh, I got you three coats, like George's."

"Great," said John, very excited. "Where are they, then?"

"I paid by check and they wouldn't let me have them till tomorrow."

"Oh," said John. "Couldn't you have said who they were for? You should have said they were for Godfrey Winn. I want them now."

"They'll be okay tomorrow," said Paul. "There's some more stuff to get tomorrow. Don't worry."

Paul then went back to his guitar and started to sing and play a very slow, beautiful song about a foolish man sitting on the hill. John listened to it quietly, staring blankly out of the window, almost as if he weren't listening. Paul sang it many times, la-la-ing words he hadn't thought of yet. When at last he finished, John said he'd better write the words down or he'd forget them. Paul said it was okay. He wouldn't forget them. It was the first time Paul had played it for John. There was no discussion.

They then lit a marijuana cigarette, sharing it between them. It was getting near seven o'clock, almost time to go round the corner to the EMI recording studios. They decided to ring Ringo, to tell him his song was finished—which it wasn't—and that they would do it that evening. John picked up the phone. After a lot of playing around, he finally got through, but it was busy. "If I hold on, does that mean I eventually get through?"

"No, you have to hang up," said Paul.

"It's Getting Better"

Another afternoon it was the first afternoon of spring—like spring, and Paul went for a walk with his dog Martha. John still hadn't arrived for the latest work on *Sergeant Pepper*.

He pushed Martha into his Aston Martin and got in beside her and started the car, but it wouldn't start. He gave it a few bangs, hoping that would do it, then he gave up and got out of the Aston Martin and into his black-windowed Mini Cooper. He revved up first time. His housekeeper man opened the large black doors and he shot through, catching all the fans by surprise. He was away before they realized he'd come out. He drove to Primrose Hill, where he parked the car and left it without locking it. He never locks his cars.

Martha ran around and the sun came out. Paul thought it really was spring at last. "It's getting better," he said to himself. He meant the weather, but the phrase made him smile because it was one of Jimmy Nichols' phrases, one they used to mock all the time in Australia.

When Ringo was once ill and unable to play, Jimmy Nichols deputized for him on part of their Australian tour. Every time one of them asked Jimmy how he was getting on, if he was liking it and was he managing okay, all he ever replied was "It's getting better."

That day at two o'clock, when John came around to write a new song, Paul suggested: "Let's do a song called 'It's Getting Better.'" So they got going, both playing, singing, improvising, and messing around. When the tune was at last taking shape, Paul said, "You've got to admit, it is getting better."

"Did you say, 'You've got to admit, it's getting better'?"

Then John sang that as well. So it went on till two in the morning. People came to see Paul, some by appointment. They were left waiting downstairs, reading, or were sent away. John and Paul stopped once for a meal, a quick fry-up.

The next evening, Paul and John went to the recording studio. Paul played the new song on the piano, *la-la*-ing the accompaniment or banging in tune to his words, to give the others an idea of what it sounded like. Ringo and George said they liked it; so did George Martin.

The first stage in the layer-cake system they now use in recording songs was to get the backing recorded on one track.

They discussed what the general sound would be like and what sort of instruments to use. They also chatted about other things. When they got bored they went off and played on their own on any instruments lying around. There was an electronic piano in the corner of the studio, left over from someone else's recording session. Someone doodled on it and the group decided to use it.

Ringo sat at his drums and played what he thought would be a good drum backing, with Paul singing the song into his ear. Because of the noise, Paul had to shout in Ringo's ear as he explained something. After about two hours of trying out little bits and pieces, they had the elements of a backing. George Martin and two studio technicians, who'd been sitting around just waiting, went up into their soundproof glass-front control room, where they continued to sit around and wait for the Beatles to get themselves organized.

Neil and Mal got the instruments and microphones arranged in one corner of the studio and the four of them at last started to sing and play "It's Getting Better." Ringo looked a bit lost, sitting slightly apart on his own, surrounded by his drums. The other three had their heads together over one microphone.

They played the song over about ten times. All that was being recorded, up in the soundproof box, were the instruments, not the voices. From time to time Paul said, "Once more, let's try it this way," or "Let's have less bass," or "More drums." By midnight they had recorded the backing.

The next day John and George assembled at Paul's house. Ringo wasn't there. They were just going to do the singing track for "It's Getting Better" and he wouldn't be needed. Ivan Vaughan, the school friend of John and Paul, was also at Paul's house. At seven thirty they all moved round to EMI where George Martin, like a very understanding housemaster, was ready and waiting for them.

A technician played the backing for "It's Getting Better" they'd recorded the night before. It was played over and over again. George Harrison and Ivan went off to chat in a corner, but Paul and John listened carefully. Paul instructed the technician which levers to press, telling him what he wanted, how it should be done, which bits he liked best. George Martin looked on, giving advice where necessary. John stared into space.

Dick James, the Beatles' song publisher, arrived wearing a camel coat. He said hello to them all, very jolly and breezy. He made a joke about there being no truth in the rumor that EMI was buying Northern Songs. He listened to the backing of "It's Getting Better" and showed no expression. Then they played him one of their other songs, about the girl leaving home. George Martin said this was the one that almost made him cry. Dick James listened and said yes, it was very good. He could do with more of them. "You mean you don't like the freak-out stuff?" Dick James said no, no, he didn't mean that. Then he left.

They played "It's Getting Better" for what seemed the hundredth time, but Paul said he wasn't happy about it. They better get Ringo in and they would do it all again. Someone went to ring for Ringo.

Peter Brown arrived. He'd just returned from a trip to America. He gave them some new American LPs, which they all jumped upon. They played him "She's Leaving Home" and a few other of the *Sergeant Pepper* songs, already recorded. Then they played him the backing track of "It's Getting Better." As it was being played, Paul talked to one of the technicians and told him to try a slightly different sound mix. The technician did so, and Paul said that was much better. It would do. They didn't need to bring Ringo in now after all.

"And we've just ordered Ringo on toast," said John. But Ringo was canceled in time and the studio was made ready to record the sound track, the voices. As it was being set up by Neil, Mal brought in tea and orange juice on a tray. Paul let his tea go cold while he played with an oscillating box he had found in a corner. By playing around with the switches, he managed to produce six different noises. He said to one of the sound engineers that if someone could produce oscillating boxes with the sounds controlled and in order, it would be a new electronic instrument.

They were ready at last. The three of them held their heads round one microphone and sang "It's Getting Better" while up in the control box George Martin and his two assistants got it all down on the track. The three Beatles were singing, not playing, but through headphones strapped to their ears they could hear the backing track. They were simply singing to their already recorded accompaniment.

In the studio itself, all that could be heard were the unaccompanied, unelectrified voices of the Beatles singing, without any backing. It all sounded flat and off key. They ran through the song about four times and John said he didn't feel well. He could do with some fresh air. Someone went to open the back door of the studio. There was the sound of loud banging and cheering on the other side. The door began to move slightly inward under the strain of a gang of fans who'd somehow managed to get inside the building.

George Martin came down from his box and told John it would be better to go up on the roof and get some air, rather than go outside. "How's John?" Paul asked into the microphone to George Martin up in the control box.

"He's looking at the star," said George Martin.

"You mean Vince Hill?" said Paul. He and George started singing "Eidelweiss" and laughing. Then John came back.

In the corner of the studios, Mal and Neil and Ivan, the friend, couldn't hear the jokes over the headphones. They'd finished their tea. Ivan was writing a letter to his mother. Neil was filling in his diary. He'd only started it two weeks earlier. He said he should have started one about five years ago.

A man in a purple shirt called Norman arrived; he used to be one of their recording engineers and now had a group of his own, The Pink Floyd. Very politely he asked George Martin if his boys could possibly pop in to see the Beatles at work. George smiled unhelpfully. Norman said perhaps he should ask John personally, as a favor. George Martin said no, that wouldn't work. If by chance he and his boys popped in about eleven o'clock, he might just be able to see what he could do.

They did pop in around eleven, and exchanged a few half-hearted hellos. The Beatles were still going through the singing of "It's Getting Better" for what now seemed the thousandth time. By two o'clock they had it, at least to a stage that didn't make them unhappy.

The "Magical Mystery Tour"

The tune and all the words of "It's Getting Better" had been worked out before they got into the recording studio, but when the Beatles arrived at the EMI studios at seven thirty one evening to record "Magical Mystery Tour," all they had was the title and a few bars of the music.

There was the usual crowd of fans waiting for them as they went in. Not screaming. Just quiet and contrite, like humble subjects subdued by the Presence. As they went in, one girl very shyly gave George a button badge that said "GEORGE FOR P.M."

"Why would Paul McCartney want you?" said John to George.

Paul played the opening bars of "Magical Mystery Tour" on the piano, showing the others how it would go. He gestured a lot with his hands and shouted *Flash, Flash,* saying it would be like a commercial. John was wearing an orange cardigan, purple velvet trousers, and a sporran. He opened the sporran and took out some pot, which he lit, then passed round. They all had a drag. Someone shouted that Anthony, John's chauffeur, wanted him on the phone.

They leaned round the piano while Paul was playing, going over and over the opening. Paul told Mal to write down the order of how they would do the song. In a very slow schoolboy hand, Mal wrote down the title and got ready for Paul's instructions. Paul said *Trumpets,* yes they'd have some trumpets at the beginning, a sort of fanfare, to go with "Roll Up, Roll Up, for the Magical Mystery Tour." Mal had better write that line down as well, as it was the only line they had. Paul told Mal to write down DAE, the first three chords of the song. Mal sucked his pencil, waiting for more of Paul's inspired words, but nothing came.

The instruments were then set up and they got ready to record the backing, which as usual was to be the first track they would do. John came back and asked Mal if he'd gotten in touch with Terry yet. Mal said he couldn't get through to him. John said it was his job to get through. Just keep on until he did.

It took a couple of hours to work out the first backing track and get it recorded. After it was done, Paul went up to see George Martin in the control room. Paul had the track played back to him, again and again.

Below, in the studio, while Paul got the technicians to do things upstairs, George got a set of crayons out of his sheepskin painted waistcoat jacket and started to draw a picture. Ringo stared into space, smoking, looking very unhappy, which is his natural expression when he's not talking. John was at the piano, sometimes playing quietly, other times jumping up, pretending to be a spastic, or thumping out loud corny tunes. No one was watching him. He smiled fiendishly to himself through his spectacles, like a Japanese gnome. Neil was reading a pile of occult weeklies which they'd all been thumbing through earlier in the evening. Mal had disappeared.

Paul was at last satisfied with the sound of the first track. He came back down and said he thought they could now add a few more things to it.

Mal reappeared carrying a big brown paper bag full of socks, all in bright self-colors. He passed the bag to John first. He grabbed it in great delight. He chose several pairs of orange terry-towelling socks, then passed the bag around for the others to have a dip. The night before he had said, just in passing, "Socks, Mal."

After the socks had been handed out, Paul asked Mal if he'd managed to get any real mystery-tour posters. Mal said he had been round the bus stations all day looking for them. But he couldn't find any. They had hoped that some real posters would have given them some ideas for the words of the song. Instead they all tried again to think of some good words apart from "Roll up, roll up," which was still all they had.

As they shouted out ideas, Mal wrote them all down. "Reservation," "Invitation," "Trip of a lifetime," "Satisfaction guaranteed." But they soon got fed up. They decided they would just sing any words that came into their heads, just to see what happened. So they did.

When they'd finished that, Paul decided that on the next track he would add a bit of bass to the backing. He put on the headphones, so he could hear what they'd done so far, and strapped on his bass guitar. After that he said they should add even more instruments. All of them, Paul, Ringo, John, George, Neil, and Mal, then picked up any old instruments that were lying around—maracas, bells, tambourines. They put on headphones and banged and played them to the music.

By two o'clock they had recorded a basic backing and had layered onto it a bass track, a lot of shouting and disjointed words and some percussion instruments. The "Magical Mystery Tour" was then forgotten about for almost six months.

The Beatles do seem to record their music in apparent chaos. It is certainly an expensive trial-and-error method, making it all up as they go along. At one time their songs were recorded at one go and on one track or at the most two. Now it takes at least four, as they continually think of another instrument or effects to add. And when a forty-piece orchestra is used, as in "A Day in the Life," the expense is enormous.

Listening to each stage of their recording, once they've done the first couple of tracks, it's often hard to see what they're still looking for, it sounds so complete. Often the final complicated, well-layered version seems to have drowned the initial simple melody. But they know it's not right, even if they can't put it into words. Their dedication is impressive, gnawing away at the same song for stretches of up to ten hours each.

Paul often appears to be the leader in all this. This is mainly because someone has to say it's not good enough, let's do it once again. They all know it. But someone has to voice the instructions. Paul does it best, as he's still the keeny. But they all have a say in any big decisions. When it's John's song, he does most of the directing; the same with George. George most of all is in complete charge of his own songs.

The recording of all the Beatles' songs follows roughly this pattern. But there is no pattern to the writing and creating of the songs in the first place. That can happen in many ways.

"The last four songs of an album are usually pure slog," says Paul: "If we need four more we just have to get down and do them. They're not necessarily worse than ones done out of imagination. They're often better, because by that stage in an LP we know what sort of songs we want."

About a third of their songs are written like this, because they've got to write a song and can't wait for any sort of inspiration. John and Paul can do these slog songs on their own, but mostly they do them together, starting at two in the afternoon and giving themselves a day to complete them.

The rest of their songs owe something, even if it's very little, to inspiration of some kind. But even when an idea has suddenly come to them, they rarely sit down and work it all out. Very often they put it away at the back of their head till they need it. Even if they are in the process of doing an album, they still tend to bring out the song for the other one to hear, or to the studio, still half-finished. It's due to laziness as much as anything else, because they want to get the others to help.

Paul's song "Eleanor Rigby" came to him when he was looking at a shop window in Bristol and liked the name—Daisy Hawkins. Playing with the name in his head, it turned into a rhythm, and then into Eleanor Rigby. He saw the tune all through his head, but he still hadn't finished the words by the time it was recorded. The last verse was thought of by all of them, making suggestions at the last minute in the studio.

The only song either Paul or John can think of which came straight out and was then recorded unaltered was John's "Nowhere Man." He's not particularly proud of it.

"I was just sitting, trying to think of a song, and I thought of myself sitting there, doing nothing and going nowhere. Once I'd thought of that, it was easy. It all came out. No, I remember now, I'd actually stopped trying to think of something. Nothing would come. I was cheesed off and went for a lie-down, having given up. Then I thought of myself as Nowhere Man—sitting in his nowhere land."

There is very little inspiration that comes simply out of the air. But a lot comes out of their immediate environment, past (like Penny Lane) or present (Lovely Rita). John particularly has taken many ideas from the media surrounding him at the time he's been looking for a song.

" 'Mr. Kite' was a straight lift. I had all the words staring me in the face one day when I was looking for a song. It was from this old poster I'd bought at an antique shop. We'd been down in Surrey or somewhere filming a TV piece to go with *Sergeant Pepper*. There was a break and I went into this shop and bought an old poster advertising a variety show which starred Mr. Kite.

"It said the Hendersons would also be there, late of Pablo Fanques Fair. There would be hoops and horses and someone going through a hogshead of real fire. Then there was Henry the Horse. The band would start at ten to six. All at Bishopsgate. Look, there's the bill, with Mr. Kite topping it. I hardly made up a word, just connecting the lists together. Word for word, really.

"I wasn't very proud of that. There was no real work. I was just going through the motions because we needed a new song for *Sergeant Pepper* at that moment."

Almost the same sort of lifted inspiration caused what many people thought was their best song on the *Sergeant Pepper* LP, "A Day in the Life."

This was the one banned by the BBC on the grounds that it contained references to drugs—"I'd love to turn you on." Even John himself is quite pleased with this song. Most of the words of the first section, the verses that begin with "I read the news today, oh boy" came from genuine pieces of news John was reading the day he wrote the song.

"I was writing the song with the *Daily Mail* propped up in front of me on the piano. I had it open at their 'News in Brief,' or 'Far and Near,' whatever they call it. There was a paragraph about 4000 holes in Blackburn, Lancashire, being discovered. There was still one word missing in that verse when we came to record. I knew the line had to go "Now they know how many holes it takes to —— something, the Albert Hall." For some reason I couldn't think of the verb. What did the holes do to the Albert Hall?

"It was Terry who said 'fill' the Albert Hall. And that was it. Perhaps

I was looking for that word all the time, but couldn't put my tongue on it. Other people don't necessarily give you a word or a line, they just throw in the word you're looking for anyway."

The film mentioned in the song wasn't in the newspaper but was a reference to his own film, which he'd just finished acting in, *How I Won the War*. The film is about the English Army winning the war. It was originally a book.

"The lucky man who made the grade" in a car accident was based, rather indirectly, on the death of a friend of John's and all the Beatles, Tara Brown. Michael McCartney, Paul's brother, was a particularly close friend of his. There was a reference to his death in the paper on the day John was writing the song.

"I didn't copy the accident. Tara didn't blow his mind out. But it was in my mind when I was writing that verse." Tara wasn't either from the House of Lords, but he was the son of a peer, Lord Oranmore and Brown, and a Guinness heir, which is the next best thing.

"Goodmorning, Goodmorning" was sparked off by listening to a corn-flakes advertisement on TV. "I often sit at the piano, working at songs, with the telly on low in the background. If I'm a bit low and not getting much done, then the words on the telly come through. That's when I heard Goodmorning, Goodmorning."

Many times the starting point of a song is a basic piece of rhythm; then words are fitted to it so that the rhythm, which originally consisted of only three or four notes, can be gone over and over and developed, either in the head or at the piano.

One day down at his home in Weybridge, John had just heard a police car going past in the distance with its siren shrieking. This consists of two notes, up and down, repeated over and over again, like a primitive wailing. The rhythm had stayed in his head and he was playing with putting words to it.

"Mis–ter, Ci–ty, p'lice–man, sit–tin, pre–tty."

He'd got as far as trying the words in a slightly different order—"Sitting pretty, like a policeman"—but hadn't got much further. He said it would be a basis for a song, but there was no need to develop now. It could be dragged out next time he needed a song. "I've written it down on a piece of paper somewhere. I'm always sure I'll forget it, so I write it down, but I wouldn't."

He'd written down another few words that day, just daft words, to put to another bit of rhythm. "Sitting on a cornflake, waiting for the man to come." I thought he said "van to come," which he hadn't, but he liked it better and said he'd use it instead.

He also had another piece of tune in his head. This had started from the phrase "sitting in an English country garden." This is what John does for at least two hours every day, sitting on the step outside his window looking at his garden. This time, thinking about himself doing it, he'd repeated the phrase over and over till he'd put a tune to it.

"I don't know how it will all end up. Perhaps they'll turn out to be different parts of the same song—sitting in an English country garden, waiting for the van to come. I don't know."

Which is what did happen. He put all the pieces together and made "I Am the Walrus." In the backing to the song can be heard the insistent rhythm of a police siren, which had sparked the song off in the first place. This very often happens. Bits of songs which have started off separately end up as the one song when the time comes to empty his head and find a new song.

Most of John's composing is done at the piano, just doodling over it for hours, letting his mind wander, almost in a trance, while his fingers go over bits of tunes. "I've got another one here, a few words, I think I got them from an advert: 'Cry baby cry, make your mother buy.' I've been playing it over on the piano. I've let it go now. It'll come back if I really want it. I do get up from the piano as if I have been in a trance. Sometimes I know I've let a few things slip away, which I could have caught if I'd been wanting something."

Paul tends to work on whole songs rather than little bits. But very often songs are left unfinished. And even when they are finished they are sometimes left around for a long time. "When I'm Sixty-four" (the age is in honor of Paul's dad) was written almost a year before it popped up as being ideal for *Sergeant Pepper*.

Sometimes when they both have a half-finished song they meld them together, to make one new whole one. The classic example of this was "A Day in the Life."

"I'd written the first section and I let Paul hear it. I said to him what we want now is fourteen bars here before we come back to the beginning. He said what about this: 'Woke up, Fell out of bed, dragged a comb across my head.' This was a song he'd written on his own, with no idea of what I was working on. I said yeh, that's it.

"Then we thought we needed some sort of connection bit, a growing noise to lead back into the first bit. We wanted to think of a good end and we had to decide what sort of backing and instruments would sound good. Like all our songs, they never become an entity until the very end. They are developed all the time as we go along.

"Often the backing I think of early on never comes off. With 'Tomorrow Never Knows' I'd imagined in my head that in the background you would hear thousands of monks chanting. That was impractical of course, and we did something different. It was a bit of a drag and I didn't really like it. I should have tried to get near my original idea, the monks singing. I realize now that was what it wanted."

It is hard enough for John, Paul, and George to get the sound they think they can hear in their heads, but it can be even harder for George Martin. They leave him with bits of tracks that can't sometimes be tied together or present him with problems that can't be solved, at least at short notice. As they thought they could hire Shepperton studios to film *Magical Mystery Tour* at a week's notice, so they still decide overnight that they'd like a forty-piece orchestra for the next evening. George Martin is expected to get it for them.

George Martin is sometimes slightly amused by their lack of musical knowledge. "They ask for such things as violins to play a middle C, which of course violins can't do." He approves and enjoys their method of piling track upon track until they get the sound they like. He's always enjoyed the electronic side of recordings, since the days of trying funny noises for his Peter Sellers records.

He thinks that they could often do with sixty-four tracks, not just four, in order to add on everything they think of.

"I once saw a film of Picasso at work. He starts with an idea, then he overlays it with something else. He still has the same basic idea, but he changes it by putting something else over it. Sometimes the original idea can get obliterated."

Complications arise when it's not just a matter of adding something to an existing track, but taking bits out of two separate tracks. "Strawberry Fields" was one of the more complicated creations, in a technical sense. They did the usual basic tracks, then John, playing it at home, decided it wasn't what he'd wanted.

"He'd wanted it as a gentle dreaming song, but he said it had come out too raucous. He said could I do him a new line-up with the strings. So I wrote a new score and we recorded that. But he didn't like it. It still wasn't right. What he would now like was the first half from the early recording plus the second half of the new recording. Would I put them together for him? I said it was impossible. They were in different keys and different tempos."

While George Martin was trying to puzzle out a way of getting around this without having to do the whole recording session all over again, he noticed that by speeding up the slower-tempo recording by 5 per cent

I love you? I love you. I love you

That's all I want to say

until I find a way

I will use the only words I know that you
understand.

Michelle

I want you, want you, want you . . . how
I think you know how
I'll get to you somehow
until I find — — —

it not only brought it to the same tempo as the other one, it also brought it into the same key. By chance he was able to meld both together without too much trouble.

Not that the Beatles have ever worried about being told things were impossible. They've also never worried when George has told them that new ideas they've thought of were very old hat. They got an idea at the end of "She Loves You" which they thought was really new. This was to go down on the last *yeh yeh* to an added sixth. "I told them it was corny. Glenn Miller was doing it twenty years ago. They said so what. That was what they wanted."

George Martin sees his work with them as having been in two stages. "At first, they needed me enormously. They knew nothing and they relied on me to produce their sound, the deafening sound they'd produced in the Cavern but which nobody was doing on record. People like Cliff and the Shadows were very quiet and subdued.

"The second stage is now, when they know what they want to put in a record, but they rely on me to arrange the start and the end. In between, I've changed from being the gaffer to four Herberts from Liverpool to what I am now, clinging onto the last vestiges of recording power." This is a half-joke, he hopes. There is a bit of teasing on both sides. The Beatles tend to mock him slightly. He in turn is slightly amused by their innocence and naïveté. He is genuinely worried that it might one day make them go too far, not in music but in films perhaps, refusing to rely on anyone experienced, such as himself. He did think they were doing too much on their TV film. From the response of the British TV critics, he was right.

George Martin still sees himself with a lot to give them, not just as an organizer and arranger, but in the field of electronics, which he's always been interested in. "I'm as fascinated by the problem of recording sounds as I've always been. I still like trying to paint pictures in sounds, using a full symphony orchestra or music concrete."

He thinks Paul has the most all-round musical talent, with an ability to turn out tunes almost to order. "He's the sort of Rodgers and Hart of the two. He can turn out excellent potboilers. I don't think he's particularly proud of this. All the time he's trying to do better, especially trying to equal John's talent for words. Meeting John has made him try for deeper lyrics. But for meeting John, I doubt if Paul could have written 'Eleanor Rigby.'

"Paul needs an audience, but John doesn't. John is very lazy, unlike Paul. Without Paul he would often give up. John writes for his own amusement. He would be content to play his tunes to Cyn. Paul likes a public. John's concept of music is very interesting. I was once playing Ravel's *Daphnis and Chloë* to him. He said he couldn't grasp it because the melodic lines were too long. He said he looked upon writing music as doing little bits which you then join up.

"This does seem to be true, judging by the way John has written many of his songs, such as 'I Am the Walrus.' " Both Paul and John have natural musical talent and originality, but they both have it in different ways. Paul can produce easy, sweet music, like "Michelle" and "Yesterday," while John's music is much bumpier and more aggressive, like "I Am the Walrus." In a way, it comes out of their personalities. As people, long before they started writing songs, John was always the rough, aggressive one and Paul the sweeter and smoother.

But perhaps the most interesting thing about them as composers is that despite writing so closely together for over ten years they are still strong individuals. Each has retained his own flavor.

If anything, their individuality has become stronger over the years. In their rock-and-roll days, their songs were much the same, but since "Yesterday," a Paul or a John song is fairly easily identifiable. They've influenced each other, in that Paul has been spurred on to try harder with his lyrics, while John has been spurred on by Paul's keenness and dedication. But they are still very different.

Their music has been constantly analyzed and praised and interpreted right from the beginning in 1963, when the *Times* music man admired their "pandiatonic clusters" and "flat submediant key switches." They have been said to have been influenced by everything from Negro blues to Magyar dances.

References to drugs have been seen everywhere, once it was known they took drugs. Even the "help" in Ringo's "A Little Help from My Friends" was said to mean pot. "Lucy in the Sky with Diamonds" was said to stand for LSD, which was just a coincidence. John's son Julian had drawn a picture for John showing Lucie, a girl in his class, in the sky. In America it was said that "meeting a girl from the motor trade" obviously meant an abortionist.

They have used drug slang in their songs, but not as much as people have said. Strangely enough, several deliberate slang obscenities have gone unnoticed. In "Penny Lane," for example, they were well aware of the phallic implications of the fireman "keeping his engine clean, it's a clean machine." The finger pie referred to is an old Liverpool obscenity used by Liverpool lads about Liverpool lasses.

They are amused by all the interpretations. John deliberately let all the verbal jokes and stream-of-consciousness–nonsense stuff stay as they

organ — Picture yourself

cymbal

F — Rhumba, int tambour + open L.hand

(D min) → guitar enter drums (middle) bass

No gap —

Lucy in the sky ... Piano, drums

organ and to A

TUDOR ST. CENEDR. 555

L.N. FOWLER + Co

Serial no 48

by

Elbert. Benjamin

Cop. 1955

DOCTRINE OF KABALIS...

BROTHERHOOD
OF LIGHT

Schneider
Life's Path
getting better
Lucy Leaving here
Kite
Fixing a hole
Lucie

Paper
Help.
Lucy
Getting
Fixing a hole

5

had come out of his head in "I Am the Walrus," knowing a lot of people would have fun trying to analyze them.

But whether they are the greatest songwriters in the world today, as some have said, or even better than Schubert, doesn't interest them. They never discuss or try to evaluate or appreciate their music. When forced to talk about it, Paul says simply that it must obviously get better all the time. "Each time we just want to do something different. After 'Please Please Me' we decided we must do something different for the next song. We'd put on one funny hat, so we took it off and looked for another one to put on.

"Why should we ever want to go back? That would be soft. It would be like sticking to gray suits all your life.

"I suppose everybody would like to do this, to try something different every time they do any work. We do, because it's just a hobby, that's all. We put our feet up and enjoy it all the time."

George doesn't think they've done any songs worth talking about yet (his song-writing is discussed later). He sees their Beatles songs as commercial and just a job.

But now and again George does yearn for the old days. "I often think it would be nice to play together again. We've never done it since we stopped touring. Perhaps one day we might hire a studio, just to play in for ourselves."

"They're good songs," says John, "but nothing brilliant. I just feel indifferent when I hear them on the radio. I never listen to them properly. Maybe if someone was attacking them, saying they were rotten, then maybe I'd work up some reaction to them."

None of them ever plays their own records, except perhaps when they're about to start a new album; then they might play the previous one through, just to see where they got up to last time. None of them sings their own songs, either before they've recorded them or afterward. When John or the others break into a chorus of "She Loves You" it's as if they're ridiculing a corny song written by someone else.

"We did all the proper listening to them, over and over again, when we wrote them," says John. "When it's finished, it doesn't matter any more.

"I actively dislike hearing bits of them which didn't come out right. There are bits of 'Lucy in the Sky' I don't like. Some of the sound in 'Mr. Kite' isn't right. I like 'A Day in the Life,' but it's still not half as nice as I thought it was when we were doing it. I suppose we could have worked harder on it. But I couldn't be arsed doing any more.

"I don't think our old songs are all that different from our new ones, as people are always saying. The words are different, but that's because they're done up differently. The tunes are much the same.

"I suppose I'm so indifferent about our music because other people take it so seriously. It can be pleasing in a way, but most of it gets my back up.

"It's nice when people like it, but when they start 'appreciating' it, getting great deep things out of it, making a thing of it, then it's a lot of shit. It proves what we've always thought about most sorts of so-called art. It's all a lot of shit. We hated all the shit they wrote and talked about Beethoven and ballet, all kidding themselves it was important. Now it's happening to us. None of it is important. It just takes a few people to get going, and they con themselves into thinking it's important. It all becomes a big con.

"We're a con as well. We know we're conning them, because we know people want to be conned. They've given us the freedom to con them. Let's stick that in there, we say, that'll start them puzzling. I'm sure all artists do, when they realize it's a con. I bet Picasso sticks things in. I bet he's been laughing his balls off for the last eighty years.

"It's sad, though. It's all a bit of a drag. Being right about art appreciation. It makes us laugh. When we're not laughing, we're conning ourselves into thinking we are important. People won't take anything as a laugh. If we said when we wrote 'She's Leaving Home' we were actually thinking about bananas, nobody would believe you. They don't want to believe you.

"It is depressing to realize we were right in what we always thought, all these years ago. Beethoven is a con, just like we are now. He was just knocking out a bit of work, that was all.

"The thing is, do Beethoven and these sort of people realize they're a con? Or do they really think they're important? Does the Prime Minister realize he's just a bloke? I don't know. Perhaps he's taken in by all this pretending to know what he's doing. The drag is he sounds as if he really thinks he knows what's going on, when he doesn't.

"People think the Beatles know what's going on. We don't. We're just doing it. People want to know what the inner meaning of 'Mr. Kite' was. There wasn't any. I just did it. I shoved a lot of words together then shoved some noise on. I just did it. I didn't dig that song when I wrote it. I didn't believe in it when I was doing it. But nobody will believe it. They don't want to. They want it to be important."

Chapter 31: John

John lives in a large mock-Tudor house on a private development full of mock-Tudor houses in Weybridge, Surrey. Ringo lives in the same development. John's house cost him in all £60,000, although it was only £20,000 to buy. He spent another £40,000 doing it up, knocking rooms around, decorating and furnishing, landscaping the garden, and building a swimming pool. He has spent too much on it, which he knows. "I suppose I'd only get half the money back if I sold it, about £30,000. I'll need to find a pop singer to sell it too, someone soft anyway."

In the garden he has a psychedelically painted caravan, matching the patterns of his painted Rolls-Royce. The house is on a slight hill, with the grounds rolling beneath. There is a full-time gardener, a housekeeper called Dot, and a chauffeur called Anthony. None of them lives in.

Inside, the front hall is dark and book-ridden, but the rooms beyond are bright and large and lushly decorated. There are long plush sofas and huge pile carpets and elegant drapes, all of which look brand-new and unused, like a Hollywood set. But among them are scattered irrelevant ornaments, old posters and bits of antiques. These look highly used and personal, obviously chosen by John rather than an interior decorator, but just dumped and forgotten about once the initial whim wore off. These reception rooms might as well be corridors. Nobody ever seems to use them, although they are kept beautifully dusted. They just walk through them to get out.

All the living is done in one little rectangular room at the back of the house. It has one wall completely made of glass and looks over the garden and trees beyond. The kitchen is next to this living room. It is about twice the size and presumably created by the same opulent color-supplement hand who did their main reception room.

John, his wife Cynthia, and their son Julian (born April 8, 1963) spend most of their time in this living room and kitchen. The surrounding opulence seems to have nothing to do with them. Dot looks after that.

Inside their quarters, Cyn looks after her family on her own, doing all the cooking for the three of them, though John sometimes makes tea. She looks after Julian by herself. She has never had a nanny, although Dot does a lot of baby-sitting.

Cyn gets worried now and again by the expense of having and not using such a big house. John, when he thinks about it, finds it a laugh. "Everything seems to cost a fortune," she says. "John spends impetuously and it's catching. I'm always feeling guilty. I have to pull myself together now and again, when I realize how much something would mean to some people. Our food and drink bill is amazing. It's just soft drinks, as we don't drink. It's mostly bread, tea, sugar and milk, and cat food. Yet it somehow comes to £120 a month. I don't know how."

Cyn and John have five cats. Their names chart the stages in John's life. There's Mimi, after his aunt, and Nel and Mal, after their road managers. Two kittens, born in 1967 at the height of their Yogi summer, are called Ying and Yang.

A lot of the regular bills, like gas and electricity, are paid directly by their accountant. Cyn pays the rest. "I sometimes open them when they arrive," says John. "If I don't like the look of them I put them away and forget about them till they start complaining. Now and again I do query them, but they just go on about 'Well sir, it's like this, sir.' You never get anywhere."

All the Beatles receive a weekly sum of £50 in fivers to cover any personal expenses, like staff. They rarely carry any money personally.

"I don't know how much money I've got," says John. "I'm not conscious of having a treasure chest full of it at the bottom of the garden. It's all hypothetical, but I know it's not as much as some people think. It's all tied up in things, in various forms. I did ask the accountant once how much it came to. I wrote it down on a bit of paper. But I've lost the bit of paper."

Their little rectangular living room is crammed high with posters, ornaments, and photographs. A large notice pinned on one wall says *Milk Is Harmless*.

They eat in this room, watch telly in this room, and when it's cold or rainy John spends most of his time, when he's not supposed to be writing a song, curled up on a small sofa in this room, doing nothing. The sofa is far too small for him. He would obviously be more comfortable on one of the lush ones from the other room. But he curls his legs around and can lie for hours.

When the weather is fine, he opens the sliding glass door and goes out and sits on a step in the garden, looking down at his swimming pool and his English country garden.

Anthony or Dot usually answers the front door, though if he's in the mood, John does. He rarely answers the telephone. It is almost impossible to get him on the telephone anyway; he has an answer-phone system which takes messages. This in itself puts off most people trying to get through to him. There is a recorded voice which says "This is Weybridge Four, Five, Wubbleyoo Dubbleyoo. Please leave your message now." His unlisted number is always being changed, which is supposed to be one way of keeping it secret. It's a secret from John anyway. He can never remember it.

An ordinary evening *chez Lennon* is ordinary. It's just like it is in millions of other south-British, two-parents-and-a-child, TV-family homes.

This particular ordinary evening, two door-to-door salesmen had come to the door, saying they were Australian students selling magazines. John happened to open the door and had let them in. They said they were in a competition to see who could get most subscriptions. The prize would help their studies. That was their story anyway. John said yeh, very good, come on then, what do you want me to do? They got out the list of the magazines and asked John to tick the ones he would like to read. He ticked a lot and the two salesmen-students said it would come to £74. John said okay, hold on till I find some money. He could only find the packet with the £50 housekeeping cash. He gave them that. They said that would do fine. They thanked him very much and left.

Cyn was making the evening meal. It was served at six thirty. They started with a slice of melon followed by a plate of cold meat with mashed potatoes and cauliflower. John didn't have the meat. He'd decided to be a vegetarian. They all drank cold milk with it.

John had a filling coming out of his tooth which he constantly played with, making a sluicing noise as he ate his food. He went to the fridge in the kitchen to get some more milk. He drank it ice-cold from the bottle. Cyn said that wouldn't do his tooth any good.

Throughout the meal, the television was on. They all turned their seats to watch it. Now and again Cyn or John would change the station. They never seemed to watch any program for more than ten minutes. John stared silently at it, lost and abstracted through his specs. Cyn was reading the *Daily Mirror* at the same time. Julian watched it and chattered. Then he got down from the table and lay on the carpet and started to do a drawing. Cyn got him some colored crayons. They both watched him, asking him what his drawing was. He said it was a bird-cage, like the one in the garden. He explained all the things happening in his drawing. John and Cyn smiled at him as he did.

John then opened the large sliding window and sat on a step to get some fresh air, looking down upon the pool. Round and round the surface of the pool went the automatic filterer, like a space ship which had just landed. Julian came out and went down to the pool. He threw some oars in, then got them out again and came back to the house. Cynthia cleared up.

Terry Doran arrived and was greeted warmly by all, including Julian, who sat on his knee.

"Do you want your dad to put you to bed?" said Cyn, smiling at John, who grinned back. "Or do you want Terry?" Julian said he wanted Terry. But she picked Julian up herself and put him to bed.

"Are you going to roll us a few, then?" said John to Terry. Terry said yes. John got up and brought out a tin toolbox which he opened for Terry. Inside was some tobacco wrapped in silver tinfoil plus some cigarette papers. Terry rolled a couple of cigarettes, which they smoked, sharing them.

This was during the pot-taking period. John was keeping it in a toolbox as he'd decided to hide it in the garden in case the police came. He had a box, but hadn't gotten around to digging a hole.

Cyn came back. The television was still on. They all sat and watched it, still changing programs all the time, until about midnight, when Cyn made some cocoa. Terry left and John and Cyn went to bed. John said he was going to read a paperback book someone had given them. Cyn said oh, she wanted to read that first.

"I'm pleased I made it young. Making it young means that I've now got the rest of my life to do what I really want. It would have been terrible to spend your whole life before you finally make it, just to find out it's meaningless. We knew it was anyway, but we had to find out for ourselves.

"For a long time we always had specific little aims, we never really looked far ahead. It was all a series of goals, to get a record made, to get a number one, to do another one, to do a film, and so on. We just sort of glimpsed it all in stages. We never thought about any big things. Now I can. I'm not interested in little stages now. Acting doesn't interest me any more. It's a waste of time for me. Writing, I've done that. I wanted to do a book and I produced one, so that was it.

"I suppose now what I'm interested in is a Nirvana, the Buddhist heaven. I don't know much about it, or really understand it enough to explain it. George knows more. Studying religion has made me try to improve relationships, not to be unpleasant. It's not a conscious move to change my personality. Perhaps it is. I don't know. I'm just trying to be how I want to be, and how I'd like others to be.

"Drugs have probably helped the understanding of myself better, but not much. Not pot. That's just a harmless giggle. LSD was the self-knowledge which pointed the way in the first place. I was suddenly struck by great visions when I first took acid. But you've got to be looking for it before you can possibly find it. Perhaps I was looking without realizing it. Perhaps I would have found it anyway. It would just have taken longer.

"The first time we took acid was really an accident. Me and George were at dinner and someone gave it to us when we didn't know much about it. We'd taken pot, but that was all. We hadn't heard of the horrors of LSD. And we weren't supervised, which you should be. We did think we were going barmy.

"But there are much better ways of getting there. I've nothing really against the ideas of Christianity and their ways. I suppose I wouldn't make that remark about Jesus today. I think about things differently. I think Buddhism is simple and more logical than Christianity, but I've nothing against Jesus. I'll let Julian learn all about Jesus when he goes to school, but I'll also tell him there have been lots of other Jesuses. I'll tell him about the Buddhist ones; they're good men as well.

"When I made the Jesus remark, lots of people sent me books about Jesus. I read a lot of them and found out things. I've found out, for example, that the Church of England isn't very religious. There's too much politics. You can't be both. You can't be powerful *and* pure. Perhaps I'll find out that the gurus are like that as well, full of politics. I don't know. All I know is that I am being made more aware by it all. I just want to be told more.

"I don't know if you have to be poor or not. I feel I could give up all this. It does waste a lot of energy. I have to wait and see what I'd be giving it up for, what I was replacing it for. I might give up all this material stuff in the end. But at the moment I want to find myself."

Cyn said she had noticed a difference in John. Perhaps he was nicer. He was quieter and more tolerant. But he still didn't communicate very much. "Perhaps I'm being selfish," she said. "It's just easier for me if he tells me things."

John admitted he'd never been one for communicating. He'd read an interview with his chauffeur Anthony in a color supplement in which

Anthony had been quoted as saying that he'd driven John for hours and hours across Spain for his film and John had never spoken to him. "I hadn't realized till then that I hadn't." John's record for not speaking, but just doing nothing and not communicating to anyone, is three days. "I'm an expert at it. I can get up and start doing nothing straight away. I just sit on the step and look into space and think until it's time to go to bed."

He doesn't consider this frittering his time away. He frittered it away even more, immediately after they stopped touring, when he never got out of bed till three in the afternoon. Now at least he tries to get up and see a bit of daylight. He says if he's doing nothing he might as well be doing it when there's some sun around.

Even when he is trying communicate, Cyn, like his aunt Mimi, often finds it difficult to know what he's on about, although he makes more of an effort these days, since Maharishi arrived, taking over from the Buddhism.

"I do find it hard to pass the time of day with people. There's no point in that sort of talk. Now and again I do it, as a game, to see if I can. How are you? What's the time? How are we getting on? Those sort of pointless things. The main thing is, there's nothing to talk about any more. I *think* communication all the time like mad, but putting it into words is a waste of time.

"We talk in code to each other as Beatles. We always did that, when we had so many strangers round us on tours. We never really communicated with other people. Now that we don't meet strangers at all, there is no need for any communication. We understand each other. It doesn't matter about the rest. Now and again, even though we feel each other, we do have a talking communication session, when we have to say things out loud, or otherwise we forget what we know we've decided among ourselves.

"I do daydream a lot. That's in the same class as idle conversation, so I suppose I shouldn't really condemn idle conversation. Just the normal daydreams, what am I going to do today, shall I get up or not, shall I write that song or not, no I'm not going to answer that phone.

"Talking is the slowest form of communicating anyway. Music is much better. We're communicating to the outside world through our music. The office in America say they listen to *Sergeant Pepper* over and over so that they know what we're thinking in London.

"I do have little spasms of talking. I go and chat to Dot, or Anthony, or the gardener, just to see if I can do it. It surprises them." The biggest change in John is the decline in his aggression brought about by success.

"It took a long, long time," says Ivan Vaughan, his friend from school. "Even a couple of years ago, the old animosities were still there, refusing to talk to anybody, being rude, slamming the door. Now he's just as likely to say to people come in, sit down."

Pete Shotton, another boyhood friend who now manages the Apple Boutique, agrees that all the chips have been smoothed down. "The good I always saw in him is now at the top. It was only people like schoolmasters who thought he was all bad. No one would ever believe what I saw in him at the time.

"It's great that he's so happy. He spent his whole childhood and all his youth trying all the time to be number one. He had to be the leader at all times, either by fighting everyone or, if they were big, by undermining them by abuse or sarcasm.

"Today John is not trying to prove anything; he doesn't have to be number one, that's why he's happy. You can even *see* the change. He used to walk like this at school and at the Art College, all hunched up, his eyes and head down, like a scared rabbit, driven into a corner but ready to lash out. You can see it in all the old pictures of him. Now he can smile in pictures.

"He's now learning because he wants to learn. At school you are forced to learn because you have to fit into society.

"But John hasn't changed in some things. He's not big-headed or vain, and he's as generous as ever. When John had a dozen sweets in a bag and there were three of us round him, he'd share them all out, three sweets each. He made me more generous, just by being with him."

John doesn't see why success should have made him big-headed or changed him in any way. Apart from thinking that success is meaningless, he also thinks anybody can do it, which Paul also thinks. Both John and Paul feel that the most important thing about success is will power. "Everyone can be a success. If you keep saying that enough times to yourself you can be.

"We're no better than anybody else. Nobody is. We're all the same. We're as good as Beethoven. Everyone's the same inside. You need the desire and the right circumstances, but it's nothing to do with talent, or with training or education. You get primitive painters and writers, don't you? Nobody told them how to do it. They told themselves they could do it and just did it.

"What's talent? I don't know. Are you born with it, do you discover you have it later on? The basic talent is believing you can do something.

Me and Paul were always drawing but George wouldn't even try because he said he couldn't draw. It took us a long time to persuade him anyone could draw. Now he's drawing all the time. And he's getting better.

"We knew that the GCE wasn't the opening to anything. We could have ground through all that and gone further, but not for me. I believed something was going to happen which I'd have to get through. And I knew it wasn't GCE. Up to the age of fifteen I was no different from any other little cunt of fifteen. Then I decided I'd write a little song, and I did. But it didn't make me any different. That's a load of crap that I discovered a talent. I just did it. I've no talent, except a talent for being happy or a talent for skivving.

"Someone wants to bust open this whole talent myth, wise everybody up. Politicians have no talent. It's all a con.

"Perhaps my guru will tell me what my real talent is, something else that I really should be doing. I never felt any responsibility, being a so-called idol. It's wrong of people to expect it. What they are doing is putting their responsibilities on us, as Paul said to the newspapers when he admitted taking LSD. If they were worried about him being responsible, they should have been responsible enough and not printed it, if they were genuinely worried about people copying.

"I only felt responsible to the public in that we tried to be as natural as we could. We did put on our social faces, but that was to be expected. But given the circumstances, we were as natural as we could be. Being asked the same questions at the same sort of places all over the world, all about the four mop tops. That was boring. And having to be social to so many people and Lord Mayors' wives. All those tasteless people who determine tastes. All those people with no standards, setting all the standards.

"Even from the beginning I hated such things as meeting the promoter's wife. People were always saying you had to go through with all the false social things. You just couldn't be yourself. They wouldn't understand if you said what you wanted to say. All you could do was make jokes, which I was expected to do anyway after a while. I don't really believe people are like that. Yet why do they go through with it all?

"I don't have to go anywhere now, perhaps a club now and again. Cyn cons me into it. We went to some opening the other night, some old friend. David Jacobs was everywhere. I went with George. He realized what it was going to be like the minute we got to the door but I didn't. I looked round and he'd gone. He never even went inside. But I was in and was stuck. It was horrible.

"I'm never conscious of being a Beatle. Never. I'm just me. I'm not famous. It's other people that do it. Until they come up and react, you've forgotten. Oh, yes, that's why they're behaving so strange; then I remember I'm a Beatle. I was more used to it a year or so ago, when we were in the thick of it, moving round the country, meeting people all the time who you knew were going to stare. I don't move around now, except with people I know, so I forget, till I go somewhere new and people stare.

"People did stare at us before we were famous. Going on a bus to the Cavern, all in leather and carrying guitars. We liked it then. It was our bit of rebellion, just to annoy all the Annie Walkers sitting in the Kardomah. I miss playing soft jokes on people. I used to do it on trains, go into people's compartments and pretend to be soft, or in shops. I still feel an urge to do that, but you can't. It would be Beatles Play Tricks. This Will Give You a Laugh.

"We were on the way to Wembley once in the van. We wrote on a piece of paper 'Which Way to Wembley.' We spoke in a foreign language and pointed to a map of Wales. Everybody went mad putting us right.

"We did all think of disguises once, so we could get around. George and I went through the customs in long coats and beards thinking no one would recognize us, but they all did. Paul was the best. He pretended to be a weird photographer, coming out with a lot of psychological gibberish. He even fooled Brian."

Most of all, John misses just going out and about and being ordinary. Even though Beatlemania is long since over, it is impossible for him or any of the Beatles to go anywhere and not be recognized. Cyn can manage on her own. Her years of avoiding all publicity have now paid off. "But we can't do a simple thing together as a family, like going for a walk. It's terrible. Sometimes I wish it had never all happened."

Of all the Beatles John is the one who most detests not being able to be a private citizen. When he thinks that perhaps he is doomed forever to be well-known, whatever he does from now on, it almost makes him scream.

"No! You don't think that would happen do you? Not famous forever? What if we disappeared for years and years, wouldn't that work? I suppose we'd then just become famous in another way, like Greta Garbo. Perhaps a new group will come along and take over from us. It would be so nice to be completely forgotten."

Toward the end of 1967 and in early 1968 the Beatles did start trying to make contact with the real world again. They found that their faces had become so famous that, like the Queen, people don't expect to see them or her in the street or in a Wimpy bar. They managed quite easily to go to little cafés in Soho during the cutting of the *Magical Mystery*

Tour. By getting in a corner with a few technicians and talking away they just looked like another group of film people. So many people at the time looked like the Beatles anyway, with sideboards and mustaches.

"I did a trial run with Ringo the other day. We went to the pictures, the first time for years and years, since we lived in Liverpool. We went to see a Morecambe and Wise film in Esher. We chose a matinee, thinking it would be quiet, but we forgot the schools were off, and it was packed. We didn't see the whole film. We had an ice cream, then left. Nobody bothered us. It was just a practice run. I might go more often now.

"Brian did use to take us to a West End theater now and again. We'd go in a party and that would be okay. People would stare, but we wouldn't be bothered too much. But I don't care about the theater, so I'm not worried about missing that. It's just five blokes on the stage pretending to be somewhere else. But I miss the cinema. I spent all my time at the pictures in Liverpool.

"Ringo and I also went on a bus. We just decided to try it, to see if we could do it. I'd never been on a London bus before. It was on the Embankment. We were on the bus twenty minutes. It was great. We got recognized, but it didn't matter too much. We were in the mood for it. We started filming all the people on the bus. The conductress told us dirty jokes. Most people didn't really believe it was us. Some newspaper rang up the office the next day. They said some woman was claiming she'd seen us on a bus. I told them to say she was wrong. It wasn't us. The next thing would have been the newspaper ringing us up and saying what was it like, John, going on a bus after all these years? I could be arsed with all that.

"What I'd like is to be completely left alone. I'm not a mixer. I've got enough friends to see me through. I just want to be left alone.

"My so-called outgoing character is all false. I kept it up for years, but I'm not a loudmouth. It was a part I put on, as a defense. I cried wolf and I'm paying for it now. I know it sounds like a moan. Perhaps it's just because the grass is always greener."

Paul and George do tend to go and see people now and again. John rarely makes an attempt to give out or make contact. Things have to come to him, or else he doesn't care about them. And the way his life is ordered, it is hard for anything to get through to him, except on the telly, which he has on nonstop.

"A couple of weeks of telly-watching is as good as pot. When I used to watch it a few years ago I couldn't stand people like Hughie Green;

now he doesn't annoy me. Everything's the same. It's like a newspaper. You read all stories and they go into your head as one.

"I think a lot when I'm watching telly. It's like looking into the fire and daydreaming. You're watching it, but your mind's not on it." The only live stimulus John gets is from the other Beatles. No one has been within light years of taking their place in his life.

At first, they naturally repelled all boarders, because they were so busy going their own way, doing their own thing together. When they became famous and people deliberately tried to get into their circle, usually for the wrong reasons, they actively and brutally repulsed all advances.

Most show-business stars change their friends as they change the size of the billing. Apart from Mick Jagger of the Rolling Stones, the Beatles have picked up no friends from the pop-music world. In their daily life, there is still only each other or Mal, Neil, and Terry.

"We have met some new people since we've become famous, but we've never been able to stand them for more than two days. Some hang on a bit longer, perhaps a few weeks, but that's all. Most people don't get across to us."

John sees Ringo most of all, since he just lives around the corner. He pops over to his place when he's bored to play in Ringo's garden or play with Ringo's expensive toys. They never make dates or proper arrangements. Things are just done as the mood takes them. Everything's on a basis of if I see you, I see you. John most of all can't be without the other three for very long, which is hard luck on Cyn. He doesn't mean it any way nastily, as he doesn't mean not talking to her or going into a semi-trance to be an insult to her. That's just him, which she has to accept.

"If I am on my own for three days, doing nothing, I almost leave myself completely. I'm just not here. Cyn doesn't realize it. I'm up there watching myself, or I'm at the back of my head. I can see my hands and realize they're moving, but it's a robot who's doing it.

"Ringo understands it. I can discuss it with him. I have to see the others to see myself. I realize then there is someone else like me, so it's satisfying and reassuring. It's frightening, really, when it gets too bad. I have to see them to establish contact with myself again and come down. Sometimes I don't come down. We were recording the other night and I just wasn't there. Neither was Paul. We were like two robots, going through the motions.

"We do need each other a lot. When we used to meet again after an interval we always used to be embarrassed about touching each other. We'd do an elaborate handshake just to hide the embarrassment. Or we did mad dances. Then we got to hugging each other. Now we do the Buddhist bit, arms around. It's just saying hello, that's all."

Now and again he gets the desire to go off somewhere, with Cyn and Julian, and of course the Beatles as well. The Greek island idea, which John was particularly keen on, greatly appealed to him at the time. "We're all going to live there, perhaps forever, just coming home for visits. Or it might just be six months a year. It'll be fantastic, all on our own on this island. There's some little houses which we'll do up and knock together and live sort of communally.

"I'm not worried about the political situation in Greece, as long as it doesn't affect us. I don't care if the government is all fascist, or Communist. I don't care. They're all as bad as here; worse, most of them. I've seen England and the U.S.A. and I don't care for either of their governments. They're all the same. Look what they're doing here. They stopped Radio Caroline and tried to put the Stones away while they're spending billions on nuclear armaments and the place is full of U.S. bases that no one knows about. They're all over North Wales."

But the Greek idea came to nothing, as did other mad ideas he's had from time to time in the last two years. One day he was all set to go to India in his caravan, though the caravan doesn't look strong enough to take him into Weybridge. He and Cyn and Julian were going to live inside it, so he said, while his chauffeur Anthony pulled them in the Rolls. Another idea was to go off and live on an island off the coast of Ireland. He did buy the island. "No, I can't remember where. Just somewhere off Ireland."

But the Greek idea was discussed for many weeks. It even got to the stage of trying to work out what to do about Julian and his schooling. John has some strong theories about the sort of schooling he wants Julian to have, but he usually forgets about them when he's contemplating six months on a deserted Greek island. He could go to a school in Greece, he told Cyn, who was obviously much more realistic about the problem than John. "What's wrong with that? He'd just spend six months of the year there and the rest here at his English school. These little Greek village schools are very good, you know. Why can't Julian go along with them? He'll soon pick up the language."

Cynthia said the chopping and changing around wouldn't do him any good. And what if he didn't pick up Greek, would the rest of his class wait for him?

John then thought of sending him to the English school in Athens where all the British diplomats and others send their kids. Cyn pointed out that would mean him boarding in Athens. They were both against that. Neither wants him to go away to boarding school.

John would prefer a council school, if possible. A council school is a free school run by the government, as opposed to private or fee-paying schools which are run and owned independently. He'd just found out that the local nursery school Julian was going to wasn't a council one, as he'd thought. Cynthia explained to him that there wasn't a council nursery school she could get him into; that was why she'd done it.

"I don't know," said John. "I suppose the fee-paying schools are no worse than the others. As long as he's happy. What does it matter if you have to pay? But I definitely won't send him to a boarding school. I wouldn't send him to Eton. They'd teach him to believe all that shit if he went to Eton. Perhaps a Buddhist school, if there is one. Or a day school, a progressive one, not far from Weybridge, that's all we want.

"We've been thinking of Julian's schooling for some time. I even got a book out about all the schools in England. All they went on about was that they could offer football and tennis. Ridiculous, isn't it? They've got all their priorities wrong. He's got to be taught to be aware of other people, that's all. He doesn't want to know how Sir Francis Drake killed all the Spaniards and that Britain invented television and all that shit fool nationalistic stuff. He wants to know how to live in this world.

"If we do go abroad, then I suppose it'll have to be a tutor, but we'll have to make sure there are other kids for him to play with. I had a happy childhood. I liked being at school. It was just that the teachers hated me and I hated teachers. But I liked school. When we're all talking about our memories it's sometimes us as the Beatles, but more often it's remembering about our school days.

"I don't think Julian could go to the sort of school I went to. I have to admit a council school might be tough for him now, thanks to me. He'd be laughed at. Millionaire pop singer's son. They'd all point at him. At least that wouldn't matter so much in a fee-paying school, where all they think about is money."

Cyn is stronger than she looks. She's been through it all before and knows where she is. She understands John's often apparent lack of consideration. He can be selfish, but not deliberately—just without thinking. All the rows they had in their early Liverpool days are long since over. They are very happy, though she still says that but for her becoming pregnant they would probably never have married. John agrees.

"John never thought of settling down in any way, just as he never thought of taking a proper job. If I hadn't got pregnant and then married, as he started touring round the world, we would just have drifted apart. I would have stuck in at the Art College and probably have become a teacher. But for Julian, it would never have happened. It kept us tied together."

She doesn't think any such thing as love would have kept them going if they'd been so far apart. "His love was for the Beatles. Without the baby he would just have gone off with the Beatles forever."

They both say they are glad the baby did happen, keeping them together. They also think it was meant to happen. It was Fate. John particularly believes in Fate.

Cyn now and again would like to try something new, to have a job, perhaps use her art-college training in some way. She and Pattie, George's wife, did discuss the idea once of opening a boutique together in Esher, but it never came to anything.

"I am becoming a bit frustrated. I don't really want to have another child at the moment, now that we can get around so much. I know that might mean leaving it too late and I would never want another.

"But I'm frustrated really because I'd like something to *do*. I do a bit of painting and dressmaking, but I often think I'd like a job. Not now, but later on. I've never had a job. I might do some designing, or perhaps teaching."

Cyn teases John about his dependence on the Beatles, and is obviously hurt by it sometimes. "I do find I suggest something and he just ignores it at the time, or says it's wrong. Then a few weeks later Ringo suggests the same thing and he's all for it. But I don't worry. I can't put it into words, but I feel strong. It's a sense. I understand things.

"What I would like is a holiday on our own, without the Beatles. Just John, Julian, and me."

"You what?" said John, smiling. "Not even with our Beatle buddies?"

"Yes, John. Don't you remember we were talking about it last week?"

"What did we say?"

"We said the three of us could just go off somewhere, not with your buddies."

"But it's nice to have your mates around."

"That really offends me. He does think it's not enough just to go with his family."

He smiled at her. She shook her head at him.

"They seem to need you less than you need them," she said.

Before he could reply to this one she got in with an example she'd obviously had all ready. "George went off to Los Angeles, just with Pattie, didn't he? *He* didn't need to get everyone to go with him."

John smiled. He agreed it did seem to be true. "I did try to go my own way after we stopped touring. I had a few good laughs and games of monopoly on my film, but it didn't work. I didn't meet anyone else I liked. I was never so glad to see the others. Seeing them made me feel normal again." Cyn looked soulfully at him.

"Okay, I know! We'll all retire to a little cottage on a cliff in Cornwall, all right?"

"No, but I can't retire. I've got these bloody songs to write. I have to work, to justify living."

Chapter 32: Paul

Paul is the only London Beatle. He lives in a large detached three-story house in St. John's Wood, near Lord's cricket ground and just round the corner from EMI's recording studios. He bought it at the end of 1966 for £40,000. He didn't do much knocking about, compared with John and Ringo. Paul spent nothing on some things, such as the garden. It became a jungle, completely overgrown, inhabited only by the prowling Martha. When he'd moved in it had been very pretty. Everybody kept on at him, especially his dad, to do something about it. He seemed to delight in its wildness and the way it annoyed some people. But at the end of 1967, he decided to start having it spruced up. He got the idea of building a magical house in it, a sort of pagoda on a raised platform with an open glass roof onto the skies.

The front of the house has a paved courtyard with an old-fashioned lamp-post. On the left, attached to the house, is a double garage in which he keeps his Mini Cooper and Aston Martin. The house is guarded by a high brick wall and large double black gates controlled from the house. You speak into a microphone, someone inside answers, and if you say the right thing, the doors swing open and then clank shut again to keep out the fans.

All the Beatle homes have fans hanging around, but Paul has most, being Paul but also being in London. They keep up a permanent watch outside, usually sitting in rows on the wall of the house opposite. From there they can just see over the wall and make out any movements around the front door. Coming into the street you can tell Paul's house by the rows of girls hanging precariously from his wall, a couple of feet off the ground, craning to look over.

The basement of the house contains a staff flat. For a long time he had a couple who both lived there, Mr. and Mrs. Kelly. She did the house-keeping and he was a sort of butler, but both really mucked about and were just there. After them, he has had a succession of people. They just seem to arrive at random and he keeps them on sometimes, however unsuitable. He could really do with a secretary, to organize his house and his visitors, but he says he would never do that. Very often he has nobody living in the house and when he's been abroad his dad Jim sometimes has to come down to look after the house and Martha.

Not that Paul worries about it. It doesn't bother him that people he's promised to see arrive and he's gone off to Africa or America. All he likes around is a nice motherly lady who serves up a fried breakfast at about one o'clock and at other hours of the day as required. When Jane is not working, she does a lot of the cooking and is very good.

The ground floor contains the kitchen which is very large and well-appointed, a large haughty dining room which looks completely unused, and his living room at the back, which is the most used of any Beatle room. This is very large and comfy with French windows opening onto the back garden. It has a large soft-green Edwardian suite, nicely faded. There is a large wooden table in this living room where most meals are served, rather than in the dining room. It is usually covered with an elderly white-lace tablecloth, very working-class posh. The room is usually in chaos, with stuff piled everywhere, ornaments, flashing lights, packages, newspapers, and bits of equipment. This is where the Beatles and Mal and Neil and others congregate before recording sessions—and in fact most times they are in London. It has a great, unpretentious lived-in feeling. "Everywhere I've lived always ends up like this. At Forthlin it was the same. Things might look a bit different now, like a big color TV, but the atmosphere's always the same."

The people around are really the same as well, the Beatles plus Mal and Neil, all speaking in the same Liverpool accents. Jane's mother and sister were there one afternoon, to watch Wimbledon on the color TV. The whole room seemed to take on a different, middle-class *persona,* with different accents and attitudes and movements. They were having strawberries and cream for tea. It seemed centuries away from the Liverpool fry-ups and bottles of sauce. Paul was enjoying it all just as much.

On the first floor is Paul's bedroom, a large L-shaped room with an extravagant bed with a large carved headboard. Jane helped him furnish this room. There are two other bedrooms. On the top floor is his workroom, where he and John do most of their hard slog together when they need some more songs to fill up an album. This is where he has the Paulozzi sculpture. Very interesting, that piece. Paulozzi was Stu Sutcliffe's hero and teacher.

The famous Martha (if you don't think she's famous you should read

Beatles Monthly) is a very large, shaggy good-natured old English sheep dog. She's good-natured even when she has a few fleas. She has her own trapdoor into the garden for her regular prowls, but Paul tries to take her a proper walk himself as often as he can. He usually goes to Primrose Hill or Regent's Park. He did go to Hampstead Heath once, but Martha had a fit and he hasn't taken her back. There are also several cats, one called Thisby, and kittens, which seem to vary in number from day to day. All the Beatles have cats (and all their births are faithfully reported in *Beatles Monthly*), but Paul is the only one with a dog.

Paul manages his walks with Martha with surprising lack of recognition. The fans never realize where he's going when he rushes out. And in the park, he usually has his jacket collar up and walks round the remotest parts with Martha, meeting only elderly dog-lovers who are more interested in the enormous Martha than in Paul.

He exchanges the time of day with other people and makes polite dog chat. He even shouts out at people he vaguely recognizes, something the other Beatles wouldn't do, not being as social as Paul. He was on the top of Primrose Hill one day when he saw an actor he knew slightly. He shouted at him, but the actor walked past, as if to say I don't know you so please don't shout, there's a good chap. He was a terribly upper-class young English-type actor. He gave a great backwards Hello when he at last recognized Paul. Paul had met him once through Jane. He'd been acting in the same play and had invited Jane and Paul to his house for dinner. Paul asked him how he was doing, then. The actor said, very coyly, that he had a chance of a play in New York. "Oh aye," said Paul. "What?"

"Can't tell," said the actor, going even coyer. "Sorry. Never do. When there's something in the offing one might spoil it by talking about it, mightn't one? Don't you find that, hmm?" Paul smiled and said yeh, he supposed so. "Well, bye then," said the actor. He breezed off, swinging his arms, looking up and breathing heavily at the lovely day. You could almost see him reading the stage directions.

"Strange, isn't it," said Paul, walking back to the car. "How somebody like that just can't relax. It's impossible for him to be natural. Yet he's okay, he's a nice-enough bloke once he relaxes and has a few drinks. By the end of that dinner we had with him he was almost normal. I feel sorry for people like that, really. It's the way they've been conditioned.

"When I was a kid of sixteen, all adolescent and awkward and shy, I was dying to be an actor like that, all smooth and in command, always coming on dead confident. But it was worth going through that awkward stage, just to be natural now. Jane has a little bit of the same trouble, with her middle-class background. She can't help it. It's how they've been brought up."

Jane and Paul make a very loving and lovely couple. Everyone agrees on this. From the very beginning, Jim said nothing would make him happier than their marriage.

Jane comes from a solid middle-class professional London family. Her father is a doctor and her mother a professor of music. She began acting, in films and on stage, as a child. She met Paul in May 1963 at a pop concert at Albert Hall. She was then seventeen and had been appearing on the TV pop-record program "Juke Box Jury." The *Radio Times* asked her to go along to the concert with a reporter and give her comments, as a teenager, on the groups. She said the only one worth screaming over was the Beatles. The Beatle she liked the look of most, when she caught sight of them in the corridors afterward, was George.

But it was Paul, who always was a star spotter, who recognized her and shouted after her, which brought the rest of them rushing round her. "We all said, 'Will you marry me,' " says Paul, "which was what we said to every girl at the time." They invited her back to their hotel, the Royal Court, for a drink. "A rare London bird, the sort we'd always heard about. We thought we were set."

The others left Paul alone in the bedroom with Jane, after a lot of winking. They spent the evening talking about gravy and what was their favorite meal. "I realized this was the girl for me. I hadn't tried to grab her or make her. I told her, 'It appears you're a nice girl.' "

"They couldn't believe I was a virgin," says Jane.

They went out many times in the next few weeks, often just walking round Soho together. Nobody yet recognized Paul in early 1963, though a lot knew Jane. When he came back from a short holiday in Rome, Jane and her mother met him at London Airport. He missed a connection back to Liverpool but Mrs. Asher said he could stay the night with them. Paul didn't want to. He didn't like the idea of staying with a girl's family. It's not the sort of thing working-class lads do. But he agreed in the end, just to stay the night. The night turned into three nights, then into three weeks, then into three years. Unbeknown to fans, Paul lived all his London life at Jane's house until at the end of 1966 he got his own house in St. John's Wood.

An evening with them, once again, is like an evening with any other young couple. Jane made the dinner. It was all vegetarian; Paul had just become one, like John and George. Jane made it and served it up beautifully, with no fuss or show. The first course was avocado vinaigrette, followed by a casserole of spaghetti, vegetables, nuts, and spices. They shared a half-bottle of white wine, which was already opened. This one had been opened for cooking. They were just finishing it up.

Throughout the meal, fans were ringing the doorbell. It was a time when Paul was between staff. Each time Jane answered them, speaking through the intercom. She was very polite. She got up nicely from her meal each time, not at all angry, and asked them if they would mind waiting as they were still eating. Paul, at this stage in the day, after dozens of doorbell fans, wouldn't have bothered. He would have stopped answering by then, as he had done that time Brian Epstein called and couldn't get in. In the end, she made Paul go, even before he'd finished his meal. He gave a twisted smile, but went out and signed for all the girls who'd been waiting.

After dinner they got out some photographs that had been taken on a Scottish holiday they'd just had. Paul has a house in a remote part of Argyllshire where they usually spend at least one week a year. Then they watched color TV and went to bed.

It was perhaps a quieter evening than normal. Paul often has some friends dropping in. People do tend to drop in a lot to see Paul, which he encourages. It happened a lot during the five months Jane was acting in America. It rarely happens to the others, partly because they live farther out. During a new album, people are coming and going all the time. Paul is now so much the leader (he was even before Brian died) in organizing many of their affairs that most things happen from his house.

Peter Blake, the artist, came to Paul's house during the discussions for the *Sergeant Pepper* cover. John was usually there as well, and so was Terry Doran. Just after Peter Blake left one afternoon, Paul's man, the one who was working in the house at the time, came into the living room to say that the Vicar of St. Mark's was at the front gate. They all laughed.

Someone said it must be a gag. Paul looked at John. John obviously didn't want to see any vicar. Paul said to his man to get rid of him. Terry said it was probably a TV actor, dressed up. They laughed. Paul said perhaps Terry should be the one to go and tell him politely that Paul was out. As Terry was halfway across the room, Paul said no, we'll let him in, eh? If he looks alright, he might be interesting. Terry came back from the front gate and said, he's foony, honest. So the electronic gates were allowed to swing open, allowing the vicar to enter.

The vicar, middle-aged and well-scrubbed, entered the living room, very nervously. Everybody smiled politely at him. Paul told him to sit down. He apologized for coming in on them when he knew they must be so busy, so frightfully busy, he knew that. He was already making their excuses for them, for whatever it was he was going to ask them to do.

He was obviously so surprised to get in. He knew it couldn't last long and he'd be straight out. Paul asked what he wanted.

The vicar turned to face Paul, having realized he must be Mr. McCartney. He'd been peering round, trying hard, but obviously unable to recognize anybody. He explained that Paul was in his parish. Mr. George McWatters would be writing to him anyway, he said, holding his hands together. It was just that they were having a garden fete and he was wondering if Paul could come along, just pop in for a second. Of course he knew how busy they were. It was marvelous, all they had done. They must be very busy people, he knew that.

"No, I never do that," said Paul. "Of course, of course," said the vicar, hurriedly, "I couldn't expect it. You're so busy. I knew it. So busy . . ."

"No, we're not," said Paul. "It's not that at all. It just wouldn't be right, would it, as I don't believe. You know?" Paul was smiling. The vicar smiled back not listening, just nodding in agreement with everything Paul said.

"Why don't you make the product better," said Paul, still smiling kindly, "instead of getting gimmicks like us?" "Oh, you're quite right, quite right. We are trying. We're trying hard to get all together. We've got an inter-denominational service next week. . . ."

"That'll be good," said Paul, "for a start. Of course, if we got going on this, we'd be here all night, wouldn't we."

"You're quite right," said the vicar. "And you're so busy. I couldn't expect you to come, you're so busy . . ."

Paul didn't bother to explain again, that that was not the reason. The vicar started to get up, smiling, and so did everyone else in the room. He went round them all, smiling earnestly and thanking them for all their time. He stared hard at everyone, trying to place them, knowing they must be placeable. Paul went with him to the door. As he left the room, he turned round again and said to everyone, "I suppose you're *all* world-famous." Then he left.

When he'd gone, everyone said how nice he was. John particularly was pleased at not being recognized. He said it was funny how people always got worried when they didn't recognize you straight ·way, as if you would be hurt, not realizing it was the opposite.

It was about five o'clock. Mrs. Mills, Paul's housekeeper at the time, served breakfast all round. Fried eggs, bacon, and black pudding. She brought in a big pile of sliced bread, already buttered, and endless tea. George and Ringo, then Neil and Mal arrived, and they all got a cup of tea. Then they went off to the recording studio.

Apart from Beatle people, or people associated in some way with the record they're working on, Paul often has a lot of his Liverpool relations staying with him. His dad and stepmother Angie and stepsister Ruth, plus his aunts and uncles, often have a week with him. Paul goes up to Liverpool most of all the Beatles. John doesn't go at all, with Mimi in Bournemouth he has no relations in Liverpool. George goes up to Warrington quite a lot to see his folks, and so does Ringo. But Paul is always going up for the weekend on a sudden whim, if Jane is away and there's no work on. Jane often goes with him as well.

Michael McCartney, Paul's brother, is probably the most frequent Liverpool visitor, especially since his own records and work began to have a London success.

The phone never seems to stop ringing. There are two numbers, both unlisted, but no matter how often the numbers are changed, fans still find out. Paul answers the phone himself, always with a funny voice. It's easy to tell a fan by the frightened silence, in which case he hangs up without speaking. "Oh, yeh, hi," he said on the phone, still keeping up his funny voice, but admitting who it was by the way he was speaking. It was a well-known disk jockey, inviting him to come down on Sunday and do some horseback riding. "Yeh, I might at that," said Paul, politely, but not definitely promising anything. He made faces down the phone as the other person smarmed on about the excellent riding. "Yeh, great, yeh. Okay, then. I might see you. Cheerio."

The phone rang again and it was his dad, asking about his proposed trip up to Liverpool at the weekend. "What time do you think you'll be coming, son?" said Jim. "Just so I can get ready."

"Ready for what?" said Paul.

"Oh you know, just get things ready."

"Don't be so stupid, Dad. I don't want you to get ready for anything. I'll arrive when I arrive."

Astrid in Germany was always suspicious of Paul's charm at first, though his relationship with Stu was also bound up in this. "It used to frighten me that someone could be so nice all the time. Which is silly. It's ridiculous to feel at home with nasty people, just because you feel that at least you know where you are with them. It's silly to be wary of nice people." A lot of Paul's niceness comes from his dad. His brother Michael has it as well. At seventeen, when the others were in revolt against their parents, Paul was the only one who listened to his dad and his little homilies—and was mocked by the others for doing so.

Paul is the easiest to get to know for an outsider, but in the end he is the hardest to get to know. There is a feeling that he is holding things back, that he is one jump ahead, aware of the impression he is giving. He is self-conscious, which the others are not. John doesn't care, either way, what people think. Ringo is too adult to think about such things, and George in many ways isn't conscious. He is above it all.

Paul himself has come to terms with himself, having gone through a stage of trying not to be so nice or to appear keen. "I do find it more of an effort *not* to make an effort. It's more false for me not to. So I might as well make the effort."

Paul's way of making an effort, by being polite and hard-working, was essential to the group. It was his public relations approach which Brian Epstein brought out. Even before that, Paul gave them any gloss they had, writing little handout letters and making little speeches. His way of making an effort has been especially vital to them since Brian Epstein died. Paul today makes most of the running. This is why it is true to say that in some ways Paul is the leader today, not John, though talking seriously about a leader of the Beatles is as pointless as it ever was. Paul is the businessman; he's the pusher, he gets things done and wheedles the rest along with him. But no big decisions are ever taken unless they all agree.

Once decisions are taken, Paul starts moving and doesn't put up with inefficiencies. There was some hold-up over a proof of the *Sergeant Pepper* cover. He hadn't received one when he should have, so he rang EMI and went through department after department till he found the person whose fault it was. He told them exactly what he thought of them. The proof was brought round immediately by car, covered by apologies.

Another time, during some other discussions with EMI, Paul rang up the boss himself, Chairman Sir Joseph Lockwood. Sir Joseph told Paul on the phone to sit tight. Then he jumped into his Rolls-Royce and came round to Paul's house personally to settle everything.

Paul is keen; he does want things to go well. He also still has a slight residue of resentment, which they all had at one time. This came from being pushed around and looked upon as pretty stupid because they were just beat-group players. He hates any insinuation that he is thick. He came back from a meeting with the Nems people one day, after he'd been trying to persuade them what a good idea Apple would be, furious at their attitude. "They think we're all thick," he said, walking round and round his living room.

The whole Apple idea and impetus is Paul's. It got going before Brian died, but it was still all Paul's creation. John and the others agree with everything and are there for all the big meetings. Paul sees it as a huge corporation, with shops, clubs, studios, and the best people in the business—from cameramen and engineers to artists, writers, and composers.

"We want to make it an environment. An umbrella where people can do things in the way they want. There's thousands and thousands of pounds going through Nems and not being properly used. They've got it all tied up for us in the Bingley Building Society or somewhere.

"But it's all just a hobby, really, like our music. We do that with our feet up. When we get Apple going big, we'll do that with our feet up. You can have business meetings which are an uplift not a bring-down."

The Magical Mystery Tour would never have got off the ground without Paul. He put his whole life into it for the fifteen weeks, directing every stage. So it was a disappointment to him at first when the British reviews were so bad. "We knew from the beginning we were just practicing. We knew we weren't taking time or doing things properly, but when you've spent a long time on something, even when it's not good enough, you begin to feel perhaps it is better than you know it is. I'm glad now it was badly received. It would have been bad to have got away with all that. It's now a challenge to do something properly."

Paul went straight from Magical Mystery Tour into thinking of subjects for full-length films. He and Jane went to see *A Man for All Seasons* and were inspired to do something with a big, lush setting. Then he thought of doing a love story. Why should they always be expected to lark around? Then he thought of doing some realism, such as Liverpool during the Depression.

Paul finds it hard not to think of ideas for the Beatles, which makes it a bit hard for Jane. This is one of the main reasons why the idea of marriage never got going all those years. They are close and happy, but there was always something between Paul and the other Beatles which Jane found hard to come to terms with.

"When they are all together, Paul is different. He isn't the same towards me as when we are alone. I want to feel that it is two of us going through life together. I don't want to be part of a gang."

Paul admits perhaps he does react differently when the others are around. "If I've seen Jane for three weeks on our own and then see the fellows for a day, then I want to talk to them."

But Paul and Jane do have more time together, on their own, than probably the other Beatle couples. They do get away together, to places like their Scottish home, thanks to Jane. She wants Paul to move to the country for good, to a quieter smaller house, not in London. Jane is a strong personality. "I always wanted to beat her down," says Paul. "I wanted her to give up work completely."

"I refused. I've been brought up to be always doing something. And I enjoy acting. I didn't want to give that up."

"I know now I was just being silly," says Paul. "It was a game, trying to beat you down." At various times, one of them wanted to get married, but the other didn't. Jane says it was usually something happening with the Beatles, just when it looked all settled, which made her change her mind. Paul says it was her acting, although he agreed when the big tour of America came up that she had to go on that.

"When I came back after five months, Paul had changed so much. He was on LSD, which I knew nothing about. All he could talk about was the spiritual experiences he'd had with John. There were fifteen people dropping in all day long. The house had changed and was full of stuff I didn't know about."

His life is much quieter and more ordered now, since Jane returned. Paul, unlike the others, is very communicative about himself. He does talk everything over with Jane. She knows what he's thinking.

"Another problem," says Paul, "was that my whole existence for so long centered round a bachelor life. I didn't treat women as most people do. I've always had a lot around, even when I've had a steady girl. My life generally has always been very lax, and not normal.

"I knew it was selfish. It caused a few rows. Jane left me once and went off to Bristol to act. I said okay, then leave; I'll find someone else. It was shattering to be without her." This was when he wrote "I'm Looking Through You." Jane has inspired several of his more beautiful songs, such as "And I Love Her."

When they got engaged on Christmas Day 1967, all these problems were in the past. Maharishi for a long time was the only little point of difference, although it was all amicable. Jane didn't fall for him when the others did. She said that she and Paul together could reach a spiritual state on their own. Paul wasn't as committed as George and John, but he still felt there was something there which would help him, which might answer his questions.

The questions he's referring to are about the purpose of life, not about the Beatles. Paul has some well-worked-out views about the Beatles, their changes, and the future. "We've gone through millions of superficial changes which mean nothing and haven't changed us.

"It's like in posh places, you get to like avocado and spinach and other way-out foods. So you have them every time. You learn about wine and that's the scene for a while. When you've done all that, then you can go back. You realize the waiter's just there to ask you what you want, not what anyone expects you to want. So if you feel like corn-flakes for lunch, you ask for them, without feeling like a Northern comedian.

"These sort of cycles are coming and going all the time. Like the mustache. I had one to amaze people, as a fun thing. I had all the fun, then one day took it off. Now I'm back to where I was. Like food; I got through it and realized what it was and came back.

"It's like meeting famous stars. You go through the being-amazed stage when you first meet them, then find out he's just like Harry Bloggs. You knew all the time he was just Harry Bloggs, but you had to go through with it to find out.

"We always come back to ourselves because we never change. We might be A plus One when One equals gray suits. That would be the gray-suit cycle. Then A plus Two when it's floral shirts. But we're always there all the time as A. Then you finish up A plus Dead. Excuse all the clever stuff. I just get carried away talking. But all the changes, you see, the physical ones are superficial. You go into a cycle, but you don't get carried away forever by it, because the more you know, the less you know. And there's always each other as safety valves.

"The thing is, we're all really the same person. We're just four parts of the one. We're individuals, but we make up together The Mates, which is one person. If one of us, one side of the mates, leans over one way we all go with him or we pull him back. We all add something different to the whole.

"Ringo—he's got a great sentimental thing. He likes soul music and always has, though we didn't see that scene for a long time, till he showed us. I suppose that's why we write those sort of songs for him, with sentimental things in them, like 'A Little Help from My Friends.'

"George—he's very definite about things and dedicated when he's decided. It makes the four of us more definite about things, just because of George. We adapt what's in him to our own use. We all take out of each of us what we want or need.

"John—he's got movement. He's a very fast mover. He sees new things happening and he's away.

"Me—I'm conservative. I feel I need to check things. I was last to try pot and LSD and floral clothes. I'm slower than John, the least likely to succeed in class.

"When a new fender guitar came along, John and George would rush out and buy one. John because it was new and George because he'd decided definitely he'd wanted one. Me, I'd hang around thinking, check I had the money, then wait a bit.

"I'm most conservative of the four of us. Not compared with outside people. Compared to my family I'm a freak-out. We still have the same basic roles, because that's what we are. But all of us will always appear to be changing, just because we don't conform. It's this not conforming, wanting to do something different all the time, which keeps our music different.

"The last generation worked all the time to attain a status in life, get certain clothes and a certain pigeonhole, and that was it. We were lucky that by the age of twenty-five we realized we could achieve any pigeonhole we fancied. I could now sit back and be a company director till I'm seventy, but I wouldn't learn as much by trying new things. You *can* learn as much about life just by plowing one furrow all the time, but it tends to make you narrow-minded.

"We've always not conformed. People told us we needed to channel ourselves, but we never believed them. People said we had to wear the school blazer. If you've enough confidence, you don't have to wear a school blazer through life, as so many people think you have to.

"We're not learning to be architects, or painters or writers. We're learning to be. That's all."

Chapter 33: George

George has a very long, low single-story brightly painted bungalow at Esher. It's on a private development, owned by the National Trust, very similar to the one where John and Ringo live. You enter the estate through a gateway from the main road, then go into what looks like the wooded gardens of a stately home. You can't see any houses at first. They are hidden from the roadway, all very secluded and lush-looking. They're named, not numbered, so it's impossible to find any of them. George's is the hardest to find. The name of his house, Kinfauns, is not even on his house or in his garden. The driveway to it looks at first to be part of another house.

The bungalow has two wings to it which enclose a rectangular courtyard at the back. In this he has a heated swimming pool. All the outside walls of the house have been painted by George, or at least sprayed, in bright luminous-looking colors. From his gardens the house looks like a psychedelic mirage.

Inside, the kitchen area is beautifully done, with lots of pinewood furniture and walls and Habitat-type utensils. It looks straight out of a color-supplement guide to a 1968 kitchen. The main living room has two huge windows, completely circular. They start at floor level and go up to the ceiling.

George has no Beatle gold disks or souvenirs in sight. The house might belong to a very contemporary young architect or fashion designer who has spent some time in the East. In the center of the living room are some very low tables. There are leather cushions on the floor beside them, for sitting on Arab fashion. There are no chairs anywhere in sight.

There is an ornate hookah beside one table. George was sitting on the floor, his legs crossed, putting new strings on his sitar. He was wearing a long white Indian shirt. A joss stick was burning from an ornamental holder on the table, filling the room with the sweet smell of incense.

"I don't personally enjoy being a Beatle any more. All that sort of Beatle thing is trivial and unimportant. I'm fed up with all this me, us, I, stuff and all the meaningless things we do. I'm trying to work out solutions to the more important things in life.

"Thinking about being a Beatle is going backwards. I'm more concerned with the future, but it would take six months of just talking to tell you exactly what I believe in—all the Hindu theories, the Eastern philosophies, reincarnation, transcendental meditation. It's when you begin to understand those things that you realize how pointless the other stuff is. To the ordinary believer in God, I know it sounds very far out."

The telephone rang. George picked it up. There was a muffled giggling noise. "Esher wine store," said George, gruffly and impatiently. "No, sorry." And he hung up.

In the kitchen, Pattie and her sister Jennie, who had just dropped in, were embroidering. They were both wearing Eastern Apple boutique clothes. They sat half-smiling, very quietly and solemnly, working away at their embroidery. The noise of George beginning his sitar lesson next door could be heard. The scene was somehow medieval.

Pattie has the least house help of any of the wives, though when she has children she will doubtless have more. They have a daily cleaning woman, Margaret. She usually has most meals with them, as part of the family, which none of the other Beatles' domestic staffs do.

Margaret does most of the cleaning and Pattie does all the cooking. Pattie usually dries all the dishes and also helps to tidy up. "It's not as big a house as it looks. It's so full of junk. If I had any more staff to help, they would just be more bother than their worth."

Pattie also does all the shopping herself, at a local supermarket. She'd just bought a bar of chocolate which she said tasted like soap. She'd sent it back with a letter of complaint. She didn't put her own name on it—she's at last learned from George to avoid any possibility of publicity. She used Margaret's. She was hoping for some free bars as compensation.

Of all the wives, Pattie is perhaps the most co-equal with her husband. They're both very modern in their marriage, the way the magazines are always telling us modern marrieds are. More than the other Beatle wives, she shares her husband's interests. She was in at the very beginning of the interest in Indian culture and shared all those developments. But she does retain some freedom and independence on her own, still doing a little bit of modeling work.

Everybody who has been close to the Beatles over the years says that George is the one who has changed most of all. Even fans who have followed George's progress over a relatively short time say he has changed. He was looked upon by many as the most handsome Beatle at one time. Now fans are always complaining about George letting his hair and mustache grow too unruly and untidy.

That is a superficial change. The inner ones are much more important. George, through being the youngest, was for a long time always considered the youngest in every sense. In comparison with John and Paul, most people who knew all three always looked upon George as just a boy. John and Paul were precocious, physically, sexually, and in their talent. They were writing songs long before George ever thought about it.

George did have a slight inferiority complex. Not seriously, more a hero-worshiping of John. Cyn remembers him always hanging around when she wanted John on his own. So does Astrid, when she was trying to be alone with Stu.

George wasn't academic at school and didn't show many signs of being clever the way Paul did. Taking an ordinary apprenticeship, compared with Paul the bright sixth-former and John the art student, made people unfairly think George wasn't as good as the others.

Ivan Vaughan, who was at the Liverpool Institute with Paul and George, admits he couldn't at first see what Paul and John saw in George. "He just didn't seem as witty or as clever." Julia, John's mother, was horrified when John dragged along another baby-faced friend to meet her. She'd already thought Paul just a kid.

"He was a lovely little boy," says Astrid, telling of their Hamburg days. "He was just little George. We never judged him in any way, the way we used to work out how intelligent or clever Stu, John, and Paul were. He didn't develop as quickly as the others had done.

"But he wasn't stupid. No one thought that for one minute. He made lovely jokes at his own expense, sending himself up for being young. I gave them all their Christmas presents one year, all wrapped up. John opened his first and it was an Olympia Press version of the Marquis de Sade. George picked up his and said 'What's in mine then, comics?' "

George of course always had his guitar, if apparently nothing else. He was even more fanatical about mastering it than Paul or John and was much better than they were. He hardly smiled onstage, he was so busy concentrating. But he wouldn't try to do anything else for a long time, such as drawing. He thought he wasn't clever enough.

But now, since the end of 1966, George is the one with so much. He was the first to rise right out and beyond Beatlemania. They all envied him his new passions in life when they themselves could find so little. He even became the leader in many things. Not by going out of his way to lead, the way John did in the Quarrymen days. The others came to George, following his interests.

George today is the Beatle who needs the other Beatles least. The others admit they all missed each other during those go-it-alone post-touring months. "I didn't miss them at all," George says. "But it was great to get home from India and tell them all about it."

"George doesn't miss anyone," Pattie says. "He's very independent and he's breaking out more and more. He's found something stronger than the Beatles, though he still wants them to share it. He's the source, but he wants them to join in." Because George's abiding passions in life today are Indian religion and Indian music, all the other trappings of being a Beatle pass over him. Yet at one time, he was the most obsessed by all the money and by the business of being a millionaire. He was the one who cross-examined Brian Epstein on all the contracts.

He can't avoid some things like autographs and the telephone. When that happens, he is often the only one who can be rude. He forgets for a minute why it has happened and is simply irritated by perfect strangers interrupting his life. On the train to Bangor he was very angry when his tea was being spoiled by women asking for his autograph. The others, who were resignedly signing away, had to restrain him and tell him not to get angry, however aggressive the fans were.

George is the one who has an absolute mania about any publicity of any sort. Anything getting into the papers about him personally makes him furious, as Pattie knows if she accidentally causes any.

Pattie is the one who is more aware of living a Beatle life, simply because she can't ignore it. She also came into it late compared with Cyn and Maureen, the other Beatle wives. Even after more than two years of marriage, Pattie is still not used to all the publicity and press attention. "I keep thinking, this time it will be okay. No one will know, and even if they do, they won't care. That trip to Los Angeles last year, I thought that would be okay. To my horror, there were TV cameras and hundreds of girls screaming.

"In 1964 when we went to Tahiti, Beatlemania was at its height and we expected it. So we went to great lengths to go secretly. Neil and I flew first to Amsterdam, under assumed names, then we flew back towards Tahiti to meet George. Even then, people still found out. It was just impossible to escape anywhere, whatever you did.

"Things are slightly better today, but it always seems to be worse out of England. You might get on a plane fairly quietly at London Airport, but the awful English press wire the press at the other end and everyone turns out.

"At night times it's not too bad. We have come out of a restaurant and walked down a couple of streets without being pursued.

"But I can't get over the fans always hanging round the house, even now. They come into the garden and rush around. They even come into the house. They got into our bedroom the other day and stole a pair of my trousers and George's pajamas."

Although George has warned her, she has on occasions inadvertently caused publicity. She received a letter through the post one day from an old man asking for people to send him used spectacle frames. He said he was getting bundles of them to send to people in Africa.

She thought it seemed a good cause, so she went out and searched round the shops and bought up all the old spectacles she could find. She took out the glass and sent the old man the frames.

"The next thing there was a story in the *Daily Mirror* about what I'd done. The old man even wrote and thanked me. He said the publicity had done his work a lot of good. George was furious."

Like all the other wives, she has come up against—to her complete surprise—physical danger purely through being a Beatle wife. "The worst time was the Christmas of 1965. They were doing their Christmas Show at Hammersmith. I went with Terry. I scraped my hair back so that I would look completely different and no one would recognize me. I don't know how anyone did, but a few did and started punching me. They took their shoes off and shouted, 'Let's go and get her.' I was hemmed in and couldn't get out. They threw things at me and screamed. Terry managed to drag me towards a side exit, with the girls kicking me as we forced a way through. Some followed me out and started kicking me again. I told them to stop. 'Who do you think you are?' they said. Then we all started fighting this time. I punched one in the face and Terry got one against a wall and held her tight. They were all shouting and swearing. Luckily we got away in the end. They were just horrid little girls. They were so tiny, only thirteen or fourteen years old. I don't know where they were from.

"It's not so bad these days, but it happens. Cyn was attacked not long ago in the street. Some girl kicked her on the legs and said she had to leave John alone, or else. Isn't it amazing, after all the years that John and Cyn have been married?

"I'm still very frightened when I see a gang of girls in the street. I can't face them. I have to go the other way. I always think perhaps they're going to hit me." Being a Beatle wife, like being a Beatle, produces difficult relationships with old friends as well as new ones. Her sister Jennie, who works in the Apple Boutique, is very close to her and spends a lot of time with her at the house. She is also very interested in Indian religion and culture. But apart from Jennie, Pattie has few close friends.

"People will suddenly make a snide remark—'It's all right for you, you can afford to do that.' That sort of thing. Old friends you would think wouldn't come out with such silly things.

"It comes out with new people you meet as well. You think, here's a nice person, then they say something which shows they think I'm different. The other day I was doing a bit of work for *Vogue* and a woman said, 'I don't think of you as a model now, you're more of a celebrity.' I'm not. I'm not an actress or a star or anything. I'm just me, as I always was.

"Some people do understand. If they've been developing a lot themselves, growing up more, they know what it's all about. Cyn was very helpful at first, telling me what to do. That was when we thought of the boutique.

"The wives have got to do something, when they're hours and hours in the recording studio. But then we went off the idea. The next thing we were all leaving Esher anyway, going off to our hundred-acres estate in the country, and then it was Greece or somewhere. There's always these mad ideas around.

"I would like to do something on my own. I took up the piano and went to lessons for a time. But it was going to take too long to be any good. I do believe you can do anything you want, if you spend enough time at it, but that was too late. Then I went to a clairvoyant who said my grandmother had played the violin and that I was meant to play it as well. I don't know how she knew my grandmother was a violinist. So I thought I'd try. I went to lessons for a while. But that was worse. You've really got to start the violin young.

"I'm now learning the dillrube—that's an Indian instrument. I'm also going to Indian dancing classes under Ram Gopal. It's lovely. Jennie and I go every day before he does his ballet rehearsals. I just don't want to be the little wife sitting at home. I want to do something worthwhile."

Pattie is involved in all things Indian, but George, as with everything he has always taken up, does it almost with a fanaticism. He used to practice the guitar till his fingers bled. Now he sometimes plays the sitar all day long. When he's not doing that, he is reading book after book on religion. He's not cranky about it. As he goes on and learns more, he becomes more humble and more light-hearted about it. He doesn't preach as much, although there is always the danger when he is being quoted of appearing more fanatical than he is. Paul and John especially would have been the first to cut down his pretensions or to mock his illusions if there had been any.

Even from the first, before Maharishi came along, as George was discovering Buddhism and Yogi for himself, they were as fascinated to hear what he'd found as he was.

"Look at this book. An Indian gave us each a copy of it when we were in the Bahamas. It's signed and dated the twenty-fifth of February, 1965. My birthday. I've only recently opened it, since I became interested in India. It's fantastic. That Indian really was something. You can tell by his name; it's really a title, showing you how learned he is.

"I now know it was part of a pattern. It was all planned that I should read it now. It all follows a path, just like our path. John, Paul, and George converged, then a little later Ringo. We were part of that action which led to the next reaction. We're all just little cogs in an action which everyone is part of.

"The only thing which is important in life is Karma, that means roughly actions. Every action has a reaction which is equal and opposite. Everything that's done has a reaction, like dropping this cushion down; see, there's a dent in it.

"Your Samsara is the recurrence of all your lives and deaths. We've all been here before. I don't know what as, though the friends you had in the previous life are the friends you have in this life. You hate all the people you hated last time. As long as you hate, there will be people to hate. You go on being reincarnated till you reach the absolute truth. But heaven and hell are just a state of mind. Whatever it is, you make it.

"We were made John, Paul, George, and Ringo because of what we did last time; it was all there for us, on a plate. We're reaping what we sowed last time, whatever it was. The reason we're here, why we're all here, is to achieve perfection, to become Christlike. This actual world is an illusion.

"It's been created by worldly minds. It doesn't matter what happens, the plan can't be affected, even having wars or dropping an H bomb; none of it matters. It's only what happens in ourselves which matters.

"I used to laugh when I read about Cliff Richard being a Christian. I still cringe when I hear about it, but I know that religion and God are the only things which exist. I know some people think I must be a nut case. I find it hard not to myself sometimes, because I still see so many things in an ordinary way. But I know that when you believe, it's real and nice. Not believing, it's all confusion and emptiness.

"Life will all work out, as long as you don't bullshit. That's what I'm trying to do. I've blacked out all the things that happened to me before I was about nineteen. I've got so much going forward now. I see so many possibilities. I'm beginning to know that all I know is that I know nothing."

Transcendental meditation came along just at this stage. George was looking for something and someone to tie all the ends together. He has never missed a day's meditation since he started, unlike the others. Now and again they forget or are too busy.

The other big part of George's life is his music. John and Paul were knocking out songs together from the day they met. But George never got round to it for a long time, although he helped with an instrumental piece they did on their Hamburg records. His songs have always been created separately from John and Paul's. He does them completely on his own. In this, as in other recent things, he has influenced them—making them aware of Eastern rhythms and instruments.

George's first song did not appear till their second long-playing record, *With the Beatles* in November 1963. It was called "Don't Bother Me." He wrote it in a Bournemouth Hotel during a tour. He had been ill and was resting.

"I was a bit run down and was supposed to be having some sort of tonic, taking it easy for a few days. I decided to try to write a song, just for a laugh. I got out my guitar and just played around till a song came. I forgot all about it till we came to record the next LP. It was a fairly crappy song. I forgot about it completely once it was on the album." He forgot about writing songs for almost two years after that. "I was involved in so many other things that I never got round to it."

George rather plays down his Beatle songs, considering them a very minor sideline. He can't remember how many he's written and isn't even clear which albums he did songs for.

His next songs were on the LP *Help!*, which appeared in August 1965. He did two for this, "I Need You" and "You Like Me Too Much." He did two songs for *Rubber Soul* in December 1965—"Think for Yourself" and "If I Needed Someone." When he was trying to think of the LPs he'd written for he forgot to mention this. Both of these were well up to the standards of the rest of the songs on that album.

For *Revolver*, which appeared in August 1966, he wrote his biggest number of songs so far on one LP, three: "Taxman," "I Want to Tell You," and "Love You Too." The last was one of the first using Indian instruments, in this case the tabla, a fashion soon copied by hundreds of pop groups in Britain and America.

His songs after this were much more Indian, reflecting his growing knowledge of the sitar and of Indian music. "Within You, without You," which has good words as well as haunting music, is perhaps his finest song to date. This appeared in *Sergeant Pepper* in April 1967. It was followed at Christmastime 1967 with "Blue Jay Way" for *The Magical Mystery Tour.*

"I began to write more songs when I had more time, especially when we began to stop touring. Having the Indian things so much in my head it was bound to come out." George has great difficulty getting the right sort of trained Indian musicians for studio sessions in London. For "Within You, without You" and "Blue Jay Way" he spent weeks finding and auditioning people who could play Indian instruments. There were no full-time professionals in England playing the instruments he wanted.

"They have jobs like bus driving during the day and only play in the evening, so some of them just weren't good enough, but we still had to use them. They were much better than any Western musician could do, because it at least is their natural style, but it made things very difficult. We spent hours just rehearsing and rehearsing."

George's sessions take even longer than the Lennon-McCartney songs. As with theirs, George Martin also helps and so do they, but George is in charge. Groups of very strange-looking Indian gentlemen with very strange-looking instruments come into the studio and sit cross-legged and play to George so that he can hear what they can do.

Up to now there has also been the problem of writing down the music for them to play. Most of them can't read Western music.

For George's early Indian songs, the Indian musicians just had to pick up the tunes by watching George play them. Not even George Martin, the trained musicologist, can read Indian music.

Now George is very well versed in Indian script. He has taught himself to write down his songs in Indian script so that the Indian musicians can play them.

"Instead of quavers and dots written across lines, Indian music is written down very simply like our tonic sol-fa. Instead of Do, Re, Mi, and so on, they sing Sa, Re, Ga, Ma, Pa, Dha, Ni, Sa. Often they don't have words for songs, but just sing those notes. You indicate how high or low, or how long each one is, by putting little marks under each note.

"The first notes of 'Within You' to go with the words 'We were talking' would go Ga Ma Pa Ni. You just need to write the first letter; that's enough. Now I can go to the Indian musicians, give them the music, play it through to let them hear it, and they can do it themselves."

George spends at least three hours a day practicing his sitar, sitting cross-legged with the end resting on the instep of his left foot, in the Indian manner. He has notebooks full of Indian music, written down in the Indian style. These are his lessons, which he has to practice. His teacher, Ravi Shankar, has sent him some tape-recorded exercises which he has on most of the time he isn't playing, even during meals. He is obviously very dedicated and hard-working. But he says Indian music will take him years and years before he is any good. He is so busy learning Indian music properly that his Beatle songs are usually written in a rush. He still forgets about his own compositions until a new LP is approaching then he thinks he should write one.

"Within You, without You" was written after dinner one night at the house of a friend—Klaus Voorman, the friend from Germany who now plays with Manfred Mann. "Klaus had a harmonium in his house, which I hadn't played before. I was doodling on it, playing to amuse myself, when 'Within You' started to come. The tune came first then I got the first sentence. It came out of what we'd been doing that evening—'We were talking.' That's as far as I got that night. I finished the rest of the words later at home.

"The words are always a bit of a hangup for me. I'm not very poetic. My lyrics are poor, really. But I don't take any of it seriously. It's just a joke. A personal joke. It's great if someone else likes it, but I don't take it too seriously myself."

A lot of critics didn't understand why there was sudden laughter after "Within You, without You" on *Sergeant Pepper*. Some said it must have been put in by the others, to mock George's Indian music. It was completely George's idea.

"Well, after all that long Indian stuff you want some light relief. It's a release after five minutes of sad music. You haven't got to take it all that seriously, you know. You were supposed to hear the audience anyway, as they listen to Sergeant Pepper's Show. That was the style of the album."

His song for the *Magical Mystery Tour,* "Blue Jay Way," was written during his visit to California in the early summer of 1967. The title comes from the street in which he and Pattie had rented a house in Los Angeles. They had just flown in from London and were waiting for their friend Derek Taylor (ex-Beatle press officer) to come and see them. "Derek

BLUE JAY WAY.
upon L.A.

There's a fog ~~on~~ ~~Blue Jay Way~~.
and my friends have lost their way.
"we'll be over soon" they said,
Now they've lost their way instead.
please don't be long
or else I'll be asleep.

Well it only goes to show...
and I told them where to go
ask a policeman on the street
there's so many there to meet.
please don't be long

Now its past my bed I know
and I'd really like to go
soon will be the break of day
Sitting here in Blue Jay way
please don't be long.

When I see you at the door
I ~~x~~ know your worth waiting for
for and the moment when you speak —
I know I'd wait here all week.

got held up. He rang to say he'd be late. I told him on the phone that the house was in Blue Jay Way. He said he'd find it okay, he could always ask a cop.

"I waited and waited. I felt really nackered with the flight, but I didn't want to go to sleep till he came. There was a fog and it got later and later. To keep myself awake, just as a joke to fill in time, I wrote a song about waiting for him in Blue Jay Way.

"There was a little Hammond organ in the corner of this rented house, which I hadn't noticed. I messed around on this and the song came." All the words directly relate to him waiting for Derek Taylor—"There's a fog upon LA, and my friends have lost their way. . . ."

When he came home to Esher, he bought himself a little Hammond organ, painted it white, and perfected the song. There is still an organ effect, very deep and booming, in the backing to the song.

In January 1968 George agreed to write his first screen music, for the film *Wonder Wall*. He has been asked to do more single songs but has usually refused. But he was working one day on one for Marianne Faithfull. She'd asked him to write one for her to sing, something like "Within You, without You." He wasn't sure how it was going to turn out. He had the song in his head, but the words were becoming jokier and jokier. He thought they might end up too silly and he'd have to dump them.

"I'd got 'You can't love me with your artichoke heart,' which is not bad." He sang and played the song on his Hammond organ. "But I'm not sure about continuing the joke—'You can't listen with your cauliflower ear' or 'Don't be an apricot fool.' I don't know. I'll just see how it turns out.

"I've got no vocal range, so I've got to keep all my songs simple. Marianne is the same, so that's all right." His voice doesn't have much range, but it has a sizable following from the fans, judging from the letters in the *Beatles Monthly*. Fans are always asking why don't John and Paul let him sing more. "It's not true they don't let me. I would if I wanted to. I just can't be bothered." He looks upon John and Paul as the composers and writers. He feels he has no need to bother when they are so good, unless he happens to have something in his head.

"I'm not sure which way I want to go now. Real Indian classical songs are so much different from the sort of Indian pop songs being turned out over here. They're just ordinary pop songs, with a little bit of Indian background.

"I'm not sure about the ones I've written. Looked at from another person's point of view, then as pop songs I like them. But looked at from my point of view, from what I really want to do, I don't like what I've done so far. I always seem to be rushed. I see things afterwards that I should have done."

George is amused by people who take Beatle music too seriously. He says the words of "Within You, without You" were meant to be true, but it was still a joke. "That's what people don't understand. Like John's 'I Am a Walrus'—'I am he as you are he as you are me.' It's true but it's still a joke. People looked for all sorts of hidden meanings. It's serious and it's not serious." George thinks they could all go a lot further and probably will in music and words. He thought John's line about taking her knickers down in "I Am a Walrus" was great.

"Why can't you have people fucking as well? It's going on everywhere in the world, all the time. So why can't you mention it? It's just a word, made up by people. It's meaningless in itself. Keep saying it—Fuck, fuck, fuck, fuck, fuck, fuck, fuck. See, it doesn't mean a thing, so why can't you use it in a song? We will eventually. We haven't started yet."

This would follow Kenneth Tynan's theory that the Beatle songs are in direct line from medieval English songs. They were all full of arses, shit, and fucking. So in one way it is true that George, John, and Paul haven't really done anything yet.

Meanwhile, back at the George Harrison ranch. It does look a bit like a ranch, with all that low-slung white wood. The telephone rang. It wasn't a fan but an ex-employee with a long complicated story about how he'd loaned Jayne Mansfield £250 and she'd died without repaying it and he was about to be evicted and could George help. George said yes, of course. He put down the phone and said, "Well, what's £250?"

George is still a Beatle. It's his job, as he says, and as with all jobs, everyone has to think about it now and again, and of the future. He is still umbilically connected with the others, despite all the sitar exercises and higher thoughts. The other Beatles are his greatest friends. As they shared his religious interest, he shares all their passions, however mundane, from long neckerchiefs to cameras.

"If one experiences something, the others all have to know about it," says Pattie. "Even just a mood, they have to rush off and tell each other about it. They have crazes, just like you have crazes at school. When a craze hits the rest of them, the whole house has to be overturned until George gets what they've got. But it keeps them all happy.

"They do waste a lot when they take up a new craze. They buy a lot of stuff they're never going to use, but it often turns out useful. They spent a lot on cameras and film equipment, but it showed them they could make films without having to know a lot.

"I know now that they are all together. I didn't realize it when I was first married. They all belong to each other. No one belongs to another person. It's no use trying to cling on, or you would just become miserable. George is my husband, but he's got to be free to go with them if he wants. It's important to him to be free.

"George has a lot with the others that I can never know about. Nobody, not even the wives, can break through it or even comprehend it. It did use to hurt me at first, as I slowly began to learn there was a part I could never be part of. Cyn talked to me about it. She said they would always be a part of each other." There is only one other minor aspect of Beatle life which Pattie in any way criticizes. Unlike the Beatles themselves, Pattie feels they should do something with all their money in the way of helping some charitable cause.

"I know they say a lot of these charities are just keeping the officials in money. I've been conditioned by George to feel this, but there must be something constructive they can do, the way Marlon Brando helps homeless children. The thing with the Beatles was that they were plagued by charities in the early days, wanting them to do things. All those crowds of crippled children that were taken to see them in their dressing rooms, as if they were faith healers. This somehow sickened them.

"I wouldn't mind organizing some charity myself, but there again the publicity would come out all wrong and spoil everything, as George says. It always does. People would think we were doing it for the wrong reasons, the way some people couldn't believe they were genuinely interested in going to listen to Maharishi. It's difficult to know what to do."

George himself says he knows what he is going to do. He has no worries about the future. His interest in spiritual things will last forever, he says. The cynics will be proved wrong. The whole interest in Indian cultures is not a passing phase.

"Reaching a godlike state is the most important thing, but I've still got to do a job, being a Beatle. We've got to do that job because we *can* do things now. We're in a position to try things, to show people. We can jump around and try new things which others can't or won't. Like drugs. People doing ordinary jobs just couldn't give the time we did to looking into all that.

"If Mick [Jagger] had gone to jail for taking pot he would have been the best person it could have happened to. It would have been much better than if it now happened to someone with no money whom it could have ruined. Being rich and famous makes it easier to go through with that sort of thing.

"We've just really started making films. *Magical Mystery Tour* was nothing. But we'll show it can be done. Anyone can make films. You don't have to do all this messing around with backers and companies and hundreds of technicians and scripts worked out to the last word.

"We'll make perhaps one or two films a year ourselves, not necessarily with us in them. We'll hire out our studios and people to anyone who wants them. We'll lend our money as well. If we ever have to use backers we'll make sure they have no influence.

"We'll go round and round in circles, doing films, trying out new things. Then after films we'll try something new. I don't know what. We didn't know we were going to make films when we started making records.

"It'll just be the same sort of scene, trying to do something new each time, going on a bit. Then we die and go on to a new life where we try again, to get better all the time. That's life. That's death.

"But as for this life, we haven't done anything yet."

Chapter 34: Ringo

Ringo lives around the corner from John in the same private housing development in Weybridge, Surrey. It is also a large mock-Tudor house. It was built in 1925 and is called Sunny Heights. It cost him £37,000, plus £40,000 to do it up. It hasn't got a swimming pool like John's or George's but it has much bigger grounds, with lots of trees and shrubs. It backs onto St. George's Hill Golf Course. Neither Ringo nor John is a member of the club and neither has ever asked to be. But when they moved in one newspaper reporter asked the club if the Beatles could be members. He was told no, there was a long waiting list. Ringo says he wouldn't join anyway. He doesn't dig walking.

Ringo's garden has had a lot of very expensive landscaping done to it. At the back, the house now looks down into a huge amphitheater dug out of the ground. It has lots of brick terraces and ponds which you walk down and into from the French windows of the main drawing room. There are little woods at either side of this amphitheater, still part of Ringo's garden. Up one tree there is a large playhouse.

Part of the rebuilding at the back, a semicircular wall, brought in a bill for £10,000, to Ringo's amazement. Like all the Beatles, for years he never asked for estimates, which of course was just leaving himself wide open. It's not that people necessarily tried to take them for a ride. They just made sure they got rid of the most expensive goods and services.

"When I walk round," said Ringo, standing looking at his vast gardens, "I often think, what's a scruff like me doing with this lot? But it soon passes. You get used to it. You get ready to argue with anyone who is trying to get too much of your money." The row over the garden wall was eventually settled—to Ringo's satisfaction, he says.

In the summer of 1967 he had built a large extension to the house which contained extra living rooms, guest rooms, a workroom, and a very long room which is used as a cinema or billiard room. The work was done by a building firm which he half-owned. This was about the only investment he has made on his own. Unfortunately, the firm had to close in mid-1967, thanks to the credit squeeze. "We built a lot of very good houses but nobody had the money to buy them. I didn't lose money when the firm closed, except that I was left with a dozen new flats and houses which stood empty for a long time."

Inside, the main drawing room is perhaps the nicest of all the Beatles' living rooms, though it's a shade dark on the garden side as there is a terrace which obscures some light. It is beautifully furnished. It has a deep-brown Wilton carpet which covers the whole room. This cost a fortune. It was made especially for Ringo in one piece, which is why it cost so much. He now shudders to think what he paid for it. He doesn't want the price repeated. It was about double what normal people pay when they're buying an entire house.

One room is a bar, all very olde-worlde and very corny, though it has genuine bar bits and pieces. Hanging up in it he has a cowboy holster which Elvis gave him.

There are various golden disks and other awards scattered throughout the house, but not too many. In his main room he has a couple of sparse bookshelves. They contain mostly well-thumbed paperbacks, some new but used-looking books on Indian religions, and some new but highly unused-looking volumes of history and Dickens. Of all the Beatles, John is the only one with proper bookshelves.

Ringo has a couple of rooms which are devoted to his own toys. They're very expensive ones, mainly film-camera equipment. He has made some excellent and ingenious films, though he is very shy about showing them and doesn't really think they're all that good. He has one 20-minute film in color which consists mainly of Maureen's eye with a background of music concrete. In it there is a scene driving down the M. 1 thruway with shots through a car window into the headlights of approaching cars. There is another excellent sequence which is weird at first, then turns out to be very simple. He'd done it by sitting on a garden swing with his camera, shooting at the house and garden as he swung up and down. He'd done all the shooting, cutting, and editing of the film himself. He was using expensive equipment, but even so the results were very interesting. One or two shots in *Magical Mystery Tour* were done by Ringo, using his own cameras.

He also does a bit of painting, but not much. His wife Maureen spends hours doing very intricate patterns and designs. She's done one based on the *Sergeant Pepper* drum which appears on the sleeve of the record, all in sequins, hundreds and hundreds of them. It took her four whole days, while she was waiting to have Jason.

Zak, their first son, was born in September 1965, Jason in August 1967. Ringo doesn't think they'll have any more for a bit. He wants to give Maureen a rest. They have a live-in nanny for the children and a daily woman for cleaning, but like John and Cyn, Ringo and his family live their self-contained life in the middle of the house. There is no outward sign of being attended on. Maureen does all the cooking for Ringo. But unlike the Lennons', the whole house has a lived-in feeling.

They both tend just to potter around when Ringo's not working. Like John, they have pop records and the TV going all the time, even in rooms they're not in. They watch TV a lot. They have six sets. From the main couch in the drawing room Ringo can change channels without getting up, just by operating a knob on the couch.

Ringo will give a smile, or just nod, when a Beatles song comes on the TV or radio, if there is anyone else with him. John and Paul don't appear to notice. George doesn't watch telly or play pop records.

"I don't play our songs myself. Maureen puts them on sometimes. She's a Beatles fan, and Frank Sinatra. In the old days we used to celebrate like mad every time we were on the radio.

"I don't mind if people attack us. We're so popular it doesn't matter now, but the critics can kill some records when a lot of people might have enjoyed them.

"When you're coming up, everyone is all for you. When you've made it, they want to knock you if they can. If only thirty people turn up at the airport to see you, people say that wasn't much of a crowd, you must be finished. They expect things to be the same as when we were touring. They think, ah the Beatles, there must be a million people round them."

Ringo is as amused as the others by those who try to see hidden meanings in their records, particularly in America. "It's bound to happen there. They have a hundred fellers doing what ten fellers do here. They're all looking for something different." Like all of them, he is trying to lead a private life for a change. He thinks that as they've stopped touring and stopped being public property, people should leave them alone. "But people just stare at us everywhere, as if we were a circus. I can understand it when I'm Ringo the Beatle. But when I'm Ritchie the person I should be freer.

"I suppose you can't expect it. They've heard so much. They want to see you. Fame, that's what it is. They don't realize we've stopped playing. They still want to gape." He and John were coming back from London one night, being driven by John's chauffeur in John's Rolls, when they passed a pub all lit up, with people sitting around in their shirtsleeves drinking. They couldn't get over it. To them it was like a scene from a fairy tale they'd dimly forgotten.

"It looked great. We were past before it had really hit us. We were in suits and felt a bit stiff. We'd been to visit Queenie [Mrs. Epstein]. It wasn't long after Brian had died. When we got home, we decided to change and go and have a drink. I took Maureen round to Cyn's to sit with her while me and John went to the pub. It was just like the old days. We brought them back potato chips and a soda.

"The pub itself hadn't changed. It was just like pubs when we used to know them, straight out of Coronation Street. The barman was very pleased when he recognized us. We had a bottle of brown each. We had to sign a few autographs, but it wasn't too bad." He thinks now, having done it once, they should be able to pop in for a quick drink more often. He's never tried going for a walk on his own, because of course he doesn't go in for walking. None of the Beatles take any exercise whatsoever, except Paul when taking Martha for a walk.

Playing billiards or his one-armed bandit is about Ringo's only exercise. "There's the garden. What's wrong with that? I often walk round the garden." He appears to need no exercise to keep fit and has kept his same weight—between nine stone and nine stone six—for the last six years. Considering the unhealthy life he led touring and his years of illness as a child, this is surprising. But the Beatles are somehow all fit, though rather pale-looking. They've had regular medical check-ups for each new film and other big contracts and nothing has been found wrong with them. John put on weight when they stopped touring, but he soon slimmed it off.

Ringo at last passed his driving test, after failing three times and driving without a license for two years. He now has three cars, a Mini Cooper, a Land Rover, and a Facel Vega. "Don't ask me how you spell it. I was away from school when they had spelling."

Apart from his parents, he has helped other relations and friends, loaning them money to buy their own houses.

"I do have a load of rubbish. I leap out and buy something, then it doesn't last a week. Camera stuff, I'm always getting it. I want some better or extra so I'm changing cameras all the time. I don't know how much I'm worth. If I said give us my money tomorrow I want it in me hand, I've no idea what it would come to."

He doesn't carry cash around with him. "Tell me, what do those pound-note thingies look like? And do they still make those cute-like half crowns? Maureen does the shopping, but she just uses a card which says this is money."

What happens when they sign a bill is that the shop sends it on to their accountant's office. He sends it back to them, for their confirmation, before he pays it. "Mine comes to about £1,000 a month. Last month it was £1,600, but I'd bought a new lens.

"I've only been caught once. We were at Brian's and me and Maureen decided to come home early. We'd come in someone else's car, so Peter [Brown] gave us his car to drive home. Halfway home, on the dual carriageway, miles from anywhere, in the middle of a Sunday night, we ran out of petrol. There was no garage and even if there had been, I had no money.

"I flagged a car down and told him I'd run out of petrol. I said could he lend us five bob so I could buy a gallon to get us home. He said are you Ringo? I said yeh. He said it would be no use loaning me money as there was no garage open anywhere around, but he'd drive us home in his car, which he did. It was great. He only turned out to be a journalist, from the *Daily Telegraph*. Well, it's those sort of unimportant things that are always getting in the papers that you don't want in. I took him into the house and gave him an LP. He never wrote about it."

They were all given checkbooks at one stage several years ago, to help in emergencies, but they never use them. "I've never signed a check in my life," says Ringo. "I don't know how to. I lost my checkbook the minute I got it. I've never been refused in a shop yet when I've asked to sign the bill, even in shops I haven't been in before. No one's ever asked me yet to prove that I really am Ringo."

He doesn't feel any urge or necessity to give money to charity and doesn't see why they should. "Brian gave stuff now and again, on behalf of us. John did Oxfam a Christmas card, didn't he? That made them a lot of money.

"I don't fancy it, really. Most of the people running charities are not nice people. What good did the Aberfan Fund do, except for all the lawyers? They gave each person £5,000 for losing a child. Ridiculous. Five million quid doesn't equal losing a child. I think a lot of people are making money out of charities. No, they're not for me.

"The Government's taking over 90 per cent of all our money anyway —we're left with one nine in the pound. The Government spends it on helping people, doesn't it? That's like helping charities. Not that the Governments are any good. They can't make anything work. Buses, trains. None of them work. I was in the car yesterday going to town and I passed five Number 7 buses, one lined up behind the other, all with just two people on. Why couldn't they all be on one bus?

"The Government takes too much on taxes. There's no initiative, you get taxed right through life. When they've left nobody rich, no one will have any money to give the Government. Everything the Government does turns to crap, not gold. The railways made profits when they were private firms, didn't they? It's like Victorian England, our Government. Outdated.

"All Governments are the same, Labour or Tory. Neither of them offers me anything. All they do is oppose each other. One says one thing and the other has to say something different. They both do it. That's all they do. Why can't they all get together and work for the country?"

They all say that Ringo is the sentimental one, although they all have bits of Ringo in them. One of the things Ringo is sentimental about is preferring England, which is something they say they don't care about. When the Greek island and other foreign ideas were being discussed, Ringo was the only one who wasn't very keen. Living all together on a hundred-acre site in Devon he would have liked, but he doesn't fancy going away for a long time to a foreign country. The others say they could do it easily.

"I couldn't live anywhere but England. That's where I'm from. That's where my family is. England's no better than anywhere else, I know that. It's just that I'm comfortable here." He does take holidays abroad and he likes to be with the others, usually John. He and Maureen wouldn't go off alone to California on a whim the way George and Pattie did. Like John, he prefers going places with his Beatles buddies. "It's nice to be together."

He's lost none of the old-fashioned Northern idea of marriage, of the man being the master at home. "That's how it is. My grandfather [Starkey] always had his seat in his house which only he sat in. I'm the same, I suppose." Both he and John have a bit of Andy Capp in them. Paul and George are much more middle-class in their domestic setting.

But Ringo is a bit alarmed that he appears more of the lord and master than he thinks he is. "Maureen was telling me the other day that the cleaning woman fears me. I don't plan or expect it. I think it's just Maureen rushing around saying we must get this ready or that done for me coming in."

When they're out, he squires Maureen in the traditional working-class way. Some years ago they once went out for dinner at Woburn Abbey, the home of the Duke of Bedford. Ringo had been friendly with his son,

Rudolph, a keen pop fan. "I thought it would be a good laugh, to see how the others lived, that's why I went." He was sat down at the baronial dining table miles away from his wife Maureen, in the traditional middle- and upper-class way, much to his alarm.

"I said oh no. Come over here, luv. They were trying to make us sit apart. Very funny people. I don't think women like to be equal. They like to be protected and in turn they like looking after men. That's how it is."

They gave up London some time ago and rarely go out at nights. "Swinging London was okay before it became swinging London. When we were just becoming famous it was nice to go around and see people knowing you, which is how all famous show-biz people are supposed to do. But it was a drag."

They don't entertain people in any formal sense at their home. Ringo has one or two friends, like Roy Tretford, from his early Liverpool days. John is the main person who pops in, then sits down for tea or whatever's going.

Maureen prefers the quiet life, although her life is really Ringo's. Anything he wants to do, she wants to do. They are very happy. She is the only Beatle wife who stays up for her husband and waits for him, no matter how late or in what condition he's likely to arrive.

"When he's recording I often stay up till four thirty in the morning. He's usually got up late the day before and perhaps not had a proper meal before going out. So I try to have something for him when he comes home, however late. Then I know at least he's got a meal inside him. They all just peck at things when they're working.

"If it turns out he has eaten a proper meal at work or with the boys, then it doesn't matter. I can easily use up the potatoes. Nothing's wasted. But I usually give him a meal. He might eat it quickly as he's tired, but he does like something when he comes home.

"I don't mind staying up for him. I might change the furniture round, to put the hours in. I just mess around, really. I spent two hours the other night deciding where to move a lamp. I might make things, curtains or clothes. I put sequins on an old lampshade the other day."

She spends a lot of time answering correspondence. Maureen takes a great interest in all Ringo's fan mail. Perhaps through having been a fan herself, she knows how much it means. Apart from Mrs. Harrison, George's mother, she is the only one in the Beatle circle who bothers. She doesn't do as much as Mrs. Harrison; she has a large house and two young children to look after.

When people send birthday cards, she still drops a little note saying thank you, adding that Ritchie is too busy working to write himself. She always calls him Ritchie, never Ringo, even writing to people who only know him as Ringo. "I don't know why, really, Ringo just seems funny. His name is Ritchie."

She gets him, in odd moments, to sign big batches of autographs. She doesn't send them to everyone who writes, because that would take too long. She just drops in his autograph with her little letter of reply when people seem really nice and polite.

"I like answering the letters. I've been doing it for five years now. I get some lovely replies back from the parents. I do get behind sometimes. When I was having Jason I got behind for a few weeks and had three shopping bags full of them.

"I don't do it just because people are polite. I know that if I liked someone enough to write a nice letter to them I would like some sort of reply. I've had letters from fans saying this is their fifteenth letter. They must feel awful. What they've been doing is writing to the office. The office gets thousands and just can't cope. Not that I want any more sent to me than I get now, thank you."

She makes quite a lot of clothes, when she is filling in the hours waiting. "I like instamatic things. I'm in such a hurry that I never use patterns. I might start off making a dress, but keep going wrong, cutting it down and down till I've ended up making a handkerchief."

When she knows she's just going to have a go at something, she always buys cheap remnants, so there won't be much waste. She's very careful when it comes to money. All her shopping is done at a Weybridge supermarket. She always gets trading stamps with everything she buys, which appears rather pointless, when she could buy anything she wanted anyway. She says she likes the idea of collecting. She likes sticking the stamps in the pages. She gets out her little book now and again to see how much she's got.

Ringo thinks it's a bit of a joke, but he's proud of the way she manages the house and looks after him. He's also very pleased by things she's made, such as the sequined Sergeant Pepper design.

They haven't started thinking about Zak's or Jason's education as they're so young. Like John, Ringo would like them to go to an ordinary council school. "But Zak's not ordinary, is he. They wouldn't let him alone. It's eased off now a bit, but he'd still get picked upon. If the only way to get him a bit of peace is to pay for it, then we'll have to. If they want to go to a boarding school, then I'll let them. But I'd rather have them at home. I just want them to be as free as possible and love one another.

"I say all those sort of things, of course, but I don't know how I'll turn out when they get older. But I don't want them to have the restrictions I had, you know, your mother telling you not to play near the window, or watch you don't break anything. You never know, do you, when it's your turn to be a parent." But he wouldn't like them to have the sort of education he had, or at least lack of education. Those lost years of illness have had some effect on him, not in any serious way, at least not what he would call serious. His spelling, for example, is non-existent, but it doesn't worry him. His knowledge of where towns and places are is also very strange.

"I know I can't spell, but I can read anything you want to give me. English is hard for anybody to spell. My maths aren't bad. But I'm best really with my hands. I can do most little jobs, if I'm just left on my own. I can eventually work things out on my own. It's when things are written down I'm no good."

Ringo came into the group last, long after all the others were settled in their positions and personalities. He felt it all was a marvelous stroke of luck. He moved in with them at the second they took off. The others never looked upon it as luck for one minute. They all knew they could be a success.

When they are all together, Ringo does tend to be the withdrawn one, stuck out on drums while the rest crowd the microphone. He's always said he wasn't the talking one. But his jokes and observations were as wise and witty as theirs. The difference is that he doesn't keep up the patter, the way Paul can, or the way George does when he's on his hobbyhorse, or the way John can make daft jokes and observations all the time. Ringo keeps quiet until he's spoken to.

In repose he does *look* withdrawn and worried. His gray streak is now grayer than it used to be. Apart from the left side of the front of his hair, it has now affected his right eyebrow as well. Some doctors think there might be psychological reasons for premature grayness, but most agree it is meaningless. It looks rather attractive.

His nose isn't as big as it can look in photographs, or of course in caricatures. It has been taken by many people as a sign that he must be Jewish. "I never realized I had a big nose till I was famous. I never even thought people were thinking I was Jewish till one day a bloke from the *Jewish Chronicle* rang me up. I had to tell him I wasn't.

"I'm beginning to see now that I am what I am because of the sort of upbringing I had, with no father and my mother always out of work. It did make me very quiet and introverted. I'm only figuring myself out now, though I was very happy at the time. I saw a program on TV the other day about the effect a long period in hospital can have on a child. It can make them very withdrawn."

Ringo isn't withdrawn. He is completely open and friendly, the sweetest of them all, really. He is not self-centered in any way. His wife Maureen thinks he could make more of himself, if he wanted to.

"It was his idea to do it with sequins, didn't he tell you? I know it's rubbish, really, but he never takes credit for things.

"I think he often underestimates himself. He does forget what good ideas he has had, because he thinks he's not creative. He says it's for the others to have the good ideas. But he is good at many things. He's a good painter. I think films will be very good for him, so I hope they come off. He's great at all things. He's a lovely dancer."

Ringo is a much stronger personality than he has appeared. He's also much handsomer in real life, with rich blue eyes. He is in no sense the buffoon of the group, or even their pet mascot. His opinions are as valid as theirs. But in the light of Paul and John's more obvious talents, he has kept himself even quieter than he is. But they rely on him a great deal. He is a vital part of the four, contributing elements they need—that old sentimentality again, but also a strong common sense, the ordinary human touch. He has some good ideas and opinions about the Beatles, and about himself.

"I think four of us together, all sort of equal, made us one whole. We're different from each other, yet alike. When you have a single star, or a leader and a backing group, you either take him or leave him. With four, you can associate with one of us, yet still like the rest of us. If you didn't like Elvis, that was that. With four of us, there's more to go on.

"There was never any competition between us, either privately or publicly, though we all have our special fans. If all four of us had to stand up there in front of a million fans and they had to line up behind the one they liked best, I think Paul would get most. John and George would be joint second. Ringo would be last. That's what I think. You can tell, from the letters and the fans screaming and mobbing.

"With John and Paul, their own fans tend not to like the other one as much. But with me, I get John fans and Paul fans as well. They all like me at the same time as their own special favorites. So perhaps if you counted second votes, I might win. They all want to mother me. I know that. It brings out the maternal bit, sentimental little Ritchie. I've always had it, as a kid. Old women like me as well as girls. Paul has a bit of this as well.

"That's me, I know it. Why change it? Now and again I do feel like being different. When people keep on asking me to do films I think I'll pick a part as a right bastard. That would be nice. Just to see the reaction.

"I'm not the creative one. I know that. But people expect I must want to be. They write and say why don't I try. I did try a couple of years ago to write two little songs, but they were such pinches, without me really realizing it.

"It can get you down, not being creative. You know people are thinking you're not the creative one. But out of four people, you wouldn't expect them *all* to be creative, would you? Fifty per cent is enough. Think of all the groups, good groups, who can't write anything at all.

"I'd love to be able to, of course. It's a bit of a bind when I realize I can't. I've got a piano, but I can't play it really. I often get a feeling. I just feel like writing a lovely song today, but I go and I can't, I don't know how to. I can knock out things in C, as long as it's twelve-bar. That's a musical joke. It means nothing. I do sometimes feel out of it, sitting there on the drums, only playing what they tell me to play. Often when other drummers of groups say to me that was great, that bit, I know the others have usually told me what to do, though I've got the credit.

"Making films is okay, but I get cheesed off with it sometimes. It's just guessing, isn't it, hoping it's going to come off and you've got something good. But I'm quite interested in films, seeing as how I'm not writing or creating that way. I might as well get in there if I can.

"I know people said I was okay in *A Hard Day's Night,* but I had no idea what was going on. That little scene with the little boy on the canal that they said was good, I was stoned out of my mind when I did that. I had a real thick head. I'd been up all the night before. I just came on with me mac on feeling dead weary. I could hardly move. Dick had to shout everything at me. But it did turn out okay. That bit where I kicked the stone along, that was my gag. Yeh, it was. But everything else was Dick's idea. I was still in a haze.

"I had lots of films offered after that, but they were all big star things, expecting me to carry the show. I nearly agreed to one about Sherlock Holmes, with me as Dr. Watson, but I thought it was too big. I don't want to try and carry anything yet. It would be awful if it was a flop. But a minor part would be okay, then I wouldn't have the responsibility. If that was okay, I could try bigger stuff.

"I took *Candy* because it wasn't too big a part and there was them other stars—Marlon Brando, Richard Burton, Peter Sellers. I thought, they'll be carrying the film, not me, and I'll learn from them. It was only a ten-day part, as the Spanish gardener, with not much dialogue.

"I can't act, of course. I don't know how to. I watch these actors on television. You can *tell* they're actors because their faces are going all the time. You should see their eyes. I can't do all that. I just don't do anything. I don't know. Perhaps that's acting." He says he wouldn't mind if it all just disappeared tomorrow. He still feels he's lucky and would be able to earn a bit of bread somehow, even if it meant going back to being a fitter.

"No, I probably wouldn't have been a fitter today. I did give that up before I finished my time, to join the groups. If Rory Storme hadn't come along and then the Beatles, I'd have continued running around in the Teddy-boy gangs. Today, well, I'd probably just be a laborer.

"I'm glad I'm not, of course. It'll be nice to be part of history, some sort of history anyway. What I'd like to be is in school history books and be read by kids."

End Bit

Doing a biography of living people has the difficulty that it is all still happening. It is very dangerous to pin down facts and opinions because they are shifting all the time. They probably won't believe half the things they said in the last four chapters by the time you've read them.

But at least with living people you can get it all firsthand, as long as they are willing to give up the time. In this case they were, though having to think about their Beatlemania days bored them stiff. Luckily, this is the most chronicled part of their lives so far.

I've tried to keep myself out of the book as much as possible, though I'm sure my prejudices have crept in all over the place. I've also tried to resist the temptation to analyze. Too many millions of words have already been trotted out by the interpreters. Someone can do a critical biography of them in fifty years' time, if anyone remembers them by then.

Naturally, I think they will. I wouldn't have done all this otherwise. But their immediate future is still very hazy. Will they do more films on their own? Will Apple come off? What will happen to Maharishi? Will they get bored and just pack it all in?

Perhaps by the time this book is out some of these questions will be answered. Already their views on Maharishi have begun to change since the last chapters were written. The Beatles have gone through so many stages that there is no reason to doubt there are more to come.

They are confident that they can succeed in films and in anything else they might try, but in the history of show business no one has yet repeated a phenomenon. Elvis Presley stood still almost immediately. Charlie Chaplin did go on, to direct some very professional films, but no one can

339

say they were phenomenal. As with Beatlemania, this little man, bewildered by the big new corporations, was right for the times. It remains to be seen whether the Beatles will be handicapped by living such isolated lives. Is art affected by lack of stimuli? According to some art experts, if Picasso had gone off and seen new people and new places, he wouldn't have messed around doing little drawings on menus.

It also remains to be seen whether they can go it alone. They had Brian Epstein when they were emerging as personalities and George Martin when they were emerging as composers.

All the experts can't see them doing it, not in a new medium and not without help.

"In their music," says George Martin, "they have an instinctive awareness of what to do. They are always ahead of everyone else. But in much of their other thinking, they tend to be juvenile psychologists.

"They are very like children in many ways. They love anything magical. If I had to clap my hands in front of John and produce a vase of flowers, John would be knocked out and fantastically impressed and I would be able to do anything with him. They like everything to be like instant coffee. They want instant recording, instant films, instant everything.

"I think they do need an organizer round them. This would allow them to be more outlandish. If they try to do everything on their own things could go wrong." They are very young, no one could deny that, which is good, because they still want to do things on their own. It's to be hoped they keep on trying.

But they could and might pack up tomorrow, live on their millions, and contemplate their navels. They haven't done badly so far. They've given us quite a lot. In return, they have got their MBEs.

Postscript

Ten years ago, when that little End Bit was written, I carefully didn't predict what I thought would happen to the Beatles. There seemed so many exciting possibilities, such as films, and exciting new creations, such as Apple. They had already started to go their separate ways, living separate lives, but I never thought for one moment that a split was imminent. And I never imagined that the end of the Beatles, whenever it happened, would simply come in a welter of legal tangles, financial quibbling, trivial personality clashes, slanging matches, ridiculous recriminations, juvenile insults, and silly squabbles. In the end, alas, they finished as so many show business partnerships have—in pathos. Gilbert and Sullivan, Britain's other great song-writing partnership, finally descended to rows and sulks. How sad that Lennon and McCartney ended their joint days as just another pair of archetypal, bickering ex-partners. Their rise has to be called phenomenal—as I hope this book has shown—but the end was rather sordid.

As sordid tales go, they don't even have the virtue of being worth retelling for the dirt. Matters became highly complicated and utterly confusing. Basically, the problems revolved around who owned who and what; and, for almost the last decade, they kept lawyers in high fees and newspaper libraries deep in reports of the latest court case. These legal rows were thought at the time by many observers to be the reason for the Beatles splitting, but they were a result, not a cause —though the personality clashes which ensued for a while were real enough. So what caused the split?

The Beatles themselves are not much help in giving exact reasons. At one time, they had contradictory theories—Paul was being blamed by the others for causing the split, while he in turn blamed them. They even argued about who actually left the Beatles first. My theory, arrived at with the benefit of hindsight, was that the split had been happening

341

for a long time. Re-reading the book makes this abundantly clear, though I can't say I realized it at the time. If there was one simple reason why they split up when they did, it was not the argument over who should run their affairs, but the arrival into John's life of Yoko Ono. That's my explanation, anyway.

The Beatles started to break up as Beatles as far back as 1966 when they gave up touring and stopped living communal lives. With living apart so much, the Lennon-McCartney numbers, however successful, became something of a misnomer. They were no longer *joint* numbers in the way they'd been in the old days, knocked out together in the back of a van. It was very easy for the fans to recognize a Lennon song or McCartney song, despite them getting equal credit. As the descriptions of *Sergeant Pepper* showed, they were by now each coming to the studio with almost every number worked out—at least in their heads.

Working in this new way was fine as long as they were still mates and nobody was getting fed up or wanting to move off in a completely different way, but petty rows did begin, based on boredom as much as anything else. In 1968 Ringo walked out on the Beatles double album. He said he was fed up being their drummer. Watching him so many times in the studio over the years, it was a pretty fed-up-making process. On stage, Ringo was equally involved and important, had his own little special bits to do, and had acquired his own faithful following among the fans. In the studio, he was virtually ignored. John and Paul would break off sometimes for hours at a time, working on an arrangement or the words or the mixing. There was often no need for Ringo to be there at all—his contribution could be dubbed on any time. However, he only walked out for a day and was persuaded to come back.

During *Let It Be* it was George who left, this time after an argument with the others. He always did have a part to play, though not as much as John and Paul, bringing in his own songs which he did most painstakingly. During the Indian phase, he was also influencing the nature of the others' compositions. George had always been the least in love with being a Beatle and was the first to put equal energy into other interests, such as religion and Indian music. But he too was persuaded to come back.

Paul was really the mainstay of the group in these later years, from about 1967 to 1969, keeping them going as composers, pushing them into new ideas, such as *Magical Mystery Tour*. He had many ideas for films and for expanding the Apple organization. He loved being a

Beatle and didn't want it to change. He came out to stay with me in Portugal in 1968 and was very full of a plan to get them all performing in public again. He wasn't thinking of touring; that had gone stale for them all. But he missed appearing in public—playing complete songs for a change, all together, in front of a live audience, trying to recapture some of the fun they had had in the early days. George was all against this, and the others weren't very keen either. But Paul at the time had high hopes of persuading them.

John, meanwhile, was letting Paul get on with directing most Beatle activities. He was tired of being a Beatle but he couldn't think of anything else he wanted to do with his life. It was obvious during those days at his home (as in Chapter 31), where he would sit for days dreaming, saying nothing, that he was utterly bored. His marriage had become a habit as much as anything else. Cynthia, as she was the first to point out, was never really on John's wavelength. She very honestly admitted that, had she not become pregnant, John would never have married her. (This remark was almost deleted from Chapter 31, because of pressure from family and business friends.) She knew he'd always loved the Beatles more than her. They had been through much together, and John couldn't think of how else he would like to live his life. Nothing better had turned up.

Then along came Yoko. He had found a kindred spirit, albeit of a very unusual kind. John was immediately sparked into life. He was away on a new plane, realizing at once that Paul, who until then had been his buddy, his only soul mate, was in many ways as conventional as Cynthia. Together, John and Yoko discovered new and all-consuming aims. The rest of the Beatles didn't matter anymore. When Paul came up with an idea for, say, a live TV show, John wasn't really interested.

Yoko moved into John's life and into his work—sitting with him during the final Beatle sessions. The others weren't exactly thrilled at her influence over John or her continual presence in the studio. George and Ringo had become bored anyway, and this took the final fun out of it. John and Yoko's own fun was centered on new and different directions. Making music as Beatles finally finished in 1969. *Let It Be* came out in 1970, but it had been recorded almost a year before.

Around the same time as John was moving into a new, exciting life with Yoko, Paul met Linda Eastman. Paul brought Linda with him during that ten-day visit with my family and myself in Portugal, where we were living at the time. We had gotten on particularly well with Jane Asher, his previous highly independent girlfriend. Watching

Linda's so obvious devotion to—nay, protection of—Paul was a surprise. I'd always presumed that an adoring fan would be the last thing he would want, having been pursued by them for so long. What I hadn't realized was that, in his enclosed life with John, whose cynicism and brutal honesty kept Paul on his toes, and with Jane Asher, who was as strong in her opinions as Paul, he could quite possibly have felt cramped and constrained. Without knowing it, he was probably in some ways jealous of John. I had first noticed this at a time when John and Brian Epstein were particularly close buddies and Paul obviously felt rather excluded.

Linda came along at the right time for Paul, just as John was moving off, and encouraged Paul not to feel inferior, to be his own man—he could do anything if he tried. She took him over but in no way became a rival. When the arguments started over Apple, both John and Paul were fueled in their attitudes by their new mates.

After Brian Epstein's death it became apparent that the Beatles' financial and business affairs had been in something of a tangle. The creation of Apple had made things even more complicated. Someone was needed to straighten things out and organize their business lives. Allen Klein, an American accountant, was brought in by John and Yoko, with the backing of George and Ringo. Paul never liked him and instead wanted his affairs to be handled by Lee Eastman, an eminent New York lawyer, who also happened to be Linda's dad. The others thought Paul was just trying to introduce his in-laws, which greatly upset Paul. He maintained they should have known him better than that. To break free from Apple, Paul discovered he couldn't sue Klein but had to sue John, George, and Ringo.

Paul had found out that none of the Beatles had control of themselves. They were owned, including their own songs, by other people and other companies. Paul maintained he was doing it all for their sake—not just his own. He didn't like the deal Klein had arranged for any of them. But, to the other three, it looked as if Paul was causing all the trouble. At this stage, they still believed Klein to be their savior. It was a very nasty few years.

The arrival of Klein was the occasion that finally and officially led to the split in the Beatles, but the polarization between John and Paul, begun by the arrival of Yoko, was already apparent.

Being caught up in court cases for so much of the last ten years took much of their energy, both physical and creative. They didn't help themselves, either, by getting into their own individual court cases at different times—divorces, drug offenses, being sued by or suing other record companies, immigration problems, and so on. At the time of this writing, all of these legal problems seem to be settled. Paul broke free from Apple. The other three are now recorded elsewhere.

Once the break was obvious, back in 1970, they naturally felt a terrible loss. Having lived such joint lives for so long, they looked forward to going it alone, but didn't quite know how. John took all the headlines in the first few years. He had done his own songs with Yoko, later forming the Plastic Ono Band, and had himself and Yoko photographed naked for *Two Virgins* (1969), which amazed and amused the pop world. They had bed-ins in different hotels around the world, giving interviews about the world's ills and how they should be cured. John forsook the puns and the whimsy of some of his Beatle songs and earlier writings, and plunged headlong into the avant-garde. He took to defending causes of all sorts, such as the Hanratty murder case, and filled his new Yoko-songs with emotional outbursts, class struggles, and political slogans. The layman was in the main amused by John's latest exploits, but there was a great deal of praise from the critics for many of the songs he was now producing on his own, such as "Imagine" (1971). He has since returned to more of his early rock-and-roll influences, though his albums seem to have lost some of his old drive and direction. Nothing new has appeared for two years. None of his records has been a hit in the Beatles sense of the word.

He married Yoko in 1969 and they had a child, Sean, in 1975, after several miscarriages. For the last five years he has lived in New York after a long legal fight to become a resident. Looking back, he has denied that Yoko broke up his marriage to Cynthia. And he thinks that the real reason for the split among the Beatles was boredom. He could be right.

John gave a lot of interviews in the early seventies about the years of Beatlemania, going into lurid details about their sex life and about drugs. He was no doubt partly trying to shock, but there was a trace of bitterness coming through, particularly against Paul, as if blaming him for perhaps having made them all conform.

His lack of any records for two years (since 1975) and his apparent lack of any activity (at least at the time of writing) is not too out of character for John, though two years is rather a long time. His recording contract expired in February 1976—with EMI in Britain and Capitol in the U.S.A.—and he didn't get round to doing anything about it. There were discussions, and promises, then nothing happened. It was common for him in the old days to have long periods of nothingness, as I noticed when I used to go down and see him in Weybridge.

Even at the height of the Beatles days, there were records on which he did very little, leaving Paul to do all the work, such as *Magical Mystery Tour*.

After some drama in his personal life—in 1974 he was parted from Yoko for almost a year—John seems to be back to a more placid, domestic life. He's still caught up in many of the Apple litigations and settlements, trying to get his share or to get things finally settled in the way he wants them settled. He's stopped his public avant-garde demonstrations, no longer getting involved in political causes. He's becoming something of the grand old man of rock, now that Elvis is dead. Elvis, of course, retreated completely from normal life; but John has only half-retreated, becoming a pop guru, holding court in New York to visiting rock-and-roll stars, giving forth his wisdom.

Some antipathy toward Paul appears still to be there, though Paul feels they are now getting on better than a few years ago. Any strain may be the result of Paul's commercial success. John may not be as financially well off as some of the Beatles (though he's not exactly poor); but he can become angry, accusing the others of charity, if there is a hint of Paul or anyone trying to help with any of his Apple complications. Unconsciously, he may deliberately be doing nothing simply because Paul is doing so much, making a point of inactivity. The other three have signed new contracts and kept working. John, as ever, is refusing to conform. He always said that but for the Beatles he would have been a bum and a layabout, doing nothing with his life.

However, no doubt he'll come alive soon. A new partner may appear, musical or otherwise, and spur him into action, unleashing his energies. Let's hope so.

Ringo worked quietly and steadily after the splitting up of the Beatles, eventually producing some nice singalong albums and singles, several of which got into the charts. He started hesitantly, obviously unaccustomed to being on his own professionally. He's never had any pretensions about his own musical skills, as a drummer or a singer, and wondered if he dared do solo records without the help of the others. He wanted to do something different, to carve out a new career, but couldn't think of what to do. He was living for a few years after the split in a big house in Highgate, not far from me, and I remember his deciding one day to learn the guitar. He thought that was what was missing. To be an all-round solo artist, playing the drums wasn't enough. He took a few lessons, then gave up.

Ringo thought for a time he would try his hand as a designer. He'd met someone whose work he liked and decided to back him. Together they produced very expensive stainless steel furniture, such as fancy fireplaces, with Ringo himself thinking up a few of them. Ringo has now taken a backseat but the firm, Ringo or Robin Ltd., is doing very well.

Ringo carried on with his film career—though there again without any pretensions to grandeur, going in for simple cameo roles where possible. He was in *The Magic Christian, Candy, 200 Motels* and played the Pope in Ken Russell's *Lisztomania.* In late 1977 he played with Mae West in "Sextet." He gets lots of offers, with people wanting his name on the cast list, but turns down most of them.

Ringo has moved around a lot in his personal life. He went from Highgate to a stately home at Ascot with 74 acres, which he took over from John who'd by then moved to New York. (The latest reports say the locals are worried because it's a historic building and seems ignored and rotting.) In 1975 he and Maureen got divorced—by which time they'd had a third child—and he went off to America. He's now based abroad for tax reasons, with a flat in Monte Carlo; he spends time each year in America.

Slowly, and perhaps to the surprise of many, Ringo has developed in the last few years as a songwriter in his own right. Though he sang the work of others in the early albums, very often using songs by George, Paul, or John, he is now doing more of his own. He was involved in three songs on his 1976 album, *Rotogravure,* and in his 1977 album, *Richard the 4th*, he has done six of them. He now has his own label, Ringo Records, and aims to keep producing an album a year, and writing (usually with a partner) more and more original songs. They're not world-shattering or very original songs, but pleasant, good-hearted, and cheerful. Just like Ringo.

George has also changed houses several times, and in 1977 he too got divorced, after eleven years of marriage to Patti. They had no children. He, like Paul, is based in Britain, living a quiet life near Henley. He started off in great style after the Beatles split, having already established for himself a new passion in life with Indian music. *All Things Must Pass* in 1970 was highly acclaimed, as was his *Concert for Bangla Desh* in 1971. Alas, he too got into court cases, the most notorious being one which alleged that he'd taken the music for his world best-seller, "My Sweet Lord," from someone else's song. In America the decision was against him, and settlements elsewhere are now taking place. He made rather cynical fun of this in a later song, which included the promise that it didn't infringe on anyone's copyright.

He continued his meditation, his vegetarianism, and his love of India, interests which at present are still strong. There's been a general rebirth of interest in transcendental meditation—TM, as it's now called—which has recovered from the overpublicity the Beatles gave it before they got bored.

George vowed he'd never tour again—but he did in 1974 in the States, a tour which wasn't very successful. He was criticized for being too experimental, though in truth people were mainly disappointed because he refused to play any Beatles songs. As ever, George is loathe to go back, and is always eager to experiment and, he hopes, move forward. "We went through so much growth as Beatles that it was limiting just being the four of us—it was too small to contain us all." He can't decide now whether having been a Beatle has been a blessing or a curse. George seems very fond of Britain, apart from the taxes, and would like everyone to rally round and be more positive.

He has his recording studio built onto his Henley house and has his own label, Dark Horse. He has spent a lot of time in the last few years trying to discover and produce records for new groups and singers, both in England and America. He still has several tied to his Dark Horse label, but none has so far made any mark on the pop scene. George does have skills as a record producer and one day they might succeed.

George and John were rather critical of Paul in public after the split, not just over the legal rows (though in the end they appear to have agreed with Paul about Klein) but over Paul's new career. They are each highly opinionated and uncompromising, and I think they'd always slightly resented Paul's being the charmer, the public relations man. George dismissed Paul's post-Beatles songs as being cute. John has put it rather more crudely.

Unlike the other three, Paul started off his independent life very shakily indeed. His wife Linda wasn't warmly received by all—and few thought it would last. Paul took the brunt of the legal troubles; he was hated by the other three for starting them and disliked by the fans who mistakenly thought he'd broken up the group. He too became a recluse —a very fashionable habit for superstars in the early seventies. One had to get away and find oneself, just to prove one existed. There were rumors at one time that Paul was dead. He had in fact retreated to a small farm he'd bought, and still has, in Argylshire, Scotland.

"When the Beatles split up, I felt on the rocks. I was accused of walking out on them, but I never did. I think we were all pretty weird at the time of the court cases. I'd ring John and he'd say don't bother me. I rang George and he was unreceptive, not at all Hare Krishna."

He did odd songs for other people, and for films, then slowly he realized that he should do what he'd always enjoyed most in life— playing with a group on stage. This had always been his ambition for the Beatles, to get them out of the studio again, at least for occasional shows. So he decided to form his own group, Wings, along with Linda, who had no previous musical experience. The pop world had a jolly chuckle at this. They started off very quietly, arriving unannounced on university campuses, but it still didn't stop the experts from criticizing Linda for her voice and for daring to muscle into Paul's group. One of Wings early singles was called "Mary Had a Little Lamb," which wasn't exactly very inspired. John was quoted as saying that Paul sounded like Engelbert Humperdink, beyond which there is no nastier comparison. He went on to kid Paul in several of his own albums. In "Imagine" he refers to Paul as "Muzak to my ears" and mentions that a "pretty face may last a year or two."

Very slowly, Wings got better. On their tours, Paul wasn't above throwing in the odd Beatles number, which everyone loved. Then with "Band on the Run" and "Venus and Mars," he started producing World Number One's again, and he almost, if not quite, repeated some of his Beatle success. His 1976 tour of the States was a sell-out and at last proved that Wings was a very successful pop group.

Paul's songs haven't perhaps reached the heights of "Yesterday" or "Eleanor Rigby," but commercially Paul is by far the most successful of the Beatles. He may lack the cutting edge which John gave him, stopping the sloppier sentiments, but he has devoted himself to seeing good ideas through. John, as ever, can still throw away a good song by getting bored and not seeing it through—or even not finishing it.

Paul says he has made more money in the last two years with Wings than he did in the whole of his Beatle career. This isn't too incredible, as so many people had shares in their lives as Beatles; but it is nonetheless remarkable.

He still lives in the same London house and is still happily married after nine years to the same wife and has now got three children, two girls and a boy. He's still a conservative, doesn't like changes, and would never leave Britain, despite taxes. He's very much the happy family man, though perhaps going out of his way a little too much at times to display his happy family (another reason for George's dismissal of him as being cute). His family is a major interest in life, having long since taken the emotional place of John and the Beatles.

As for the other characters in the Beatle drama, Neil Aspinall, their roadie, went on to be an executive in Apple and produced the *Let It Be* film. He's still there, though Apple these days doesn't seem to have much to do or produce, apart from legal arguments. He is married with five children. Mal Evans, on the other hand, who always seemed so relaxed and contented compared with the rather nervy Neil, ended his life in tragedy. He'd left his wife and family and had moved to America when he was shot in an incident with the police in Los Angeles in 1976. Paul's father Jim has also died, as have John's father Fred and George's mum, Louise.

George Martin went on to become a successful independent music producer, though without discovering anyone else on the scale of the Beatles. His remarks in the End Bit, warning that the Beatles could go wrong if they went on their own, have in some ways been prophetic. All four Beatles have been active and productive so far, but only Paul has really flourished on his own—but then his temperament, energy, and his lyrical abilities were always the most suited for survival in the pop world.

Will they ever play again? They're now quieter and calmer after all the rows, though not exactly soul mates. They don't make a point of seeking each other out but are friendly when by chance their paths cross. Their relationships are more like old school friends who at one time went through a lot, even if they now know they haven't much in common. They are continually being asked to appear in public again, usually by promoters desperate for self-promotion who offer 50 million dollars for one concert, knowing full well it won't happen. It's a regular newspaper story, especially during the silly season. One promoter even said he'd give all his profits away from such a concert, and would also ask every fan to bring along money and clothes for the world's needy. Shades of those mad days in the sixties when it was honestly thought by some that the Beatles could save the world. I don't think such a concert will ever happen, regardless of how many millions of dollars may be offered. John does say he's not got a great deal of money, but none of them is by any means hard up and they should never again have to fall into the hands of another promoter.

All the same, I have a feeling that one day the Beatles will play together—just once, completely informally, if only for their own fun. During my days with them, which was at the height of Beatlemania, they loved talking about the early days in Liverpool and Hamburg, about the awful things they did, the irresponsibility of it all, the messing about, on stage and off it, not caring really what the world thought. That was their adolescence. And they were genuinely fond of their very early songs. Before the drag of the big deal touring, they did love being Beatles. I think one day they might try to recapture that early atmosphere and have their own old boys' reunion, even if it's in private.

But I can't see them ever composing together again, which of course would be best of all. Things have gone too far. They've all moved on. Paul and John, as their respective music shows, have become totally different personalities, producing different types of music, which, for better or for worse, are essentially their own. They can never capture what they did together, how they once affected each other, how their talents intermingled and overlapped, producing something which was so much finer and stronger and more original than the sum of their parts. What they produced as Beatles is what we shall have to content ourselves with. I, for one, am still very happy with what they did. The Beatles are dead. Long may they live.

APPENDIX

The Beatles' Songs:

All compositions by Lennon and McCartney unless otherwise noted

Germany, 1961

As the backing group for singer Tony Sheridan the Beatles recorded ten numbers. Only one was an original composition, an instrumental number called "Cry for a Shadow," written by Lennon and Harrison. On one other, "Ain't She Sweet," John Lennon was the lead singer. On the other eight they were the backing group: "My Bonnie," "The Saints," "Kansas City," "Sweet Georgia Brown," "If You Love Me Baby," "What'd I Say," "Why," "Nobody's Child."

Single-playing records by the Beatles issued by Parlophone Records in England

TITLE	DATE	HIGHEST CHART POSITION
Love Me Do / PS I Love You	Nov 62	17
Please Please Me / Ask Me Why	Jan 63	1
From Me to You / Thank You Girl	April 63	1
She Loves You / I'll Get You	Aug 63	1
I Want to Hold Your Hand / This Boy	Nov 63	1
Can't Buy Me Love / You Can't Do That	March 64	1
A Hard Day's Night / Things We Said Today	July 64	1
I Feel Fine / She's a Woman	Nov 64	1
Ticket to Ride / Yes It Is	April 65	1
Help! / I'm Down	July 65	1
Day Tripper / We Can Work It Out	Dec 65	1
Paperback Writer / Rain	June 66	1
Yellow Submarine / Eleanor Rigby	Aug 66	1

354

Penny Lane / Strawberry Fields Forever	Feb 67	1
All You Need Is Love / Baby, You're a Rich Man	July 67	1
Hello, Goodbye / I Am the Walrus	Nov 67	1

Long-playing records issued by Parlophone, England

PLEASE PLEASE ME (April 63):
I Saw Her Standing There
Misery
Ask Me Why
Please Please Me
Love Me Do
PS I Love You
Do You Want to Know a Secret
There's a Place
*Anna
*Chains
*Boys
*Baby It's You
*A Taste of Honey
*Twist and Shout

WITH THE BEATLES (Nov 63):
It Won't Be Long
All I've Got to Do
All My Loving
Don't Bother Me (Harrison)
Little Child
Hold Me Tight
I Wanna Be Your Man
Not a Second Time
*Till There Was You
*Please Mister Postman
*Roll Over Beethoven
*You Really Got a Hold on Me
*Devil in Her Heart
*Money

A HARD DAY'S NIGHT (Aug 64):
A Hard Day's Night
I Should Have Known Better
If I Fell

* Songs not composed by the Beatles.

I'm Happy Just to Dance with You
And I Love Her
Tell Me Why
Can't Buy Me Love
Any Time at All
I'll Cry Instead
Things We Said
When I Get Home
You Can't Do That
I'll Be Back

BEATLES FOR SALE (Nov 64):
No Reply
I'm a Loser
Baby's in Black
I'll Follow the Sun
Eight Days a Week
Every Little Thing
I Don't Want to Spoil the Party
What You're Doing
*Rock and Roll Music
*Honey Don't
*Mr. Moonlight
*Kansas City
*Words of Love
*Everybody's Trying to Be My Baby

HELP! (Aug 65):
Help!
The Night Before
You've Got to Hide Your Love Away
I Need You (Harrison)
Another Girl
You're Going to Lose That Girl
Ticket to Ride
It's Only Love
You Like Me Too Much (Harrison)
Tell Me What You See
I've Just Seen a Face
Yesterday
*Act Naturally
*Dizzy Miss Lizzie

* Songs not composed by the Beatles.

RUBBER SOUL (Dec 65):
Drive My Car
Norwegian Wood
You Won't See Me
Nowhere Man
Think for Yourself (Harrison)
The Word
Michelle
What Goes On
Girl
I'm Looking Through You
In My Life
Wait
If I Needed Someone (Harrison)
Run for Your Life

REVOLVER (Aug 66):
Taxman (Harrison)
Eleanor Rigby
I'm Only Sleeping
Love You Too (Harrison)
Here, There and Everywhere
Yellow Submarine
She Said She Said
Good Day Sunshine
And Your Bird Can Sing
For No One
Dr. Robert
I Want to Tell You (Harrison)
Got to Get You into My Life
Tomorrow Never Knows

SERGEANT PEPPER'S
LONELY HEARTS CLUB BAND (April 67):
Sergeant Pepper's Lonely Hearts Club Band
With a Little Help from My Friends
Lucy in the Sky with Diamonds
Getting Better
Fixing a Hole
She's Leaving Home
Being for the Benefit of Mr. Kite
Within You, without You (Harrison)
When I'm Sixty-four

Lovely Rita
Good Morning, Good Morning
A Day in the Life

MAGICAL MYSTERY TOUR (Two EPs) (Dec 67):
Magical Mystery Tour
Your Mother Should Know
I Am the Walrus
Fool on the Hill
Flying (Lennon, McCartney, Harrison, Starkey)
Blue Jay Way (Harrison)

Single Beatle Records Issued in U.S.A.

ISSUED BY SWAN RECORDS   August 1963
  She Loves You / I'll Get You   May 1964
  Sie Liebt Dich

ISSUED BY VJ   In 1963 and
  Please Please Me / Ask Me Why   early 1964
  From Me to You / Thank You Girl
  Do You Want to Know a Secret
*Twist and Shout
  Love Me Do / PS I Love You

ISSUED BY CAPITOL
  I Want to Hold Your Hand / I Saw Her Standing
    There   January 1964
  Can't Buy Me Love / You Can't Do That   March 1964
  A Hard Day's Night / I Should Have Known Better   July 1964
  I'll Cry Instead / I'm Happy Just to Dance
    with You   July 1964
  And I Love Her / If I Fell   July 1964
*Slow Down / Matchbox   August 1964
  I Feel Fine / She's a Woman   November 1964
  By the Beatles (EP)   February 1965
      *1. Honey Don't
      2. I'm a Loser
      *3. Mr. Moonlight
      *4. Everybody's Trying to Be My Baby
  Eight Days a Week / I Don't Want to Spoil the
    Party   February 1965

* Songs not composed by the Beatles.

Ticket to Ride / Yes It Is	April 1965
Help! / I'm Down	July 1965
*Act Naturally / Yesterday	September 1965
We Can Work It Out / Day Tripper	December 1965
Nowhere Man / What Goes On	February 1966
Paperback Writer / Rain	May 1966
Yellow Submarine / Eleanor Rigby	August 1966
Strawberry Fields Forever / Penny Lane	February 1967
Baby You're a Rich Man / All You Need Is Love	July 1967
Hello, Goodbye / I Am the Walrus	November 1967
Lady Madonna / The Inner Light (Harrison)	March 1968

ISSUED BY APPLE

Hey Jude / Revolution	August 1968
Get Back / Don't Let Me Down	May 1969
The Ballad of John and Yoko / Old Brown Shoe (Harrison)	June 1969
Come Together / Something (Harrison)	October 1969
Let It Be / You Know My Name (Look Up My Number)	March 1970
The Long and Winding Road / For You Blue (Harrison)	May 1970

Long-playing Beatle Records Issued in U.S.A.

ISSUED BY VJ

Introducing the Beatles: Songs, Pictures and Stories of the Fabulous Beatles	1964
Jolly What!: The Beatles and Frank Ifield on Stage	

ISSUED BY UNITED ARTISTS

A HARD DAY'S NIGHT   June 1964

A Hard Day's Night
I Should Have Known Better
If I Fell
I'm Happy Just to Dance with You
And I Love Her
Tell Me Why
Can't Buy Me Love
Any Time at All
I'll Cry Instead
Ringo's Theme (This Boy)

* Songs not composed by the Beatles.

ISSUED BY CAPITOL RECORDS

MEET THE BEATLES: January 1964
  I Want to Hold Your Hand
  I Saw Her Standing There
  This Boy
  It Won't Be Long
  All I've Got to Do
  All My Loving
  Don't Bother Me
  Little Child
*Till There Was You
  Hold Me Tight
  I Wanna Be Your Man
  Not a Second Time

THE BEATLES' SECOND ALBUM: April 1964
*Roll Over Beethoven
  Thank You Girl
*You Really Got a Hold on Me
*Devil In Her Heart
*Money
  You Can't Do That
*Long Tall Sally
  I Call Your Name
*Please Mister Postman
  I'll Get You
  She Loves You

SOMETHING NEW   July 1964
  I'll Cry Instead
  Things We Said Today
  Any Time at All
  When I Get Home
  Slow Down
*Matchbox
  Tell Me Why
  And I Love Her
  I'm Happy Just to Dance with You
  If I Fell
  Komm Gib Mir Deine Hand

* Songs not composed by the Beatles.

THE BEATLES' STORY—ON STAGE WITH   November 1964
THE BEATLES
  How Beatlemania Began
  Beatlemania in Action
  Man behind the Beatles—Brian Epstein,
    John Lennon
  Who's a Millionaire?
  The Beatles Look at Life
  "Victims" of Beatlemania
  Beatle Medley
  Ringo Starr
  Liverpool and All the World!
  Beatles Will Be Beatles
  Man behind the Music—George Martin,
    George Harrison
  A Hard Day's Night
  Paul McCartney, Sneaky Haircuts

BEATLES '65   December 1964
  No Reply
  I'm a Loser
  Baby's in Black
*Rock and Roll Music
  I'll Follow the Sun
*Mr. Moonlight
*Honey Don't
  I'll Be Back
  She's a Woman
  I Feel Fine
*Everybody's Trying to Be My Baby

THE EARLY BEATLES   March 1965
  Love Me Do
*Twist and Shout
*Anna
*Chains
*Boys
  Ask Me Why
  Please Please Me
  PS I Love You
*Baby It's You
* Songs not composed by the Beatles.

*A Taste of Honey
Do You Want to Know a Secret

BEATLES VI   June 1965
  Kansas City
  Eight Days a Week
  You Like Me Too Much
  Bad Boy
  I Don't Want to Spoil the Party
  Words of Love
  What You're Doing
  Yes It Is
*Dizzy Miss Lizzie
  Tell Me What You See
  Every Little Thing

HELP!   August 1965
  Help!
  The Night Before
  From Me to You Fantasy
  You've Got to Hide Your Love Away
  I Need You (Harrison)
  In the Tyrol
  Another Girl
  Another Hard Day's Night
  Ticket to Ride
  The Bitter End
  You Can't Do That
  You're Going to Lose That Girl
  The Chase

RUBBER SOUL   December 1965
  I've Just Seen a Face
  Norwegian Wood (This Bird Has Flown)
  You Won't See Me
  Think for Yourself (Harrison)
  The Word
  Michelle
  It's Only Love
  Girl
  I'm Looking Through You
  In My Life
* Songs not composed by the Beatles.

Wait
Run for Your Life

"YESTERDAY" . . . AND TODAY   June 1966
Drive My Car
I'm Only Sleeping
Nowhere Man
Dr. Robert
Yesterday
*Act Naturally
And Your Bird Can Sing
If I Needed Someone
We Can Work It Out
What Goes On
Day Tripper

REVOLVER   August 1966
Taxman (Harrison)
Eleanor Rigby
Love You Too (Harrison)
Here, There and Everywhere
Yellow Submarine
She Said She Said
Good Day Sunshine
For No One
I Want to Tell You (Harrison)
Got to Get You into My Life
Tomorrow Never Knows

SERGEANT PEPPER'S LONELY   June 1967
HEARTS CLUB BAND
Sergeant Pepper's Lonely Hearts Club Band
A Little Help from My Friends
Lucy in the Sky with Diamonds
Getting Better
Fixing a Hole
She's Leaving Home
Being for the Benefit of Mr. Kite
Within You without You (Harrison)
When I'm Sixty-four
Lovely Rita
Good Morning, Good Morning
* Songs not composed by the Beatles.

Sergeant Pepper's Lonely Hearts Club Band—reprise
A Day in the Life

MAGICAL MYSTERY TOUR   November 1967
Magical Mystery Tour
The Fool on the Hill
Flying (Lennon, McCartney, Harrison, Starkey)
Blue Jay Way (Harrison)
Your Mother Should Know
I Am the Walrus
Hello Goodbye
Strawberry Fields Forever
Penny Lane
Baby, You're a Rich Man
All You Need Is Love

ISSUED BY APPLE

THE BEATLES   November 1968
Back in the U.S.S.R.
Dear Prudence
Glass Onion
Ob-La-Di, Ob-La-Da
Wild Honey Pie
The Continuing Story of Bungalow Bill
While My Guitar Gently Weeps (Harrison)
Happiness Is a Warm Gun
Martha My Dear
I'm So Tired
Blackbird
Piggies (Harrison)
Rocky Raccoon
*Don't Pass Me By
Why Don't We Do It in the Road?
I Will
Julia
Birthday
Yer Blues
Mother Nature's Son
Everybody's Got Something to Hide Except Me
    and My Monkey
Sexy Sadie

* Songs not composed by the Beatles.

Helter Skelter
Long, Long, Long (Harrison)
Revolution
Honey Pie
Savoy Truffle (Harrison)
Cry Baby Cry
Revolution (No. 9)
Good Night

YELLOW SUBMARINE   January 1969
Yellow Submarine
Only a Northern Song (Harrison)
All Together Now
Hey Bulldog
It's All Too Much (Harrison)
All You Need Is Love
Pepperland
Medley: Sea of Time and Sea of Holes
Sea of Monsters
March of the Meanies
Pepperland Laid Waste
Yellow Submarine in Pepperland

ABBEY ROAD   October 1969
Come Together
Something (Harrison)
Maxwell's Silver Hammer
Oh! Darling
*Octopus's Garden
I Want You (She's So Heavy)
Here Comes the Sun (Harrison)
Because
You Never Give Me Your Money
Sun King
Mean Mr. Mustard
Polythene Pam
She Came in Through the Bathroom Window
Golden Slumbers
Carry That Weight
The End
Her Majesty

* Songs not composed by the Beatles.

HEY JUDE   February 1970
  Can't Buy Me Love
  I Should Have Known Better
  Paperback Writer
  Rain
  Lady Madonna
  Revolution
  Hey Jude
  Old Brown Shoe (Harrison)
  Don't Let Me Down
  The Ballad of John and Yoko

LET IT BE   May 1970
  Two of Us
  I Dig a Pony
  Across the Universe
  I Me Mine (Harrison)
  Dig It (Lennon/McCartney/Harrison/Starkey)
  Let It Be (version two)
  Maggie Mae (arr. Lennon/McCartney/Harrison/Starkey)
  I've Got a Feeling
  One After 909
  The Long and Winding Road
  For You Blue (Harrison)
  Get Back (version two)

THE BEATLES 1962–1966   April 1973
  Love Me Do
  Please Please Me
  From Me to You
  She Loves You
  I Want to Hold Your Hand
  All My Loving
  Can't Buy Me Love
  A Hard Day's Night
  And I Love Her
  I Feel Fine
  Ticket to Ride
  Yesterday
*James Bond Theme
  Help!

* Songs not composed by the Beatles.

You've Got to Hide Your Love Away
We Can Work It Out
Day Tripper
Drive My Car
Norwegian Wood (This Bird Has Flown)
Nowhere Man
Michelle
In My Life
Girl
Paperback Writer
Eleanor Rigby
Yellow Submarine
Strawberry Fields Forever
Penny Lane
Sgt. Pepper's Lonely Hearts Club Band
With a Little Help from My Friends
Lucy in the Sky with Diamonds
A Day in the Life
All You Need Is Love
I Am the Walrus
Hello Goodbye
The Fool on the Hill
Magical Mystery Tour
Lady Madonna
Hey Jude
Revolution
Back in the U.S.S.R.
While My Guitar Gently Weeps (Harrison)
Ob-La-Di, Ob-La-Da
Get Back
Don't Let Me Down
The Ballad of John and Yoko
Old Brown Shoe (Harrison)
Here Comes the Sun (Harrison)
Come Together
Something (Harrison)
*Octopus's Garden
Let It Be
Across the Universe
The Long and Winding Road

* Songs not composed by the Beatles.

ISSUED BY POLYDOR   May 1970

THE BEATLES—CIRCA 1960—IN THE BEGINNING
*Ain't She Sweet
  Cry for a Shadow (Lennon/Harrison)
  Let's Dance
*My Bonnie
*Take Out Some Insurance on Me, Baby
  What'd I Say
*Sweet Georgia Brown
  The Saints
  Ruby Baby
*Why
*Nobody's Child
  Ya Ya

ISSUED BY CAPITOL   1976

THE BEATLES ROCK 'N ROLL MUSIC
*Twist and Shout (Russell-Medley)
  I Saw Her Standing There
  You Can't Do That
  I Wanna be Your Man
  I Call Your Name
*Boys
*Long Tall Sally
  Hey Bulldog
  Birthday
  Get Back
*Rock N' Roll Music
*Slow Down
*Kansas City
*Money (That's What I Want)
*Bad Boy
*Matchbox
*Roll over Beethoven
*Dizzy Miss Lizzie
  Any Time at all
  Drive My Car
*Everybody's Trying to Be My Baby
  The Night Before
  I'm Down

* Songs not composed by the Beatles.

Revolution
Back in the U.S.S.R.
Helter Skelter
Taxman
Got to Get You into My Life

ISSUED BY ATLANTIC   1977

THE BEATLES LIVE AT THE STAR CLUB IN HAMBURG, GERMANY 1962

*I'm Gonna Sit Right Down and Cry over You (Thomas-Biggs)
*Roll Over Beethoven
*Hippy Hippy Shake
*Sweet Little Sixteen
*Lend Me Your Comb
*Your Feets Too Big
  Where Have You Been All My Life
*Mr. Moonlight
*A Taste of Honey
*Besame Mucho
*Till There Was You
*Kansas City/Hey, Hey, Hey, Hey
  Ain't Nothin Shakin (Like the Leaves on a Tree)
*To Know Her Is to Love Her
*Little Queenie
*Falling in Love Again
*Sheila
*Be Bop-A-Lulu
*Hallelujah I Love Her So
*Red Sails in the Sunset
*Everybody's Tryin' to Be My Baby
*Matchbox
*Talkin 'bout You
*Shimmy Shake
*Long Tall Sally
*I Remember You

ISSUED BY CAPITOL   1977

THE BEATLES LIVE AT THE HOLLYWOOD BOWL

*Twist and Shout
  She's a Woman
*Dizzy Miss Lizzie

* Songs not composed by the Beatles.

Ticket to Ride
Can't Buy Me Love
Things We Said Today
*Roll over Beethoven
*Boys
A Hard Day's Night
Help!
All My Loving
She Loves You
*Long Tall Sally

SOLO ALBUMS BY EX-BEATLES

Paul McCartney

McCARTNEY   Apple   April 1970
(all compositions by McCartney)
The Lovely Linda
That Would Be Something
Valentine Day
Every Night
Medley: Hot As Sun; Glasses; Suicide
Junk
Man We Was Lonely
Oo You
Momma Miss America
Teddy Boy
Singalong Junk
Maybe I'm Amazed
Kreen-Akrore

RAM   Apple   May 1971
Too Many People (McCartney)
3 Legs (McCartney)
Ram On (McCartney)
Dear Boy (Paul and Linda McCartney)
Uncle Albert/Admiral Halsey (Paul and Linda McCartney)
Smile Away (McCartney)
Heart of the Country (Paul and Linda McCartney)
Monkberry Moon Delight (Paul and Linda McCartney)
Eat at Home (Paul and Linda McCartney)
Long-Haired Lady (Paul and Linda McCartney)
Ram On (version two) (McCartney)

* Songs not composed by the Beatles.

The Back Seat of My Car (McCartney)

WILD LIFE   Apple   December 1971
  Mumbo (P. and L. McCartney)
  Bip Bop (P. and L. McCartney)
  Love Is Strange
  Wild Life (P. and L. McCartney)
  Some People Never Know (P. and L. McCartney)
  I Am Your Singer (P. and L. McCartney)
  Bip Bop (reprise) (P. and L. McCartney)
  Tomorrow (P. and L. McCartney)
  Dear Friend (P. and L. McCartney)

RED ROSE SPEEDWAY   Apple   April 1973
(all compositions by McCartney)
  Big Barn Bed
  My Love
  Get on the Right Thing
  One More Kiss
  Little Lamb Dragonfly
  Single Pigeon
  When the Night
  Loup (1st Indian on the Moon)
  Medley: Hold Me Tight: Lazy Dynamite; Hands of Love; Power Cut

BAND ON THE RUN   Apple   December 1973
(All compositions by McCartney except "No Words")
  Band on the Run
  Jet
  Bluebird
  Mrs. Vandebilt
  Let Me Roll
  Mamunia
  No Words (with Denny Laine)
  Helen Wheels
  Picasso's Last Words (Drink to Me)
  Nineteen Hundred and Eighty-Five

VENUS AND MARS   Capitol   May 1975
(all compositions by McCartney except "Medicine Jar" and
"Crossroads Theme")
  Venus and Mars
  Rock Show

Love in Song
You Gave Me the Answer
Magneto and Titanium Man
Letting Go
Venus and Mars (reprise)
Spirits of Ancient Egypt
Medicine Jar (Jimmy McCulloch/Colin Allen)
Call Me Back Again
Listen to What the Man Said
Medley: Treat Her Gently; Lonely Old People
Crossroads Theme (Tony Hatch)

ISSUED BY CAPITOL   1976

WINGS AT THE SPEED OF SOUND
(all songs by Linda or Paul unless specified)
Let 'Em in
The Note You Never Wrote
She's My Babby
Beware My Love
Wino Junko (McCulloch-Allen)
Silly Love Songs
Cook of the House
Time to Hide (Laine)
Must Do Something about It
San Ferry Anne
Warm and Beautiful

ISSUED BY CAPITOL   1976

WINGS OVER AMERICA
(all songs by Linda or Paul unless specified)
Venus and Mars/Rock Shot/Jet
Let Me Roll it
Spirits of Ancient Egypt
Medicine Jar (McCulloch-Allen)
Maybe I'm Amazed
Call Me Back Again
Lady Maddona
The Long and Winding Road
Live and Let Die
Picasso's Last Words
Richard Cory (Paul Simon)
Bluebird

I've Just Seen a Face
Blackbird
Yesterday
You Gave Me the Answer
Magneto and Titanium Man
Go Now (Banks-Bennett)
My Love
Listen to What the Man Said
Let 'Em In
Time to Hide (Laine)
Silly Love Songs
Beware My Love
Letting Go
Band on the Run
Hi, Hi, Hi
Soily

John Lennon

UNFINISHED MUSIC NO. 1—   Apple   November 1968
TWO VIRGINS
(all compositions by John Lennon and Yoko Ono)
Two Virgins No. 1
Together
Two Virgins No. 2
Two Virgins No. 3
Two Virgins No. 4
Two Virgins No. 5
Two Virgins No. 6
Hushabye Hushabye
Two Virgins No. 7
Two Virgins No. 8
Two Virgins No. 9
Two Virgins No. 10

UNFINISHED MUSIC NO. 2:   Apple   May 1969
LIFE WITH THE LIONS
(all compositions by John Lennon and Yoko Ono)
"Cambridge 1969"
Song for John
Cambridge 1969
Let's Go Flying
Snow Is Falling All the Time

Mummy's Only Looking for Her Hand in the Snow
No Bed for Beatle John
Baby's Heartbeat
Two Minutes Silence
Radio Play

WEDDING ALBUM   Apple   October 1969
(all compositions by John Lennon and Yoko Ono)
John and Yoko
Amsterdam

THE PLASTIC ONO BAND—   Apple   December 1969
LIVE PEACE IN TORONTO
*Blue Suede Shoes
*Money (That's What I Want)
*Dizzy Miss Lizzie
 Yer Blues
 Cold Turkey (Lennon)
 Give Peace a Chance
*Don't Worry Kyoko (Mummy's Only Looking for Her Hand
    in the Snow)
*John, John (Let's Hope for Peace)

JOHN LENNON/   Apple   December 1970
PLASTIC ONO BAND
(all compositions by John Lennon)
 Mother
 Hold On (John)
 I Found Out
 Working-Class Hero
 Isolation
 Remember
 Love
 Well Well Well
 Look at Me
 God
 My Mummy's Dead

IMAGINE   Apple   September 1971
(all compositions by John Lennon except as noted)
 Imagine
 Crippled Inside

* Songs not composed by Lennon.

Jealous Guy
It's So Hard
I Don't Want to Be a Soldier, Mama, I Don't Want to Die
Give Me Some Truth
Oh My Love (Lennon/Yoko Ono)
How Do You Sleep?
How?
Oh Yoko!

SOMETIME IN NEW YORK CITY Apple   June 1972
  Woman Is the Nigger of the World (Lennon/Yoko Ono)
  Sisters, O Sisters (Yoko Ono)
  Attica State (Lennon/Yoko Ono)
  Born in a Prison (Yoko Ono)
  New York City (Lennon)
  Sunday Bloody Sunday (Lennon/Yoko Ono)
  The Luck of the Irish (Lennon/Yoko Ono)
  John Sinclair (Lennon)
  Angela (Lennon/Yoko Ono)
  We're All Water (Yoko Ono)
  Cold Turkey (Lennon)
  Don't Worry Kyoko (Yoko Ono)
  Well . . . (Baby Please Don't Go) (Walter Ward)
  Jamrag (Lennon/Yoko Ono)
  Scumbag (Lennon/Yoko Ono/Frank Zappa)
  Au (Lennon/Yoko Ono)

MIND GAMES   Apple   November 1973
(all compositions by John Lennon)
  Mind Games
  Tight A$
  Aisumasen (I'm Sorry)
  One Day (At a Time)
  Bring on the Lucie (Freda Peeple)
  Nutopian International Anthem
  Intuition
  Out the Blue
  Only People
  I Know (I Know)
  You Are Here
  Meat City

WALLS AND BRIDGES   Apple   September 1974
(all compositions by John Lennon except as noted)
Going Down on Love
Whatever Gets You Thru the Night
Old Dirt Road (Lennon/Harry Nilsson)
What You Got
Bless You
Scared
No. 9 Dream
Surprise, Surprise (Sweet Bird of Paradox)
Steel and Glass
Beef Jerky
Nobody Loves You (When You're Down and Out)
Ya Ya (Morris Robinson/Clarence Lewis/Lee Dorsey)

ROCK 'N' ROLL   Apple   February 1975
*Be-Bop-A-Lula
*Stand by Me
*Medley: Rip It Up; Ready Teddy
*You Can't Catch Me
*Ain't That a Shame
*Do You Want to Dance
*Sweet Little Sixteen
*Slippin' and Slidin'
*Peggy Sue
*Medley: Bring It on Home to Me; Send Me Some Lovin'
*Bony Moronie
*Ya Ya
*Just Because

SHAVED FISH   Apple   October 1975
Give Peace a Chance
Cold Turkey (Lennon)
Instant Karma! (We All Shine On) (Lennon)
Power to the People (Lennon)
Mother (Lennon)
Woman Is the Nigger of the World (Lennon/Yoko Ono)
Imagine (Lennon)
Whatever Gets You Thru the Night (Lennon)
Mind Games (Lennon)
No. 9 Dream (Lennon)
Medley: Happy Xmas (War Is Over) (Lennon/Yoko Ono); Give
     Peace a Chance
* Songs not composed by Lennon.

George Harrison

WONDERWALL MUSIC   Apple   December 1968
(all compositions by George Harrison)
 Microbes
 Red Lady Too
 Medley: Tabla and Pakavaj; In the Park
 Medley: Drilling a Home; Guru Vandana
 Medley: Greasy Legs; Ski-ing and Gat Kirwani
 Dream Scene
 Party Seacombe
 Medley: Love Scene; Crying
 Cowboy Museum
 Medley: Fantasy Sequins; Glass Box
 On the Bed
 Wonderwall to Be Here
 Singing Om

ELECTRONIC SOUND   Zapple   May 1969
(all compositions by George Harrison)
 Under the Mersey Wall
 No Time or Space

ALL THINGS MUST PASS   Apple   November 1970
(all compositions by Harrison except as noted)
 I'd Have You Anytime (Harrison/Bob Dylan)
 My Sweet Lord
 Wah-Wah
 Isn't It a Pity (version one)
 What Is Life
 If Not for You (Bob Dylan)
 Behind That Locked Door
 Let It Down
 Run of the Mill
 Beware of Darkness
 Apple Scruffs
 Ballad of Sir Frankie Crisp (Let It Roll)
 Awaiting on You All
 All Things Must Pass
 I Dig Love
 Art of Dying
 Isn't It a Pity (version two)
 Hear Me Lord
 Out of the Blue

It's Johnny's Birthday
Plug Me in
I Remember Jeep
Thanks for the Pepperoni

THE CONCERT FOR   Apple   December 1971
BANGLA DESH
  George Harrison/Ravi Shankar Introduction
  Bangla Dhun: Star and Sarod Duet; Dadratal; Teental
  Wah-Wah (Harrison)
  My Sweet Lord (Harrison)
  Awaiting on You All (Harrison)
  That's the Way God Planned It (Billy Preston)
  It Don't Come Easy (Starkey)
  Beware of Darkness (Harrison)
  Introduction of the Band
  While My Guitar Gently Weeps (Harrison)
  Medley: Jumpin' Jack Flash (Mick Jagger/Keith Richard);
     Youngblood (Jerry Leiber/Mike Stoller/Doc Pomus)
  Here Comes the Sun
  A Hard Rain's Gonna Fall (Bob Dylan)
  It Takes a Lot to Laugh/It Takes a Train to Cry (Bob Dylan)
  Blowin' in the Wind (Bob Dylan)
  Mr. Tambourine Man (Bob Dylan)
  Just Like a Woman (Bob Dylan)
  Something (Harrison)
  Bangla Desh (Harrison)

LIVING IN THE   Apple   May 1973
MATERIAL WORLD
(all compositions by George Harrison)
  Give Me Love (Give Me Peace on Earth)
  Sue Me, Sue You Blues
  The Light That Has Lighted the World
  Don't Let Me Wait Too Long
  Who Can See It
  Living In the Material World
  The Lord Loves the One (That Loves the Lord)
  Be Here Now
  Try Some, Buy Some
  The Day the World Gets 'Round
  That Is All

DARK HORSE   Apple   December 1974
(all compositions by George Harrison unless noted)
  Hari's on on Tour (Express)
  Simply Shady
  So Bad
  Bye Bye, Love (Felice Bryant/Boudleaux Bryant—parody lyrics by
     George Harrison)
  Maya Love
  Ding Dong; Ding Dong
  Dark Horse
  Far East Man (Harrison/Ron Wood)
  It Is "He" (Jai Sri Krishna)

EXTRA TEXTURE—   Apple   September 1975
READ ALL ABOUT IT
(all compositions by Harrison)
  You
  The Answer's at the End
  This Guitar (Can't Keep from Crying)
  Ooh Baby (You Know That I Love You)
  World of Stone
  A Bit More of You
  Can't Stop Thinking about You
  Tired of Midnight Blue
  Grey Cloudy Lies
  His Name Is Legs (Ladies & Gentlemen)

33⅓   Dark Horse   September 1976
(all compositions by Harrison)
  Woman Don't You Cry for Me
  Dear One
  Beautiful Girl
  This Song
  See Yourself
  It's What You Value
  True Love
  Crackerbox Palace
  Learn How to Love You

Ringo Starr

SENTIMENTAL JOURNAL   Apple   April 1970
(no songs composed by Ringo)
  Sentimental Journey

Night and Day
Whispering Grass (Don't Tell the Trees)
Bye Bye Blackbird
I'm a Fool to Care
Star Dust
Blue, Turning Grey Over You
Love Is a Many-Splendored Thing
Dream
You Always Hurt the One You Love
Have I Told You Lately That I Love You?
Let the Rest of the World Go By

BEAUCOUPS OF BLUES　　　Apple　　September 1970

(no songs composed by Ringo)
Beaucoups of Blues
Love Don't Last Long
Fastest Growing Heartache in the West
Without Her
Woman of the Night
I'd Be Talking All the Time
$15 Draw
Wine, Women and Loud Happy Songs
I Wouldn't Have You Any Other Way
Loser's Lounge
Waiting
Silent Homecoming

"RINGO"　　　Apple　　November 1973

(Ringo wrote all or part of four songs)
I'm the Greatest (Lennon)
Hold on (Have You Seen My Baby) (Randy Newman)
Photograph (Starkey/Harrison)
Sunshine Life for Me (Sail Away Raymond) (Harrison)
You're Sixteen (Richard Sherman/Robert Sherman)
Oh My My (Starkey/Vini Poncia)
Step Lightly (Starkey)
Six O'Clock (Paul and Linda McCartney)
Devil Woman (Starkey/Vini Poncia)
You and Me (Babe) (Harrison/Mal Evans)

ISSUED BY APPLE　　　November 1974

GOODNIGHT VIENNA

(no songs composed by Ringo except as noted)

Occapella
Oo-Wee (Starkey/Vini Poncia)
Husbands and Wives
Snookeroo
All by Myself
Call Me
No No Song
Only You and You Alone
Easy for Me
Goodnight Vienna (reprise)

ISSUED BY APPLE   December 1975

BLAST FROM YOUR PAST
You're Sixteen
No No Song
It Don't Come Easy
Photograph (Starkey/Harrison)
Back off Boogaloo
Only You
Beaucoup de Blues
Oh My My (Starkey/Poncia)
Early 1970
I'm the Greatest

ROTOGRAVURE
Las Brises (Starkey/Andrews)
Lady Gaye (Starkey/Poncia/Ward)
Cryin (Starkey/Poncia)
Cookin (Lennon)
I'll Still love you (Harrison)
Pure Gold (McCartney)

ISSUED BY ATLANTIC   September 1977

RICHARD THE 4th
Wings (Starkey/Poncia)
Gave It All Up (Starkey/Poncia)
Out on the Streets (Starkey/Poncia)
It's No Secret (Starkey/Poncia)
Gypsies in Flight (Starkey)
Simple Love Song (Starkey/Poncia)

About the Author

Hunter Davies was born in Renfrew, Scotland, and attended University College, Durham. After graduating, he joined Thomson Newspapers, serving first as a reporter on the *Manchester Evening Chronicle*. In 1960 Mr. Davies joined the *Sunday Times* of London, where he remains as staff writer. From 1965 to 1967 he penned the celebrated Atticus column for that newspaper. In 1975 he became Editor of the *Sunday Times* of London magazine. He is author of twelve books, including *The New London Spy, Here We Go Round the Mulberry Bush* (novel and screenplay) and *The Other Half*. Margaret Forster, Mr. Davies' wife, is well known as the author of the novel and screenplay *Georgy Girl* and for the *Travels of Maudie Tipstaff*. Hunter Davies lives in London with his wife and three children.